The Neuropsychology of Dreams
A Clinico-Anatomical Study

INSTITUTE FOR RESEARCH
IN BEHAVIORAL NEUROSCIENCE

Jason W. Brown, Series Editor

BROWN
Neurology of Visual Perception

GOLDBERG
Contemporary Neuropsychology and the Legacy of Luria

PERECMAN
Integrating Theory and Practice in Clinical Neuropsycholgoy

KOHN
Conduction Aphasia

CHRISTENSEN AND UZZELL
Brain Injury and Neuropsychological Rehabilitation:
International Perspectives

UZZELL AND STONNINGTON
Recovery After Traumatic Brain Injury

SOLMS
The Neuropsychology of Dreams:
A Clinico-Anatomical Study

The Neuropsychology of Dreams
A Clinico-Anatomical Study

Mark Solms
London Hospital Medical College
and
University College London

Routledge
Taylor & Francis Group

LONDON AND NEW YORK

First Published 1997 by
Lawrence Erlbaum Associates, Inc.

Published 2016 by Routledge
2 Park Square, Milton Park, Abingdon, Oxfordshire OX14 4RN
711 Third Avenue, New York, NY 10017

First issued in paperback 2015

*Routledge is an imprint of the Taylor and Francis Group,
an informa business*

Cover design by Kathryn Houghtaling

Library of Congress Cataloging-in-Publication Data

Solms, Mark.
    The neuropsychology of dreams : a clinico-anatomical
study / Mark Solms
        p. cm.
    Includes bibliographical references and index.
    1. Dreams.   2. Neuropsychology.   I. Title.
QP426.S65   1996
154.6'3—dc20   96-21693
                                            CIP

ISBN 13: 978-1-138-98958-0 (pbk)
ISBN 13: 978-0-8058-1585-6 (hbk)

Publisher's Note
The publisher has gone to great lengths to ensure the quality of this reprint
but points out that some imperfections in the original may be apparent.

This book is dedicated to the beloved memory
of Douglas Leonard de Gier Solms

Contents

Foreword

Jason W. Brown
New York University Medical Center

The goal of clinical research in perception has been to study and, it is hoped, account for the different forms of object breakdown that occur with brain damage. Toward this goal, research has centered on disturbances of object perception, for example, in the visual modality, on disorders of form, shape, or movement detection, or in the recognition of colors, faces, or routes. The strategy has been to identify a specific deficit, localize it in the brain, distinguish it from associated conditions, and tease out any contaminants of language, memory, or attentional deficit. This approach assumes, of course, that naked percepts arriving in sensory cortex are subsequently associated to other areas for naming, recognition, spatial relations, and so on.

During this early—or *taxonomic*—phase, it was already clear that many disorders of object perception could not be readily distinguished from, say, disorders of memory. Cases were reported of visual agnosia with deficits in memory or imagery, such as inability to describe from memory or visualize an object that could not be identified. There were cases of perceptual deficits with intrusive phenomena such as illusions and hallucinations, for example, visual hallucination in the acute stage of cortical blindness. A variety of intact and altered image types were reported, including after-images, eidetic (or palinoptic) images, and imagination or thought images. Of these reports, the works of Paul Schilder, G. de Morsier, Morris Bender, Jean Lhermitte, Otto Pötzl, and Macdonald Critchley stand out, for me, as among the more important. Their observations suggested a relation between memory, imagery, and object perception that was not adequately explained by classical theory, that is, sensory or association psychology.

In order to preserve the classical theory and safeguard the autonomy of the conditions that had been described, cases with defects of both imagery and object perception were interpreted as collections or aggregates of both functions resulting from damage to contiguous neurologic systems. With damage to the perceptual system alone, imagery was preserved, or, in the case of hallucination, released from inhibition. Strangely, it was not noticed that the same explanation served for both intact and pathological imagery. With damage to the imagery system alone, a pure disorder of imagery (irreminiscence) was postulated. To date, however, this condition has not been adequately documented.

The relegation of the image system to a gray zone between the perceptual and memory areas accompanied and promoted a somewhat dismissive attitude toward imagery research. Imagery was treated as a perceptual disorder by those working in memory and as a memory disorder by those working in perception. For everyone else, it was a fuzzy, subjective content, hard to pin down, heavily dependent on verbal report, and, as with other introspective data, a not altogether respectable field of study. As a result, interest in imagery declined and the old literature was largely forgotten.

In recent years, this decline has been reversed in large part by cognitivist studies of normal thought and imagination images. The work of Kosslyn, Shepard, and others has been widely cited in this regard. One feature of some cognitive studies and, incidentally, a measure of their distance from the clinical literature, was their preoccupation with the claim that images have propositional content, that is, that images are language equivalents.

I confess that I have never fully grasped the basis or the importance of this position. It seemed that one could entertain the notion that an image is propositional content only in thought images where the image is like an idea. Moreover, the imagery tests that were used were clearly language-infected. The question of whether an image is an idea is not uninteresting, but that the image is *only* an idea ignores the entire history of work on pathological imagery. I recall a seminar at Rockefeller University on this topic in a group biased toward a linguistic interpretation, when George Miller, in frustration with the discussion, asked, "What is the propositional content of a phantom limb?" None of the participants responded and the debate continued as before. This was, to my way of thinking, exactly the right question! To this day, the supposed connection between images and propositions plays a role in its (erroneous) localization by some to the left temporal lobe.

Because the work in normal cognitive psychology largely has neglected pathological imagery of the type seen in brain-damaged patients, including dreams, phantoms, hallucinations, and palinoptic images, the relevance of this work to neuropsychology is uncertain. Still, research on imagery in normal subjects did contribute new methods of investigation to the study of brain-damaged populations and has had the effect, salutary in my view, of suggesting that common mechanisms underlie central aspects of both imagery and perception, a conclusion that is in conformity with a century of forgotten clinical research.

In spite of these advances, the clinical material was in a state of disrepair. What was sorely needed was not a collation of cases from the standpoint of lesion location but a rethinking of the case reports in relation to other intact and defective capacities, and in relation to the change in symptomatology over time. The richness of the old reports, as Mark Solms so beautifully demonstrates, is not, as many psychologists assume, a gratuitous elaboration on a core deficit. Instead, this richness is the context around the deficit that is omitted in most psychologies. In the right hands, as in Solms' book, a study of the context of a disorder is the key to an interpretation of the meaning of the symptom and its relation to normal cognition. The temporal relatedness is especially important because, without it, imagery is subject to the same fate as object perception; that is, defective or intrusive images are decontextualized, localized, objectified as interior (intact or lost) "mental solids," and, as a result, their role in the process of object formation is missed completely.

What exactly is the relation of an image to an object? For me, the lesson of clinical study is that an image is not a revival of a perception or an aid to a developing object but is a segment in the perceptual process that reappears when the object development is incomplete. The imaginal segment persists in a certain sense as a virtual phase in a normal perception. For example, the symbolic relations of conceptual transformations that discharge directly in a dream hallucination remain behind, so to say, as conceptual, affective, and experiential content at intermediate stages in a waking perception. Conversely, an object is an image that with its space is derived outward to form the world of perception. The role of sensation in this process is to parse a mental representation so that it models the "out there" in the world. Put differently, sensation delimits the free play of an endogenous system of dream and mental image generation.

The study of pathological imagery and patterns of perceptual breakdown confirms that an image is the underpinning of the object at successive phases. Damage to phases in a multitiered system of space formation gives rise to disorders of imagery and/or object perception. The pathological image is an attenuation of the object from the viewer's standpoint. The pathological object is a deficiency in the perception from the standpoint of an external observer. For example, a lesion of the limbic–temporal area in either hemisphere can lead to a formed hallucination in which transformations are related to the meaning content of the image. This is a momentary expression of a phase in the forming object where meaning is established. This lesion—especially if bilateral—also can lead to a disorder of object perception in which the selection of the object through a phase of meaning relations is disturbed. The object is adequately perceived but is no longer familiar to the subject or is misrecognized. This is one form of visual agnosia. The agnosia reveals the conceptual deficiency that is expressed as a symptom in the hallucination. Similarly, lesions of the occipito-parietal area can give rise to disorders of perception in which an impairment of object form is the most prominent deficit (visuospatial agnosia), or they can give rise to disorders of imagery in which a deviance of form is the most prominent symptom (metamorphopsias and other illusory phenomena). The same derailment of process that involved the selection of meaning now involves the selection of form. In both examples, the image exposes or is a positive symptom of a phase in the object that is a deficit in the agnosia.

From the pathological material we can reconstruct the series of microtemporal events that constitute the process of normal visual perception. In this process, the initial stage encodes shape and location information in a two-dimensional space about the body. At subsequent stages, meaning and experiential memory (recognition) are established in an intrapersonal volumetric space. The succession of stages in object formation corresponds with that in the image: from sleep, to dreams, to illusions, to elementary hallucinations or after-images. The development is from an intra- to an extrapersonal space, from past to present, from private meaning to public fact, from self to world.

The hypothesis that an image is sculpted to an object brings the image to the forefront of research on object perception. A sensation is not the building block of an object but a constraint on the process of mental representation (imagery). A lack of sensory regulation of a developing object exposes a covert image that traverses the disturbed segment. Image phenomena in sensory deprivation, cortical blindness, or dream can be explained in this way.

Dream is a perceptual world across modalities with an internal coherence similar to waking perception. In dream as in wakefulness, the modalities conspire to authenticate the image. We see, hear, and touch the dream image, as we do the waking perception. Reality for the individual is whatever deposits at a given moment, whether dream or perception, as long as there is consistency across the different modalities. A hallucination in one modality may not undermine the observer's world; that is, it may be recognized as a hallucination, because an external object can be achieved through other perceptual channels. This is a fragile process. In the waking state, an observer may not accept a visual hallucination as real until the other modalities are engaged. This is observed in cases where a false hallucination of a face is acknowledged as real as soon as the hallucinated figure begins to speak. Auditory and visual hallucinations are congruent and the observer has no way to disconfirm the reality of the image. Put differently, an image becomes the perceptual world of the viewer when its imaginal content is distributed across the different perceptual modalities. We learn from such cases that dream does not have a purely protective or restitutive function. It is necessary to dream because imaginal phases constitute the greater part of a perception. Indeed, a complete theory of perception is unimaginable without a theory of the dream.

In this book, Mark Solms has undertaken to provide the "missing link" of perceptual study, namely, a neuropsychology of dream and related phenomena. The topic is of vital importance and his approach is an exciting departure from what is customary in neuropsychology. He has taken on the difficult and ambitious project of describing the syndromes of disordered dream-imagery in a dynamic framework and in relation to associated changes in cognition and personality. The focus is on the complexity of the clinical picture that accompanies and surrounds the image disorder. This complexity is buried in the deficit and is usually ignored in experimental studies.

An approach to the whole person is essential if research in imagery, not to mention the field of neuropsychology in general, is to progress beyond mere enumeration. It is my view that the process of cognition is a recurrent transform that leads from context to item or whole to part. If this is true, the process can only be discovered in the relation of the context to the item, or the whole to the part, not in the study of the parts alone. Goethe realized this a long time ago when he wrote that science should proceed "not by concentrating on the separate and isolated elements of nature but by portraying it as alive and active with its efforts directed from the whole to the parts" (Goethe, 1790/1988). The recovery of this process, which is the binding of the parts, will invigorate a neuropsychology of the future, one in which this exceptional work should play a pivotal role.

Preface

As a result of the neuropsychological investigations of the past century, which were based primarily on the clinico-anatomical method, we now have a complex understanding of the neurological organization of many aspects of mental life. This knowledge has advanced greatly our scientific understanding of the human mind, and it has been put to practical use in the diagnosis and treatment of neurological disease. However, there is one important mental function that neuropsychology has neglected and to which the clinico-anatomical method has not yet been systematically applied. This function is dreaming—a function that has attracted great psychological interest in the past. In this book I report a study in which the clinico-anatomical method was applied systematically to dreaming for the first time.

The purpose of this study was to place disorders of dreaming on an equivalent footing with those of other higher mental functions, such as the aphasias, apraxias, and agnosias. Modern knowledge of the neurological organization of human mental functions was grounded on systematic clinico-anatomical investigations of these functions under neuropathological conditions. It therefore seemed reasonable to assume that equivalent research into dreaming would provide analogous insights into the cerebral organization of this important but neglected function. Accordingly, the main purpose of this study was to identify changes in dreaming that were systematically associated with focal cerebral pathology and to describe the clinical and anatomical characteristics of those changes. The goal, in short, was to establish a nosology of dream disorders with neuropathological significance.

Unless dreaming turned out to be organized in a way fundamentally different from other mental functions, there was every reason to expect that this research would cast light on the cerebral organization of the normal dream process. Accordingly, I felt justified in advancing a number of theoretical formulations on normal dreaming in this book, based on the clinico-anatomical findings. However, I am under no illusions as to the durability of these formulations. Clinico-anatomical correlations represent but the first step in the neuroscientific investigation of a complex mental function. This step lays the essential descriptive groundwork for the more focused experimental research that must follow if we are to adequately understand the described phenomena. For this reason, just as the post hoc explanations offered by the early clinical investigators of the aphasias, apraxias, and agnosias have long since been surpassed, I realize that few of the formulations advanced in this book are likely to survive future experimental investigations. I sincerely hope that my colleagues will use the full range of technological aids now available to confirm, extend, and correct the preliminary, clinical formulations that are set out in the following pages. They will thereby devote to the problem of dreaming the detailed neuroscientific attention that it certainly deserves; for at the present stage in the development of mental science, few would disagree with Zeki's timely remark that "dreams and hallucinations, up until now the preserve of the psychoanalyst, are legitimate areas of inquiry for the neurobiologist" (Zeki, 1993, p. 343).

The study reported in this book was conducted over a period of several years, starting in 1985. It was completed in all essentials by 1991, but for a variety of reasons the process of preparing it for publication has been unusually protracted. During this period I have accumulated large debts of gratitude to many individuals and institutions. I would like especially to acknowledge the contributions of the following people: Dr. Karen Kaplan-Solms, who contributed fundamentally to the whole scientific project of which the present study forms a part; Professor Michael Saling, who helped me plan this study; Dr. Oliver Turnbull, who assisted me in almost every aspect of this research; Mr. Percy Miller, who made available the vast clinical material at his disposal; Dr. Estelle Doctor, who guided me through many bureaucratic channels; Mr. Michael Whiteside, translator extraordinaire; Mrs. Beryl Bailey, librarian at the Institute of Neurology; Dr. Jason Brown, editor of the IRBN series, and Ms. Amy Olener, Editor with the publishers.

—*Mark Solms*

1

Introduction

There can be little doubt that the neglect of dreaming in neuropsychology is largely attributable to the special methodological problems that this subject poses for the neurological scientist. Changes in dreaming differ from analogous changes in language, praxis, and gnosis in one important respect: dreams are entirely subjective phenomena. This fact prompted Zeki (1993) to write that "most [neuroscientists] would shrink in horror at the thought of investigating what appears so impenetrable a problem" (p. 343). Nevertheless, in conducting the present study I started from the observation that certain neurological patients complained of specific changes in their dreams, the onset of which they dated to the beginning of their illnesses. This was a simple clinical fact, as deserving of serious attention as any other. There was no a priori reason to doubt either the veracity of these patients' reports or the reality of the experiences they described. I therefore decided to treat the reports as I would any other clinical complaint. The scientific task, in my view, was to discover whether or not these reports displayed any degree of uniformity and whether or not typical subjective descriptions tended to co-occur with particular clinical presentations and pathological–anatomical findings. Only then would it be possible to form a considered opinion on the scientific value of the reports. Starting from this premise, I systematically investigated changes in dreaming following neurological disease, using the subjective reports of a large series of neurological and neurosurgical patients as my primary data. With all of its limitations, this method provided the only direct access to the subject matter of the present research, namely, changes in dreaming as experienced and reported by neurological patients.

The subjective experience of dreaming is not to be confused with the physiological state known as rapid eye movement (REM) sleep. REM sleep, unlike dreaming, has been the subject of considerable neuroscientific attention ever since Aserinsky and Kleitman (1953, 1955) first discovered its existence. The clinico-anatomical method was long ago applied to REM sleep. The scientific yield of that research was the identification of an intricate network of neural mechanisms that regulate REM and other sleep phenomena. It is often assumed that this research simultaneously identified the neural mechanisms underlying dreaming, but this is in fact both logically and empirically erroneous. Despite the fact that REM and dreaming frequently co-occur (Dement & Kleitman, 1957a, 1957b), they are distinct entities that can equally well occur independently (Labruzza, 1978; Vogel, 1978; Wasserman, 1984). It therefore cannot simply be assumed that the neurological mechanisms underlying the physiological phenomena of REM sleep regulate the concomitant conscious experiences of dreaming. An empirical investigation of the neurological organization of the conscious experiences themselves is necessary before the causal mechanisms underlying the two classes of phenomena can be equated directly.

In order to access the conscious experiences, one has no alternative but to obtain a subjective report. Because my own interest in this subject started from the observation that certain neurological patients themselves complained of specific changes in their dreams, I decided to extend this simple method of observation into a systematic clinico-anatomical study. I began to ask all my neurological and neurosurgical patients, during routine assessments, about the quality of their dreams. After doing this for 4 years, I systematically correlated the subjective reports that I had obtained from 361 patients with the available clinical and pathological–anatomical data for the same cases, in order to discover whether or not these reports displayed any degree of uniformity and whether or not typical subjective descriptions tended to co-occur with particular clinical presentations and pathological–anatomical findings.

Bedside assessments in behavioral neurology and neuropsychology do not typically involve an investigation of a patient's dreams. The omission of this line of questioning presumably reflects a widespread belief among practitioners that it would not be clinically useful. However, if that belief exists, it is not entirely justified. Although there have been no systematic clinico-anatomical studies, there is a substantial body of published evidence that suggests that neurological diseases do indeed result in specific alterations of dreaming experience. Moreover, this literature suggests that changes in dreaming can provide useful diagnostic indicators as to the location and (in some instances) the nature of a neuropathological process. I was able to trace 73 such publications in the world literature, in which subjective changes in dreaming following specific cerebral insults were described. Most of these reports consisted of incidental observations that were buried in studies devoted primarily to other subjects. I could find only 28 publications that were devoted explicitly to the effects that cerebral lesions have on dreaming, and only 25 of these appeared in English-language journals. Furthermore, the data was largely anecdotal and was limited to descriptions of single cases. Isolated reports of this kind do not carry the weight of evidence that the body of literature as a whole represents. The evidence linking specific changes in dreaming with specific brain changes has therefore not received the attention that it deserves from neurological scientists and clinicians, and the prevailing opinion remains that "there is virtually nothing on this subject in the literature" (Sacks, 1991, p. 29).

In the following pages, I exhaustively review the scattered literature that does exist in order to demonstrate that there is in fact good reason for us to take this subject seriously. The reader should be aware, however, that in subjecting this literature to review I am artificially imposing order and coherence upon a body of data that in reality is disjointed and fragmentary. I should also warn the reader in advance that the crude statistical observations I make in relation to this literature may be misleading. They are made on the basis of data that was collected and recorded by others, often inadequately and incompletely, from small and unequal groups of cases, most of which were studied only because of some remarkable aspect of their dreaming or visual functioning. It is obvious that a meta-analytic procedure such as this is subject to serious sources of error. The conclusions that I reach on the basis of my review of the literature are therefore intended only to provide a foothold on the existing material. Accordingly, they serve as a set of hypotheses for consideration in the light of the empirical findings that are reported in the later chapters of this book.

2

The Classic Case Reports of Charcot–Wilbrand Syndrome

CHARCOT'S CASE

The possibility that dreaming might be altered in specific ways by neurological disease was first introduced more than 100 years ago in a celebrated lecture by Charcot (1883), in which he described a highly unusual case. Charcot's patient (Monsieur X.) gradually became aware, over an 18-month period, of increasing forgetfulness and malaise. This culminated in a sudden paroxysm of confusion, which resulted in a near-total loss of what the patient himself described as "visual memory." By this description the patient meant that he was no longer able to consciously conjure up any visual mental images—a subjective state that he accounted for in the following terms:

> Now, even with the strongest desire in the world, I cannot picture to myself the features of my children or my wife, or any other object of my daily surroundings. Hence, when you realise that I have absolutely lost this power of mental vision, you will readily understand that my impressions are changed in a corresponding fashion. No longer being able to represent visible objects, and yet having com-

pletely preserved my abstract memory, I daily experience astonishment at seeing things which I have known so well for a long time. (Charcot, 1883/1889, p. 158)

The patient complained of various other, apparently related deficits, the most noteworthy of which (from our point of view) was the following: "The faculty of picturing objects within myself being absolutely wanting, *my dreams are correspondingly modified. At the present time I dream simply of speech, whereas I formerly possessed a visual perception in my dreams* [italics added]" (p. 158). Charcot's diagnosis of this case is not known, but the clinical evidence suggests a vascular process in the distribution of the posterior cerebral arteries.[1]

WILBRAND'S CASE

Four years after the publication of Charcot's report, Wilbrand (1887) described a similar case, although there were important differences between the two presentations. Wilbrand's patient, Fräulein G., passed into a "curious state" (after an abrupt loss of consciousness), wherein she could not recognize her physician, and she confused people, animals, and inanimate objects. She was initially regarded as blind but, as the patient herself soon realized, her visual deficit was actually somewhat more complex: "When people stood at my bedside and spoke with pity of my blindness, I said to myself, 'You can't really be blind because you are able to see the cloth with the blue border on the table in the sick-room'" (Critchley, 1953, p. 313). When she was allowed to get up several weeks later, she found herself in the "strange condition of not seeing and yet being able to read" (p. 313). Various other remarkable symptoms were noted, including the following: "Before her illness she dreamt a great deal in pictorial images, *now she dreams almost not at all anymore* [italics added]. Recently however she saw the image of her late sister in a dream" (Wilbrand, 1887, p. 54; Solms, Kaplan-Solms, & Brown, 1996). At autopsy, bilateral infarction in the occipito-temporal region was found (Wilbrand, 1892).

CHARCOT–WILBRAND SYNDROME IN THE LITERATURE

In the classical literature these two cases are grouped together under the nosological heading *Charcot–Wilbrand syndrome* (Critchley, 1953; Nielsen, 1946; Pötzl, 1928). Pötzl (1928) defined this syndrome as "mind-blindness with disturbance of optic imagination" (p. 306). Nielsen (1946) defined it as "visual agnosia plus loss of the ability to revisualise images" (p. 74). According to Critchley's (1953) definition (which is the one most commonly cited), the term *Charcot–Wilbrand syndrome* refers to a condition "whereby a patient loses the power to conjure up visual images or memories, and furthermore, ceases to dream during his sleeping hours" (p. 311). Deficient revisualization (which is called *visual irreminiscence* in the nomenclature of Nielsen, 1946) was the fundamental symptom of the complex. Cessation of dreaming ("or at least, an alteration in the vivid visual component of the dreaming state," Critchley, 1953, p. 311), prosopagnosia, and topographical agnosia or amnesia, were considered to be more or less necessary corollaries of the fundamental revisualization deficit. The locus of the lesion responsible for this configuration of symptoms was never exactly defined, but the occipital cortex (particularly Brodmann's area 19) was typically implicated, usually bilaterally (Critchley, 1953; Gloning & Sternbach, 1953; Nielsen, 1946, 1955).

The nosological category of Charcot–Wilbrand syndrome was generally accepted in classical neurology, and although the whole subject of dreaming has since slipped into obscurity, the syndrome still remains in current nosological usage (cf. Botez, 1985; Botez, Olivier, Vézina, Botez, & Kaufman, 1985; Epstein, 1979; Murri, Arena, Siciliano, Mazzotta, & Murarorio, 1984; Peña-Casanova, Roig-Rovira, Bermudez, & Tolosa-Sarro, 1985). A recent definition of the Charcot–Wilbrand syndrome reads: "the association of loss of the ability to conjure up visual images or memories and the loss of dreaming . . . [indicating] a lesion in an acute phase affecting the posterior regions" (Murri et al., 1984, p. 185). Research on the Charcot–Wilbrand syndrome has in fact provided the mainstream of literature on the neuropsychology of dreams over the past century.

A careful reading of the original case reports, however, reveals that both the designation and the definition of the Charcot–Wilbrand syndrome were based upon a misconception. Critchley (1953) was under the impression that Wilbrand's case "could not visualize the streets of Hamburg where she had been brought up" (p. 311). Nielsen (1946, p. 74), Gloning and Sternbach (1953, p. 305) and Farah (1984, p. 260) were under the same impression. However the original report stated only that her topographical memory (*Ortsgedächtniss*) of Hamburg was defective (Wilbrand, 1887, p. 52), and this deficit was described in terms which would nowadays be defined as topographical agnosia: "As she told her attendant . . . 'If you insist that this is the Jungfernstieg, and that is the Neuenwall, and that the Rathaus, I suppose I must take your word for it, but I can't recognize them at all'" (Critchley, 1953, p. 311). When Wilbrand specifically questioned the patient about her visual imagery she reported: "I could quite well walk through Hamburg with my eyes closed, but when I actually stand in the street I don't know which way to turn; with my eyes shut I see the old Hamburg in front of me again" (Critchley, 1953, p. 311).

It is evident from these excerpts that Wilbrand's case actually lacked the cardinal symptom of the so-called Charcot–Wilbrand syndrome; she suffered an abnormality of visual recognition rather than one of visual imagery. If the patient did initially complain of defective visual imagery, this fact was not mentioned in the published report of the case, and when Wilbrand himself examined her, he specifically commented upon the vivacity (*Lebhaftigkeit*) of her imagery (Wilbrand, 1887, p. 53).

The deficit in Charcot's (1883) case appears to have been quite different. His patient clearly described a striking absence of inner vision (*vision intérieure*), whereas the alteration in his external visual perception was limited to a sense of strangeness and unfamiliarity (p. 570).

It seems likely that the conflation of these two presentations in the secondary literature arose out of the ambiguity of the term *memory* (*Gedächtniss*) in the context of the early *mind-blindness* (*Seelenblindheit*) concept, when it was assumed that the symptom of visual agnosia was caused by a loss of visual memory images. It is interesting to note that Wilbrand himself was well aware of the distinction between the two classical cases with respect to their visual imagery (Wilbrand, 1887), as were many other early commentators (Brain, 1954; Lange, 1936; Müller, 1892; Pötzl, 1928). The subsequent nosographic confusion was apparently caused by theoretical advances in the agnosia concept (Solms et al., 1996).

There was another important difference in the symptomatology of Charcot and Wilbrand's cases, a difference that is of greater interest to us because it concerns their dreaming. This fact has also not attracted the scientific attention that it deserves. Charcot's patient ceased to dream in visual images, but he continued to dream in words. Wilbrand's (1887) patient, on the other hand, dreamed "almost *not at all* [italics added] anymore" (p. 54). However, on at least one occasion some years after her stroke she did experience a visual dream. In other words, whereas Charcot's patient lost the visual aspect of his dreams, Wilbrand's patient either totally lost the faculty of dreaming for a period of time and then regained it, or else she dreamed much less frequently than before. In either event there was no mention of her having nonvisual dreams, which is what Charcot's patient unequivocally described.

In 1892, Müller reported another case of Charcot–Wilbrand syndrome. Müller's patient (Frau Anna Hoffmann) suffered irreminiscence and visual agnosia, among other symptoms, following bilateral occipital hemorrhages. This patient "had *no further dreams* [italics added] since her illness, whereas previously she not infrequently had vivid dreams and saw all sorts of things in them" (Müller, 1892, p. 868). This was an unambiguous description of complete cessation of dreaming—which confirms the distinction between Charcot's and Wilbrand's cases in this respect.

The two varieties of the dream abnormality described by Charcot on the one hand and Wilbrand and Müller on the other were often reported in the literature of the present century. At least 11 cases of patients with loss of visual dreaming have been reported, together with 4 patients who reported selective deficits of visual dream imagery that are highly reminiscent of the disorder described by Charcot (see Table 2.1). Moreover, Brown (1972), Efron (1968), and Kerr, Foulkes, & Jurkovic (1978), confirmed the retrospective subjective

TABLE 2.1
Case Reports of Cessation or Restriction of Visual Dream Imagery

Source	Case	Lesion	Charcot–Wilbrand Symptoms	Dreams
Charcot [Bernard] (1883)	Monsieur X	[No information — ?Bilat. med. Occip-Temp. (thrombosis)]	Irreminiscence, Prosopagnosia, Topograph. agnosia	Cessation of visual imagery
Grünstein (1924)	Patient N., 23-yr f.	L. lat. Occip.[a] (thrombosis)	Irreminiscence, Prosopagnosia, Topograph. agnosia	Cessation of visual imagery
Adler (1944, 1950); Sparr, Jay, Drislane, & Venna (1991)	H.C., 22-yr f.	Bilat. Occip-Par.[a] (CO poisoning)	±Irreminiscence, Prosopagnosia, Topograph. amnesia	Cessation of visual imagery, with subsequent global cessation of dreaming
Brain (1950, 1954)	Case 1, 36-yr m.	Front., Occip.[a] (trauma)	Irreminiscence, Topograph. amnesia	Cessation of visual imagery
Gloning & Sternbach (1953)	W. Josef, 53-yr m.	L.[b] Thalam.[a] (hemorrhage).	None	Cessation of visual imagery
Schindler (1953)	Case 89	Bilat. deep Front.[c] (leukotomy)	[No information][e]	Global cessation of imagery [dream feeling without imagery]
	Case 111	Bilat. deep Front.[c] (leukotomy)	[No information]	Global cessation of imagery [dream atmosphere without imagery]
Macrae & Trolle (1956)	32-yr m.	Bilat. Par.[a] (trauma)	Irreminiscence, Prosopagnosia	Cessation of visual imagery[a]
Tzavaras (1967)	Monsieur P. Maurice, 54 yrs	L. Occip-Temp., R. Temp.[a] (hemorrhage)	Irreminiscence for faces, Prosopagnosia, Topograph. amnesia	Cessation of facial imagery
Efron (1968); Benson & Greenberg (1969); Brown (1972)	25-yr m. [Brown's Case 13]	Bilat. Occip-Par.[a] (CO poisoning)	Irreminiscence, Prosopagnosia	Non-visual nightmares for 1 wk; residual cessation of visual imagery or global cessation of dreaming [descriptions ambiguous][f]

TABLE 2.1
(*Continued*)

Source	Case	Lesion	Charcot–Wilbrand Symptoms	Dreams
Kerr et al. (1978)	21-yr f.	?R. Par.[a] [Not localiz-able] (Turner's syndrome)	Irreminiscence	Absence of visual imagery
Botez, Olivier, Vézina, Butez, & Kaufman (1985)	38-yr m.	?R.[b] hemisphere, ?Corp. callosum (?dysgenesis)[d]	Irreminiscence, ±Prosopag-nosia, Topograph. agnosia or Topograph. amnesia [description ambiguous]	Reduction or absence of facial imagery [description ambigu-ous] and absence of hypna-gogic imagery
Sacks (1985)	Dr. P., m.	"visual parts of his brain" (tumor or atrophy)[a]	?Irreminiscence [description ambiguous], Prosopagnosia	Cessation of visual imagery
Sacks & Wasser-man (1987)	Jonathan I., 65-yr m.	Bilat. med. Occip-Temp.[a] (trauma)	Irreminiscence for color	Cessation of color imagery and reduction of tonal gradation
Sacks (1991)	[No infor-mation]	"diffuse damage to the occipital cortex"[a] (Alzheimer's disease)	[No information]	Cessation of visual imagery

[a] Clinical localization or diagnosis.
[b] Left-handed or ambidextrous patient.
[c] Localization or diagnosis based on intraoperative observation.
[d] Localization or diagnosis based on in vivo imaging techniques.
[e] Unless otherwise indicated, it is assumed that the authors comprehensively investigated and reported the neuropsycho-logical status of their cases.
[f] Benson & Greenberg (1969, p. 85) described this patient as a case of global cessation of dreaming and reported that "the patient denied dreaming" upon REM awakening, whereas Brown (1972, p. 210) stated that "a REM study was normal in character but revealed absence of *visual elements* [italics added] in his dreams."

reports by means of the REM awakening method. More than 40 cases have been reported with global cessation of dreaming (or gross reduction in frequency of dreaming) of the type described by Wilbrand and Müller (see Table 2.2). Michel and Sieroff (1981) and Schanfald, Pearlman, and Greenberg (1985) confirmed these subjective reports too by means of the REM awakening method. There were also a number of reports of neurological patients in which preservation of dreaming and dream imagery was described (see Table 2.3a).[2] Negative cases such as these form an important group in the characterization of any syndrome. Table 2.3b lists additional cases in which subjective dream reports were elicited by awakening neurological patients from REM sleep. Because there is no guarantee that the latter patients would have reported normal dreaming in the context of a bedside interview, they have been tabulated separately.

This literature not only confirms the fact that dreaming can be disrupted in specific ways by neurological disease, as the classical concept of Charcot–Wilbrand syndrome suggested, it also confirms that this concept conflated two different neurogenic dream disorders. In short, there appear to be two types of Charcot–Wilbrand syndrome. This conclusion forms the first hypothesis to be investigated in the present study: The Charcot–Wilbrand syndrome is not a unitary entity; two types of "loss of dreaming" exist, each of which is part of a distinct neuropsychological syndrome with separate anatomical correlates.

An alternative possibility exists: Charcot's variant of the syndrome may be an incomplete form of Wilbrand's variant. This implies that the lesion sites producing the two variants of the classical syndrome should overlap, as should their clinical phenomenology. It is therefore important to know, from both a clinical and a scientific point of view, what pathological–anatomical features are associated with these different changes in dreaming and what their neurobehavioral correlates are. If we can establish that the two phenomena regularly coincide with lesions to specific brain regions then we will have identified not only two focal symptoms with some clinical usefulness, but also two important components of the neuroanatomical substrate of normal dreaming. Likewise, if the changes in dreaming regularly co-occur with other specific neurocognitive deficits then we will have identified two focal syndromes, the analysis of which should isolate one or more of the elementary psychological functions underlying the normal process of dreaming. This will be the clinical and scientific yield if a double dissociation of function (Teuber, 1955, 1959) can be established between nonvisual dreaming and global cessation of dreaming.

These issues are considered in the following chapters, in relation to the existing literature, before I approach them afresh in relation to my own research.

TABLE 2.2

Case Reports of Global Cessation or Reduction of Dreaming

Source	Case	Lesion	Charcot–Wilbrand Symptoms	Dreams
Wilbrand (1887, 1892)	Fräulein G.	R. med. Occip-Temp., L. deep Occip. (thrombosis).[a]	Prosopagnosia, Topograph. agnosia	Either global cessation with recovery over approx. 4 yrs or gross reduction in frequency [description ambiguous]
Müller (1892)	Frau Anna Hoffmann, 50 yrs	Bilat. Occip. (hemorrhage)[b]	Irreminiscence, Prosopagnosia, Topograph. amnesia	Global cessation
Grünstein (1924)	[p. 420]	[L. lat. Temp.]	None	Global cessation
	[p. 420]	[L. lat. Temp.]	None	Global cessation
Lyman, Kwan, & Chao (1938)	42-yr m.	L. deep Occip-Par. (meningioma)[d]	Irreminiscence	Global cessation
Piehler (1950)	Case 1, 49-yr m.	Bilat. deep Front.[d] (leukotomy)	None	Global cessation with recovery after approx. 6 wks; global cessation again after 2nd op. with recovery after approx. 2 yrs; residual reduction in frequency, narrative complexity, and intensity
	Case 2, 36-yr m.	Bilat. deep Front.[d] (leukotomy)	None	Global cessation with gradual recovery after approx. 4 months
	Case 3, 34-yr f.	Bilat. deep Front.[d] (leukotomy)	None	Global cessation with recovery after approx. 3 months; residual reduction in frequency

(Continued)

11

TABLE 2.2
(Continued)

Source	Case	Lesion	Charcot–Wilbrand Symptoms	Dreams
[Piehler (1950)]	Case 4, 33-yr f.	Bilat. deep Front.[d] (leukotomy)	None	Global cessation with recovery after approx. 3 months
Humphrey & Zangwill (1951)	Case 1, 26-yr m.	R. Par.[e] (trauma)	Irreminiscence, Topograph. amnesia	Global cessation with partial recovery or gross reduction in frequency [description ambiguous]
	Case 2, 21-yr m.	Bilat. lat. Par.[e] (trauma)	Irreminiscence, Topograph. amnesia	Global cessation and cessation of hypnagogic imagery
	Case 3, 32-yr m.	R.[f] [lat?] Par.[d] (trauma)	Irreminiscence, Topograph. amnesia	Global cessation with recovery after approx. 5 yrs
Oldfield (Humphrey & Zangwill, 1951) [p. 324n]		R. Occip-Par. (abscess)[d]	[No information][c]	Global cessation
Gloning & Sternbach (1953)	S. Johann, 48-yr m.	R. deep Front-Temp. (glioma)[d]	None	Increased proprioceptive-vestibular imagery (falling & flying); residual reduction in frequency
	L. Josef, 64-yr m.	L. med. Occip-Temp., R. post. Occip. (thrombosis)[a]	Irreminiscence	Global cessation
	K. Franz, 56-yr m.	L. med. Occip-Temp. (thrombosis)[b]	Irreminiscence	Global cessation with recovery after approx. 1 yr; residual reduction of visual imagery
	W. Karl, 52-yr m.	R.[e] Front.[b] [& Temp-Par.] (thrombosis)	None	Global cessation
	M. Klara, 32-yr f.	R. deep Front-Par. (glioma)[d]	None	Global cessation

TABLE 2.2
(Continued)

Source	Case	Lesion	Charcot–Wilbrand Symptoms	Dreams
[Gloning & Sternbach (1953)]	Sch. Gertrude, 56-yr f.	Bilat. deep Front. (glioma)[d]	None	Increased vivacity, later becoming global cessation
	M. Josef, 24-yr m.	R. deep Par-Temp. (hemorrhage)[e]	None	Gross reduction in frequency
	E. Ernst, 57-yr m.	L. Occip-Thalam. (thrombosis)[b]	Topograph agnosia or amnesia [description ambiguous]	Global cessation with gradual recovery over approx. 3 yrs
	N. Johann, 51-yr m.	L. Thalam. (thrombosis)[b]	None	Global cessation with recovery after 5 months
	[p. 318]	Bilat. deep Front. (leukotomy)[d]	[No information]	Global cessation
	[pp. 318–9]	Bilat. deep Front. (leukotomy)[d]	[No information]	Global cessation
Boyle & Nielsen (1954); Nielsen (1955)	E. S., 31-yr m.	3rd. ventric. (cyst) [with hydroceph.],[e] L. deep Occip-Temp.,[b] R. Occip.[d] (surgical trauma)	Irreminiscence	Global cessation
Nielsen (1955)	Harley S., m.	L. Occip. (glioma)[d]	Irreminiscence, Topograph. agnosia or amnesia [description ambiguous]	Global cessation
	[p. 52]	L. Occip. (tumor)	Irreminiscence	Global cessation
	[p. 52]	L. Occip. (tumour)	Irreminiscence	Global cessation
	f.	Bilat. Occip.[d] (trauma)	None	Global cessation

(Continued)

TABLE 2.2
(Continued)

Source	Case	Lesion	Charcot–Wilbrand Symptoms	Dreams
Ettlinger et al. (1957)	N. H., 57-yr m.	R. Occip–Temp.[a] (metastatic tumor)	Irreminiscence, Topograph. amnesia	Global cessation
Ritchie (1959)	Douglas Ritchie, 50-yr m.	L. (thrombosis)[b]	None	Global cessation with recovery after approx. 2 yrs
Farrell (1969); Neal (1988)	Patricia Neal, 39-yr f.	L. Temp[-Par.] (hemorrhage)[d]	Irreminiscence	Global cessation
Feldman (1971)	36-yr f.	Ventral pons. (thrombosis)[b]	None	Global cessation
Moss (1972)	C. Scott Moss, 43-yr m.	L. (thrombosis)[b]	None	Global cessation with recovery after 4 months
Wapner, Judd, & Gardner (1978)	J. R., 73-yr m.[f]	Bilat. Occip. (thrombosis)[e]	Irreminiscence, Prosopagnosia, Topograph. amnesia	Global cessation
Epstein (1979)	Patient 1, 56-yr f.	L.[f] med. Par-Occip. (thrombosis)[b]	Irreminiscence, Prosopagnosia	Global cessation with gradual recovery after approx. 5 months
Basso, Bisiach, & Luzzatti (1980)	M. G., 63-yr m.	L. med. Occip–Temp, cerebellum (thrombosis)[e]	Global irreminiscence [affecting all modalities], Prosopagnosia, Topograph. agnosia	Global cessation and cessation of hypnagogic imagery
Epstein & Simmons (1983)	Case 1, 47-yr f.	L. Front–Temp. (hemorrhage)[d]	None	Global cessation
	Case 2, 35-yr f.	L. Front. (thrombosis)[e]	None	Global cessation
	Case 3, 33-yr m.	L. Front–Temp. (thrombosis)[e]	None	Global cessation
	Case 4, 56-yr f.	L. (thrombosis)[b]	None	Global cessation

TABLE 2.2
(Continued)

Source	Case	Lesion	Charcot–Wilbrand Symptoms	Dreams
[Epstein & Simmons (1983)]	Case 5, 52-yr f.	L. (thrombosis).[b]	None	Global cessation
	Case 6, 43-yr f.	L. (thrombosis)[b]	None	Global cessation
	Case 7, 59-yr f.	L. deep Par-Occip. (thrombosis)[e]	None	Global cessation
Peña–Casanova, Roig-Rovira, Bermudez, & Tolosa-Sarro (1985)	A. R., 47-yr m.	L. med. Occip-Temp. [thrombosis][e]	Irreminiscence	Global cessation with gradual recovery after approx. 5 months
Habib & Sirigu (1987)	Case 2, 26-yr f.	R.[f] med. Temp. (thrombosis)[e]	Topograph. agnosia	Either global cessation or specific amnesia [description ambiguous]
Farah, Levine, & Calviano (1988)	R. M., 64-yr m.	L. med. Occip-Temp. (thrombosis)[e]	Irreminiscence	Global cessation

[a]Autopsy-confirmed localization.
[b]Clinical localization or diagnosis.
[c]Unless otherwise indicated, it is assumed that the authors comprehensively investigated and reported the neuropsychological status of their cases.
[d]Localization or diagnosis based on intraoperative observation.
[e]Localization or diagnosis based on in vivo imaging techniques.
[f]Left-handed or ambidextrous patient.

TABLE 2.3A
Case Reports of Normal Dreaming

Source	Case	Lesion	Charcot–Wilbrand Symptoms[b]	Dreams
Mach (1906/1959)	Self-report	L. (thrombosis)[a]	None	Present, with [?visual] imagery
Brain (1941)	Howard G., 15-yr m.	[Diffuse][a] (systemic)	±Irreminiscence, ±Prosopagnosia, ±Topograph. agnosia	Present, with visual imagery
Gloning & Sternbach (1953)	P. Anton, 33-yr m.	R. Temp.[d][-Occip.][a] (trauma, abscess)	None	Present, no abnormality detected
	P. Hilde, 31-yr f.	R. Temp. (dermoid cyst)[c]	None	Present, no abnormality detected
	P. Anna, 45-yr f.	R. Thalam. [thrombosis][a]	None	Present, no abnormality detected
	K. Theodora, 64-yr f.	R. Thalam. (thrombosis)[a]	None	Present, no abnormality detected
	D. Leopold, 54-yr m.	R. med. Par-Occip., R. Thalam. (thrombosis)[a]	Topograph. agnosia or amnesia [description ambiguous]	Present, no abnormality detected
Pallis (1955)	A. H., 51-yr m.	Bilat. Occip. (thrombosis)[a]	Topograph. agnosia, Prosopagnosia	Present, with visual imagery, with possible reduction in frequency [description ambiguous]
Dahlberg & Jaffe (1977)	C. Clay Dahlberg, 55-yr m.	L. (thrombosis)[d]	None	Present, apparently normal [description ambiguous]
Shuttleworth, Syring, & Allen (1982)	Case 2, 49-yr f.	Bilat. Occip-Temp-Par. (trauma)[c]	Prosopagnosia, ±Irreminiscence	Present, with visual imagery

[a] Clinical localization or diagnosis.
[b] Unless otherwise indicated, it is assumed that the authors comprehensively investigated and reported the neuropsychological status of their cases.
[c] Localization or diagnosis based on intraoperative observation.
[d] Localization or diagnosis based on in vivo imaging techniques.

TABLE 2.3B

Case Reports of Normal Dreaming (Dream Reports Elicited by REM Sleep Awakening)[a]

Source	Case	Lesion	Charcot–Wilbrand Symptoms	Dreams
Greenwood, Wilson, & Gazzaniga (1977)	J. K. N., m.	Corp. Callosum (±commissurotomy)	None	Present, with visual imagery
	J. K., m.	Corp. Callosum (±commissurotomy)	None	Present, with visual imagery
	J. H., m.	Corp. Callosum (commissurotomy)	None	Present, with visual imagery
Schanfald et al. (1985)	LFP, m.	L. Front-Par. (cerebro-vascular accident; CVA)	None	Present, apparently normal
	LF, m.	L. Front. (CVA)	None	Present, apparently normal
	LFTP, m.	L. Front-Temp-Par. (CVA)	None	Present
	LTP, m.	L. Temp-Par. (CVA)	None	Present, apparently normal
	RTP, m.	L. Temp-Par. (CVA)	Prosopagnosia	Present, apparently normal
	RAVM, m.	R. (AVM)	None	Present, apparently normal
Murri, Massetani, Siciliano, & Arena (1985)	Case 1, 57-yr f.	L. Front.[b] (tumor)	[No information][d]	Present, apparently normal
	Case 2, 74-yr f.	R. Front.[b] (tumor)	[No information]	Present, apparently normal
	Case 3, 51-yr f.	L. Front.[b] (tumor)	[No information]	Present, apparently normal
	Case 4, 66-yr f.	R. Front.[b] (tumor)	[No information]	Present, apparently normal
	Case 5, 69-yr f.	R. Front.[b] (CVA)	[No information]	Present, apparently normal
	Case 6, 71-yr f.	L. Temp-Par-Occip.[c] (CVA)	[No information]	Present, apparently normal

(Continued)

TABLE 2.3B
(Continued)

Source	Case	Lesion	Charcot–Wilbrand Symptoms	Dreams
[Murri, Massetani, Siciliano, & Arena (1985)]	Case 7, 53-yr f.	R. Front.[b] (CVA)	[No information]	Present, apparently normal
	Case 9, 50-yr m.	R. Temp-Par-Occip.[c] (tumor)	[No information]	Present, apparently normal
	Case 14, 57-yr m.	L. Temp-Par-Occip.[c] (CVA)	[No information]	Present, apparently normal
	Case 16, 63-yr m.	R. Temp-Par-Occip.[c] (tumor)	[No information]	Present, apparently normal

[a]Brown's (1972) Case 11, who reported preserved dreaming and dream-imagery upon REM awakenings, is excluded from this table because it seems reasonably certain from the published account that the patient's dreams were abnormal.

[b]Lesion defined as "outside the temporo-parieto-occipital area"—which could imply either a frontal or a deep lesion, or a combination of the two.

[c]Lesion defined as "inside the temporo-parieto-occipital area"—which could imply a lesion in any one or any combination of the other three lobes.

[d]Unless otherwise indicated, it is assumed that the authors comprehensively investigated and reported the neuropsychological status of their cases.

18

NOTES

[1]It is of historical interest to note that Freud—who had an opportunity to speak with this patient and who later translated Charcot's report of the case into German (Charcot, 1886/1890)—was of the opinion that his condition was hysterical (Schilder, 1961). This opinion was shared by Bay, among others (Bay & Lauenstein, 1948).

[2]Doricchi and Violani (1992) cited further case reports of this type, which I have been unable to trace.

3

Charcot's Variant
of the Charcot–Wilbrand Syndrome:
Cessation or Restriction
of Visual Dream-Imagery

Does nonvisual dreaming have regular pathological–anatomical correlates? Charcot's original case never came to autopsy; nor did any of the subsequently reported cases of the nonvisual type. However, a number of cases with defective revisualization in general (irreminiscence) did come to autopsy. Because the symptom of irreminiscence was the central feature of Charcot's case, the autopsy data pertaining to irreminiscence is relevant to the question under consideration. In two well-known reviews of this data, Nielsen (1946, 1955) concluded that a lesion in area 19 of the occipital lobes of either hemisphere was necessary for the occurrence of this symptom. On this basis some classical authors described irreminiscence as *"l'amnesie des occipitaux"* (Critchley, 1953, p. 304). The occipital localization of disorders characterized by a total loss of visual mental imagery has been confirmed by modern investigators using in vivo imaging techniques (see Farah 1984, 1989a, 1989b, for reviews). However, recent research—which has focused on specific components of visual imagery, such as form, color, faces, letters, and spatial relationships—has begun to reveal more complex anatomical correlations (see Goldenberg, 1993, for review).

CHAPTER 3

PATHOLOGICAL–ANATOMICAL CORRELATES
OF DISORDERED DREAM-IMAGERY

I focus my review of the literature on the pathological–anatomical correlates of disordered dream-imagery. Table 2.1 shows that there was a strong tendency for the symptom of nonvisual dreaming to be associated with bilateral cerebral lesions. Eight of the 15 published cases of this type were considered by their investigators (on clinical and radiological grounds) to have bilateral cortical lesions. Of the remaining 7 patients, one sustained a high-velocity head injury (Brain, 1950, 1954), another was diagnosed with Turner's syndrome (Kerr et al., 1978), a third was thought to have had "a massive tumour or degenerative process" (Sacks, 1985, p. 17), a fourth presented with an obscure congenital abnormality (Botez et al., 1985), and a fifth was a patient with Alzheimer's disease who was described as having "diffuse damage to the occipital cortex" (Sacks, 1991, p. 31). All of these cases are likely to have been instances of bilateral disease. Only Grünstein (1924) and Gloning and Sternbach (1953) reported nonvisual dreaming in association with unilateral cerebral lesions. However, Grünstein's case had a clinical history suggestive of meningovascular syphilis (with positive Wasserman reaction) and had neurobehavioral symptoms that are commonly associated with bilateral cerebral disease (e.g., prosopagnosia; Ettlin et al., 1992). There was nothing that positively suggested a bilateral affection in Gloning and Sternbach's case with a cerebral hemorrhage, but because hemorrhages are space-occupying lesions, the possibility of a bilateral lesion cannot be excluded in this case.

In addition to the lesions' being bilateral, they were also shown, in published cases of this type, to frequently involve the posterior cerebral zones, (Table 2.1 demonstrates this point). Involvement of the medial occipitotemporal region is a particularly common feature. There are only two patients in whom this region was definitely not implicated (Schindler, 1953, Cases 89 & 111). In these two cases the dream-imagery deficit was associated with prefrontal leukotomy. However, these cases displayed some unique features. The patients reported that they experienced dream atmospheres or dream feelings (*Traumstimmungen oder Gefühl eines Traumes*) with a total absence of dream-imagery in any modality. None of the other patients listed in Table 2.1 reported these experiences; in all the other cases the imagery deficit was restricted to the visual modality. This discrepancy between Schindler's cases and the others calls into question their inclusion under the heading of cessation or restriction of visual dream-imagery. It also raises the possibility that the dream symptomatology in his cases was attributable to their serious psychopathology rather than to their psychosurgical lesions. Lewin (1946, 1953) has described identical phenomena ("blank dreams") in purely functional cases. Therefore, Schindler's observations do not undermine our putative localization of nonvisual dreaming to the occipito-temporal region.

This results in a second hypothesis for the present investigation: Cessation or restriction of visual dream-imagery indicates a bilateral lesion in the medial occipito-temporal region. It is noteworthy that this localization partly overlaps with the localization that was given in the classical literature for the Charcot–Wilbrand syndrome as a whole (i.e., area 19 of either hemisphere; Nielsen, 1946).

NEUROBEHAVIORAL CORRELATES
OF NONVISUAL DREAMING

The classical definition of the Charcot–Wilbrand syndrome included three symptoms in addition to cessation of dreaming itself: irreminiscence, prosopagnosia, and topographical agnosia or amnesia (Critchley, 1953; Nielsen, 1946). Some authors also considered visual (object) agnosia to be part of the Charcot–Wilbrand syndrome (Adler, 1944, 1950; Boyle & Nielsen, 1954; Broughton, 1982; Gloning & Sternbach, 1953; Greenwood, Wilson & Gazzanga, 1977; Grünstein, 1924; Nielsen, 1946; Pötzl, 1928). However, this was disputed by other authors (Basso et al., 1980; Botez et al., 1985; Brain, 1950, 1954; Humphrey & Zangwill, 1951; Macrae & Trolle, 1956; Murri et al., 1984; Murri et al., 1985).

Irreminiscence

Irreminiscence was the focus of Charcot's (1883) original case report. This symptom was subsequently considered to be the basic deficit (*Grundstörung*) underlying the entire Charcot–Wilbrand syndrome (Critchley, 1953; Nielsen, 1946; Pötzl, 1928). Table 2.1 shows that almost all cases of nonvisual dreaming reported in the literature (91%) suffered this basic deficit. In view of the obvious phenomenological similarity between the inability to generate a visual image and cessation of visual dream-imagery, the strong correlation between them reasonably suggests that irreminiscence and nonvisual dreaming arise from a common underlying deficit. The only evidence not supporting this conclusion consists of Gloning and Sternbach's case W. Josef (see Table 2.1), who apparently experienced nonvisual dreaming in the absence of irreminiscence, and Brain's (1941) and Brown's (1972) cases of irreminiscence, who apparently experienced preservation of visual dream-imagery. However, in view of the elusive subjectivity of phenomena such as mental imagery and dream-imagery, isolated exceptions to a rule should not be overemphasized. In these circumstances a 91% correlation is extremely high. Kerr and Foulkes's (1981) case report (described in chapter 12) demonstrates that a patient's initial description of his or her dreams is sometimes flatly contradicted or heavily qualified upon systematic questioning.

The conclusion that irreminiscence and nonvisual dreaming arise from a common underlying deficit is further supported by the observation that partial disruptions of visual dream-imagery are regularly accompanied by correspondingly partial irreminiscences. Tzavaras (1967) reported a patient who lacked facial dream-imagery and who suffered prosopagnosia and irreminiscence for faces in waking life. Sacks and Wasserman (1987) reported the case of an artist with loss of color-imagery in dreams, who had central achromatopsia and irreminiscence for colors in waking life. Basso et al. (1980) reported the case of a patient with global cessation of dreaming who complained of waking irreminiscence in all modalities (see Table 2.2). Harrison (1981) reported the case of a person with transient aphasia associated with transient alexia in a dream (see Table 7.3). Kerr and Foulkes (1981) reported a patient who was "[unable] to represent extrapersonal space kinematically" (p. 605) and described her dreams as "lacking specifically in *continuous* [italics added] visual imagery;" the occasional visual images that did appear were "fragmentary and static in nature" (p. 608). These associations are reminiscent of the fractionation of visual imagery into form, color, faces, letters, and spatial relationships by modern researchers (see Goldenberg, 1993, for review).

Agnosias

The correlations between cessation of visual dream-imagery and the other classical elements of the Charcot–Wilbrand syndrome do not appear to be as strong as the association between nonvisual dreaming and irreminiscence. Seventy-three percent of the cases listed in Table 2.1 suffered prosopagnosia and only 50% of them suffered either topographical agnosia or amnesia or visual (object) agnosia. Furthermore, Brain (1941) reported one case of a man with associative visual agnosia who was able to generate meaningful visual perceptions in his dreams, Schanfald et al. (1985) reported a case of a patient with simultanagnosia and prosopagnosia who experienced clear visual dream-imagery—including images of familiar faces—and Brown (1972) reported two cases of people with apperceptive agnosia (Cases 11 & 12), both of whom experienced at least some visual dream images. Pallis (1955) reported similar observations in a case of prosopagnosia and topographical agnosia. It is evident from these reports that prosopagnosia and topographical agnosia (or topographical amnesia) are not necessary correlates of irreminiscence. This implies that although irreminiscence may be the *Grundstörung* underlying the symptom of nonvisual dreaming itself, it does not explain the entire Charcot–Wilbrand syndrome—which is what Pötzl (1928), Nielsen (1946) and Critchley (1953) originally suggested.

Other Symptoms:
Achromatopsia and Hypoemotionality

Charcot's prototypical patient presented with two further symptoms that were not subsequently included in the Charcot–Wilbrand syndrome but neverthe-less deserve further comment. The first of these was central achromatopsia. Because this symptom is rather rare, it is noteworthy that 33% of the cases listed in Table 2.1 presented with achromatopsia (Charcot, 1883; Macrae & Trolle, 1956; Sacks & Wasserman, 1987; Tzavaras, 1967). The patient in the case of Basso et al. (1980; discussed previously; see Table 2.2) adds further weight to this association.

There is little reason to believe that central achromatopsia is an integral part of the syndrome of nonvisual dreaming. However, because the cortical lesion producing central achromatopsia has been localized to a highly circum-scribed region—namely, area V4 on the fusiform gyrus bilaterally (Zeki, 1990, 1993)—its association with nonvisual dreaming may shed additional light on the localization of the latter symptom. Similar considerations apply to prosopagnosia, the critical lesion for which lies in close proximity to region V4 on the fusiform gyrus, and therefore frequently accompanies central achro-matopsia (Ettlin et al., 1992; Zeki, 1993). Prosopagnosia was present in 73% of the cases listed in Table 2.1 (Adler, 1944; Botez et al., 1985; Charcot, 1883; Efron, 1968; Grünstein, 1924; Macrae & Trolle, 1956; Sacks, 1985; Tzavaras, 1967). These observations support our putative localization of the lesion re-sponsible for nonvisual dreaming to the bilateral medial occipito–temporal region (Hypothesis 1).

The second of the two symptoms that deserve further attention is hypo-emotionality. This symptom was described by Charcot's (1883) patient in the following remarkable passage:

> A singular result of the loss of this mental faculty . . . is a great change in my character. . . . I am much less affected by grief and disappointment. I may men-tion that having lately lost one of my relatives, for whom I had a sincere attach-ment; I experienced a much less intense grief than if I had still possessed the power of representing, by my internal vision, the face of the relative, the phases of the disease through which he had gone; and especially, if I had been able to picture within myself the outward effects produced by his premature death on the other members of our family. (Charcot, 1883/1889, p. 159)

A symptom of this nature can have a complex determination; it therefore does not necessarily have any special relationship to irreminiscence or nonvisual dreaming. For example, a relationship appears to exist between functional de-pression and loss of visual imagery (see Schilder, 1934). Although functional mood disorders have never been associated with nonvisual dreaming, there is at least one report in the literature of a depressed patient who reported global cessation of dreaming (Styron, 1990). Notwithstanding these considerations, it is interesting to observe that Botez et al.'s (1985) patient with nonvisual dreaming (Table 2.1) had a similar complaint to Charcot's patient:

> When his present girlfriend leaves their apartment, he has no kind of visual im-age of her and, therefore, fails to experience the relevant feeling. He said: *"L'ab-*

sence des images visuelles empêche le prolongment des émotions" (the absence of visual images disrupts the continuity of emotional feelings). (p. 378)

Hypoemotionality was not mentioned in any of the other case reports of non-visual dreaming.[1] However, the fact that it was not mentioned does not necessarily imply that it was absent in those cases; indeed only highly articulate and introspective patients are likely to report experiences of this sort spontaneously. A direct investigation is therefore required of the relationship between loss of visual dream-imagery and hypoemotionality.

Because there is insufficient evidence to include the last-mentioned symptoms in a definition of the syndrome of nonvisual dreaming, our putative definition (and a third hypothesis for the present study) reads as follows: Cessation or restriction of visual dream-imagery typically occurs in combination with a corresponding deficit of visual imagery in general (irreminiscence) and it is also commonly associated with prosopagnosia, topographical agnosia or amnesia, and visual agnosia. However, we should also pay special attention to the relationship between nonvisual dreaming on the one hand and central achromatopsia and hypoemotionality on the other, when we consider the results of the present study (see chapter 13, this volume).

NEUROPSYCHOLOGICAL MECHANISMS OF NONVISUAL DREAMING

Before leaving the topic of nonvisual dreaming in order to discuss the global (Wilbrand–Müller) variant of the Charcot–Wilbrand syndrome, I briefly review the literature on the neuropsychological mechanism of nonvisual dreaming. In fact very little has been written about the mechanism of this syndrome. Charcot (1883) reported the phenomenon of nonvisual dreaming as a simple clinical fact that was incidental to the main thrust of his argument, without making any specific theoretical comments. Most subsequent authors have followed this example. Nevertheless, it is clear from Charcot's general discussion of his case that he conceptualized the syndrome as a modality-specific memory disorder. Charcot's (1889) conclusion was the following:

> This necessarily leads one to admit that the different groups of memories have their seat in circumscribed regions of the encephalon. And this in turn becomes added to the proofs which go to establish that the hemispheres of the brain consist of a number of differentiated "organs," each of which possesses its proper function. (pp. 162–163)

The explanation of nonvisual dreaming in terms of damage to a cortical center for visual memory images has been either implicitly or explicitly endorsed by most subsequent authors. There have been only three additions to Charcot's original conceptualization of the syndrome, all of which may be understood as elaborations of his theory.

Grünstein's Elaboration of Charcot's Theory

The first of these elaborations came from Grünstein (1924) who observed that whereas visual dream-imagery is lost in cases of visual agnosia and irreminiscence (i.e., in cases with damage to visual association cortex), it is not affected in cases of cortical blindness (i.e., in cases with damage to primary visual cortex). Grünstein predicted on this basis that analogous modality-specific dream disorders should arise from damage to secondary cortex in any sensory modality. For example, patients with lesions in secondary auditory cortex should experience nonauditory (or nonverbal) dreams. In other words, Grünstein extended Charcot's theory of visual dream-imagery to the other modalities. However, Grünstein himself was unable to confirm his prediction in two cases of what he described as *auditory agnosia* (actually they were cases of pure word-deafness), for both of the patients reported that they had stopped dreaming completely (see Table 2.2). Grünstein's hypothesis therefore remains of theoretical interest today, as it has still not been systematically investigated. (It is investigated in chapter 14, this volume.)

The important observation on which Grünstein's hypothesis was based— namely that dream-imagery is preserved in cases of cortical blindness but not in cases with higher visual disturbances—was evidently overlooked by Zeki (1993) when he wrote the following passage:

> We have already alluded to the visual normality of most dreams and hallucinations, to the fact that they are integrated, centrally generated images which must somehow be fed back into the cortex as if they were coming from outside. If dreams and hallucinations depend upon feed-back into V1 and V2, the above assumption can be readily tested, at least in patients with a damaged V1 and V2, or so one would imagine. Unfortunately the task is not that simple and *direct proof of this supposition is in fact lacking* [italics added] (p. 342)

In fact, Grünstein's observation of vivid visual dreaming in a case of cortical blindness has often been repeated (e.g., Brown, 1972, pp. 208–209). Formed visual hallucinations have also been reported in cases of total cortical blindness (e.g., Simmonds & Mackenzie, 1957) and in blind fields with hemianopia (Cogan, 1973; Lance, 1976; Riddoch, 1935; Schröder, 1925; Seguin, 1886). Today it is generally accepted that formed visual hallucinations and vivid visual dreams are common at the onset of cortical blindness (Brown, 1989, p. 246; Hécean & Albert, 1978, pp. 173–174). However, Zeki (1993) went on:

> If it can be shown that *formed visual hallucinations are possible in the absence of areas V1 and V2* [italics added], then the implications from the viewpoint of cortical neurobiology are very important. For such a demonstration would imply that in-

tegration and the maintenance of topographic relationships that are such important features of hallucinations could be established without reference to areas
with a highly detailed map of the retina. (p. 343)

This important theoretical issue, which Zeki described as "fundamental to an
understanding of how the visual cortex functions" (p. 343; cf. Crick, 1994;
Edelman, 1989) will be taken up in chapter 15, in relation to the findings of
the present study.

Gloning and Sternbach's Elaboration of Charcot's Theory

The second elaboration of Charcot's theory came from Gloning and Sternbach (1953). These authors reported on a patient with posterior thalamic disease who experienced nonvisual dreaming in the absence of irreminiscence or
visual agnosia (case W. Josef; see Table 2.1). According to Charcot's theory,
this configuration of symptoms should not be possible. Gloning and Sternbach therefore amended the theory to account for their observation. The
amended theory was predicated upon two major assumptions about the neuroanatomy of dreaming, namely (a) that dreams are stimulated by hypothalamic
impulses arising during sleep, and (b) that these impulses are conveyed (by
way of modality-specific thalamic nuclei) to the secondary cortical zones,
where they generate conscious dream-images in the various modalities. On
this basis, Gloning and Sternbach reasoned that a lesion in the posterior thalamus or pulvinar, which disconnects the diencephalon from the visual association cortex (areas 18 and 19), would result in nonvisual dreaming. However,
because the visual cortex itself is not disrupted by subcortical (thalamic) lesions, there would be no irreminiscence or agnosia during waking consciousness in these cases.

   This elaboration of Charcot's theory assumes that loss of visual imagery
during waking life (irreminiscence) and loss of visual imagery during sleep
(nonvisual dreaming) are produced by different cerebral mechanisms. In accordance with the general theoretical assumptions of classical German neurology, Gloning and Sternbach apparently assumed that waking visual
imagery—being a voluntary phenomenon—must be cortically generated. As
we have seen already, the evidence available today does not support the assumption that irreminiscence and nonvisual dreaming are produced by different mechanisms. Most modern theorists believe with Farah (1989b) that "waking and dream imagery are the products of a single common system for image
generation" (p. 406). However, Gloning and Sternbach's theory never was systematically tested. We therefore return to it in later chapters of the present
study (see chapter 14, this volume). Gloning and Sternbach (1953) also made
a number of specific proposals regarding the relationship between nonvisual

dreaming and global cessation of dreaming. These proposals were based on a theory of hemispheric dominance for dreams, which are considered in chapter 4.

Farah's Modern Cognitive Theory of Dreaming

The modern cognitive theory of dreaming proposed by Farah and her co-workers (e.g., Farah, 1984, 1989a, 1989b; Greenberg & Farah, 1986) may also be described as an elaboration of Charcot's original theory.[2] According to cognitive psychologists, visual perception involves external (bottom-up) activation of visual representations, and visual imagery involves internal (top-down) activation of the same representations (Finke, 1980; Hebb, 1968; Kosslyn, 1980; Shepard, 1978). Farah and her coworkers adopted this intuitively appealing theory to explain dreaming, which they equated with visual imagery. (This is a problematic equation, as dreams differ from waking images in a number of important respects; cf. Doricchi & Violani, 1992, p. 120). However, Farah acknowledged that her theory is contradicted by the clinical fact that irreminiscence frequently occurs in the absence of visual agnosia (see the foregoing discussion). In an attempt to account for this fact, Farah appealed to Kosslyn's (1980) componential analysis of image generation. She postulated two separate cognitive modules, one for the (latent) representation of visual images in long-term memory and another for the (explicit) generation of those images in the short-term visual buffer. Farah localized her hypothetical image generation module to the left parietal region and her image representation module to the bilateral occipital region.[3] According to this model, damage to the image-generation module results in impaired imagery but does not affect the underlying representations, whereas damage to the image representation module results in both visual agnosia and irreminiscence. This accounts for cases of irreminiscence without agnosia. However, surprisingly, Farah failed to recognize the fact that the reverse pattern of symptoms also occurs, namely, visual agnosia without irreminiscence (Behrmann, Wincour, & Moscovitch, 1992; Brain, 1941; Brown, 1972; Goldenberg, Mamoli, & Binder, 1985; Jankowiak, Kinsbourne, Shalev, & Bachman, 1992; Levine, 1978; Morin, Riurain, Eustache, Lampert, & Courtheoux, 1984; Riddoch & Humphreys, 1987; Schanfald et al., 1985; Wilbrand, 1887, 1892).[4] Her model cannot account for this configuration of symptoms. Because she attributes visual agnosia to a defect in the visual representations themselves, visual agnosia should always be accompanied by irreminiscence (see Behrmann et al., 1992; Goldenberg, 1993; Solms et al., 1996). It is evident that a more complex theory is required to account for the full range of clinical phenomena that are associated with nonvisual dreaming. These issues will be taken up again later (in chapter 15), in relation to the findings of the present study.

NOTES

[1]Bauer (1982) described a case of related interest. The patient—who had bilateral medial occipito-temporal lesions—"reported that he could no longer become emotionally or sexually aroused by visual stimuli, and that his visual world had become drab and uninteresting" (p. 702). This patient suffered prosopagnosia and topographical agnosia in addition to visual hypoemotionality, but no mention was made of his dreams or visual imagery.

[2]It could also be described as an elaboration of Munk's (1878) theory of vision, and of the philosophy of mind of Locke (1689) and Hume (1739).

[3]Kosslyn (1994) subdivided these modules and localized them to a distributed network of cortical zones.

[4]Farah (1984) acknowledged the existence of Brain's (1941) and Brown's (1972) case reports, but she considered them to be inadequately investigated.

4

Wilbrand's Variant of the Charcot–Wilbrand Syndrome: Global Cessation or Reduction of Dreaming

I was able to trace 47 published reports of global cessation of dreaming (see Table 2.2)[1] but only 15 reports of nonvisual dreaming (see Table 2.1). This creates the impression that global cessation of dreaming is considerably more common than nonvisual dreaming. However, this is not necessarily correct, as there are many factors that could influence differentially the number of reported cases. For example, patients might be more likely to spontaneously report a complete cessation of dreaming than a change in the quality of their dreams. The incidence of the two different variants of the Charcot–Wilbrand syndrome therefore requires direct empirical investigation.

This question has not been addressed previously in the literature. The sum total of knowledge in this regard consists of two passing comments, by Weinstein (1963) and Murri et al. (1984). Weinstein (1963) observed that in his clinic "we ask about dreams routinely, and of 100 patients with histories of traumatic brain involvement, dreams were reported by 16" (p. 87). This comment seems to imply that loss of dreaming is an extremely common consequence of traumatic brain injury. However, the context of Weinstein's remark suggests that the patients he referred to were unable to recall and report specific dreams on request, not that they reported a global cessation of dreaming. Similarly, in the context of a large, controlled study of the capacity of neurological patients to report specific dreams on request, Murri et al. (1984) remarked that the Charcot–Wilbrand syndrome may be "not . . . as rare as it is presently considered to be" (p. 185).[2] I reconsider these incidental remarks later, in relation to the findings of the present study (chapter 16, this volume).

ARE THERE TRULY TWO VARIANTS OF CHARCOT–WILBRAND SYNDROME?

I now return to the initial question as to whether or not the Charcot–Wilbrand syndrome can be subdivided meaningfully into two variants. In the previous chapter I noted that the neurobehavioral symptomatology of Charcot's variant of the syndrome closely resembled that of the original undifferentiated Charcot–Wilbrand syndrome. This applied especially to the symptom of irreminiscence, which is strongly correlated with nonvisual dreaming. What are the neuropsychological correlates of global cessation of dreaming?

The frequency analysis reported in Table 4.1 demonstrates that the classical Charcot–Wilbrand symptoms (irreminiscence, prosopagnosia, topographical agnosia, or topographical amnesia) do not have a particularly strong association with global cessation or reduction of dreaming. The same applies to visual agnosia, which some authors included in the classical syndrome, as well as to achromatopsia, which we discussed in relation to nonvisual dreaming. (Aphasia and amnesia, which are also included in Table 4.1, are discussed later.) The incidence of all of these symptoms in global nondreamers does not appear to be essentially different from that found in neurological patients with preserved dreaming (see Table 4.1), except in the case of irreminiscence. Irreminiscence was observed in 42% of global nondreaming cases. Although this does not represent a particularly high incidence in itself, it is somewhat higher than the 20% incidence among cases with preserved dreaming.[3] This suggests that although irreminiscence is by no means a necessary correlate of global cessation of dreaming, there may nevertheless be some overlap between the two variants of the Charcot–Wilbrand syndrome insofar as the capacity to generate visual images is concerned.

Our preliminary conclusion (and fourth hypothesis), then, is the following: Global cessation or reduction of dreaming has no special relationship with any element of the classic Charcot–Wilbrand syndrome.

This does not mean that global cessation of dreaming has no special relationship with any other neurobehavioral symptoms; it is neither a random nor a nonspecific phenomenon. Global cessation of dreaming has repeatedly been linked in the literature with two specific symptoms, but these were not in-

TABLE 4.1
Neuropsychological Correlates of Cessation of Dreaming

Type of Case	Irreminiscence	Prosopagnosia	Topographic	Object Agnosia	Aphasia	Amnesia	Achromatopsia
Charcot[a]	91%	73%	50%	50%	50%	16%	33%
Wilbrand[b]	42%	12%	26%	19%	52%	21%	12%
Normal[c]	20% (12%)	30% (24%)	30% (16%)	11% (5%)	22% (42%)	0% (21%)	11% (5%)

[a]Cf. Table 2.1.
[b]Cf. Table 2.2.
[c]Cf. Table 2.3a (figures in brackets refer to Tables 2.3a & 2.3b combined).

cluded in the original Charcot–Wilbrand concept. These symptoms are amnesia and aphasia.

AMNESIA AND CESSATION OF DREAMING

The possible link between cessation of dreaming and amnesia raises an obvious question: If a patient claims that he or she no longer dreams, does that reflect an absence of dreams or an inability to remember dreams? In other words, is loss of dreaming a disorder of dreaming or a disorder of memory?

This question can itself be interpreted in various different ways. As we have seen, Charcot (1883) explained his case of nonvisual dreaming in terms of defective visual memory. The patient was considered to be unable to generate visual dream-images because his visual memory was destroyed. By similar reasoning, classical neurologists reduced all of the aphasias, apraxias, and agnosias to material-specific disturbances of memory; aphasia was explained as a loss of verbal memory-images, apraxia as a loss of motor memory-images, and agnosia as a loss of visual memory-images. However, if memory is defined in this way, the question as to whether or not global cessation of dreaming is a memory disturbance assumes a different meaning. It becomes a question of whether or not cessation of dreaming is a disturbance of gnosis or imagery (rather than a disturbance of memory as such). The relationship between cessation of dreaming and gnosis and imagery (agnosia and irreminiscence) has been discussed already. The pertinent issue now is whether or not nondreamers are actually having dreams but then forgetting them, that is, whether or not global cessation of dreaming is illusory. The question therefore becomes: Are nondreaming patients amnesic in the modern sense of the word?

However, even when it is restated in this way, the question is still not a simple one. The modern concept of amnesia is complex (Moscovitch, 1982). Although we do not speak of amnesia in relation to short-term and modality-specific disorders of memory (which is how we would today describe the disorder that Charcot postulated), we do use the term in relation to material-specific disorders of memory. Moreover, in recent years cognitive neuropsychologists have argued that the so-called semantic memory system can be fractionated into multiple subsystems which can be impaired selectively (Warrington & McCarthy, 1987; Warrington & Shallice, 1984). In this climate, it is not impossible that some contemporary theorists might conceptualize cessation of dreaming as a category-specific amnesic syndrome. It is therefore necessary to state that since the pertinent issue is whether or not nondreamers are actually having dreams but then forgetting them, we need only concern ourselves with the so-called episodic memory system. Moreover, because it is morbid cessation of dreaming (as opposed to premorbid absence of dreaming) that we are considering, we need only concern ourselves with anterograde disorders of that system. This means that we need to establish whether or not global cessation of dreaming may be attributed to what modern clinical researchers describe as recent memory disorder.

How can this be achieved? Due to the subjective nature of dreams, it is obviously impossible to determine directly (objectively) whether or not a particular patient is actually experiencing dreams. Nevertheless, the question can be approached indirectly by means of two different methods. First, because it is generally accepted that most people experience dreams during REM sleep, nondreamers can be subjected to REM-sleep awakenings in order to give the investigator the closest proximity to the actual dream situation. This minimizes the potential for forgetting, as even the most severe amnesiacs are able to recall what happened to them a few seconds ago. Second, because patients who forget that they dream should also forget other experiences, nondreamers can be subjected to formal neuropsychological assessment in order to obtain an objective measurement of the state of their memory functions. The assessment findings can then be extrapolated to the dream situation.

Both of these methods have been used in previous research. Two studies using the REM-sleep paradigm have been reported. Jus et al. (1973) awakened 9 patients who claimed to have stopped dreaming from all REM-sleep periods during two nights in a sleep laboratory. Despite apparently normal sleep cycles and normal incidences of REM (66 episodes altogether), only one of these patients reported dreams upon REM awakening. The patient concerned reported two dreams. Thus only two dream reports could be elicited from these 9 patients over a total of 66 REM awakenings. This is an incidence of only 3% (where 80% is normal). Similarly, Murri et al. (1985) subjected 12 patients who had previously been unable to recall any dreams over a 10-day observation period, together with 7 patients who had been able to recall dreams during the same period, to sleep-laboratory investigation. All 7 dream-recallers regularly reported dreams upon REM awakenings (75% of awakenings elicited dream reports), whereas only 3 of the 12 nonrecallers reported dreams (17% of awakenings elicited dream reports). There were no differences in the sleep profiles between the two groups (including the amount of REM). However, Murri et al. (unlike Jus et al.) did not study patients who had stopped dreaming altogether; rather they studied patients who did not recall any dreams during a 10-day observation period, and these patients reported no dreams during a 2-night laboratory investigation. This important methodological distinction is discussed in detail at the end of the present section.

The results of these two studies suggest that, in contrast to the neurotic inability to recall dreams (Goodenough, Shapiro, Holden, & Steinschreiber, 1959), in neurological patients who report global cessation of dreaming the absence of dreams is confirmed by REM sleep awakening. This conclusion was supported in clinical studies by Michel and Sieroff (1981) and Schanfald et al. (1985). The findings of these authors strongly support the view that neurogenic loss of dreaming is a disorder of dreaming rather than a disorder of memory.

The neuropsychological assessment paradigm for evaluating the memory of nondreamers, however, yielded mixed results. Five experimental investigations using this paradigm have been reported. Cathala et al. (1983) reported strongly positive correlations between various graded tests of visual and verbal memory on the one hand and frequency and informative richness of dream-recall on the other. Arena, Murri, Piccini, and Muratorio (1984) found that absence of dreaming was related to poor long-term verbal recall (and to aphasia) but not to short-term verbal recall or to short-term or long-term visual recall. On the other hand, Murri et al. (1984) found that absence of dreaming was related to poor visual recall (and to aphasia), although this association was not statistically verifiable. In a follow-up study, Murri et al. (1985) found no relationship between dreaming and memory. In the fifth study, Jus et al. (1973) found no difference in the mnestic abilities of dreaming and nondreaming leukotomy patients. The results of these investigations are far from satisfactory and no definite conclusion can be drawn from them.

The situation is complicated further by the fact that general amnesic syndromes have repeatedly been associated with poor dream-recall in the clinical literature. Talland (1965) reported that 10 patients in a series of 20 Korsakoff amnesiacs claimed that they never dreamed and that a further 8 claimed that they dreamed only rarely. These claims were supported by sleep laboratory studies. Greenberg, Pearlman, Brooks, Mayer, and Hartman (1968) elicited only one dream report from 7 Korsakoff amnesiacs during several nights in a sleep laboratory, with a total of 34 REM awakenings (a 3% recall rate). Torda (1969) obtained only 51 dream reports from 180 REM awakenings over 2 nights from a group of 6 postencephalitic amnesiacs (a 28% recall rate), as compared with 135 (75%) from a matched control group. Kramer, Roth, and Trinder (1975) obtained recall rates of between 8% and 57% from 21 cases of what they (inaccurately) described as dementia. The recall rate was inversely correlated with age and severity of dementia.[4] These studies suggest that subjective reports of global cessation of dreaming might well be artifacts of general amnesia. However these results are contradicted by the fact that global cessation of dreaming has only rarely been associated with general amnesic disorder (see Table 4.1). In 79% of the cases reported in the literature, at least, the cessation of dreaming was not associated with general amnesia. In other words, although many amnesiacs apparently do not dream, very few non-dreamers are amnesiacs. The explanation for this discrepancy might be that although amnesia frequently produces subjective cessation of dreaming, subjective cessation of dreaming is only rarely caused by amnesia. In other words, although some cases with loss of dreaming may be dreaming but then forgetting their dreams, in the majority of cases the dream disorder occurs independently of amnesia. This suggests that global cessation of dreaming might not be a unitary syndrome with a single underlying mechanism.

However, it is important to emphasize another possible explanation for the discrepancies in this aspect of the literature. There are significant methodological differences between the *clinical* literature that I reviewed earlier (summarized in Tables 2.2 and 4.1) and the experimental literature that I have just reviewed (Arena, Murri, Piccini, & Muratorio, 1984; Cathala et al., 1983; Greenberg et al., 1968; Kramer et al., 1975; Murri et al., 1984; Murri et al., 1985; Torda, 1969). These differences have already been alluded to above. In the clinical studies, patients were described as nondreamers if they themselves reported a global cessation of dreaming. However, in the experimental studies subjects were described as nondreamers if they were unable to report specific dreams during the administration of a morning dream-recall questionnaire over a given number of days, or during REM-sleep awakenings over a given number of nights. The subjective complaint of global cessation of dreaming is not the same as a failure to report specific dreams during a time-limited experiment. It therefore seems likely that these two bodies of literature in fact studied two rather different groups of patients.

The relationship between global cessation or reduction of dreaming and memory disorder has clearly not yet been adequately evaluated. This question will have to be reconsidered later, on the basis of the empirical findings of the present research see chapter 18, this volume). With this purpose in mind, a testable hypothesis can be formulated: Global cessation or reduction of dreaming is a primary phenomenon, independent of any disturbance of memory.

APHASIA AND CESSATION OF DREAMING

It has often been suggested that global cessation of dreaming might be a consequence of aphasic disorder (Anan'ev, 1960; Broughton, 1982; Doricchi & Violani, 1992; Epstein & Simmons, 1983; Foulkes, 1978; Jakobson, 1973; Moss, 1972; Zinkin, 1959). These authors differed in their views on the specific nature of the relationship between cessation of dreaming and aphasia. However, they were united by the claim that the language disorder not only prevents patients from verbally reporting or recollecting their dreams, but also makes it impossible for them to actually generate dreams. Moss (1972) stated this position most vividly in his autobiographical account of aphasia:

> During the daytime I had no words to express what was happening and at night I had no dreams. . . . [This was due to] a complete and total vacuum of self-speech [rather than memory disorder]. . . . How else would one account for the fact that even today I hold many waking memories from my period of hospitalization and the first few months when I had no words to describe these events

even to myself, but at the same time do not remember having dreamed at all during these four months. Further evidence is that as I recovered my internal verbalizations, the memory of nocturnal mentation began to recur. (p. 9)[5]

On this view, loss of the ability to generate language necessarily implies loss of the ability to generate dreams, which are considered to be a form of nocturnal "self speech." This tallies well with Greenberg and Farah's (1986) localization of the dream-generation module to the left hemisphere.[6] However, this viewpoint also indirectly implies that cessation of dreaming should always be accompanied by aphasia, which is in fact not supported by the available evidence; only 52% of nondreamers reported in the literature were aphasic (see Table 4.1). Moreover, aphasia is equally common in cases of nonvisual dreaming (50%). Any theory of the relationship between dreaming and language must account for this association too. The failure of previous authors to distinguish between the two variants of the Charcot–Wilbrand syndrome has frequently undermined their attempts to explain loss of dreaming.

Recent authors have attempted to explain the low incidence of aphasia among nondreamers by postulating linguistic–semantic disorders which do not produce manifest aphasia but nevertheless prevent dreaming. The following passage illustrates some of the theoretical complexities involved:

> Lack of dreaming could depend not only on a mnemonic deficit or on a defective verbalization of dream experience, but also on deficits in cognitive decoding of the dream during its actual nocturnal development, since the lesions [which lead to cessation of dreaming], besides affecting linguistic functions, also affect cognitive processes that are *nonlinguistic but functionally linked to language* [italics added] and probably indispensable to the full perceptual–cognitive processing of internally generated information. (Doricchi & Violani, 1992, p. 122)

For example, cessation of dreaming in aphasiacs and nonaphasiacs alike could be attributed to an alteration in "the semantic top-down parsing of endogenously generated information" (Doricchi & Violani, 1992, p. 120).[7] On this view, even in the absence of manifest aphasic symptomatology, cessation of dreaming may be attributed to deficits in cognitive processes that are functionally linked to language. However, this theoretical viewpoint is unsatisfactory insofar as it can explain all disconfirmatory presentations by postulating ad hoc connections with language (cf. Müller, 1992). Moreover, Cathala et al. (1983), Murri et al. (1984) and Schanfald et al. (1985)—the latter having specifically investigated the relationship between aphasia and dreaming—all demonstrated that aphasiacs are able to generate dreams. Cathala et al. (1983) and Schanfald et al. (1985) even demonstrated that at least some aphasiacs with lesions in auditory and sensorimotor association cortex are able to generate normal audioverbal dream-imagery. (This contradicts Grünstein's [1924] prediction that modality-specific dream-imagery deficits should accompany lesions to modality-specific association cortex.) However, the presence of dreams in some cases of aphasia does not preclude the converse relationship; the absence of dreams in other cases can still be caused by aphasia. This suggests once again that global cessation of dreaming might not be a unitary syndrome with a single underlying mechanism. A more detailed, controlled neuropsychological study of this question is clearly necessary.

For now, in consideration of the fact that a causal relationship between language disorder and cessation of dreaming has not yet been demonstrated, we shall confine ourselves to a purely descriptive hypothesis: Global cessation or reduction of dreaming is commonly (but not invariably) associated with aphasia. It is too early to draw theoretical inferences from this statistical observation.

PATHOLOGICAL–ANATOMICAL CORRELATES
OF DREAM CESSATION

Evidence was presented in the previous chapter to suggest that nonvisual dreaming typically arises from bilateral lesions in the medial occipito-temporal region. It was suggested that the two variants of the Charcot–Wilbrand syndrome may overlap and that the circumscribed dream-imagery deficit of Charcot's variant might be an incomplete form of the global deficit in Wilbrand's variant of the syndrome. Although the latter suggestion was not supported by the neuropsychological evidence, there did seem to be a degree of overlap between the two variants, particularly with regard to the symptom of irreminiscence. Considered from the anatomical viewpoint, if nonvisual dreaming were an incomplete form of global cessation of dreaming, then the site of the lesion producing the global deficit should include the medial occipito-temporal region bilaterally. Is this prediction confirmed by the available evidence?

Three cases with global cessation of dreaming have come to autopsy (Ettlinger, Warrington, & Zangwill, 1957; Gloning & Sternbach [case L. Josef], 1953; Wilbrand, 1892). Two of these cases were found to have extensive bilateral occipito-temporal lesions and the third case had a massive, space-displacing lesion in the medial occipito-temporal region of the right hemisphere (which may well have had bilateral effects). This evidence supports the above prediction. However, a different picture emerges when one considers the remainder of the cases in this group. Among the 47 cases listed in Table 2.2, there was clinical, surgical or radiological evidence of unilateral cerebral disease in 32 cases. This suggests, notwithstanding the limited autopsy evidence, that bilateral involvement is probably not necessary for global cessation of dreaming. This contradicts the view that nonvisual dreaming is a partial or incomplete form of global cessation of dreaming.

The existence of unilateral cases with cessation of dreaming also has implications for the supposed link between this symptom and aphasia. If cessation of dreaming is caused by an aphasic disorder, then it should never occur with unilateral right-hemisphere disease (unless the definition of *aphasic disorder* is broadened to an extent which renders it meaningless; see the foregoing discussion). Table 2.2 shows that unilateral cases of right-hemisphere lesions with global cessation of dreaming do indeed exist; 7 (dextral) cases of this type have been reported in the literature (Humphrey & Zangwill's [1951] Case 1; Oldfield's case [cited in Humphrey & Zangwill, 1951]; Gloning & Sternbach's [1953] cases S. Johann, W. Karl, M. Klara, & M. Josef; Ettlinger et al.'s [1957] case N.H.). In fact, the existence of these cases of unilateral right-hemispheric disease led some authors to propose, in direct contrast to the hypothesis that loss of dreaming is caused by language disorder, that the right hemisphere might be dominant for dreaming. This proposal—which is intuitively appealing insofar as it seems to account for many of the peculiarities of dream mentation—attracted considerable attention in the literature. It was first suggested by Bogen (1969) in a well-known series of papers on hemispheric specialization. Bogen drew attention to the involvement of the right hemisphere in all of Humphrey & Zangwill's (1951) cases (he was apparently unaware of the numerous contradictions to this rule that had already been published), and he added his own observation that a number of commissurotomy patients stopped dreaming following disconnection of the two cerebral hemispheres. The latter observation was explained by both Galin (1974) and Bakan (1976) as the result of a disconnection between the articulate left hemisphere and the dreaming right hemisphere, which made it impossible for the patient to consciously recall and report dream experiences. On this basis, Bakan (1976) coined a memorable phrase to the effect that "the right hemisphere is the dreamer" (p. 66).

A number of studies have since specifically investigated this hypothesis, using a variety of methodologies, but they have produced little evidence in support of it (see Table 4.2). In fact, Bogen's original observations on commissurotomy material have never been replicated. Nevertheless, some authors still claimed a dominant role for the right hemisphere in dreaming, on grounds that the dreams of commissurotomy and right hemispherectomy patients are in one way or another impoverished (Hoppe, 1977; Kerr & Foulkes, 1981). However, the evidence in support of this latter view is questionable, for the patients described by these authors did not themselves complain of any changes in their dreaming; it was the authors who considered their dream reports to be impoverished. This distinction (between subjective awareness of change and an objective normative opinion) is obviously important, especially in view of the absence of appropriate control groups in these two studies.

Goldstein, Burdick, and Lazslo (1970; Goldstein, Stoltzfus, & Gardocki, 1972) observed asymmetrical, right-dominant cerebral activation during REM sleep. This has been cited in support of the right-dominant theory of

TABLE 4.2
Studies of Laterality in Cessation of Dreaming

Source	Subjects	Methodology	Percentage Nondreamers (R.)	(L.)	Quality of Dreams
Bogen (1969)	"Several"[a]	Clinical interview	"Some"	—	—
Greenwood et al. (1977)	3[a, g]	Sleep laboratory (1–4 nights)	0%	—	Contained visual imagery
Hoppe (1977)	13 (1,[b] 12[a])	Clinical interview	0%	—	Sparse, lacked narrative (symbolic) complexity
Kerr & Foulkes (1981)	1[a,b]	Sleep laboratory (2 nights)	0%	—	Lacked kinematic visual imagery
Epstein & Simmons (1983)[d]	7[c]	Clinical interview	—	100%	—
Arena et al. (1984)	52 (19 R., 33 L.)[c]	Morning diary (10 nights)	79%	55%	—
Murri et al. (1984)[e]	53 (21 R., 32 L.)[c]	Morning diary (10 nights)	38%	31%	—
Murri et al. (1985)[e]	19 (11 R., 8 L.)[c, g]	Sleep laboratory (2 nights) & Morning diary (10 nights)	46%	50%	Mean score on a 7 point scale of dreamlike fantasy was 2.3 for R. & L. alike
			64%	63%	
Schanfald et al. (1985)	8 (2 R., 4 L., 2 Bilat.)[c, g]	Sleep laboratory (1–5 nights)	0%	0%	—[f]

[a]Commissurotomy.
[b]Hemispherectomy.
[c]Subtotal hemispheric lesion.
[d]Also listed in Table 2.2.
[e]Also listed in Table 4.3.
[f]Both bilateral patients were nondreamers.
[g]Also listed in Table 2.3b.

dreaming. However, Goldstein's findings are highly controversial; they were replicated by some authors (e.g., Hirshkowitz, Ware, & Karacan, 1980; Rosenkind, Coates, & Zarcone, 1979) but not by others (e.g., Antrobus, Ehrlichman, & Weiner, 1978; Moffitt et al., 1982; Pivik, Bylsma, Busby, & Sawyer, 1982). The reader may consult Bertini and Violani (1992) for a full discussion of this controversy.

Some of these studies are difficult to interpret in view of the different definitions of *loss of dreaming* that are used in the experimental and clinical literature. If we focus on the clinical literature (and therefore define *cessation of dreaming* as a subjective symptom), the fact remains that only 7 of the 29 dextral patients with unilateral lesions listed in Table 2.2 had right hemisphere lesions (24%). In other words, there appears to be a clear lateral bias in the leftward direction, with 22 of the 29 unilateral cases (76%) having damage restricted to the left hemisphere. In an extensive review of this question, Greenberg and Farah (1986) concluded that the generation of dreams is an exclusively left-hemispheric phenomenon. However Greenberg and Farah restricted their review to the English-language literature and were therefore not aware of Gloning and Sternbach's (1953) report of four cases with unilateral right-hemisphere lesions. Also, these authors discounted Humphrey and Zangwill's (1951) patient with a right-hemisphere lesion on the grounds that he did not suffer a total loss of dreams, and they failed to notice the cases of Oldfield (cited by Humphrey & Zangwill, 1951) and Ettlinger et al. (1957).

In a subsequent and more comprehensive review, Doricchi and Violani (1992) recognized the existence of unilateral right-hemisphere cases with cessation of dreaming. On this basis they concluded that simple right-dominant versus left-dominant theories of dreaming were "too generic and potentially misleading" (p. 121). They attributed functional roles to both hemispheres, with the right hemisphere providing the "perceptual 'hard grain' . . . which is probably indispensable for the sensorial vividness of the dream experience" (p. 121) and the left hemisphere providing the "cognitive decoding of the dream during its actual nocturnal development" (p. 122). A similar viewpoint was articulated by Kerr and Foulkes (1981), who suggested that the visual–imagistic components of dreaming are mediated by the posterior divisions of the right hemisphere, whereas the narrative structure of dreaming is contributed by the left frontal lobe (see also Antrobus, 1987, and Foulkes, 1978, 1987). These more complex hypotheses are consistent with recent conceptualizations of mental imagery in general (Kosslyn, 1994).

Doricchi and Violani (1992) also pointed out that the preponderance of left-hemisphere lesions among published cases of cessation of dreaming might not accurately reflect the relative frequency of left- versus right-hemisphere cases in the general clinical population. A basic epidemiological study has never been undertaken. If it had, it would have had to make allowances for the tendency of patients with lesions of the right hemisphere to deny their deficits (anosognosia), which renders these patients less likely than their counterparts with left-hemispheric lesions to spontaneously complain of changes in their nocturnal mentation.

For the moment, therefore, all that can be said with confidence about the pathological–anatomical correlates of global cessation of dreaming is that it can occur with strictly unilateral lesions in either hemisphere. This distinguishes it from nonvisual dreaming, which apparently occurs only with bilateral lesions. However, the fact that global cessation of dreaming can occur with damage to either hemisphere does not necessarily imply that it has any less localizing value than nonvisual dreaming; it could simply mean that the localization of the lesion producing the former symptom is different from that producing the latter symptom. In this respect it is interesting to observe that Doricchi and Violani (1992) detected marked intrahemispheric differences in their review of the published clinical cases. For example, they noted that cessation of dreaming occurs only with left frontal lesions (never with right frontal lesions) and then only in association with aphasia; that it seldom occurs with temporal convexity lesions; that it occurs with equal frequency with bilateral, left and right parietal lesions (but tends to recover more slowly in the latter cases); that it has never been reported in a case of unilateral-right occipital disease; and that it is always associated with visual–verbal disconnection symptoms in patients with left (or bilateral) occipital lesions. Evidently, the pathological–anatomical correlates of global cessation of dreaming are far more complicated than at first they appeared to be.

INTRAHEMISPHERIC ANATOMICAL CORRELATES

Wilbrand's (1887) prototypical case was found at autopsy to have a bilateral occipito-temporal lesion (Wilbrand, 1892), as was Gloning and Sternbach's (1953) case L. Josef. Ettlinger et al.'s (1957) case had a massive space-displacing lesion in the right occipito-temporal area. These three cases suggest that nonvisual dreaming and global cessation of dreaming share a common anatomical localization. However, the pathological–anatomical data for the other cases listed in Table 2.2 suggest that this localization is by no means typical of cases with global cessation of dreaming. In 15 of the 41 cases in which intrahemispheric localizing information was available (37%), the symptomatic lesion was situated outside of the medial occipito-temporal region (which is the region that was associated with nonvisual dreaming). Nevertheless, most of these cases did have lesions located in the general vicinity of the medial occipito-temporal region; that is to say, there was a clear posterior bias in the site of the lesions associated with global cessation of dreaming. Among the 35 cases with suitably circumscribed lesions listed in Table 2.2, the damage was restricted to the posterior cerebral region in 27 cases (77%). This posterior bias has been

TABLE 4.3
Studies of Posterior Versus Anterior Lesions in Cessation of Dreaming

Study	Methodology	Percentage Nondreamers		
		(Posterior)	(Anterior)	(Control)
Cathala et al. (1983)	Sleep Laboratory (1 night)	69% (25/36)	35% (9/26)	16% (11/69)[a]
Murri et al. (1984)	Morning Diary (10 days)	67% (14/21)	12% (4/32)	14% (4/28)
Murri et al. (1985)	Morning Diary (10 days) Sleep Laboratory (2 nights)	91% (10/11) 64% (7/11)	25% (2/8) 13% (1/8)	— —

[a]The figures for Cathala et al.'s study refer to proportion of awakenings producing no dream reports; those in Murri et al.'s studies refer to proportion of subjects producing no dream reports.

confirmed in three experimental studies that directly investigated the relative frequency of anterior versus posterior lesions in loss of dreaming (see Table 4.3). One of these studies (Murri et al., 1984) classified 14% of normal subjects as nondreamers. This might create the erroneous impression that the clinical value of cessation of dreaming is very limited. The high incidence of nondreamers among normal subjects probably arises from the fact that the authors listed in Table 4.3 defined loss of dreaming according to limited experimental criteria; they did not study true clinical cases of global cessation of dreaming.

On the basis of the available evidence, it seems reasonable to conclude that subjective cessation of dreaming is a symptom of some localizing value, although the critical lesion site has not yet been precisely determined. In the vast majority of reported cases, subjective cessation of dreaming is associated with a lesion somewhere in the *posterior cortical convexity*. This is the conclusion which Doricchi and Violani (1992) reached after their exhaustive review of the clinical and experimental literature:

> Both in the individual [clinical] reports of patients with loss of dreaming and in the groups of brain-damaged subjects studied by other [experimental] investigators, cases of frontal damage are significantly fewer than cases with damage to the posterior lobes. Conversely, frontal cases are significantly more frequent among patients who maintained the experience of [normal] dreaming. (p. 109)

Combining this sort of evidence with the previously mentioned evidence regarding the (predominantly leftward) laterality of lesions associated with global cessation of dreaming, Greenberg and Farah (1986) concluded that "a region of the posterior dominant hemisphere is critical for dreaming" (p. 319). It seems reasonable to frame a provisional anatomical hypothesis along these lines, in the hope that the present investigation will yield more precise and reliable information. However, before doing so, another body of evidence must be considered. This body of evidence seriously undermines the notion of a unitary focal syndrome characterized by global cessation of dreaming.

NOTES

[1]Doricchi and Violani (1992) cited further case reports of this type, which I have been unable to trace (Corda, 1985; Michel & Sieroff, 1981).

[2]The contradiction in the Charcot–Wilbrand syndrome is apparent from the following comment by these authors: "Curiously enough, the earliest case reports [of Charcot–Wilbrand syndrome] frequently noted a loss of *visual* dream content, while subsequent authors reported a *total* loss of dreaming" (Murri et al., 1984, p. 185; italics added).

[3]The incidence of irreminiscence and other posterior-cortical symptomatology is likely to be artificially high among published cases with preserved dreaming (i.e., among those included in Table 2.3a) in comparison with the neurological population in general. In the published cases, the presence of visual symptomatology usually provided the rationale for investigating the patient's dreams in the first place.

[4]Kramer et al.'s (1975) study embodied serious methodological flaws that make it difficult to meaningfully interpret the results. It is mentioned here only for the sake of completeness.

[5]See also a personal communication by Moss (1975), quoted by Foulkes (1978, p. 164).

[6]However, Greenberg and Farah (1986) did not equate image generation with language generation. Their disagreement with Doricchi and Violani (1992) on this point reflects a long-standing controversy in the cognitive literature as to whether mental images are propositional or depictive representations.

[7]Freud (1900/1953) postulated a similar process under the name of *secondary revision*. However, secondary revision was not considered to be an essential component of the dream work. It is unlikely that a failure of secondary revision in Freud's model would produce a global cessation of dreaming.

5

The Neglected Psychosurgical Literature

In a survey of 200 cases of prefrontal leukotomy, Frank (1946) observed that a common result of this psychosurgical procedure was "a poverty or entire lack of dreams, and a thinning, or disappearance of dereistic [fantasy] experience" (p. 508). In a later report on the same series of cases—then comprising more than 300 subjects—Frank (1950) confirmed and elaborated upon his earlier finding:

> To the observation of the infrequency of dreams and daydreams after lobotomy, should be added the simplification of the manifest dream content, when dreams do occur. The dreams have the character of direct wish fulfillment like those of children. . . . Lobotomized patients dream of delicacies, of getting rich, and so on, and have occasional pollution dreams. The manifest dream content also becomes tamed after lobotomy. For example a . . . [schizophrenic patient] complained before the operation about a recurring nightmare in which he was surrounded by wild animals in an arena; after lobotomy the dream lions did not roar and were not frightening any longer but walked away silently. (p. 38)

Confirmation of these unexpected observations was soon forthcoming from other authors who reported similarly large series of leukotomy cases (see

TABLE 5.1

Global Cessation of Dreaming in Clinical Series of Prefrontal Leukotomy

Source	Series	Dreams
Frank (1946)	100 cases, 22–26 yrs, 100 m., 100 f.	Global cessation and decreased frequency or narrative complexity (description ambiguous) in an unspecified number of cases
Frank (1950)	300+ cases	Global cessation or decreased frequency (description ambiguous) and decreased narrative complexity and emotional intensity in an unspecified number of cases
Piehler (1950)	58 cases, 21 m., 37 f.	Global cessation in 11 cases; recovery over 1 yr with residual reduction in frequency, vivacity, narrative complexity, and emotional intensity in 8 of these
Partridge (1950)	300 cases	Global cessation or gross reduction in frequency (description ambiguous) in several cases; recovery over 6 months to 1 yr in an unspecified number of cases
Slater (cited in Humphrey & Zangwill, 1951)	"A number of patients."	Global cessation or reduction in frequency (description ambiguous)
Schindler (1953)	150+ cases	Global cessation in 134 cases; recovery over several months to 1 yr with residual reduction in narrative complexity in an unspecified number of cases
Jus et al. (1973)	13 cases, 31–63 yrs, 1 m., 12 f.; 13 matched (schizophrenic) controls	Global cessation in 9 cases (sleep lab. confirmed in 7 of these); global cessation claimed by 3 controls (disconfirmed in lab)
Freeman (cited in Jus et al., 1973)	No information	Global cessation or reduction in frequency (description ambiguous)

Table 5.1). However, Frank and his psychiatric colleagues made no attempt to link their findings with the existing (neurological) literature on the subject of dreams; indeed they did not seem to be aware of its existence. Likewise—with the exception of Humphrey and Zangwill (1951) and Gloning and Sternbach (1953)—subsequent neurological researchers working on dreams have uniformly neglected this psychosurgical literature.

There can be no doubt that the psychosurgical evidence has far-reaching implications for the concept of the Charcot–Wilbrand syndrome. We must accommodate our conceptions to the fact that cessation of dreaming—which in the neurological literature was regularly associated with posterior cortical damage—also frequently occurs after prefrontal leukotomy, where the lesion is anterior by definition. This suggests two new possibilities. Either (a) the symptom of loss of dreaming has no localizing value at all, because it can accompany damage to any of the lobes of the brain (and to both hemispheres) without preference, or (b) loss of dreaming does have localizing value but it is not a unitary symptom (that is, it occurs with lesions in a limited number of different but specific locations). Everything that is known about the cerebral organization of mental functions—in other words everything that has been learned in the past from the neuropsychological investigation of other mental faculties—points to the second of these two possibilities. In fact, this possibility was raised already in relation to the evidence linking cessation of dreaming with aphasia and amnesia. (I speculated that cessation of dreaming might be caused by language or memory disorder in some cases but not in all cases.) I shall now review the previous data in relation to this new line of evidence.

Before the prefrontal leukotomy literature was introduced, it seemed justifiable to conclude that in the majority of cases cessation of dreaming indicated a lesion in the posterior divisions of the left cerebral hemisphere. This conclusion is incompatible with the notion that loss of dreaming has no localizing value. It therefore implies either (a) that the initial conclusion was incorrect, or (b) that Frank (1946, 1950) and his colleagues identified a second lesion site that produces the same symptom. The latter situation is common in neuropsychology. Consider, for example, the localizing value of such well-established focal symptoms as alexia and agraphia, where the site of the lesion is indicated not so much by the presence or absence of the symptom itself as by the quality of the symptom and the configuration of associated symptoms and signs (e.g., pure alexia, agraphic alexia, aphasic alexia). In these conditions the focal symptom only achieves true localizing significance in the context of a recognizable syndrome.

The distributed nature of focal symptomatology reflects the fact that—contrary to the expectations of 19th-century neurologists—complex mental faculties such as reading and writing (and, we might add, dreaming) are not localized within circumscribed cortical centers, the destruction of which results in the isolated loss of a whole mental faculty. Modern neuropsychological research demonstrated conclusively that mental faculties are subserved by complex functional systems or networks, which consist of constellations of cortical and subcortical structures working together in a concerted fashion. Such systems or networks can be disrupted by damage to any one of their component parts. Moreover, the anatomical structures subserving different mental faculties overlap. Damage to a particular structure therefore does not disrupt a single mental faculty in isolation; focal lesions typically disrupt a number of psychological faculties simultaneously. For example, the agraphia produced by inferior left parietal lesions is typically accompanied by defective oral spelling, alexia, and ideomotor apraxia; thus the faculty of writing is disrupted simultaneously with the faculties of spelling, reading, and voluntary action. Psychological analysis of a constellation of symptoms and signs such as this identifies the underlying common factor that was shared by the different faculties and that was subserved by the anatomical structure in question. In this way the primary symptom attains its clinical localizing value, and, moreover, the functional architecture of the brain and the elementary structure of mental faculties is laid bare (cf. Luria, 1973; Luria & Majovski, 1977; Mesulam, 1985b; Walsh, 1991, 1994).

Against this theoretical background, it seems plausible to suppose that the faculty of dreaming may be lost by both posterior and anterior lesions without this necessarily disqualifying cessation of dreaming as a focal symptom. The task therefore is to discover whether cessation of dreaming is linked with damage to two specific lesion sites within these broad anatomical divisions and with two different constellations of associated symptoms and signs.

We have already seen that a relatively specific region of the cortex was implicated in the majority of published cases with cessation of dreaming (namely, the left posterior convexity). How can this be reconciled with the additional facts reported in the psychosurgical literature? The published evidence in this regard seems, at first sight, to be completely contradictory. On the one hand, Frank (1946, 1950), Piehler (1950), Partridge (1950), Schindler (1953), and Jus et al. (1973) all described cessation of dreaming as a relatively common consequence of prefrontal leukotomy. On the other hand, Humphrey and Zangwill (1951), Cathala et al. (1983), Murri et al. (1984), and Murri et al. (1985) all found a relatively low incidence of nondreamers among their subjects with frontal lobe lesions. Likewise Doricchi and Violani (1992) described a lack of association between loss of dreaming and frontal lesion as their "most robust and consistent conclusion" (p. 118). This apparent contradiction is resolved by a closer analysis of the anatomical data. A review of the relevant cases listed in Table 2.2 reveals the following. Six of the eight cases with loss of dreaming from pure anterior lesions were cases of prefrontal leukotomy. The seventh was a case of butterfly glioma, in which the site of the lesion coincided almost exactly with the lesion produced by the prefrontal leukotomy procedure of Freeman and Watts (Gloning & Sternbach, 1953, Case Sch. Gertrude;

cf. Freeman & Watts, 1942; Stuss & Benson, 1983). In the eighth case the patient presented initially with a hemisensory impairment; therefore the possibility cannot be excluded that the loss of dreaming was in fact due to posterior cerebral involvement in that case (Epstein & Simmons, 1983, Case 2). In other words, all of the unequivocally anterior cases reported in the literature had frontal lobe lesions in a highly specific location, namely the white matter surrounding the frontal horns of the lateral ventricles bilaterally. This localization is confirmed by the numerous series of cases listed in Table 5.1. It therefore seems likely that the low incidence of loss of dreaming among the frontal cases that was reported by Humphrey and Zangwill (1951), Cathala et al. (1983), Murri et al. (1984), Murri et al. (1985), and Doricchi and Violani (1992) was due to the fact that the lesions in the cases that were studied by these authors implicated a different aspect of the frontal lobes. In fact, in both of Murri et al.'s studies (1984, 1985) cases with bilateral lesions were expressly excluded. Cathala et al.'s sample included four patients with bifrontal lesions, but no specific information was provided regarding the incidence of dreaming in these cases. Pertinent information was also lacking in Humphrey and Zangwill's (1951) report. Doricchi and Violani (1992), who entirely overlooked cases of this type in their otherwise comprehensive review, noted that cessation of dreaming can occur with left frontal convexity lesions in the context of nonfluent aphasia. However, the cases they cited in support of this viewpoint (Epstein & Simmons, 1983, Cases 1–6) all had lesions extending into posterior cerebral structures. The available data therefore neither confirms nor disconfirms the putative hypothesis that bilateral white matter lesions in the frontal lobes (and left posterior lesions) produce loss of dreaming, whereas frontal lobe lesions sparing these structures do not. The issue can only be resolved on the basis of further research. For this purpose, a formal hypothesis can now be formulated: Global cessation or reduction of dreaming indicates either (a) a left posterior cortical lesion or (b) a deep bilateral frontal lesion.

It remains to consider whether or not the postulated anatomical varieties of cessation of dreaming are linked with two different clinical syndromes. In the absence of any literature directly relevant to this question, it may be addressed indirectly by way of an apparently unrelated issue. I have described the symptom under discussion in this and the previous chapter as global cessation or reduction of dreaming. I use this rather cumbersome designation for the following reasons. First, in some of the clinical reports reviewed in these chapters it was impossible to determine from the authors' description whether or not their patients had actually stopped dreaming completely. Wilbrand's (1887, 1892) case, a patient who dreamed "almost not at all anymore" (1887, p. 57), was the prototypical example of this type (see also the cases of Frank, 1950, and Humphrey & Zangwill, 1951.) Second, in the experimental reports reviewed in the previous chapter, patients were classified as dreamers or nondreamers according to the number of dreams they reported over a limited number of days; this made it impossible to determine whether or not the latter group of subjects were true nondreamers as opposed to merely infrequent dreamers. In the studies reported by Greenberg et al. (1968), Torda (1969), Kramer et al. (1975), Cathala et al. (1983), Arena et al. (1984), Murri et al. (1984), and Murri et al. (1985) it seems likely that they were merely infrequent dreamers. Third, when some of the patients with global cessation of dreaming listed in Table 2.2 recovered, they were left with a residual reduction in the frequency of dreaming (e.g., Gloning & Sternbach, 1953 [Case K. Franz]; Piehler, 1950 [Cases 1 & 3]). In other words, in some cases at least, cessation of dreaming can transform itself into reduction of dreaming. On these grounds, it seems reasonable to assume that global cessation of dreaming and reduced frequency of dreaming are somehow related, although the precise nature of the relationship has not yet been determined.

Against this background it is interesting to observe that reduced frequency of dreaming seems to occur especially commonly in cases with posterior cerebral lesions (Epstein, 1979; Gloning & Sternbach, 1953 [Cases S. Johann & M. Josef]; Humphrey & Zangwill, 1951 [Case 1]; Peña-Casanova et al., 1985; Wilbrand, 1887). Infrequent dreaming has seldom been reported in cases with bifrontal lesions (Piehler, 1950 [Cases 1 & 3]). Moreover, the reverse seems to apply with respect to another symptom associated with cessation of dreaming: Reduced narrative (or symbolic) complexity and emotional intensity of dreaming has been associated with frontal lobe lesions by a number of authors (Frank, 1946, 1950; Humphrey & Zangwill, 1951; Piehler, 1950; Torda, 1969). The meaning of the phrase *reduced narrative (or symbolic) complexity and emotional intensity of dreaming* is best illustrated by the following quotation, which I have cited once before:

> To the observation of the infrequency of dreams and daydreams after lobotomy, should be added the *simplification* [italics added] of the manifest dream content, when dreams do occur. The dreams have the character of direct wish fulfillment like those of children. . . . Lobotomized patients dream of delicacies, of getting rich, and so on, and have occasional pollution dreams. The manifest dream content also becomes *tamed* after lobotomy. For example a . . . [schizophrenic patient] complained before the operation about a recurring nightmare in which he was surrounded by wild animals in an arena; after lobotomy the dream lions did not roar and were not frightening any longer. (Frank, 1950, p. 38)

All of the reported cases of this type had frontal lesions; an unequivocal case with a posterior lesion has never been reported. Moreover, a number of cases have been described where cessation of dreaming following bifrontal lesions recovered and the patients were left with residual symptoms of this type (Piehler, 1950; Schindler, 1953). In fact, Piehler (1950) observed that cessation of dreaming after prefrontal leukotomy is frequently a transient phenomenon. He also noticed that recovery of dreaming in these cases coincides with clinical (psychiatric) relapse, and he suggested that absence of dreaming might therefore serve as an index of the success of the operation. Schindler (1953) refined this conception and noted that the recovery of dreaming is only a poor prognostic sign if it occurs early—during the so-called "labile affect" postsurgical phase—whereas later recovery of dreaming is typical and benign.

Reduced frequency of dreaming and reduced intensity and complexity of dreaming (both of which are linked with global cessation of dreaming) therefore appear to be associated with posterior and anterior lesions, respectively. This provides limited support for the notion that global cessation of dreaming might occur in the context of two distinct syndromes, for if a symptom recovers in two different ways it is possible that it has two different mechanisms. The whole issue of recovery from cessation of dreaming clearly deserves careful attention. However, in the absence of pertinent data in the published literature, I defer further consideration of it to later chapters (chapter 16 and 24, this volume).

THE MECHANISM OF
GLOBAL CESSATION OF DREAMING

As was the case with nonvisual dreaming, very little has been written about the mechanism of global cessation of dreaming. Most authors describe global cessation of dreaming as a simple clinical fact that was incidental to the main thrust of their argument, without making any specific theoretical comments. In fact, very few authors even distinguished between nonvisual dreaming and global cessation of dreaming. In the earliest case reports, global cessation of dreaming was implicitly conceptualized in exactly the same way as nonvisual dreaming. That is, global cessation of dreaming, too, was attributed to the destruction (or disconnection) of visual memory centers (Müller, 1892; Wilbrand, 1887). Most subsequent authors have followed this same conceptualization, either explicitly or implicitly (Basso et al., 1980; Epstein, 1979; Epstein & Simmons, 1983; Farah, 1984, 1989a, 1989b; Greenberg & Farah, 1986; Grünstein, 1924; Nielsen, 1955; Peña-Casanova et al., 1985).

The first theoretical attempt to account for the obvious differences that exist between nonvisual dreaming and global cessation of dreaming came from Gloning and Sternbach (1953). These authors suggested that global cessation of dreaming results from damage to the same anatomical structures as nonvisual dreaming. However global cessation of dreaming—instead of nonvisual dreaming—arises if the patient is of the visual type (i.e., if his or her premorbid cognitive style was predominantly visual). On this view, if a patient is of the visual type then his or her thought processes will be disrupted globally by damage to the center for visual memory images (and there will be global cessation of dreaming); whereas if the patient is of the verbal type then damage to the center for visual memory images will disrupt only the visual component of cognition (and there will be nonvisual dreaming). Gloning and Stern-bach's (1953) conception of the Charcot–Wilbrand syndrome therefore im-plied that Charcot's variant of the syndrome was a partial form of Wilbrand's variant. In effect, it implied that the two variants are the same syndrome in two degrees of severity. However, as I pointed out already, the available clini-cal and anatomical evidence does not support this conclusion. Moreover Charcot's case, who was an extreme example of the visual type, did not suffer global loss of dreaming.

A second group of theories revolved around the issue of lateral specializa-tion of function. Gloning and Sternbach (1953)—deeply embedded as they were in the conceptual traditions of classical German neurology—were the first to propose that both variants of the Charcot–Wilbrand syndrome arose from dominant (left) hemisphere lesions. This reflected their belief that the center for visual memory-images was to be found in area 19 of the dominant hemisphere. Modern cognitive theorists (Greenberg & Farah, 1986) made a similar claim, when they localized the module for image generation to the left parietal region. Other authors (reviewed in preceding chapters) linked global cessation of dreaming with left-hemispheric disease on the basis of a theory that conceptualizes dreaming as a linguistic–semantic process. Another group of authors have claimed that the nondominant (right) hemisphere is special-ized for dreaming. This reflects their view that the right hemisphere is spe-cialized for visuospatial thinking and for nonanalytical processes in general (Bogen, 1969).

The early proponents of this theory assigned an almost exclusive role to the right hemisphere in dreaming (Bakan, 1976; Galin, 1974). Some of these au-thors went so far as to claim that dreams were the product of a functional dis-connection between the hemispheres (Bakan, 1977–1978). In other words, dreams were thought to arise from isolated right-hemisphere activity. In this way, many of the peculiarities of normal dream phenomenology were suppos-edly accounted for. When the notion that dreaming was an exclusively left- or right-hemispheric phenomenon proved untenable, after repeated empirical disconfirmation (see the foregoing chapters), strong lateralized theories of dreaming were replaced by weaker versions of these theories, which claimed only that the two hemispheres make unequal contributions to the process (Doricchi & Violani, 1992; Foulkes, 1978; Hoppe, 1977; Kerr & Foulkes, 1981). I reviewed the anatomical and clinical evidence for and against all of these (lateralized) theories of dreaming in the previous chapter, as well as the theory that loss of dreaming is primarily an amnestic disorder. These theories will therefore not be considered again.

All of the theories discussed thus far were unable to account for the fact that prefrontal leukotomy frequently causes global cessation of dreaming. When Frank (1946) first documented this association he implicitly attributed it to the emotional asymbolia of the leukotomized patient (see also Frank, 1950). Gloning and Sternbach (1953) placed this implicit, clinical theory on an explicit, anatomical footing. Their theory was based upon two assumptions. The first assumption was that dreams are triggered by affects. The second assumption was that affective impulses are generated in the dorsomedial nuclei of the thalamus, and then projected to areas 9 through 12 of the frontal lobes (where they are experienced consciously). On this basis Gloning and Sternbach proposed (a) that complete, bilateral lesions of the dorsomedial thalamus or its frontal projections produce global cessation of dreaming, due to ablation or disconnection of the primary instigator of dreams, and (b) that incomplete or unilateral thalamo-frontal disconnections produce reduced frequency, complexity, or emotional intensity of dreaming, due to an incomplete disruption of the same mechanisms. Therefore, reduced frequency, complexity, or emotional intensity of dreaming were considered to be partial forms of global cessation of dreaming. (Gloning and Sternbach proposed a similar framework to explain the changes in dreaming that are associated with posterior lesions. This aspect of their theory has been reviewed already.) In short, Gloning and Sternbach (1953) attributed all dream deficits either to lesions of or disconnections between thalamic and cortical centers for affect and vision. Gloning and Sternbach are the only authors to date who attempted to explain the fact that cessation of dreaming arises from lesions in completely different locations. However, their theory (and the article in which it was published) was ignored by almost all subsequent investigators.

All subsequent attempts to accommodate the frontal lobes in theories of global cessation of dreaming have therefore been relatively deficient. For example, Schindler (1953) conceptualized postleukotomy cessation of dreaming in terms of thalamo-frontal disconnection of affects from consciousness, but he ignored the posterior variants of the syndrome. Greenberg et al. (1968) proposed a similar theory to account for the infrequency and blandness of dream-reports in Korsakoff amnestics, but they made no attempt to link it with global cessation of dreaming. Partridge (1950) explained cessation of dreaming in leukotomized patients as a result of the unusual depth of sleep that prefrontal leukotomy was supposed to produce. Jus et al. (1973) suggested that loss of dreaming in patients with frontal lobe disorders might be due to a failure of active searching behavior, but they did not articulate this theory in any detail. Both of these latter theories cannot account for cessation of dreaming with posterior lesions. Kerr and Foulkes (1981) speculated that whereas the visual–imagistic components of dreaming are mediated by the posterior divisions of the right hemisphere, the narrative structure of dreaming is contributed by the left frontal lobe (see also Foulkes, 1978). This theory was tacitly endorsed by Doricchi and Violani (1992). These authors were apparently unaware of the substantial body of literature (reviewed earlier) that demonstrates that the critical lesion site in frontal lobe cases with cessation of dreaming is not the left frontal convexity but rather the white matter surrounding the anterior horns of the lateral ventricles bilaterally.

6

The Problem of REM Sleep

Following the discovery of rapid eye movement (REM) sleep in the mid-1950s by Aserinsky and Kleitman (1953, 1955) and the discovery that it is systematically correlated with the subjective experience of dreaming (Dement & Kleitman, 1957a, 1957b), the widespread assumption arose that REM was the physiological equivalent of dreaming. In other words, it was widely assumed that the physiological state known as REM sleep and the subjective state known as dreaming were one and the same thing described from two different points of view. It followed from this assumption that the neurological mechanisms that produced REM sleep were simultaneously the neurological mechanisms that produced dreaming.

A great many theoretical models of the mechanism of REM sleep have been advanced (e.g., by Hobson, 1988; Jouvet, 1973; and Sakai, 1980). From the anatomical viewpoint, all of these models attribute a pivotal role in the regulation of the REM cycle to deep brainstem nuclei. The validity of this localization has been confirmed repeatedly, most notably in studies of human subjects in whom REM was severely disrupted or even abolished (Adey, Bors, & Porter, 1968; Chase, Moretti, & Prensky, 1968; Cummings & Greenberg,

1977; Feldman, 1971; Freemon, Salinas-Garcia, & Ward, 1974; Guillemi-nault, Cathala, & Castaigne, 1973; Lavie, Pratt, Scharf, Peled, & Brown, 1984; Markand & Dyken, 1976; Osorio & Daroff, 1980). From the psychological viewpoint, all of these models attribute the subjective experience of dreams to brainstem activation during sleep of higher cortical structures (see Antrobus & Bertini, 1992; Hobson, 1988). It follows from this that destruction of the brainstem nuclei that generate the REM cycle should simultaneously abolish both REM and dreaming. It is therefore very striking that among all of the studies reviewed in chapters 4 and 5, only two (viz., Feldman, 1971, and Schanfald et al., 1985) reported cases in which the cessation of dreaming could be attributed to a disruption of REM sleep or to the destruction of deep brainstem nuclei. The many other cases listed in Table 2.2 implicated cortical structures and connections. The same applies to the large series of cases listed in Tables 4.2, 4.3 and 5.1. Furthermore, despite the vast literature that has accumulated around the phenomenon of REM sleep, it has in fact never been demonstrated that the abolition of REM is accompanied by a cessation of the subjective experience of dreaming.[1] Conversely, it has repeatedly been demonstrated that cessation of dreaming is compatible with the preservation of a normal REM cycle (Benson & Greenberg, 1969; Brown, 1972; Efron, 1968; Jus et al., 1973; Kerr et al., 1978; Michel & Sieroff, 1981).

These observations cast serious doubt on our conventional assumptions regarding the relationship between REM sleep and dreaming. However, the disparity between the published neurophysiological and neuropsychological data does not seem to have been noticed before, as it has not attracted any attention in the previous literature. The obvious inference to be drawn from this disparity is the following: Although there is a statistical correlation between the physiological state of REM sleep and the conscious state of dreaming, dreaming is not causally dependent on REM. If we nevertheless assume that all conscious states are dependent on physiological processes, this implies that the physiological mechanisms that produce dreams are independent of those that produce REM. In other words, although the neural processes that regulate REM sleep usually co-occur with those that produce dreams, the two processes can also occur independently; the mechanisms that produce REM are neither necessary nor sufficient for the conscious experience of dreaming. The following question then arises: What is the neural mechanism of dreaming (as opposed to that of REM) and why do the two processes co-occur with such regularity?

Definitive answers to these questions require sleep laboratory investigations of focal neurological patients with and without cessation of REM sleep and dreaming. Experiments of this type transcend the stated aims and methods of the present clinico-anatomical study. Nevertheless, I can make a preliminary contribution to this important theoretical problem by investigating the following interrelated hypotheses: (a) Deep brainstem lesions are not commonly associated with global cessation of dreaming, and (b) Global cessation of dreaming is not commonly associated with deep brainstem lesions.

I can also contribute to this problem by identifying precisely the lesion sites associated with global cessation of dreaming, and thereby begin to clarify the neuropsychological mechanism of dreaming per se.

The possibility that REM sleep and dreaming are causally independent processes introduces a related question of great theoretical interest: What is the function of dreaming? This question received much scientific attention ever since Freud (1900/1953) first suggested that dreams were the guardians of sleep. Many alternative hypotheses have been advanced since, but most of them have failed to distinguish between the function of REM sleep and the function of dreaming. The following quotation from an influential article illustrates this trend:

> The primary motivating force for dreaming is not psychological but physiological since the time of occurrence and duration of dreaming sleep [i.e., REM sleep] are quite constant, suggesting a preprogrammed, neurally determined genesis. In fact, the neural mechanisms involved can now be precisely specified. This conclusion does not, of course, mean that dreams are not also psychological events. . . . But it does imply that the process is much more basic than the psychodynamically determined, evanescent, "guardian of sleep" process that Freud had imagined. (Hobson & McCarley, 1977, p. 1346)

By similar reasoning, empirical investigations of this question have inferred the function of dreams from the effects of REM-sleep deprivation (e.g., Berger & Oswald, 1962; Dement, 1960, 1963; Dement, Henry, Cohen, & Ferguson, 1967). The drawback of this paradigm is that the sequelae of dream deprivation are readily conflated with those of REM deprivation and sleep deprivation. Nevertheless, the paradigm was popular because it is difficult (if not impossible) to achieve pure dream deprivation experimentally with normal subjects. The clinical phenomenon of cessation of dreaming therefore provides unique opportunities to isolate the sequelae of dream deprivation from those of REM and sleep deprivation, and therefore to cast new light on the function of dreaming per se. Surprisingly, no attempt has ever been made to study nondreaming patients from this point of view. The following hypothesis is a first attempt to rectify this situation. It is designed to test Freud's original theory, which seems the appropriate place to start: Global cessation of dreaming is typically associated with disrupted sleep.

An adequate test of this hypothesis requires objective studies of the quality and quantity of sleep in dreaming and nondreaming patients. Once again, experiments of this type transcend the stated aims and methods of the present clinical study. Nevertheless, I report some pertinent preliminary observations in a later chapter (chapter 18, this volume).

The body of literature that we have considered thus far represents the mainstream of previous research on the neuropsychology of dreams. However, our review of the literature is not yet complete. Nonvisual dreaming and global cessation of dreaming do not exhaust the range of clinical phenomena that are reported in the existing neuroscientific literature. Various other changes in dreaming following neurological insult were also reported.

NOTE

[1]The following exceptions apply. Starr (1967) reported a case of a patient with Huntington's disease, with absence of rapid eye movements, who reported only 1 dream during 25 awakenings from (otherwise normal) paradoxical sleep. However, the nature and extent of the pathological process in Huntington's disease makes it impossible to attribute the paucity of dreams in this case to brainstem mechanisms. Osorio and Daroff (1979), in an oblique turn of phrase, mentioned that absence of REM in 2 cases of patients with spinocerebellar degeneration (whom they studied in a sleep laboratory over 3 consecutive nights) "included all the concomitant phenomena" (p. 278). Taken in context, this comment seems to imply that the 2 patients reported no dreams on the 3 consecutive mornings in question. Similarly, Lavie et al. (1984, p. 118) described a case of localized pontine lesion who awoke spontaneously during REM sleep on one occasion in a sleep laboratory, and "could not recall any dreams" on that one occasion. These observations do not constitute instances of *cessation* of dreaming. Indeed, even Schanfald et al.'s (1985) patients, who were more pertinently described as cases of "absence of dream recall" (p. 246), were studied over (a maximum of) only 5 sleep laboratory nights; and the authors themselves admitted that "such absence of recall [i.e., in a time-limited sleep laboratory context] has also been observed in subjects without apparent brain damage" (Schanfald et al., 1985).

7

Other Abnormalities
of Dreaming Described
in the Literature

Two other abnormalities of dreaming have been mentioned already, and they will therefore be discussed first: reduced frequency of dreaming, and reduced narrative complexity and emotional intensity of dreaming.

REDUCED FREQUENCY OF DREAMING

It was suggested in a previous chapter that reduced frequency of dreaming might have a special relationship with global cessation of dreaming of posterior origin, and that this (residual) symptom might therefore distinguish between loss of dreaming following posterior versus anterior lesions. This suggestion was made for two reasons, first because some cases of loss of dreaming with posterior lesions resolved into cases of decreased frequency of dreaming and, second, because the two conditions were indistinguishable in some cases. Furthermore, Cathala et al. (1983), Murri et al. (1984), and Murri et al. (1985) reported that patients with posterior lesions dream less frequently than patients with anterior lesions. However, no systematic clinical studies of the relative frequency of dreaming with different lesion sites have been undertaken to date.

In this respect it is noteworthy that numerous instances of infrequent dreaming were described in cases with lesions outside of the posterior cortical region. First, two cases of reduced frequency of dreams with pure frontal lesions have been reported (Piehler, 1950 [Cases 1 & 3]). Second, Hoppe (1977) reported that commissurotomy patients dream unusually infrequently. Third, in Talland's (1965) study of a series of 20 Korsakoff amnesiacs, 8 patients "professed to having dreams rarely" (p. 54). Last, in the experimental studies of Greenberg et al. (1968), Torda (1969), Jus et al. (1973) and Kramer et al. (1975) infrequent dream recall upon REM awakening was reported for subjects with lesions in a variety of nonposterior locations. These results call into question the localizing value of reduced frequency of dreaming, as well as its value for differentiating loss of dreaming of posterior versus anterior origin. The following hypothesis is designed to test this conclusion: Reduced frequency of dreaming has no localizing significance.

Research has never been conducted into the neurobehavioral correlates of reduced frequency of dreaming. The only relevant data in this regard is the observation that amnesiacs have an unusually low dream recall rate upon REM sleep awakening (Greenberg et al., 1968; Torda, 1969). It is difficult to interpret this observation because amnesiacs have a low recall rate by definition. The following hypothesis therefore is formulated on the grounds that it is the natural corollary of the previous one: Reduced frequency of dreaming has no specific neurobehavioral correlates.

Notwithstanding these two hypotheses, some patients with neurological disorders apparently do complain of reduced frequency of dreaming. If this is a valid clinical observation, then this symptom no less than any other should reveal something about the neural organization of dreaming. In the absence of any definite data on the anatomical and neurobehavioral correlates of infrequent dreaming, however, there is no point in speculating on its possible theoretical implications.

REDUCED NARRATIVE COMPLEXITY AND EMOTIONAL INTENSITY OF DREAMING

I have suggested, on the basis of Frank's (1950) observations (which were subsequently confirmed by others; cf. Table 5.1), that this phenomenon is closely related to the variant of cessation of dreaming caused by deep bifrontal lesions. However, there is also good reason to doubt that suggestion. Torda (1969) reported reduced narrative complexity and emotional intensity of dreaming in amnestic patients who had recovered from encephalitis, Hoppe (1977) reported it in cases of commissurotomy and right hemispherectomy (cf. Table 4.2), and Kramer et al. (1975) reported it in an undifferentiated sample of patients with "organic" disorders. Furthermore, Cathala et al. (1983) reported that the dream reports of patients with frontal lobe lesions are significantly more emotional than those of controls (i.e., they found the exact opposite of what was previously claimed). It is also important to note that in all the reports just mentioned the observation of reduced narrative complexity and emotional intensity of dreaming was not made by the patients themselves; rather, it was inferred by the authors from the patients' descriptions of their dreams. The shortcoming of this method for establishing subjective changes in dreaming is obvious. The status of this phenomenon as a clinical entity therefore remains uncertain, pending further investigation. The following two hypotheses were designed for that purpose: (a) Reduced narrative (or symbolic) complexity and emotional intensity of dreaming has no localizing significance; and (b) Reduced narrative (or symbolic) complexity and emotional intensity of dreaming has no specific neurobehavioral correlates.

With regard to the second of these hypotheses, however, it should be noted that Frank (1946, 1950), Piehler (1950), Schindler (1953), and Hoppe (1977) all reported that patients with reduced narrative complexity and emotional intensity of dreaming also had reduced complexity and intensity of daytime fantasies.

OTHER CHANGES IN DREAMING

Two further changes in dreaming were reported in the neurological literature. These are increased frequency and vivacity of dreaming and recurring nightmares.

Increased Frequency and Vivacity of Dreaming

Grünstein (1924) was the first to describe a patient who complained of increased frequency and vivacity of dreaming. In the case of this patient, who had sustained a penetrating missile wound, the increased vivacity of dreaming gradually resolved over a period of three weeks, leaving the patient with a residual increase in the frequency of dreaming. Gloning and Sternbach (1953) confirmed Grünstein's observation by reporting five similar cases. Whitty and Lewin (1957) then documented three further cases and provided more detailed clinical observations. In addition to increased vivacity of dreaming, they noted that their patients sometimes had difficulty in distinguishing dreams from reality and that they reported increased frequency of dreaming. Some of their patients also experienced continuous dreams (that is, the same dream continued throughout the night, despite intervening periods of wakefulness). Lugaresi et al. (1986), Gallassi, Morreale, Montagna, Gambetti, and Lugaresi

(1992), Morris, Bowers, Chatterjee, and Heilman (1992), and Sacks (1995) reported further cases, with symptoms similar to those described by Whitty and Lewin (1957). These cases, which have not previously been collated, are summarized in Table 7.1.

A case reported by Berti, Arienta, and Papagno (1990) is of related interest. This patient (a 43-year-old female with a septum pellucidum cyst, which was excised by a transcallosal approach, and with a small infarct of the right cingulate gyrus) reported that "she was living as if in a dream . . she was never sure whether she had seen people or places in real life or had dreamt of them" (p. 922). Similarly, Damasio, Graff-Radford, Eslinger, Damasio, and Kassell (1985) described a series of five patients with basal forebrain lesions who reported fabricated memories, "some of which were acquired through . . . dreaming" (p. 269). Whitty and Lewin (1960), Morris et al. (1992), and Sacks (1995), among others, reported similar cases, with loss of the sense of reality in association with "a sort of waking or public dream, in which dreamlike fancies . . . proliferate and weave themselves into the waking perceptions of the mind" (Sacks, 1995 [Case Greg F.], pp. 53–54). Unfortunately, these authors made no comment upon their patients' actual dreams. Whitty and Lewin (1957) made the interesting observation that such experiences are considered to be normal in young children (under 5 years of age). Similar phenomena have been observed under pathological conditions in narcolepsy (Broughton, 1982), in delirium (Lipowski, 1990), in migraine (Sacks, 1985), in various types of pharmacological intoxication and withdrawal (Sacks, 1990), at the onset of psychosis, and in REM rebound states (Sacks, 1991). These reports have not been included in the present review due to the lack of demonstrable cerebral lesions in such cases.

What are the anatomical correlates of this symptom-complex? Morris et al. (1992) suggested that it was associated with basal forebrain lesions. However, the anatomical data summarized in Table 7.1 suggests a slightly broader localization. The lesion was bilateral in at least eight of the 11 cases in which anatomical data were available, and the lesion involved the limbic system (and specifically the anterior limbic structures) in all but one instance. The anterior limbic region was also involved in the cases reported by Whitty and Lewin (1960), Damasio et al. (1985) and Sacks (1995). The single exception (Grünstein, 1924) was the case of a patient with a penetrating missile wound, in which the possibility of a distal vascular or other complication affecting deep structures cannot be excluded. Increased frequency and vivacity of dreaming therefore appears to be a focal symptom-complex. My next hypothesis is designed to test this conclusion: Increased frequency and vivacity of dreaming indicates a lesion (usually but not invariably bilateral) in the anterior parts of the limbic system.

As far as the neurobehavioral correlates of this syndrome are concerned, three factors emerge from the literature. First, there is some evidence to sug-

TABLE 7.1

Case Reports of Increased Frequency and Vivacity of Dreaming

Source	Case	Lesion	Dreams
Grünstein (1924)	Patient N., 21-yr m.	Bilat. Occip. (trauma)	Increased vivacity, recovering gradually over approx. 3 wks; residual increased frequency
Gloning & Sternbach (1953)	M. Johanna, 27-yr f.	Hypothalam. (tumor)	Increased vivacity
	H. Therese, 27-yr f.	Bilat. med. Front. (meningioma)	Increased vivacity (with nightmares), gradually decreasing in frequency over 2 yrs
	S. Josef, 54-yr m.	Hypothalam., Thalam. (craniopharyngioma)	Increased frequency and vivacity (with nightmares), recovery after approx. 1 yr
	E. Gustav, 44-yr m.	R. Thalam. (thrombosis)	Increased vivacity
	K. Rudolf, 50-yr m.	R. Thalam. (thrombosis)	Increased frequency and vivacity
Whitty & Lewin (1957)	Case 1, 58-yr m.	Bilat. med. Front. (cingulectomy)	Continuous dreaming with increased vivacity, blurred fantasy/reality distinction; recovery over approx. 4 days
	Case 2, 31-yr f. (cingulectomy)	Bilat. med. Front.	Continuous dreaming with increased vivacity, blurred fantasy/reality distinction; recovery over approx. 2 days
	Case 3, 60-yr m.	Bilat. med. Front. (cingulectomy)	Continuous dreaming with increased vivacity, blurred fantasy/reality distinction; recovery over approx. 4 days
Lugaresi et al. (1986), Gallassi et al. (1992)	S. S., 53-yr m.	Bilat. Thalam. (atrophy)	Increased vivacity with enactment, gradually increasing in frequency over approx. 6 months, becoming continuous
Gallassi et al. (1992)	L. S., 29-yr f.	No information	Increased vivacity, gradually increasing in frequency
Morris et al. (1992)	S. J., 51-yr m.	R. Hypothalam. (astrocytoma)	Increased vivacity; blurred fantasy/reality distinction
Sacks (1995)	Franco Magnani, 54-yr m.	No information (febrile illness)	Increased frequency (continuous dreaming?) and increased vivacity; blurred fantasy/reality distinction

gest that unusually vivid dreaming might in certain cases have a special relationship with cerebral blindness. In Grünstein's (1924) Patient N., Gloning and Sternbach's (1953) case of M. Johanna, and Sacks's (1995) case of Greg F., the onset and course of the changes in dreaming coincided with a period of cerebral blindness. The possible association between increased frequency and vivacity of dreaming and cerebral blindness in these cases suggests that a subclassification within this symptom-complex might be necessary (i.e., cases with and without cerebral blindness might experience the same changes in dreaming but for different reasons). It is well known that de-afferentation of the visual system can provoke visual hallucinations. This provides an alternative explanation for the (possibly nonlimbic) site of the lesion in Grünstein's case. The following descriptions by Brown (1972) of two cases with cerebral blindness (which resolved into apperceptive agnosias) appear to support this suggestion:[1]

> During the immediate post-coma period [i.e., at the onset of cortical blindness], he reported having a series of nightmares, these having a definite visual character. Subsequently, the nightmares disappeared, and he offered that he had some decline in dream recall. (Case 11, p. 208)

> He reported that around the time of onset of blindness, and for the following week or so, he was having terrific nightmares. On questioning, it appeared that these were of a striking visual character, and they were vividly described by him. (Case 12, p. 209)

The second of the two factors mentioned previously is affective disinhibition. This symptom was reported in eight of the published cases with increased frequency and vivacity of dreaming (Gloning & Sternbach, 1953 [Cases H. Therese, S. Josef, E. Gustav, K. Rudolf]; Lugaresi et al., 1986; Morris et al., 1992; Whitty & Lewin, 1957 [all cases]).

The third factor proves to be of more far-reaching importance. In at least seven of the published cases there was a breakdown of the distinction between fantasy and reality. These patients found it difficult to distinguish their dreams from real experiences. Some of them also suffered from vivid daydreams, which bordered on hallucination. Others experienced their waking thoughts as if they were lived occurrences. One of Whitty and Lewin's (1957) patients described this state of mind in the following terms:

> In response to a question as to what he had been doing that day, he replied: "I have been having tea with my wife." Without further comment from the questioner, he continued: "Oh, I haven't really. She's not been here today. But as soon as I close my eyes the scene occurs so vividly, I can see the cups and saucers and hear her pouring out, then just as I am lifting the cup for a drink I wake up, and there's no one there."
> *Q.* Do you sleep a lot, then?
> *A.* No, I am not asleep—it's a sort of waking dream . . . even with my eyes

open sometimes . . . My thoughts seem to be out of control, they go off on their own—so vivid. I am not sure half the time if I just thought it or it really happened. (Case 1, p. 73)

On the basis of the three factors enumerated in the preceding paragraphs, the following hypothesis is advanced for later investigation: Increased vivacity and frequency of dreaming usually occurs in conjunction with cerebral blindness, disturbed affective disinhibition or reality monitoring.

An interesting feature of this condition is that it seems to represent the mirror image of the state of mind described by nonvisual dreamers. This contrast applies (a) to the dreams of these patients (increased vivacity or intensity of dream-imagery is the opposite of cessation or restriction of visual dream-imagery), (b) to their cognition (intense thoughts that are automatically visualized are the opposite of irreminiscence, or inability to visualize thoughts), and (c) to their emotionality (affective disinhibition is the opposite of the hypoemotional state described by some Charcot syndrome patients).

As regards the neuropsychological mechanism of these phenomena, only two theories have been formulated in the literature. First, Damasio et al. (1985) and Morris et al. (1992) attributed the syndrome to a disruption of basal-forebrain innervation of the hippocampus. Second, Whitty and Lewin (1957), who also attributed the syndrome to temporal lobe mechanisms, suggested that increased frequency and vivacity of dreaming may be an epileptic phenomenon. They speculated that the symptoms may be the result of abnormal temporal lobe activity, provoked by an irritative limbic focus. The notion that abnormal dream phenomena may have an epileptiform basis leads directly on to the next topic.

Recurring Nightmares

By comparison with the obscure symptoms already described, it is relatively well established in clinical neurology that seizure disorders may be associated with recurring nightmares. De Sanctis (1896) is usually credited with being the first to describe this association. Freud (1900/1953) cited a contemporaneous article by Thomayer (1897). Temkin (1971) described nightmares in cases of epilepsy dating back to antiquity. The earliest actual case reports that I have been able to trace were published by Clarke (1915). Following the early reports, Penfield (1938) described an important case in which he established a causal relationship between epilepsy and recurring nightmares. (This case was also documented by Penfield & Erickson, 1941, and Penfield & Rasmussen, 1955.) The patient (J.V.) suffered a single infantile seizure associated with transient left hemiparesis. At the age of 7 she witnessed a frightening scene in a meadow. Thereafter she suffered a recurring nightmare in which the frightening scene was repeatedly re-experienced. By the age of 11 full-blown epilepsy had developed and the nightmare began to occur in the form of an of an hallucinatory aura. When the case came to surgery Penfield observed dural-arachnoidal adhesions in the right temporo-occipital zone (particularly in Brodmann's area 19). Stimulation of this general region (i.e., the right temporal lobe) evoked conscious reminiscences of the same stereotyped scene. Penfield and Erickson (1941) reported similar observations in a second case (Case C. Ft.). A causal relationship between (right) temporal lobe irritation and a stereotypical dream was again demonstrated by surgical stimulation. At least 20 further cases of this type have been reported in the literature (Table 7.2). In many cases there was an admixture of increased vivacity and frequency of dreaming, which suggests a degree of overlap between this disorder and the previous one. It is difficult to classify some cases that seem to belong in both categories.[2]

Complaints of recurring nightmares sometimes preceded the onset of frank epilepsy (as in Penfield's case); at other times the nightmares occurred simultaneously with the onset of (nocturnal or complex-partial) seizures, or they immediately preceded the seizures themselves, as dreamy-state aurae. In some cases no obvious relationship between the dreams and the seizures could be demonstrated (Epstein, 1964).

Recurring nightmares are not confined to the epileptic population (cf. Epstein, 1973). For example, they are conspicuous in post-traumatic stress disorder.[3] Formal studies have not been conducted on the relative incidence of recurring nightmares in epileptics versus nonepileptics. In fact normative studies are lacking for all of the dream phenomena reviewed in previous chapters. However, the relevant question for nosological purposes is not whether or not (or how commonly) these phenomena occur in the normal population, but rather whether or not a significant change in the dreams of individual patients have neuropathological implications. The following hypothesis is to be understood in this sense: Recurring nightmares are frequently associated with seizure disorder.

The available literature suggests that the symptom-complex of recurring nightmares with epilepsy has definite anatomical correlates. The right hemisphere was affected in 17 of the 19 cases listed in Table 7.2 for whom localizing information was available (89%) and the disorder was also linked specifically with a temporal lobe seizure focus in 17 of the 19 cases. The perceptual content of the nightmares in these cases was consistent with a temporal focus (they typically included smells, affects, and reminiscences). In both of the nontemporal cases (Snyder, 1958; Epstein, 1967 [Case 2]) parietal lobe foci were established by surface-electrode EEG recording (which is an inexact method for localizing purposes.) The rightward lateralization of this disorder is inconsistent with my earlier observation (based upon the literature on cessation of dreaming) that "a region of the posterior dominant [left] hemisphere is critical for dreaming" (Greenberg & Farah, 1986, p. 319). Nevertheless, the next hypothesis is formulated in accordance with the evidence pertinent to

TABLE 7.2
Case Reports of Recurring Nightmares Associated with Epilepsy

Source	Case	Lesion	Dreams
Clarke (1915)	Case 3, 24-yr m.	No information	Repetitive nightmares, with subsequent development of manifest epilepsy associated with recurrent dreams which sometimes culminated in seizures
	Case 8, 35-yr m.	No information	Recurring nightmare, disappearing with onset of manifest epilepsy
Kardiner (1932)	Case 4 (A. R.) 13-yr f.	No information	Repetitive nightmares of sudden onset, with subsequent development of manifest epilepsy
	Case 5, 21-yr f.	No information	Repetitive nightmares, sometimes continuous, with subsequent development of manifest epilepsy
Naville & Brantmay (1935)	Case 18, 11-yr f.	No information	Frequent nightmares associated with onset of epilepsy
Penfield (1938)	J. V., 14-yr m.	R. lat. Temp-Occip. (hemorrhage)	Recurring nightmare, later becoming hallucinatory aura; reproducible by R. Temp. stimulation
Penfield & Erickson (1941)	C. Ft., 27-yr m.	R. deep Temp. (glioma)	Repetitive series of dreams, typically culminating in nocturnal seizure; reproducible by R. Temp. stimulation
Rodin, Mulder, Faucett, & Bickford (1955)	Case 3, 23-yr f.	(Bilat. Temp. EEG foci, R. > L.)	Dreams of recurring (unpleasant) form, typically culminating in nocturnal seizure
Ostow (1954b)	Case 3, 36-yr f.	(R. Temp. EEG focus)	Recurring (unpleasant) dreams, related in content to compulsive waking-thoughts and seizure automatisms
	Case 4, 38-yr m.	(Bilat. Temp. EEG slowing, L. > R.)	Nightmares of recurring form, related in content to compulsive waking thoughts
Epstein & Ervin (1956)	H. D., 35-yr f.	(R. Temp. EEG focus)	Recurring nightmares, related in content to compulsive waking thoughts and seizure automatisms
	L. E., 22-yr. f.	R.[a] (Bilat. Temp EEG slowing)	Repetitive nightmares, being nocturnal seizures, related in content to waking complex-partial seizures
Snyder (1958)	A. M., 9-yr m.	(R. Par. EEG focus)	Nightmares of sudden onset, with confusion or complaints of headache on awakening, controlled by anticonvulsant medication

TABLE 7.2
(Continued)

Source	Case	Lesion	Dreams
Epstein (1964)	38-yr m.	(L. Temp. EEG focus)	Recurring nightmare, later becoming hallucinatory seizure or aura (description ambiguous)
	23-yr f.	(R. Temp. EEG focus)	Recurring nightmares, gradually becoming more frequent and vivid, later becoming nocturnal seizure or aura with blurred fantasy/reality distinction; controlled by anticonvulsant medication
Epstein & Hill (1966)	35-yr f.	R. Temp. (encephalitis)	Recurring nightmares, typically culminating in or being nocturnal seizure; associated with R. Temp. spiking during REM sleep
Epstein (1967)	Case 1, 41-yr f.	(Bilat Temp. EEG foci, R. > L.)	Nightmares of recurring form, typically being nocturnal seizures
	Case 2, 20-yr f.	(R. Par. EEG focus)	Recurring nightmare, disappearing with onset of manifest epilepsy, later becoming hallucinatory aura
Boller, Wright, Cavalieri, & Mitsumoto (1975)	65-yr m.	R. Temp. (thrombosis)	Frequent nightmares with enactment; controlled by anticonvulsant medication
Epstein (1979)	Patient 2, 27-yr m.	(R. Temp. EEG focus)	Recurring nightmares, with same content as compulsive waking thoughts and aura
	Patient 3, 35-yr f.	(Bilat. Temp. EEG foci; hemangiomatosis)	Recurring nightmare, sometimes being or culminating in nocturnal seizure; associated with spiking during REM sleep
	Patient 4, 27-yr f.	(L. Temp. EEG focus)	Recurring nightmare, sometimes culminating in nocturnal seizure; associated with spiking during REM sleep
	Patient 5, 30-yr f.	(Bilat. Temp. EEG foci)	Recurring nightmares, typically being nocturnal seizures; associated with R. Temp-Occip. spiking during REM sleep
Epstein & Freeman (1981)	38-yr m.	R. Temp. (gliosis)	Recurring nightmares, with content related to seizure aura; partially controlled by anticonvulsant medication

aClinical localization.

TABLE 7.3
Miscellaneous Case Reports of Abnormal Dreaming

Source	Case	Lesion	Dreams
Grünstein (1924)	(5)	Pons, medulla (acoustic neuroma)	Increased frequency with increased acoustic imagery
	(6)	Conus medullaris (tabes)	Increased erotic imagery
Gloning & Sternbach (1953)	S. Franz, 9-yr m.	Pons, cerebellum (glioma)	Increased proprioceptive–vestibular imagery (falling & flying); recovery with (?) residual decreased frequency (description ambiguous)
Torda (1969)	6 cases, 36–56 yrs; 6 matched controls	Bilat. med. Temp. (herpes simplex encephalitis)	Decreased frequency, length, narrative complexity, and emotional intensity; cessation of recent mnemic material (i.e., exclusively pre-morbid mnemic content)[a]
Harrison (1981)	37-yr m.	L. (transient ischemic attack, aneurysm)	(Transient) cessation of verbal–graphic imagery (concurrent with nocturnal transient ischemic attack [TIA])

[a]Objective assessment of dream transcripts of patients versus controls.

this particular disorder: Recurring nightmares indicate a discharging lesion in the region of the right temporal lobe.

As far as the neurobehavioral correlates of recurring nightmares are concerned, no pertinent observations at all have been published to date. Our conclusions in regard to the clinical correlates of this disorder must therefore be limited to the hypothesis already formulated, to the effect that it is frequently associated with epilepsy. Likewise, few specific proposals regarding the mechanism of (epileptogenic) recurring nightmares have been published. However, Penfield and Erickson (1941) alluded to a theory of the neurological organization of dreaming in general, which was based upon these phenomena, when they wrote the following words:

> In dreams under normal circumstances there may be a sort of patterned neuronal activity within the temporal cortex of one or perhaps both sides. *One may be said to dream with his temporal lobe* [italics added]. (Penfield & Erickson, 1941, p. 133; see also Penfield & Rasmussen, 1950)

Subsequent reports of epileptogenic nightmares have been conceptualized in almost identical terms, and many authors have directly quoted this passage. Alternative explanations of this disorder have not been advanced. The intimate connections between the limbic temporal lobe and the anterior limbic structures which were implicated in the previous disorder (increased frequency and vivacity of dreaming) lend some credence to Whitty and Lewin's (1957) suggestion that the two disorders might share a common mechanism. However, what is perhaps most striking about Penfield's viewpoint that "one may be said to dream with his temporal lobe" is its apparent incompatibility with the other models of dreaming that were reviewed earlier (which were based upon other abnormalities of dreaming and upon the REM sleep literature). No attempt has yet been made to conceptualize all of these disorders within a unitary conceptual framework. Epstein and Freeman (1981) did supplement Penfield's viewpoint with the proposal that reciprocal activation might occur between uncinate seizure foci and the deep brainstem structures that regulate REM sleep, but this proposal is contradicted by the fact that nocturnal seizures in fact occur most commonly during NREM sleep (Janz, 1974).

Miscellaneous Abnormalities

I conclude this review of the neuroscientific literature on abnormalities of dreaming with the inevitable observation that some cases have been described which do not fit into any of the broad categories that I have identified. These cases are listed in Table 7.3. However, not all of these reports have been replicated or confirmed. It is therefore not surprising that some of them are less convincing than others. Additional problems arise in relation to experimental studies in which patients' dreams were characterized by the investigators rather than by the patients themselves. For example, Torda (1969) asserted that the dreams of amnesiacs contain material drawn solely from remote memory and that their dreams are shorter in length than normal. Similarly Cathala et al. (1983) considered the dreams of their patients with parietal lesions to be less spatially elaborated than those of controls. Kramer et al. (1975) arrived at some rather absurd conclusions in this way; for example, they claimed that neurologically impaired patients are more likely than controls to dream of females and of family members, and that they tend to dream of more friendly social interactions. Claims such as these do not warrant serious scientific consideration. However it is important to recognize in this regard that a systematic, open-ended survey of the dreams of neurological patients has never yet been conducted. All but one of the clinical studies reviewed here were based upon the spontaneous accounts of individual patients, and all of the existing experimental studies investigated predetermined parameters of dreaming (e.g., presence versus absence of dreams). The only open-ended investigation of the dreams of neurological patients was that of Gloning and Sternbach (1953). However, their sample was small and limited to a restricted range of lesion sites. The possibility therefore remains that any number of dream abnormalities might exist that have not yet been identified. This is the final hypothesis for investigation in the present study: A variety of neuropathologically significant dream phenomena exist that have not yet been identified in the literature.

NOTES

[1]These two cases are not listed in Table 7.1 because it is unclear from the published accounts whether or not the patients themselves considered the vivacity of their dreams to be different from usual.

[2]Similar problems arise with the other disorders discussed in this book, as they probably do in all nosography. Thus Adler's (1944, 1950) case, which was classified in Table 2.1 on the basis of the initial presentation, could have been classified in Table 2.2 on the basis of her later presentation (see also Sparr, Jay, Drislane, & Venna, 1991). Gloning and Sternbach's (1953) cases S. Johann and Sch. Gertrude, listed in Table 2.2, could have been included in Tables 7.3 and 7.1 respectively. Similarly, Gloning and Sternbach's cases H. Therese and S. Josef, which were included in Table 7.1, might also belong in Table 7.2. Epstein's (1964) second case, which was listed in Table 7.2, could equally well have been listed in Table 7.1. Similarly, Efron's (1968), Benson and Greenberg's (1969) and Brown's (1972) case in Table 2.1 might also have been classified in Table 2.2. I already indicated that Schindler's (1953) cases 89 and 111 (included in Table 2.1) should perhaps rather have been listed in Table 2.2. Similarly Basso et al.'s (1980) case M. G. (in Table 2.2) and Harrison's (1981) case (in Table 7.3) could both have been included in Table 2.1. Further examples abound.

[3]It is interesting to note in this regard that many 19th-century neurologists considered traumatic emotional experiences to be an etiological factor in epilepsy (Temkin, 1971).

8

Summary of Provisional Conclusions and Hypotheses

In this chapter the provisional conclusions that are reached on the basis of the foregoing review of the existing literature are briefly summarized. This enables us to take our bearings for the empirical investigations that are reported in the following chapters.

The world literature on abnormalities of dreaming following neurological insult is not a very large body of work. It consists of 73 publications, 60 of which describe individual clinical cases and 13 of which report groups of cases. Two methodologies were employed. In one of these, clinical investigators reported patients' own descriptions of subjective changes in their dreaming; in the other, experimental researchers reported objective features of a sample of dreams (from which they drew inferences about the patients' dreams in general). The results obtained by these two methods are not directly comparable (i.e., the subjective experience of global cessation of dreaming is not the same thing as an objective failure to report dreams during three nights in a sleep laboratory).

Notwithstanding these methodological difficulties, there can no longer be much doubt that a number of specific abnormalities of dreaming do exist in the neuropathological population. These abnormalities can be divided into two broad categories, namely deficits and excesses of dreaming or dream-imagery. These broad categories include at least two symptom-complexes each. These are (a) cessation or restriction of visual dream-imagery, (b) global cessation or reduction of dreaming, (c) increased frequency and vivacity of dreaming, and (d) recurring nightmares.

The bulk of the existing literature is devoted to the first two symptom-complexes (i.e., deficits of dreaming and dream-imagery). These phenomena have traditionally been classified under the nosographic rubric of Charcot–Wilbrand syndrome—a syndrome that is classically characterized by cessation of dreaming, visual irreminiscence, topographical agnosia or amnesia, prosopagnosia, and (according to some authors) visual agnosia. The first case of this type was described by Charcot in 1883, the second by Wilbrand in 1887, the third by Müller in 1892, and numerous further reports have appeared throughout this century. Despite early opposition from Freud and Bay and others, currently the Charcot–Wilbrand syndrome enjoys universal acceptance among specialists in the field—although it is not widely utilized in clinical practice. Despite its general acceptance, the small literature devoted to this syndrome is fraught with controversy and contradiction (although the contradictions are not always recognized).

From the outset, there was disagreement over the exact definition of the syndrome (specifically, over whether or not it is a form of agnosia). However, modern investigators have ignored the early debates, and have tended to use the term *Charcot–Wilbrand syndrome* indiscriminately to refer to almost any condition which is characterized by a loss, reduction, or restriction of dreaming or dream-imagery. Thus, for example, cessation of visual dream-imagery, congenital absence of facial dream-imagery, global cessation of dreaming, and reduced frequency of dreaming have all been described as Charcot–Wilbrand syndrome by modern authors. The same applies to the anatomical correlates of the syndrome. Whereas the earlier neurological reports favored a relatively circumscribed localization for the disorder (viz., area 19 of the occipital lobes), modern researchers claim only that it is associated with posterior cortical disease. This broad localization is generally accepted, but there is considerable disagreement about the lateralization of the (posterior) lesion site responsible for the syndrome. Moreover, the general acceptance of a posterior localization ignores the fact that a second body of literature exists which describes loss of dreaming as a common consequence of prefrontal leukotomy. This last fact casts serious doubt on the diagnostic significance and localizing value of loss of dreaming, unless it is accepted that the same symptom may arise from two completely different lesion sites.

The failure to recognize that loss of dreaming can arise from various lesions has created widespread confusion in regard to the neuropsychological status of the disorder. Some investigators believe that loss of dreaming is an illusion; they suggest that loss of dreaming is in fact an amnesia for dreams (although the precise nature of this amnesia is ill-defined). Others have suggested that loss of dreaming is a secondary manifestation of aphasic disorder. According to the latter authors, loss of dreaming may be attributed to loss of the ability to verbally encode or decode mental images. However, a third group of authors have expressed a viewpoint that directly contradicts the previous one. They claimed that dreaming is predominantly a right hemispheric activity. Some of them have even gone so far as to assert that "the right hemisphere is the dreamer" (Bakan, 1976, p. 66). The situation is complicated still further by the existence of a fourth group of authors who assert that loss of dreaming is a visual–verbal disconnection syndrome. The empirical evidence for and against these various claims is inconclusive, partly as a result of the foregoing methodological and definitional inconsistencies but also partly due to contradictory empirical findings.

Very little has been written about the Charcot–Wilbrand syndrome from the viewpoint of the light that it might cast on the neural mechanisms of normal dreaming. Most authors limited their theoretical comments to simple localizationist or disconnectionist explanations of the clinical phenomena themselves. This approach produced a variety of elementary (and frequently contradictory) theories, each of which explain isolated aspects of the dream process but none of which accounts for the process as a whole. Little attempt has been made to integrate this research with the vast experimental and theoretical literature on the phenomenon of REM sleep. Few authors considered its implications for the controversial question of the function of dreams. In fact, there was a general tendency among most authors to relate their findings to only a fraction of the existing literature (if indeed they placed them in any context at all).

In the previous chapters, the literature on this syndrome has been comprehensively reviewed for the first time. This review resulted in a number of preliminary conclusions, which were fashioned into hypotheses for further investigation in the present study. These hypotheses are enumerated below.

EIGHTEEN HYPOTHESES

1. The classical definition of the Charcot–Wilbrand syndrome was unable to accommodate the different clinical phenomena which have actually been observed. These phenomena seemed to fall naturally into two groups. Therefore my first hypothesis stated that *the Charcot–Wilbrand syndrome is not a unitary entity; two types of loss of dreaming exist, each of which is part of a distinct neuropsychological syndrome with separate anatomical correlates.*

2. The first type of loss of dreaming was characterized by cessation or restriction of visual dream-imagery, whereas dream-imagery in the other mo-

dalities (and therefore dreaming itself) was preserved. A careful review of the anatomical data for the 15 cases of this type that were reported in the literature suggested that this symptom-complex had rather precise localizing significance: *Cessation or restriction of visual dream-imagery indicates a bilateral lesion in the medial occipito-temporal region.*

3. Nonvisual dreaming also had regular neurobehavioral correlates. These coincided roughly with the classical definition of the Charcot–Wilbrand syndrome: *Cessation or restriction of visual dream-imagery typically occurs in combination with a corresponding deficit of visual imagery in general (irreminiscence) and it is also commonly associated with prosopagnosia, topographical agnosia or amnesia, and visual agnosia.*

4. The second type of loss of dreaming was more global than the first; it represented a true cessation of dreaming. However, from the neuropsychological viewpoint this symptom-complex seemed to be quite different from the classical Charcot–Wilbrand syndrome: *Global cessation or reduction of dreaming has no special relationship with any element of the classical Charcot–Wilbrand syndrome.*

5. The question as to whether or not global cessation of dreaming was a secondary manifestation of amnestic disorder arose in relation to the second variant. A review of the available evidence in this regard (which was far from adequate) led to the tentative conclusion that *global cessation or reduction of dreaming is a primary phenomenon, independent of any disturbance of memory.*

6. The evidence suggesting a possible relationship between cessation of dreaming and aphasia was equally equivocal. The sixth hypothesis reflected this fact: *Global cessation or reduction of dreaming is commonly (but not invariably) associated with aphasia.*

7. The two variants of the Charcot–Wilbrand syndrome seemed to be unrelated from the anatomical viewpoint as well. Whereas nonvisual dreaming appeared to have precise localizing significance, the global variant of the disorder was linked with damage to a wide range of brain structures. Nevertheless, an aggregation of the lesion sites that have been reported led to the following conclusion: *Global cessation or reduction of dreaming indicates either (a) a left posterior cortical lesion or (b) a deep bilateral frontal lesion.*

8. From the theoretical point of view, there was a remarkable lack of overlap between this localization of the lesions producing global cessation or reduction of dreaming and those which produced cessation or reduction of REM sleep. This observation led to the following reciprocal hypotheses: *Deep brainstem lesions are not commonly associated with global cessation of dreaming and global cessation of dreaming is not commonly associated with deep brainstem lesions.*

9. Finally, in the absence of any attempts to relate the available data on the Charcot–Wilbrand syndrome to the important theoretical questions surround-

ing the function of dreams, an hypothesis was formulated to test Freud's original theory in this regard: *Global cessation of dreaming is typically associated with disrupted sleep.*

The question then arose as to whether or not two other changes in dreaming (which appeared to be closely related to global cessation of dreaming) had any clinico-anatomical significance in their own right. Specifically, starting from the observation that cessation of dreaming following posterior or anterior lesions frequently resolved into residual reduced frequency of dreaming or reduced narrative complexity and emotional intensity of dreaming, respectively, it seemed that these two clinical phenomena might distinguish between the two localizations (and thereby shed further light on the different mechanisms involved in posterior versus anterior deficits of dreaming). However, my review of the limited data did not yield positive results. This generated the following set of hypotheses:

10. *Reduced frequency of dreaming has no localizing significance.*

11. *Reduced frequency of dreaming has no specific neurobehavioral correlates.*

12. *Reduced narrative (or symbolic) complexity and emotional intensity of dreaming has no localizing significance.*

13. *Reduced narrative (or symbolic) complexity and emotional intensity of dreaming has no specific neurobehavioral correlates.*

A further category of disorders, described here as excesses of dreaming, was divided into two symptom-complexes (although there was a degree of overlap between them). The first of these was characterized by increased vivacity and frequency of dreaming. This disorder was not defined as such in the existing literature, but it was possible to arrive at the following conclusions on the basis of the published case reports:

14. *Increased vivacity and frequency of dreaming indicates a lesion (usually but not exclusively bilateral) in the anterior parts of the limbic system.*

15. *Increased vivacity and frequency of dreaming usually occurs in conjunction with cerebral blindness, disturbed reality monitoring, or affective disinhibition.*

The second disorder in this group was characterized by recurring nightmares.

16. It was not possible to identify any specific neurobehavioral correlates for this disorder. Nevertheless it was evident that *recurring nightmares are frequently associated with seizure disorder.* This hypothesis was formulated with due regard to the fact that similar complaints frequently occur in the normal population. The possible neuropathological significance of subjective change in this regard was emphasized.

17. The available evidence pointed to a definite localization of the lesion site responsible for this disorder: *Recurring nightmares indicate a discharging le-*

sion in the region of the right temporal lobe. The contradiction between this assertion and the previous conclusion regarding the predominance of posterior left hemispheric lesions in cases of cessation of dreaming was noted.

Penfield made a far-reaching inference regarding the neural substrate of dreaming on the basis of this last disorder. He concluded that "one may be said to dream with his temporal lobe" (Penfield & Erickson, 1941, p. 133). This conclusion was incompatible with much of the existing evidence pertaining to other disorders of dreaming—which underlines the fact that a serious attempt has not yet been made to integrate the disparate knowledge based on the various disorders of dreaming into a unitary conceptual framework.

18. Our review of the literature ended with the observation that an open-ended evaluation of the dreams of a large, unselected neurological population has never been undertaken. This raised the possibility that *a variety of neuropathologically significant dream phenomena exist that have not yet been identified in the literature.*

RATIONALE FOR THE PRESENT STUDY

By collating the results of all previously published studies, I arrived at a set of 18 provisional conclusions that will serve as a basis for the present study. It is true that these conclusions deserve to be heavily qualified. They embody approximations and aggregations, some of them are mutually incompatible, many of them are open to empirical contradiction, and almost all of them are subject to weighty methodological objections. Although it seems reasonable to conclude that the clinical existence of neurogenic abnormalities of dreaming has now been established beyond reasonable doubt (by virtue of repeated, independent observations and descriptions over a period of 100 years), the reader nevertheless has every justification to conclude that the nature, number, incidence, course, localizing significance, neurobehavioral correlates, diagnostic value, theoretical implications, and so on, of these phenomena—in short, their whole clinical significance and scientific meaning—still remain essentially obscure.

If the true significance of the Charcot–Wilbrand syndrome and kindred disorders is to be realized, then the dreams of a large, unselected clinical population, representing a broad range of lesion sites and types, across varying degrees of severity and chronicity—together with adequate controls—must be systematically investigated. Any abnormalities of dreaming that emerge must be qualitatively defined, possible associations between these phenomena and other neurobehavioral symptoms and signs must be determined, and their relationships with the underlying pathological anatomy must be established. The results of such an inquiry must then be classified nosologically in accordance with the various distinguishing characteristics and patterns of interrelationship that emerge. Ultimately, they must be explained within a unitary conceptual framework. This would represent a definitive clinico-anatomical study, which would pave the way for experimental investigations into the neuropsychological mechanisms and functions of dreaming. Despite repeated calls for such a study (Broughton, 1982; Cathala et al., 1983; Doricchi & Violani, 1992; Epstein, 1979; Epstein & Simmons, 1983; Greenberg & Farah, 1986; Greenwood, Wilson, & Gazzaniga, 1977; Grünstein, 1924; Harrison, 1981; Humphrey & Zangwill, 1951; Murri et al., 1985; Sacks, 1991; Zeki, 1993), nothing approaching it has ever been conducted. In the remaining chapters of this book the first attempt to conduct such a study is reported.

9

Description of
the Present Research

This study builds upon existing knowledge regarding the neuropsychology of dreams. Data from previous research was collated and reviewed in the first seven chapters and summarized in the eighth chapter in the form of 18 hypotheses for further research. The fact that most of these hypotheses consisted of simple nosological statements reflects the current state of our knowledge in this field, which in turn reflects the relative neglect of the subject of dreaming during the progression from classical neurology to modern neuropsychology. In the neuropsychology of dreams we are still engaged in the basic scientific task of observing, describing, and classifying phenomena. The scope and design of the present study reflects this fact.

AIMS

The aims of the study were the following: (a) to confirm the existence of the previously reported neurogenic changes in dream phenomenology, (b) to search for other, kindred phenomena, (c) to characterize the behavioral–

neurological and pathological–anatomical correlates of these phenomena and thereby to establish their clinical significance, (d) to compile a taxonomy of such phenomena, and (e) to formulate on this basis a preliminary model of the normal dream process. The following question now arises: how should one set about achieving these aims?

METHODS

In the course of reviewing the existing literature, it became apparent that two different methods were employed in previous investigations in this field. For the sake of brevity, I designated them as the *clinical* and *experimental* methods, respectively. The clinical approach represented the mainstream of previous research. It was simply the classical behavioral–neurological technique of systematic clinical observation, applied to subjective reports of dreams. In this approach patients were questioned (usually in the context of the general clinical examination) about changes which may have occurred in their dream-life as a whole, in comparison with their personal premorbid norm, following the onset of the neurological illness. The subjective changes were treated qualitatively, as clinical symptoms. They were then correlated with other neurobehavioral symptoms and signs and with the nature and localization of the underlying pathological process. The experimental approach, on the other hand, represented the application of standardized psychometric assessment techniques to dreams. In this approach a sample of dreams was collected by an objective method over a given period of time (either in a sleep laboratory setting or by means of a standardized morning-recall questionnaire). The sample of dreams was then compared across predetermined parameters with an established population norm. The deviations that emerged were treated quantitatively, as abnormalities of dreaming. These abnormalities were then correlated with other normative measures of psychological deficit and with the site of the underlying lesion.

The methodological divergence between these two approaches reflects a basic divergence that exists within neuropsychology as a whole (see Luria & Majovski, 1977, passim; Walsh, 1991, pp. 2–33). This is not the place to consider these broader methodological issues. What is important for our purposes is that the different approaches in the previous literature on the neuropsychology of dreams have produced apparently contradictory results. This is because subjective descriptions of symptoms and statistical measures of abnormality were prematurely conflated. For example, patients who were unable to recall any specific dreams over 2 or 3 days in laboratory studies were equated directly with patients who claimed retrospectively in clinical interviews that they had stopped dreaming altogether (e.g., Arena et al., 1984; Cathala et al., 1983; Murri et al., 1984; Murri et al., 1985). This resulted in confusion between the notions of reduced frequency of dreaming and of cessation of dreaming. Moreover, the conflation of subjective reports and objective measures is not justified in a field in which the distinction between explicit and implicit knowledge is sometimes of critical importance (cf. Schacter, McAndrews, & Moscovitch, 1988). In disorders of dreaming, for which conscious awareness is a defining feature, clinical description must precede objective measurement. This does not mean that qualitative description is superior to quantitative measurement, but only that clinical disorders of this type cannot be scrutinized experimentally before they have been characterized clinically.

Against this background, it seemed appropriate to base my own study on the methodology best suited to the basic scientific task of observing, describing, and classifying subjective phenomena. The qualitative techniques of the clinical approach are better suited to this task than those of the experimental approach. The former (clinical) approach was therefore used in the present study. This made it possible for me to build directly upon the mainstream of existing research in this area—which employed a primarily clinical–descriptive methodology. However, it also implies that the results reported in the following chapters embody all the weaknesses of a purely clinical method. For, although it is true that subjective neurobehavioral phenomena (like any other natural phenomena) cannot be systematically studied before they have been adequately described and defined, it is also true that science does not progress by descriptions and definitions alone. For this reason the wide latitude that I have assumed in the collection and analysis of clinical data in the present study is based on the assumption that future investigators will use these descriptive findings as the necessary basis for more focused and precise studies, employing more rigorous, experimental methodologies.

SUBJECTS

In basic nosological research it is desirable (for obvious reasons) to study a large series of cases representing the widest possible cross-section of the clinical population. I therefore considered for inclusion in the present study every patient that I assessed during routine clinical work over a continuous 4-year period. This resulted in a target population of 434 cases. I attempted to include as many of these cases as possible in the study. Nevertheless, I was forced to exclude 73 of them for various reasons.[1] This left a final series of 361 cases. Tables 9.1, 9.2, 9.3, and 9.4 summarize the range of demographic characteristics, pathologies, lesion localizations, and neurobehavioral disorders included in this series.

Controls

There are significant differences between a clinical series and a statistical sample or experimental group. The composition of the present clinical series was

TABLE 9.1
Demographic Characteristics of the Clinical Series[a]

Average Age (in years) 35.8
Average Education (in years). 8.6
Sex
    Males. 221
    Females. 132
Ethnicity
    Asian 14
    African. 184
    European 139
    Mixed/Other. 20
Handedness
    Right (dextral) 265
    Left (sinestral or ambidextral). . . . 29

[a]Excludes cases in which the relevant data was not available.

TABLE 9.2
Pathological Characteristics of the Clinical Series

Pathology	$N =$
Benign Cyst	11
Cerebrovascular Disease	83
Congenital Malformation.	3
Degenerative or Systemic Disease.	11
Idiopathic Epilepsy	5
Idiopathic Hydrocephalus	8
Infection.	14
Neoplasm.	79
Trauma.	108
Control.	29
Chronicity	$\bar{x} =$
Weeks since onset of symptoms.	99.5
Weeks since last neurological insult . . .	54.6

determined by the number and range of patients that were referred during the continuous period over which this study was conducted, rather than by any statistical or experimental criteria. It is important to recognize the implications of this for the control group. The latter consisted of all the patients that were referred to me for neuropsychological assessment during the course of the study, in whom cerebral illness was initially suspected but ultimately excluded.[2] They were therefore drawn from the same clinical population as the other patients, and subjected to the same extraneous influences (such as acute

TABLE 9.3
Anatomical Characteristics of the Clinical Series

Lesion Quality	$N=$[b]
Diffuse	114
Focal	209
Laterality	
Bilateral	42
Unilateral	149
Left	76
Right	73
Localization[a]	
Brainstem[c]	61
	(11)
Limbic Lobe[d]	59
	(16)
Occipital Lobe	33
	(2)
Parietal Lobe	93
	(10)
Temporal Lobe[e]	55
	(5)
Frontal Lobe[f]	120
	(22)

[a]The following classifications are not exclusive (pure cases are indicated in parentheses).

[b]Excludes cases for whom the relevant data was not available.

[c]Includes the cerebellum and rostral brainstem (mesencephalon and diencephalon). See Figure 9.1.

[d]Defined as the entire gyrus fornicatus (cingulate, retrosplenial and parahippocampal cortex) with its underlying nuclei and fibre-bundles (including the hippocampal formation, amygdaloid complex and basal forebrain nuclei). Excludes brainstem structures.

[e]Excludes limbic structures.

[f]Excludes limbic structures; includes the basal ganglia.

illness and a hospital milieu). They were not significantly different from the other patients in terms of age, sex, handedness, and educational level. From the statistical point of view a larger and less heterogenous control group would certainly have been preferable. However, if the group is considered from the clinical viewpoint (i.e., if it is considered as just another diagnostic category, as it is in Table 9.2), it provided a suitable control group in the sense that it represented the range of neuropsychologically normal cases that are typically referred for differential diagnostic assessment in a routine clinical situation. The study of such controls is of direct clinical (and therefore nosological) relevance.

PROCEDURE

The Dream Interview

I asked each of the 361 patients included in this study whether or not their dreams had changed since the onset of their neurological illness, and, if so, I asked them to describe in their own words the manner in which they had changed. Thereafter the patients were asked a series of questions about specific aspects of their dreams, excluding those aspects which they might have described already. The questions were asked according to the following basic plan, which was adapted in consideration of each patient's individual circumstances. (The requirement of flexibility when assessing the subjective experience of a seriously ill neurological population is obvious, especially in view of the fact that it was desirable to study a wide cross-section of cases.)

   1. Patients were asked how they were sleeping at night, and whether or not their sleep had been affected by their illness. Responses were classified under

TABLE 9.4
Neurobehavioral Characteristics of the Clinical Series

Symptom or Sign[a]	$N=$[b]
Acalculia	35
Adynamia	70
Agraphia	52
Alexia	29
Anosognosia	83
Aphasia	61
Apraxia	24
Central Achromatopsia	2
Constructional Apraxia	58
Disinhibition	95
Disorientation (to time, place, or person)	51
Disturbed Problem-Solving	89
Finger Agnosia	18
Hemispatial Neglect	46
Hypoarousal	34
Long-Term Memory Disorder	68
Perseveration	87
Prosopagnosia	4
Right–Left Disorientation	19
Short-Term Memory Disorder	46
Topographical Agnosia	1
Topographical Amnesia	14
Visual Agnosia	6
Visual Irreminiscence	6

[a]See appendix for definitions.
[b]Excludes cases for whom the relevant data was not available.

four headings: (a) Sleep was considered to be *better* since the onset of illness, (b) sleep was considered to have been *disrupted* since the illness, (c) sleep was considered to be *unaffected*, or (d) patients were *unsure* as to whether or not there had been any change in the quality of sleep.

2. Patients were asked whether or not they still dreamed at night. If the response was negative, the patient was carefully questioned to determine whether or not this had also been the case prior to the onset of the illness. (No patients reported premorbid absence of dreaming; all patients who claimed that they never dreamed premorbidly, when closely questioned in this regard, qualified their initial statements and said that they seldom dreamed or that they never remembered their dreams.) Subsequent changes from a patient's personal baseline were then determined. Patients were classified under three headings, namely, (a) those who *continued* to dream, (b) those in whom all dreaming had *ceased*, and (c) those who were *unsure* as to whether or not they were still dreaming.

Many patients had great difficulty framing definite responses to some of the following questions, which pertained to the more elusive aspects of dreaming. In such cases the responses were classified as *unsure*.

3. Patients were asked about their ability to recall dreams. Many who had initially claimed that they had stopped dreaming corrected their observations at this point to state that although they were aware that they still experienced dreams, they could no longer remember them in the morning. In all cases of alleged cessation of dreaming this distinction was carefully explored. Here patients were classified in terms of (a) *better*, (b) *worse*, or (c) *unchanged* morning dream-recall, or they were classified as (d) *unsure* if there was no definite response.

4. The difficult matter of narrative complexity of dreaming was then addressed. Patients were asked whether or not their dreams seemed more simple, more straightforward, or more banal than usual, whether or not they were more bizarre, incredible, or convoluted, and whether or not they appeared to be derived more or less directly from real daytime experiences than they used to be. A great deal of clarification and discussion of responses was necessary before patients could be classified with confidence. The four headings used for classification of dreams were, (a) *more* simple, straightforward, banal, and mundane than before; (b) *less* simple, straightforward, banal, and mundane than before (i.e., more bizarre, incredible, convoluted, and strange); (c) dreams that were *unchanged* in these respects; and (d) *unsure* responses.

5. The emotional intensity of dreams was also difficult to assess. The difficulty in obtaining definite responses to this and the previous question underlines the methodological differences between this study and some of those in the existing literature. The literature is devoid of any report of a patient who

actually reported decreased narrative (or symbolic) complexity and emotional intensity of their own dreams. In every instance it was the investigator who characterized the patient's dreams in such terms. In the present study, the patients were asked whether or not they themselves felt that their dreams were (a) *more pleasant* or (b) *more unpleasant* than before, as opposed to being (c) *unchanged* from the affective point of view. The majority of patients were unable to provide unequivocal answers to these questions, and they were therefore classified as (d) *unsure* about this point. A subset of patients specifically complained of recurring nightmares at this stage in the interview. This symptom was classified separately (see item 6).

6. Subjects were asked about the (a) *presence* versus (b) *absence* of recurring nightmares. Care was taken to ascertain whether or not recurring nightmares were also present premorbidly. Few patients reported uncertainty about this criterion.

7. Next, patients were asked whether or not the frequency of their dreaming had changed since the onset of their illness; that is, they were asked whether they dreamed more or less often than they used to. Responses were classified under four headings: (a) *more* frequent dreams, (b) *less* frequent dreams, (c) *unchanged* frequency of dreams, and (d) *unsure*.

8. Patients were then asked whether or not there had been any change in the visual imagery of their dreams. In this respect, patients were classified according to whether visual dream-imagery was (a) *absent* or (b) *present*. Any qualitative variations in imagery were recorded descriptively. Discussion of the quality of dream-imagery led naturally to the next category (item 9).

9. Subjects were questioned about the vivacity of their dream-imagery. A significant number of patients described dreams of decreased or increased perceptual clarity. Others described their dreams as being more realistic than before. The latter concept was initially introduced as a separate category; however it soon became apparent that the designation *reality*, when applied to dreams, was synonymous with *clarity* and *vivacity*, and that the patients were using these terms interchangeably to describe a single aspect of dream experience. Patients were therefore classified in accordance with their responses as having (a) *more* or (b) *less* vivid (or real) dream-imagery, (c) as having dreams of *unchanged* vivacity (or reality), or (d) as being *unsure* about this aspect of their dreams.

10. Actual inability to distinguish between dreams and reality is not the same as increased vivacity or reality of dream-imagery. Cases reporting this distinctive symptom were classified separately, in terms of (a) *presence* versus (b) *absence* of dream–reality confusion.

11. Continuity or duration of dreams (which was also related in the literature to increased vivacity of dreaming) was then explored. Patients were asked whether or not their dreams tended to be unusually long or to display unusual

continuity over a single night, or, alternatively, whether or not they seemed uncharacteristically short and clipped. Responses were classified under four headings: (a) *longer*, (b) *shorter*, (c) *unchanged* or (d) *unsure*. The phenomenon of continuous dreaming (see chapter 7) turned out to be unrelated to the factor of duration of dreams. Nevertheless, both phenomena were covered in the present part of the interview.

12. An assessment of recency versus remoteness of mnemic material in dreams (as described by Torda, 1969) was extremely difficult to obtain. Cases of individuals who clearly recognized (a) more *recent* mnemic material in their dreams than before, or who recognized (b) more *remote* material than before, or (c) who felt sure that their dreams were *unchanged* in this respect, were classified as such, but the majority of cases had to be classified as (d) *unsure*.

13. Finally, patients were asked whether they had noticed any other changes in their dreams that had not yet been discussed. At this point many patients clarified previous responses. Also, some patients made miscellaneous observations that could not be classified meaningfully (e.g., "I dream more about money" or "I dream more about my husband," etc.).

The main features of this interview are summarized in Table 9.5.

TABLE 9.5
Summary of Dream Classification

	Classification			
Category	*Excesses*	*Deficits*	*Normality*	
Sleep	Better	Worse	Unchanged	Unsure
Dreams		Absent[a]	Present[b]	Unsure
Dream-Recall	Better	Worse	Unchanged	Unsure
Narrative Complexity	Increased	Decreased	Unchanged	Unsure
Emotional Intensity	More Pleasant[a]	More Unpleasant[a]	Unchanged	Unsure
Recurring Nightmares	Present[a]		Absent[b]	Unsure
Dream Frequency	Increased	Decreased	Unchanged	Unsure
Visual Imagery		Absent[a]	Present[b]	Unsure
Dream Vivacity	Increased	Decreased	Unchanged	Unsure
Reality Confusion	Present[a]		Absent[b]	Unsure
Dream Duration	Increased	Decreased	Unchanged	Unsure
Mnemic Material	Recent[a]	Remote[a]	Unchanged	Unsure
Miscellaneous	—[c]			

[a]I.e., change in this direction.
[b]I.e., unchanged.
[c]This data was not tabulated; it is reported in discursive form, with reference to individual cases, in the main body of the text.

Neuropsychological Assessment

Once the typical ways in which dreaming was altered by neurological disease had been defined, the next step was to ascertain whether or not regular relationships existed between these changes and other neurobehavioral symptoms and signs. Because the present study approached the neuropsychology of dreams from a clinical-descriptive viewpoint, it correlated changes in dreaming with conventional nosological categories rather than with psychometric test scores. The nosological classification of a clinical performance depends on the extent to which it approximates qualitatively to an established pattern of abnormality rather than the extent to which it deviates quantitatively from a statistical measure of normality (McFie, 1960). For this reason, unlike psychometric scores which are obtained by fixed and standardized methods of investigation, clinical symptoms and signs are demonstrated in variable ways. Different patients may achieve the same test score for different reasons, and it is necessary to investigate each performance in depth before it is possible to categorize it nosologically (Luria & Majovski, 1977). However, the qualitative categorization of symptoms depends on clinical acumen and experience, and is therefore subject to error. Difficulties of nosological classification also arise from definitional controversies, which abound in the history and theory of neuropsychology. The reader is therefore referred to the appendix at the end of this book for clarification of the manner in which the nosological conventions used in this study were defined and operationalized. More detailed clinical information (concerning individual cases and small groups of cases) is presented in the text wherever appropriate.

Anatomical Data

The pathological–anatomical substrata of the clinical findings were classified by projecting computerized tomographic (CT) and magnetic resonance imaging (MRI) scans onto detailed templates, according to the standard method described by Damasio and Damasio (1989). These templates were derived from the anatomical atlases of Montemurro and Bruni (1988) and Damasio and Damasio (1983). The templates are represented schematically in Fig. 9.1. All subsequent figures in this book are based on Fig. 9.1; the reader should therefore refer back to it in order to identify anatomical details in the later figures.

Template projection is not a purely mechanical process; a fair amount of interpretation is frequently called for. Errors of localization commonly associated with this technique are usually due to the neglect of dynamic and contextual factors (cf. Damasio & Damasio, 1989; Damasio & Geschwind, 1985; Frederiks, 1985; Kertesz, 1983). For this reason gross localizations in the pres-

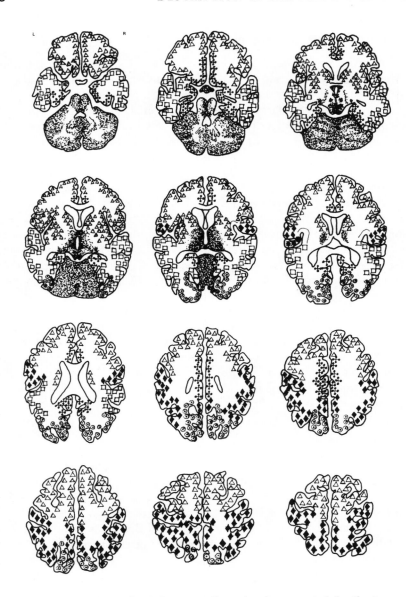

FIG. 9.1.   Templates of typical scan cuts illustrating the anatomical classification of lesions in the present study. For cytoarchitectural details, compare Damasio and Damasio (1983, pp. 239 & 241). L = left; R = right; △ = frontal lobe; □ = temporal lobe; ◆ = parietal lobe; ☉ = occipital lobe; ✢ = limbic lobe; ⣿ = brainstem. (See Table 9.3 for definitions.)

ent study were supplemented by additional information, such as information concerning the type and date of onset of pathology and the date of last neurological insult (which is not always synonymous with the date of onset of pathology). The presentation of anatomical data in subsequent chapters starts with gross classifications that are progressively qualified and refined as more specific clinico-anatomical questions are considered. In individual cases and small groups of patients, these data are also represented visually, using the anatomical templates.

Statistics

From the viewpoint of data analysis, most of the hypotheses summarized in the previous chapter have a similar basic structure; they form a series of a priori planned contrasts. They could therefore be accommodated within a classical 2×2 chi-square framework, used in conjunction with step-wise discriminant analyses in order to determine the relative predictive power of interrelated variables.[3] However, in some instances the phenomena under study turned out to be extremely rare, making it impossible to apply multivariate techniques meaningfully (despite the ample size of the original sample). Clinical methods of description and classification were therefore heavily relied upon to supplement the formal statistical analyses.

I am now in a position to begin to consider the results of the present study.

NOTES

[1] Six aphasic patients were excluded for reasons of insurmountable communication difficulties, 4 amnesiacs could not remember anything about their postmorbid dreams, 8 further amnesiacs provided information that was too confabulatory or confused to be used, 7 patients were too agitated or disinhibited to cooperate in a meaningful way, 2 patients flatly refused to cooperate, 1 patient claimed that he had no knowledge of any kind about his dreams, and 17 patients were excluded for ethical reasons (they were considered to be too ill to participate in research of this type). In addition, 28 cases were lost to the study when excessive clinical pressures precluded the persual of research interests.

[2] This included 3 pseudoneurological cases, 2 cases with benign headache, 2 cases of cranial tumor without impingement on the cranial contents, 7 cases of concussion with complete spontaneous recovery, and 15 cases with exclusively spinal or peripheral nerve lesions.

[3] Many of the patients in this study were assessed more than once, in order to track the natural history of their disorders. Unless otherwise indicated, data derived from the *first* assessment was used in the statistical analyses reported in subsequent chapters. Analyses based upon follow-up assessments are clearly identified as such.

10

The Charcot–Wilbrand Syndrome Reconsidered

In chapter 2, after some preliminary comments and a review of the classical cases, I expressed the view that both the concept and the designation of the Charcot–Wilbrand syndrome (a syndrome that represents the mainstream of neuropsychological research on dreaming) may have been based upon a misconception. This led to the formulation of Hypothesis 1: The Charcot–Wilbrand syndrome is not a unitary entity; two types of loss of dreaming exist, each of which is part of a distinct neuropsychological syndrome with separate anatomical correlates. This hypothesis became the premise for eight further hypotheses, each of which made specific predictions about the clinical and anatomical correlates of the proposed varieties of loss of dreaming.

This chapter provides a brief summary of the broader issues raised by this first hypothesis and an initial overview of my findings with regard to it, before I present in detail the empirical evidence for these findings and consider the specific clinico-anatomical issues arising from them in relation to the subsequent eight hypotheses.

As regards the first hypothesis, the essential questions raised by the review of the literature were the following: (a) Is nonvisual dreaming (i.e., loss of dreaming of the type described by Charcot) a distinct nosological entity with separate clinical and anatomical correlates that are clearly distinguishable from those associated with global cessation of dreaming (i.e., loss of dreaming of the type described by Wilbrand and Müller); or (b) is the phenomenon of nonvisual dreaming an incomplete form—a subset—of the primary syndrome of global cessation of dreaming? If the second alternative is the correct one, the lesion site associated with global cessation of dreaming should overlap with (indeed include) the lesion site that is typically associated with nonvisual dreaming. Similarly, the characteristic neurobehavioral features of the former syndrome should in some way incorporate those of the latter syndrome. On the other hand if the first alternative is the correct one, there should be minimal overlap between the two phenomena; they should be independent entities from both the clinical and the anatomical points of view. This situation would accord with the requirements of the clinico-anatomical principle of double dissociation (Teuber, 1955, 1959).

What light does the present research cast upon these fundamental questions? In the entire series of 361 cases, it was possible to identify only two cases with cessation or restriction of visual dream-imagery (i.e., loss of dreaming of the Charcot type). This suggests that nonvisual dreaming is an extremely rare clinical phenomenon. In agreement with trends observed in the existing literature, the disorder of dream-imagery in both of these cases occurred in conjunction with an analogous disorder of waking visual-imagery (irreminiscence) and an associated short-term memory deficit. However, there were differences in the quality of the dreams of these two patients.

In the first case there was a complete cessation of visual dream-imagery, whereas in the second case isolated elements of visual dreaming were preserved. As was the case in previous reports in the literature, the differences in dream-imagery in these two cases were paralleled by differences in the quality of their waking imagery. There was a complete loss of waking visual imagery in the first case but isolated elements were preserved in the second case. Also in agreement with the previous literature, the medial occipito-temporal region was compromised in both of these cases.

However, definitive conclusions cannot be reached on the basis of such a small number of cases. Moreover, the pathology in the first case (a right parietal arterio-venous malformation draining from the posterior cerebral circulation bilaterally) was not suitable for precise localizing purposes; and in the other case (a right medial occipito-temporal glioma), the lesion was unilateral. This is inconsistent with previously reported cases, in which the lesion was typically bilateral. All that can be said with confidence, therefore, is that my two cases do not contradict the medial occipito-temporal localization that was hypothesized on the basis of the literature. My cases also raise the possibility that there are an as yet undefined number of incomplete forms of nonvisual dreaming associated with various circumscribed (and possibly unilateral) localizations within the medial occipito-temporal region. This possibility—and other matters of detail—are addressed in chapter 12.

An entirely different picture emerged in relation to loss of dreaming of the (global) type described by Wilbrand and Müller. First, global cessation of dreaming was far more common than nonvisual dreaming; a full 112 patients reported global cessation of dreaming (whereas only two patients reported nonvisual dreaming). Second, global cessation of dreaming was unequivocally associated with lesions outside of the medial occipito-temporal region. The lesion sites associated with the latter syndrome were (a) the parietal convexity (of either hemisphere)—perhaps involving the inferior parietal lobule in particular—and (b) the periventricular frontal white matter (bilateral). Neither of these anatomical sites was implicated in my single case of the Charcot type for whom precise localizing data was available; however, the right parietal convexity was involved in the other case of nonvisual dreaming (right parietal arterio–venous malformation; AVM). Third, neither irreminiscence (which was present in both of our Charcot-type cases) nor any other element of the classical Charcot–Wilbrand syndrome correlated significantly with global cessation of dreaming. A small number of cases ($N = 12$) presented with one or more elements of the classical syndrome (irreminiscence, prosopagnosia, topographical amnesia or agnosia, visual object agnosia), but none of these symptoms appeared frequently enough to be statistically significant. The neurobehavioral symptoms and signs, which did correlate significantly with global cessation of dreaming, were, in the cases of patients with parietal lesions, right–left disorientation, finger agnosia, and visuospatial short-term memory deficit. In the cases of patients with frontal lesions, disinhibition, adynamia, and perseveration correlated significantly with cessation of dreaming. In other words, two subtypes of global cessation of dreaming emerged, each with different clinical and anatomical correlates. Both of these subsidiary syndromes were distinct from the syndrome of nonvisual dreaming, although one of them shared a common element with it (viz., visuospatial short-term memory deficit).

Taken together, these findings support the first hypothesis. The Charcot–Wilbrand syndrome is indeed a nosological hybrid; two types of loss of dreaming exist, each of which is part of an independent syndrome with separate anatomical correlates. There is a small degree of overlap between the two syndromes, but considering the anatomical proximity of the lesion-sites involved, this is not surprising.

I am now in a position to consider in detail the evidence for these preliminary conclusions in relation to the more specific clinico-anatomical hypotheses.

11

Two Patients
With Nonvisual Dreaming

Cases presenting with cessation or restriction of visual imagery were identified by question 8 of the interview schedule described in chapter 9. Only 186 patients provided a definite answer to this question. (Questions concerning dream-imagery did not arise for the 112 patients who reported global cessation of dreaming, and 34 patients gave equivocal responses.) The fact that only two patients in the effective sample of 186 reported a cessation or restriction of visual dream-imagery suggests that the incidence of this disorder in the neurological population is very low (1.1%).[1] None of the 29 control subjects reported this disorder.

CASE 1: CESSATION OF VISUAL DREAM-IMAGERY
(PATIENT NO. 201)[2]

This patient was a 26-year-old dextral female and homemaker with 7 years' formal education. Her difficulties began with headache, insidious development of left-sided paresis, somatosensory defect, and a slowly progressive loss of vision in the left field that culminated in sudden onset of blindness and global aphasia. Computerized tomography (CT) identified a high-density mass (arterio–venous malformation; AVM) in the right parietal lobe, with an abnormal vessel in the right lateral ventricle. There was considerable surrounding edema that extended across the midline into the posterior quadrant of the left hemisphere (see fig. 11.1). Four-vessel angiography demonstrated that the AVM was draining primarily from the posterior cerebral circulation.

The patient's visual perception and speech recovered rapidly. Her vision passed through a phase of dense visual agnosia (apperceptive agnosia) followed by prosopagnosia and topographical disorientation. At the time of the first systematic neurobehavioral examination (which took place 2 months post-ictus) the patient reported that she still could not recognize people facially—for the most part she depended on clues from their voices or clothing. She was also aware that she frequently got lost and that she still could not speak properly. However, her subjective account of these deficits suggested that they fluctuated somewhat.

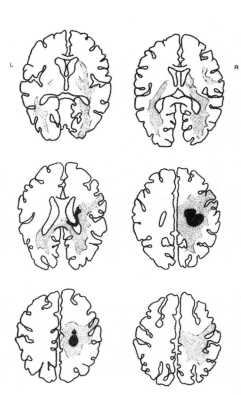

FIG. 11.1.   Facsimile of a CT scan in Case 1 (cessation of visual dream-imagery) illustrating the approximate location and extent of the right parietal AVM and surrounding bilateral edema.

Neurobehavioral Examination

There were no visual field defects on confrontation testing. The patient was able to recognize everyday objects, simple line drawings, and colors. However, she displayed considerable difficulty identifying complex visual material. For example, the Poppelreuter figures (Poppelreuter, 1917–1918) were quite incomprehensible to her, and a photograph depicting a dinner party was described as follows: "A picture of a person. I don't think it's a . . . it's a man, and this is a glass." She also could not recognize photographs of relatively amorphous objects, such as a cloudy sky, the sea, and a mountain-range. Her subjective experience of these difficulties was that she could not see very well "out of the left eye" and that things "sometimes look dark and vague." She typically failed to recognize visitors at first sight and she frequently misidentified the examiner. Visual imagery was also impaired. The patient herself was unsure as to whether or not she was able to generate visual images of objects, but when asked to describe specific objects from internal visualization her performances were clearly deficient. For example, her description of a dog was: "It has four feet, two ears and a mouth." When asked to supplement this description with more detail, she could only say that "dogs have rough skins." A chicken was described as follows: "It has two feet, a beak, a head, and wings." A car: "Four wheels, a steering-wheel, and four seats." Her home: "It has five rooms; two bedrooms, one sitting-room, a kitchen, and an outside."

In contrast, her descriptive abilities in relation to subjects that did not require revisualization skills (such as the history of her illness and the features of concrete objects presented visually) were full and relatively fluent. Her intact ability to describe the features of objects that she perceived externally suggests that this patient's deficit should be attributed to deficient visual imagery per se, rather than to visual–verbal disconnection (notwithstanding the mild dysnomia described later). This interpretation was supported by her poor performance on Binet's cube analysis task (Terman & Merrill, 1937), which is considered to be a suitable test of visual–spatial imagery in patients with limited verbal skills (see McFie & Zangwill, 1960; Newcombe, 1969; Warrington & Rabin, 1970).

At the time of assessment the patient's speech and language performance corresponded to the syndrome of conduction aphasia (Goodglass, 1992). Comprehension was intact, spontaneous production was fluent with occasional literal paraphasias, and repetition was fluent but very paraphasic.[3] There was no obvious word-finding difficulty in spontaneous speech but a moderate deficit emerged on confrontation-naming tasks (Boston Naming Test; Kaplan, Goodglass, & Weintraub, 1983). There was a mild abnormality of written language, consistent with her speech deficit (aphasic paragraphia to dictation) and an atypical form of alexia (recognition of individual letters and words was entirely unaffected, but the patient had great difficulty deciphering sentences and short passages). It is interesting to note how the patient herself experienced the latter deficit: "I can understand what I am reading, but I can't *keep* it. . . . I lose what I read while I'm still busy reading it."

This statement suggests that her ability to read was compromised by her imagery deficit. Her audioverbal short-term memory span was slightly restricted (5 digits forward), as was immediate recall of nonrepresentational figures (Complex Figure Test, copy trial = 25/36, immediate recall = 9/36; Osterrieth, 1944; Rey, 1941). This deficit was limited to immediate and working memory; it did not extend to long-term material (Complex Figure Test, delayed recall = 10/36; Hidden Objects Test = no abnormality detected; Strub & Black, 1986). There was no evidence of everyday forgetfulness (e.g., the patient was able to give a detailed and accurate account of the first day's assessment 24 hours after the event). Constructional praxis was moderately impaired, as was calculation, but the assessment of these functions was complicated by the other deficits I have described. Right–left orientation, finger gnosis, stereognosis, graphesthesia, and all forms of higher motor activity were intact. The planning and regulation of action were completely unimpaired. Also, there was no evidence of hemispatial neglect or true anosognosia. However, the patient's emotional disposition was distinctly bland. She described all aspects of her long and difficult illness, including the effects it had on her family and personal life, entirely without manifest emotion (anosodiaphoria). She conveyed an impression of detached bewilderment, perhaps even depersonalization. On direct questioning she was incapable of offering any introspective comments on her affective state; she said only that she felt "dull."

She was, however, able to offer some striking observations on her dreams. In response to a question about the quality of her sleep (question 1; see chapter 9) she spontaneously mentioned that in the first weeks after her cerebrovascular accident (CVA) she dreamed unusually frequently and that her dreams had since become "very strange." When asked for clarification on the nature of this strangeness she gave the following description:

> I know that I am dreaming but I don't know what it is that I'm dreaming. I can't keep anything. I know that I'm dreaming but I see nothing, nothing happens. . . .
> I used to be able to see and hear all sorts of things in my dreams but now they are not the same, they're very strange. I see nothing. I know I am dreaming but I see nothing in them. . . . [In response to a further question:] Yes, I hear voices and things but I don't *see* anything.

On the day following this interview, the patient was asked to describe her dreams of the night before. She confirmed that she had experienced at least one dream but she could not recall any specific content. Asked again if it was unusually difficult for her to remember her dreams since her illness began (she had denied this the day before), she reported the following: "No, it's not more difficult, it's just that now I *see* nothing in them; now I just hear things all through my dreams." She felt that her dreams were unchanged in other respects (apart from an initial increase in dream frequency, already mentioned).

CASE 2: RESTRICTION OF VISUAL DREAM-IMAGERY (CESSATION OF "KINEMATIC" IMAGERY) (PATIENT NO. 208)[4]

This patient was a 31-year-old dextral male; he was unemployed, with 12 years of formal education. His notes reflected a 9-year history of uncontrolled generalized epilepsy. A right medial occipito-temporal tumor (mixed astrocytoma/oligodendroglioma) had been surgically resected just over 2 years previously. The tumor was situated in the fusiform gyrus (Brodmann's areas 36 & 37), and it extended anteriorly into the white matter beneath the parahippocampal gyrus (see Fig. 11.2). The epilepsy persisted postsurgically. At the time of

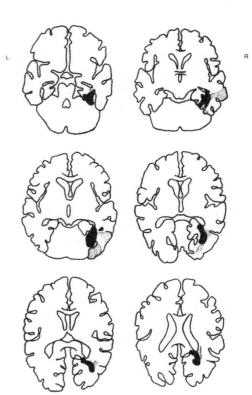

FIG. 11.2. Combined facsimile of two CT scans in Case 2 (restriction of visual dream-imagery) illustrating the original site of the right occipito-temporal glioma and the approximate location and extent of postsurgical low density.

neurobehavioral assessment the patient complained of poor visual acuity, photophobia, hyperacusia, and severe depression.

Neurobehavioral Examination

There was an upper-left quadrantanopia on confrontation testing. Visual recognition of objects and faces appeared normal, but the patient insisted that he frequently had difficulty recognizing people whom he knew well. This could not be verified objectively, but a severe impairment in the recognition of unfamiliar faces was documented (Benton, Hamsher, Varney, & Spreen, 1983, Facial Recognition Test = 32/54). This deficit did not extend to other aspects of visuo-spatial perception and judgment (e.g., Poppelreuter's figures = n.a.d.; Judgment of Line Orientation Test = 30/30; Benton et al., 1983). However, his performance on tests involving the transformation and inspection of visual images were deficient (e.g., Binet's Cube Analysis Test = 8/14).

Subjectively, the patient reported an inability to revisualize familiar faces and a general impoverishment of visual mental imagery. He gave full descriptions of the appearance of common objects and animals, but he reported that he could only picture them "in parts" and that his internal representations therefore had to be built up "out of parts." For example:

> If I think about my room, first I see my hi-fi [set] on the left . . . actually I see all the numbers and the red and green lights . . . lights, then next I see my bed [etc.]. . . . The cupboard is against the other wall, but I can't see them both together. I can't picture how the room [as a whole] looks.

In the process of discussing this subjective deficit, the patient spontaneously reported a change in his dream-imagery; he complained that he no longer saw anything in his dreams and that his dreams now took the form of "thinking rather than dreaming." Asked to give an example to illustrate this change, he reported the following dream from the previous night:

> My mother and another lady were holding me down. It seemed to last the whole night. But I didn't see anything. . . .
> [*How did you know that it was your mother who was holding you down?*]
> I just knew it was her, and the other lady was J. . . . In the morning I thought it might really have happened and I said, "Mommy, did I have another blackout last night?"
> [*Are your dreams more realistic than they used to be?*]
> No, they're more like thinking-dreams. . . .
> [*Could you actually feel them holding you down in that dream?*]
> Yes I think so.
> [*But usually when people are thinking they don't actually experience the things they are thinking about.*]

It's hard to explain. It's like working myself up over something, like how much of a burden I am to Mommy. It's like running myself down over something and things like that; but I'm sleeping, so I dream what I'm thinking.

However, a dream reported on the following morning contradicted the impression that his dreams were totally devoid of visual imagery. This confirms Kerr and Foulkes' (1981) observation to the effect that a patient's initial description of his or her dreams is sometimes flatly contradicted or heavily qualified on systematic investigation.

I dreamed about the doctor. I was thinking that he didn't like me, that he thought I was wasting his time. I thought he might want me to leave because he needed my bed for someone else. . . .
[*How did you know it was the doctor?*]
I saw his white coat and his tie.

Further questioning confirmed that the patient did actually see the white coat and tie in this dream; these were not thoughts. Similar instances of isolated, static dream-images were described on subsequent days.

This patient also complained of other changes in his dream mentation. Specifically, he stated that he dreamed less frequently than before and that his dreams were more difficult to remember. On the other hand, he also complained that some (unpleasant) dreams seemed to "last the whole night." He also suffered recurring nightmares with stereotyped content, but there was some uncertainty as to whether his dreams had actually changed in this last respect. The patient himself felt that he had suffered repetitive nightmares all his life.

The reported difficulty in remembering dreams was accompanied by generalized subjective memory loss. This was only partially confirmed on formal assessment (Wechsler Memory Scale, Wechsler, 1945; Logical Memory Subtest = 12.5/23 [16,9 immediate recall; 9,7 delayed recall]; Associate Learning Subtest = 6,1; 6,3; 6,4). For figural material there was a mild immediate recall deficit, with excellent subsequent retention (Complex Figure Test, Copy Trial = 32/36, Immediate Recall Trial = 16/36, Delayed Recall Trial = 16/36).

In addition to the above, there was mild dyscalculia (of the spatial type; Hécaen, Angelergues, & Houillier, 1961), and there were equivocal signs of left hemispatial neglect in the visual modality. There was no evidence of topographical amnesia or agnosia, color imperception, amusia or constructional apraxia (although the patient's approach to constructional tasks was unusually ponderous and methodical). Right–left orientation, tactile gnosis, the body image, speech and language function, and planning and regulation of motor activity were all completely intact. Anosognostic signs were not in evidence; on the contrary, this patient was unusually preoccupied with all his deficiencies. There was abundant depressive and self-critical ideation and affect, with some obsessive–compulsive features.

TABLE 11.1

Cases with Cessation or Restriction of Visual Dream-Imagery

Case	Lesion	Relevant Symptoms and Signs	Dreams
Case 1, 26-yr f.	R. deep Par. AVM[a] [Bilat. Occip–Temp–Par][b]	Restriction of L. visual field, Irreminiscence, Prosopagnosia, Topographical amnesia, Simultanagnosia, Hypoemotionality, Material nonspecific short-term memory deficit, Fluent dysphasia	Initial increased frequency, Cessation of visual imagery
Case 2, 31-yr m.	R. med./deep Occip-Temp. Glioma[a]	Generalized epilepsy, L. upper Quadrantanopia, ±Irreminiscence, Unfamiliar face recognition Deficit, Visuospatial short-term memory deficit, Depressive ideation with obsessive-compulsive features	Gross reduction in visual imagery (cessation of kinematic imagery), Reduction in frequency and recall, Repetitive nightmares, Occasional continuous dreaming

[a]Localization based on in vivo imaging techniques.
[b]Clinical localization.

The main characteristics of the two cases just reported are summarized in Table 11.1.

NOTES

[1]The incidence figures given throughout this study refer to the incidence of positive cases in the effective sample studied. The effective samples exclude the 29 control cases, which are considered separately.

[2]The patient number denotes the position of a case in the original consecutive series of 361 patients (see chapter 9).

[3]These difficulties are not reflected in the quotations provided, which are translations into English. Paraphasic errors cannot be easily translated but the following sample conveys something of the character of this patient's deficit.

Spontaneous Production:

Examiner: *Waar is ons nou?* [Where are we now?]

Patient: *By die Bara Hospitaal in Diepkloof.* [At the Bara Hospital in Diepkloof]

Repetition:

Examiner: *Die bed is in die hospitaal.* [The bed is in the hospital]

Patient: *Die bed opdiespitaal.* [The bed onthespital]

Examiner: *Dit is mooilik om te praat.* [It is difficult to speak]

Patient: *Ek is mooilik dikter praat.* [I am difficult dulter speak]

[4]The use of the term *kinematic* reflects the similarity between this patient's disorder and a disorder that Kerr and Foulkes (1981) described by that term. This disorder is not to be confused with cerebral akinetopsia, which has different clinical characteristics and anatomical correlates. (According to Zeki, 1991, 1993, human V5 is located at the junction of Brodmann's areas 19 and 37, on the *lateral* occipito-temporal surface.)

12

Anatomical Correlates of Nonvisual Dreaming

The following hypothesis was advanced in chapter 3 (Hypothesis 2): Cessation or restriction of visual dream-imagery indicates a bilateral lesion in the medial occipito-temporal region. In the light of the case material described in the previous chapter, this hypothesis can now be considered from two points of view: (a) Did both patients with cessation or restriction of visual dream-imagery have lesions in this area? and (b) Did all cases in the series with lesions in this area have cessation or restriction of visual dream-imagery? When considering the hypothesis from these two points of view, we should also bear in mind that it makes two separate predictions: (a) that nonvisual dreaming is invariably associated with bilateral cerebral lesions, and (b) that the lesions always include the medial occipito-temporal region.

We begin this chapter by considering Cases 1 and 2 in relation to these two predictions. Next we examine the cases in my series with bilateral medial occipito-temporal lesions who did *not* present with nonvisual dreaming. Finally, we consider a group of cases of related interest; in these cases, visual dream-imagery was preserved, but the patients reported a reduction in the vivacity of the imagery.

CASE 1

The pathology in Case 1 (the only case in our series with complete cessation of visual dream-imagery) did not lend itself to precise anatomical localization. Nevertheless, a few broad statements can be made with some justification. First, although the primary lesion in this case was localized to the right cerebral hemisphere, and it therefore appears at first sight to contradict the bilateral hypothesis, there was nevertheless good clinical and radiological evidence of bilateral cerebral involvement. The AVM itself was situated in the right parietal lobe, but AVMs are nonlocalizable due to their widespread hemodynamic effects, and in this particular case there was also radiological evidence of considerable left-hemispheric edema. In addition, there were clinical features typical of both left hemispheric dysfunction (aphasia) and bilateral cortical dysfunction (cerebral blindness, which resolved into simultanagnosia and prosopagnosia). Second, it seems reasonably certain that the pathology in this case affected both medial occipito-temporal surfaces. This was suggested by the location and extent of the edema on scan, by the fact that the AVM was draining primarily from the posterior cerebral arteries, and by the presence of symptoms typically associated with bilateral medial occipito-temporal lesions (e.g., prosopagnosia). It is less clear what additional anatomical structures were involved, although the clinical presentation (conduction aphasia) implicated at least some aspect of the left posterior convexity and the radiological evidence certainly implicated the right parietal lobe.

The value of this case from the viewpoint of localization, therefore, is that the pathological anatomy *does not contradict* either of the predictions made in Hypothesis 2. Due to the imprecise localization of the lesion, this case adds very little to the conclusions that were reached in chapter 3 on the basis of the existing literature. However, it is at least consistent with those conclusions. This case also confirms the very existence of a clinical phenomenon characterized by complete cessation of visual dream-imagery in the context of otherwise normal dream phenomenology. In addition, it gives an indication of the statistical rarity of this phenomenon. In our entire series of 361 patients, only one example was found. This confirms the impression conveyed by the literature. Only 12 examples of truly nonvisual dreaming were documented in a period of more than 100 years (Table 2.1).[1] The case reported in the present study is the 13th.

This symptom was not reported by any of our control patients. In view of the now-established rarity of the phenomenon, and considering the relatively small size of the control group, this observation cannot be considered definitive. Nevertheless, unless and until a contradictory observation is actually documented, we are justified in concluding that nonvisual dreaming is invariably associated with cerebral pathology.

CASE 2

In Case 2, although the symptom of nonvisual dreaming was less complete than it was in Case 1, the localization of the lesion was easier to establish. Whereas the lesion in Case 1 was relatively diffuse, the lesion in Case 2 was unequivocally situated in a highly circumscribed location, namely the right medial occipito-temporal region (fusiform gyrus). This is consistent with the second of the two predictions mentioned previously. However, whereas the evidence in Case 1 pointed to bilateral cortical involvement, in Case 2 all of the evidence—radiological, surgical and clinical—indicated that the lesion was unilateral. We may therefore answer in the affirmative the question as to whether or not all patients in the series who presented with cessation or re-striction of visual dream-imagery have lesions in the medial occipito-temporal area, but we cannot confirm that these lesions were invariably bilateral.

The presence of a unilateral lesion in Case 2—and the incomplete nature of the dream-imagery deficit in that case—suggests that dream-imagery might be selectively impaired with unilateral lesions in the medial occipito-temporal region. This raises the possibility that, whereas complete cessation of visual dream-imagery is associated with bilateral medial occipito-temporal disease, partial cessation (or restriction) of such imagery is associated with uni-lateral pathology in this area.

Is this conclusion supported by the literature? In fact, none of the three previously reported cases with selective loss of an aspect of visual dream-imagery (Botez et al., 1985; Sacks & Wasserman, 1987; Tzavaras, 1967; see Table 2.1) had unilateral damage.[2] Although the pathological process was ill-defined in two of these cases (Botez et al., 1985; Sacks & Wasserman, 1987)—and the possibility of unilateral right-hemispheric involvement therefore could not be definitely excluded—there was an autopsy-proven bilateral lesion in the third case (Tzavaras, 1967). It also seems unlikely, on clinical grounds, that the lesion in Sacks and Wasserman's (1987) case was restricted to a single hemisphere; central achromatopsia typically is associated with bi-lateral disease (Green & Lessel, 1977; Pearlman, Birch, & Meadows, 1979; Damasio, Yamada, Damasio, Corbett, & McKee, 1980; Zeki, 1990). The liter-ature therefore does not support the conclusion that partial cessation (or re-striction) of visual dream imagery is associated with unilateral lesions in the medial occipito-temporal region. However, it is important to recognize that the cases that I have grouped together under the heading of partial cessation (or restriction) of visual dream-imagery do not form an homogenous group. Tzavaras's (1967) and Botez et al.'s (1985) patients reported absence of facial dream-imagery, Sacks and Wasserman's (1987) patient reported cessation of color imagery in dreams, Harrison's (1981) patient reported a transient inabil-ity to image letters, and the case described in the present study (Case 2) lost the kinematic aspect of visual dream-imagery. (The fact that all of these cases suffered analogous disorders of waking perception or imagery is discussed in chapter 13.)

Comparison with Kerr and Foulkes' (1981) Case

The deficit in Case 2 was very similar to that described in a case report by Kerr and Foulkes (1981).[3] Their report will therefore be examined in some detail. During a single night in a sleep laboratory, the patient (a 44-year-old male of superior intellect) described his dreams as being like "a complicated story going on rather than a complicated movie going on" (p. 605) and as something that he "felt" rather than something that he actually "saw" (pp. 605–606). Such comments are characteristic of nonvisual dreamers, and similar descriptions were offered by both of our own patients (see chapter 11). However, unlike patients with complete cessation of visual dream-imagery, Kerr and Foulkes's patient did experience some isolated visual dream-images:

> For example, when asked about the visual nature of a dream about buying dresses for a friend, he reported that he could see the pattern of the dress material, but only as a static image focused on the material itself, and in the absence of any larger visual context or setting. (p. 606)

This account is strikingly reminiscent of the description given by our Case 2 (the dream of the surgeon's white coat and tie). Kerr and Foulkes summarized their patient's disturbance in the following terms, which describes exactly the dream disorder in our Case 2: "The subject's dream-reports were typically sequential and narrative in form, but lacking specifically in continuous visual imagery. The occasional visual images that appeared . . . [were] fragmentary and static in nature" (p. 608).[4]

Did Kerr and Foulkes' (1981) case, like Case 2, have a unilateral lesion? The authors' description of the pertinent data is somewhat ambiguous. However it appears from the published account that a right temporal AVM was removed by incomplete lobectomy when the patient was 16 years old, resulting in left-sided hemianopia, and that there was a subsequent left hemiparesis following a CVA (Kerr & Foulkes, 1981). It therefore seems probable that the symptomatic lesion in this case was unilateral (right hemispheric) and that it involved the medial occipito-temporal aspect of the hemisphere. This is the precise region that was involved in Case 2.

This leads to the conclusion that at least some forms of selective dream-imagery deficit do arise from unilateral lesions and, more specifically, that the variant of this disorder which is characterized by cessation of kinematic visual dream-imagery is associated with unilateral lesions in the medial occipito-temporal aspect of the right cerebral hemisphere. The localizations of the other known forms of partial cessation of visual dream-imagery (faces and colors) appear to be bilateral, and to be situated in the same general area. However, there is insufficient data at this stage to clarify the finer anatomical distinctions that may differentiate these selective dream-imagery disorders. (See Goldenberg, 1993, for a discussion of similar issues with respect to components of waking imagery.)[5]

The nosological value of Case 2, therefore, is that it confirms the existence of a group of subsyndromes characterized by the disruption of selective aspects of visual dream-imagery, and it suggests that specific lesion sites within the medial occipito-temporal region are responsible for these disorders. It also contradicts Doricchi and Violani's (1992) assertion that cases with loss of dreaming (in the broad sense of the classical Charcot–Wilbrand syndrome) never have been observed in association with circumscribed right occipito-temporal lesions. This is a new finding, that qualifies our earlier conclusion to the effect that all cases of patients with nonvisual dreaming have bilateral medial occipito-temporal lesions (Hypothesis 2). The evidence now available suggests that only *complete* cessation of visual dream-imagery is invariably associated with bilateral lesions in this area.

NEGATIVE CASES

This paves the way for the second question raised at the beginning of this chapter: Did all cases with bilateral medial occipito-temporal lesions have cessation of visual dream-imagery? My series included four patients with definite (radiologically confirmed) bilateral lesions in this area who did not report nonvisual dreaming. How did the lesions in these cases affect visual dream-imagery?

Case 3: Global Cessation of Dreaming (Patient No. 19)

This patient was a 36-year-old dextral male; he was an artisan with 9 years formal education. Five months prior to the neurobehavioral assessment, the patient complained of headache and deteriorating vision. A CT scan demonstrated ventricular dilation, 5 small bilateral mediobasal occipito-temporal cysticerci, and 1 large right parietal cyst. A ventriculo-peritoneal shunt was inserted and a course of Praziquantel was administered. This resulted in significant clinical improvement. Ophthalmological investigations revealed a residual left-superior quadrantanopia and a right peripheral-field scotoma. His IQ was very superior. At 20 weeks postonset, a neurobehavioral examination revealed a visual material-specific memory deficit (Complex Figure Test; copy trial = 35/36, immediate recall = 10.5/36, delayed recall = 4/36). At that stage the patient was *unsure* as to whether or not he was dreaming. No other deficits were documented. He was discharged but readmitted 3 weeks later complaining of deteriorating memory and vision. He now felt sure that dreaming had ceased completely. A new CT scan demonstrated a large right basal temporal cyst. Once again, he was medicated with successful result. On reassessment (3 weeks later; i.e., 26 weeks after the initial onset) the left-superior quadrantanopia was again observed and a mild, visual-material-specific deficit of memory was documented (Complex Figure Test; copy trial = 36/36, immediate recall = 16/36, delayed recall = 9/36). At this last assessment the patient reported that his dreaming had recovered but that there was residual reduction in dream frequency, dream recall, and vivacity of visual dream-imagery. (It seems likely that the latter symptom is related to nonvisual dreaming. This possibility is addressed later.)

Case 4: Global Cessation of Dreaming (Patient No. 123)

This patient was a 37-year-old sinistral male; he was a manual laborer with 8 years' formal education. He was admitted with headache, nausea, drowsiness, and ataxia following an assault (blow to the occiput). CT investigation at the time of admission demonstrated large, bilateral supratentorial subdural hemorrhages and an extradural hematoma in the posterior fossa. A craniotomy was performed immediately. Neurobehavioral assessment (2 weeks later) was limited to a bedside examination of vision and memory. No gross abnormalities were detected in these functions. At that point the patient reported global cessation of dreaming since the date of the trauma.

Case 5: Global Cessation of Dreaming (Patient No. 189)

This patient was a 49-year-old dextral female; she was a nursing sister with 16 years' formal education. She had a congenital atrial-septal defect and took Warfarin for many years. Her complaints included a 3-year history of severe headache with scintillating scotoma and nausea, progressive memory loss, visual disturbances, anxiety attacks, and a single olfactory hallucination. CT and MRI investigations revealed evidence of multiple lacunar infarcts, bilaterally in the medial occipito-temporal region (in the distribution of the posterior cerebral artery). An electroencephalogram (EEG) was considered normal. Neurobehavioral assessment revealed mild, material nonspecific, recent memory dysfunction (e.g., Complex Figure Test, immediate recall trial = 10.5/32; Babcock Story Recall Test [Babcock, 1930], immediate recall trial = 6/21), subclinical apperceptive agnosia (Luria's Neuropsychological Investigation, Test G [1]; Christensen, 1974) and a marked decline in visual–spatial reasoning (Gottschaldt's, 1928, Figures, this assessment = 6/42, premorbid assessment = 12/42; Raven's, 1960, Progressive Matrices, this assessment = 20/38, premorbid assessment = 31/38).[6] This patient reported global cessation of dreaming.

Case 6: Global Cessation of Dreaming (Patient No. 318)

This patient was a 35-year-old sinistral female; she was a shop assistant with 8 years' formal education. She was unconscious on admission. Her relatives reported that she had been involved in a motor vehicle accident 1 year previously (with loss of consciousness), but they insisted that she had made a complete recovery. This was confirmed by the hospital records. The present admission followed an assault consisting of an axe wound in the midoccipital region. CT investigation demonstrated a left occipital depressed fracture with a fresh intracerebral hemorrhage, a right medial occipito-temporal acute subdural hemorrhage and an area of low density in the right mediobasal frontal region suggestive of an old infarct (possibly gliosis from the previous motor vehicle accident). The patient regained consciousness after 5 days but she remained disoriented. There was severe nonfluent aphasia for approximately 2 weeks. Two weeks later (5 weeks posttrauma) she was transferred to the rehabilitation unit. At neurobehavioral assessment (3 weeks after her transfer) the following deficits were documented: right hemianopia, disorientation for time and place, visual material-specific recent memory deficit, associative visual agnosia, constructional apraxia, unilateral (right) neglect, adynamia, and global cessation of dreaming.

The fact that dreaming stopped completely in all of these cases is not without nosological significance. As mentioned in chapter 10, it suggests that there may be a degree of overlap between the syndromes of nonvisual dreaming and global cessation of dreaming (the two variants of the Charcot–Wilbrand syndrome). The fact that dreaming stopped completely in these cases also lends indirect support to Hypothesis 2. None of the patients with definite bilateral medial occipito-temporal lesions reported preservation of visual dream-imagery. Visual dream-imagery is lost, by definition, in cases with global cessation of dreaming. We may therefore answer in the affirmative the question as to whether or not all cases in the series with bilateral medial occipito-temporal lesions had cessation of visual dream-imagery.

PATIENTS WITH REDUCED VIVACITY OF DREAMING

We turn finally to the third group of patients mentioned at the beginning of this chapter. Cases presenting with the disorder described as cessation or restriction of visual dream imagery (or nonvisual dreaming) were identified by question 7 of the dream interview. This question simply asked patients whether visual imagery was currently *absent* or *present* in their dreams.

We have seen already that only two patients reported a subjective *absence* of visual dream-imagery in response to this question. However, a significant proportion of the other 184 patients who provided a definite response to this question (and stated that visual dream-imagery persisted) went on to qualify their answers when they responded to question 9 of the interview, which probed the vivacity of dream imagery. Of the 116 patients who gave a definite response to this question, 36 patients described their dreams as being relatively *less vivid* than they were premorbidly (31% of the effective sample).[7] Because this subjective change might represent a tendency in the direction of nonvisual dreaming, it might be appropriate to group these patients together under a subclinical heading, and to consider what additional light they might cast on our pathological–anatomical findings concerning the full (clinical) form of the disorder.

However, before doing so, it is important to recognize that 3 control subjects reported reduced vivacity of dream-imagery (Patient No. 40, a case of psychogenic pain; Patient No. 83, a paraplegic; and Patient No. 313, a paraplegic). Nineteen controls gave a definite description of their visual dream-imagery, which means that the incidence of reduced vivacity of dream-imagery among controls was 15.7%. This is somewhat lower than the 31% incidence among cerebrally impaired patients, $\chi^2 = 2.73$, $p < .1$. Nevertheless, the fact that controls reported this phenomenon suggests that vivacity of dream-imagery can also be altered by purely functional factors.

What then were the pathological–anatomical correlates of this phenomenon? Nine of the 36 patients had diffuse cerebral pathology. These cases were unsuitable material for localizing purposes. Of the remaining 27 (focal) cases, the majority had unilateral lesions (10 left, 10 right, 7 bilateral). It is seen from Table 12.1 and Figure 12.1 that these lesions clustered around the occipito-limbic axis. Stepwise discriminant analysis confirmed this tendency; occipital and limbic involvement discriminated modestly between patients with and without reduced vivacity of dream-imagery, $p < .1$. However, once the variance contributed by the limbic lobe, $F = 4.33$, $p < .05$, was partialled out of the discriminant analysis, the occipital lobe lost most of its predictive power (combined occipital and limbic lesion: $F = 3.13$, $p = .08$; occipital lesion alone: $F = 1.86$, $p = .18$). This means that the limbic lobe was the more powerful of these two discriminators.

If it is conceptually legitimate to describe reduced vivacity of dream-imagery as a subclinical tendency in the direction of nonvisual dreaming, then these anatomical observations add weight to our localization of nonvisual dreaming to the medial occipito-temporal region (which is contiguous with the occipito-limbic region). We might speculate on this basis that the relative importance of the limbic lobe reflects a link between vivacity of dream-

TABLE 12.1
Anatomical Correlates of Reduced Vivacity of Dream-Imagery[a]

	Vivacity Reduced		Vivacity Not Reduced[c]	
Location[b]	N	%[d]	N	%[d]
Brain Stem	8	34.8	15	65.2
Occipital	13	52.0	12	48.0
Limbic	8	61.5	5	38.5
Temporal	7	38.9	11	51.1
Parietal	12	38.7	19	61.3
Frontal	18	34.6	34	65.4

[a]These lesion sites are not exclusive.
[b]See Table 9.3 for definitions of anatomical categories.
[c]Unchanged or increased vivacity of dream-imagery.
[d]Percentages of cases with or without reduced vivacity of dream-imagery by anatomical category.

imagery and an unspecified emotional variable (cf. the hypoemotionality described by Charcot, 1883, and Botez et al., 1985). This would account for the fact that reduced vivacity of dream-imagery also occurs in purely functional cases. However, it must be emphasized that these suggestions are based on modest statistical correlations. Reduced vivacity of dream-imagery in the individual case does not reliably indicate a lesion in the medial occipito-temporal region, whereas actual cessation of visual dream-imagery (or aspects thereof) evidently does. Therefore, although reduced vivacity of dream-imagery may be a suggestive empirical phenomenon, it is not a reliable clinical symptom.

NOTES

[1]If Schindler's (1953) two cases were subtracted from this total (as it seems that they should be; see chapter 2) then Basso et al. (1980) and Kerr and Foulkes' (1981) two cases could be added to it.

[2]Unless Harrison's (1981) aphasic case with transient dream-alexia is included in this category (see Table 7.3).

[3]This case was not included in Table 2.1 for methodological reasons. The patient was not asked to comment upon the quality of his dream life in general; instead his dreams were studied in the context of a limited sleep laboratory experiment which sought to establish the specific role of the right hemisphere in dreams. The case was therefore classified in Table 4.2 rather than Table 2.1.

[4]A case reported by Deleval, De Mol, & Noterman (1983) was also strikingly reminiscent of our Case 2, in respect of his waking imagery. The patient had unilateral (left) posterior damage and apparently could not integrate the parts of an image together:

> When I try to imagine a plant, an animal, an object, I can recall but one part, my inner vision is fleeting, fragmented; if I'm asked to imagine the head of a cow, I know that it has ears and horns, but I can't revisualize their respective places. (p. 71, Farah & Koening's translation; cited in Kosslyn, 1994, p. 313)

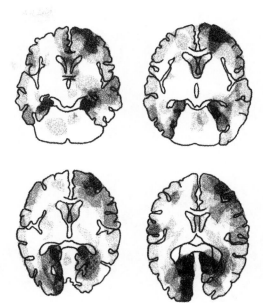

FIG. 12.1. Combined facsimile of CT scans in 21 cases with reduced vivacity of dream-imagery, illustrating the relative preponderance of medial occipito-temporal–limbic lesions.

Compare the following remarks by our Case 2:

> If I think about my room, first I see my hi-fi [set] on the left . . . actually I see all the numbers and the red and green lights . . . lights, then next I see my bed [etc.]. . . . The cupboard is against the other wall, but I can't see them both together. I can't picture how the room [as a whole] looks.

Deleval et al. (1983) evidently did not ask their patient about changes in dreaming.

[5]Goldenberg (1993) distinguishes between imagery for letters, forms, colors, faces, and spatial relationships. The disorder described here as loss of kinematic imagery (after Kerr & Foulkes, 1981) shares many attributes with the disorder that Goldenberg describes as loss of imagery for spatial relationships. Kosslyn (1994) described similar phenomena under the heading of *coordinate spatial relations* encoding. The choice of an appropriate nosological term for this disorder (or group of disorders) awaits further investigation of its fundamental nature. However, it is important to note in this regard that Goldenberg (1993) and Kosslyn (1994) conflated subjective changes in mental imagery with defective performances on objective tests which measure imagery-dependent behaviors (cf. chapter 9 and appendix).

[6]Premorbid values were kindly provided by the National Institute for Personnel Research (NIPR), where this patient was tested 11 years previously (scores refer to NIPR adaptations of these well-known tests).

[7]One hundred-and-two patients gave equivocal or *unsure* responses. A further 114 cases could not respond to question 9 because they had reported global cessation of dreaming or visual dream-imagery in response to questions 2 and 8.

13

Clinical Correlates of Nonvisual Dreaming

In chapter 2 we predicted not only that cessation or restriction of visual dream-imagery would correlate with bilateral medial occipito-temporal lesions (Hypothesis 2) but also that the dream-imagery disorder would co-occur with a corresponding disorder of waking visual imagery (irreminiscence), and that it would also correlate—to a lesser extent—with prosopagnosia, topographical agnosia or amnesia and visual agnosia (Hypothesis 3). These symptoms comprised the classical Charcot–Wilbrand syndrome. In the present chapter I consider these predictions in relation to each of the symptoms in turn.

IRREMINISCENCE

Irreminiscence was present in both of our symptomatic cases, but it took a different form in each case. Case 1 was unsure subjectively whether or not she was able to generate visual imagery, but indirect evidence from the clinical examination of this faculty suggested that she was not. Her descriptions of familiar objects and animals were very schematic and they contained no references to unequivocally visual elements such as color and shape. It is unlikely that these impoverished descriptions were due to aphasia or visual–verbal disconnection (cf. Doricchi & Violani, 1992), as the patient was capable of providing full and vivid descriptions of things that she saw (as opposed to imaged) and of nonvisual mnemic material. It seems reasonable to conclude that visual imagery was defective in this case. This is consistent with the previous literature, in which 91% of reported cases with total cessation of visual dream-imagery also suffered complete visual irreminiscence in waking imagery (Table 4.1).[1]

Case 2 reported a somewhat different and more circumscribed deficit. He was unable to revisualize familiar faces and he reported a subjective impoverishment of visual imagery in general. This took the form of a fragmentation or deconstruction of the visual scene, which prevented him from revisualizing spatial relationships between isolated visual elements. In other words, the nature and extent of the irreminiscence in this case corresponded closely to the nature and extent of his dream-imagery deficit. This confirms a tendency that was noticed with regard to the existing literature. Tzavaras (1967) documented the case of a patient reporting absence of facial dream-imagery who also reported prosopagnosia and irreminiscence for faces in waking life. Sacks and Wasserman (1987) reported the case of an individual with loss of color-imagery in dreams who also had central achromatopsia and irreminiscence for colors in waking life. Basso et al. (1980) reported the case of a patient with global cessation of dreaming who complained of waking irreminiscence in all modalities (see Table 2.2). Harrison (1981) reported a case of a patient with transient aphasia associated with transient alexia in a dream (see Table 7.3). Kerr and Foulkes (1981) reported the case of a patient who was "[unable] to represent extrapersonal space kinematically" (p. 605) and who described her dreams as "lacking specifically in continuous visual imagery;" the occasional visual images that did appear were "fragmentary and static in nature" (p. 608). Our Case 2 described an almost identical association between akinematic irreminiscence and akinematic visual dream-imagery. These associations are reminiscent of the fractionation of visual imagery into form, color, faces, letters, and spatial relationships by modern researchers (see Goldenberg, 1993, for review). Taken together, these facts strongly support the notion that irreminiscence is the basic deficit (*Grundstörung*) underlying the syndrome of nonvisual dreaming (Critchley, 1953; Nielsen, 1946; Pötzl, 1928).

Negative Cases

However, if irreminiscence is indeed the *Grundstörung* underlying Charcot's variant of the Charcot–Wilbrand syndrome, then not only should nonvisual dreaming always be accompanied by irreminiscence, but also irreminiscence should always be accompanied by nonvisual dreaming. Our series yielded 4 cases with irreminiscence who did not report the latter symptom. Three of these patients reported global cessation of dreaming. In the fourth case, normal visual dream-imagery persisted, although the performance of this patient on some clinical tests casts doubt on her subjective incapacity to generate visual images. These 4 cases are described briefly.

Case 7: Global Cessation of Dreaming (Patient No. 139). This patient was a 23-year-old dextral male; he was unemployed with 11 years' formal education. He was admitted unconscious with lacerations and bruising in the right frontal region, suggestive of assault. He regained consciousness within hours of admission, but 6 weeks posttrauma the following physical deficits were still evident on examination: seventh nerve palsy on the right, left superior quadrantanopia and athetoid movements of the left hand. He also complained of poor vision and memory. Neurobehavioral assessment revealed a material nonspecific recent-memory disorder (Complex Figure Test, copy trial = 32/36, immediate recall = 2/36; Auditory–Verbal Learning Test, recall trials = 4/6/5/6/9/4/4, recognition = 4; Rey, 1964; Taylor, 1959). Prosopagnosia and topographical amnesia were also demonstrated (see the following discussion). The patient was completely unable to revisualize. He provided an unambiguous subjective description of this symptom. There were no other localizing signs. This patient reported global cessation of dreaming. Although he conceded that his ability to judge whether or not he was dreaming was compromised by his memory difficulties, he nevertheless felt sure that he was actually not dreaming.

Case 8: Global Cessation of Dreaming (Patient No. 207). This patient was a 37-year-old male; he was a bus driver with 10 years' formal education. He was assaulted by a mob and received repeated blows to the head. There was protracted loss of consciousness. A fractured base of skull was visible on X-ray. Hospital records indicated that there were "multiple intracranial hemorrhages," but the original CT scan had been misplaced by the time that he was seen for neuropsychological assessment (2½ years posttrauma). At the time of the assessment, complete left hemiplegia and fixed left hemianopia were still present. On examination, he was severely adynamic and there was limited critical awareness. He displayed material nonspecific recent memory disturbance, unilateral (left) neglect in all modalities, dense prosopagnosia, topographical amnesia, and achromatopsia. He was unable to generate any visual images subjectively. He said that he could "picture" smells and tastes but not visual qualities. His descriptions of the appearance of a bus and of a traffic light were grossly deficient. He reported that he had not experienced a single dream since the assault, although he had been a frequent dreamer previously.

Case 9: Preservation of Visual Dreaming (Patient No. 200).   This patient
was a 33-year-old dextral female; she was an artist with 15 years' formal education. She had a lifelong history of refractory complex-partial epilepsy, with a
right temporal focus on EEG. After one generalized seizure in childhood
there had been transient left hemianesthesia and hemianopia. She described
occasional nocturnal enuresis and she complained of recurring nightmares
(described in chapter 22). She also reported episodic depersonalization and
derealization, "confusion," occasional horrifying visual and auditory hallucinations, and bouts of suicidal depression. Neurobehavioral examination
elicited evidence of mildly deficient memory and spatial judgment but no
other localizing signs. This patient reported absence of visual waking imagery,
but specific questioning in this regard yielded some equivocal responses. For
example, she described the British flag as "Red, white, blue, with lots of inter-
connected crosses." Her pet dog (a dachshund) was described as follows: "It
has a long body, four legs, a tail, its ears flop down from the top of its head, and
it is covered in short brown fur." A canary was described thus: "Smallish, with
two legs, a feathered tail and wings, small black eyes, pointed nose . . . usually
yellow." [*Can you picture it to yourself?*] "No." Her father: "He is big and fat,
bald, with brown eyes . . . he's about 5' 10" and he's got gray hair." [*Can you picture his face?*] "No, I'm not picturing anything. I'm thinking about him." This
patient reported frequent sleep-onset hypnagogic hallucinations (typically visual images of a disembodied face). Her dreams were described as being rich
in visual elements.

Case 10: Global Cessation of Dreaming (Patient No. 346).   This patient
was a 45-year-old sinistral male; he was a delivery man with 8 years' formal education. He was involved in a MVA with subsequent anoxic complications due
to a severe chest injury. His behavior in the ward, especially at night, was bizarre. Occasional generalized seizures ensued. The EEG displayed an irregular, nonspecific abnormality. CT and MRI scans demonstrated a small calcific
lesion in the right parietal white matter. The patient complained of deficient
vision and memory. Neurobehavioral examination (8 months post trauma) revealed severe prosopagnosia. He could not identify photographs of familiar
faces, including one of himself (see the following section). However, recent
memory per se was only mildly defective (visual memory was better than verbal). There was associated topographical amnesia, achromatopsia, constructional apraxia, and bimanual nonfluency with severe motor perseveration. A
complete visual irreminiscence was noted. The patient reported global cessation of dreaming and subjective inability to generate visual mental images (the
latter was indirectly corroborated by asking him to describe well-known faces
and places). There were no other clinical features of note.

The reader will observe that, once again, these patients were not negative cases in the strict sense; they did not report actual preservation of visual dream-imagery in association with irreminiscence. Rather, the majority of them reported global cessation of dreaming, which necessarily implied cessation of visual dream-imagery. We were therefore unable to confirm the observations of Brain (1941) and Brown (1972), who reported cases of patients demonstrating irreminiscence with apparent preservation of visual dream-imagery. This supports our earlier conclusion to the effect that disorders of visual imagery in waking life are typically associated with corresponding disorders of dream imagery. The viewpoint that a primary disorder of visual imagery is the *Grundstörung* of the nonvisual variant of the Charcot–Wilbrand syndrome may therefore be upheld. Nonvisual dreaming and visual irreminiscence are simply manifestations of the same underlying deficit, during sleep and wakefulness, respectively. This deficit may affect visual imagery as a whole or circumscribed aspects thereof. However, the preservation of waking imagery in other modalities among the negative cases with global cessation of dreaming demonstrates that global cessation of dream imagery is not always associated with an equivalently global disorder of waking imagery (as it was in the case of Basso et al., 1980). The close association between waking imagery and dream imagery therefore appears to be a modality-specific phenomenon. This issue is discussed further in chapter 14.

PROSOPAGNOSIA

This symptom was not present in both symptomatic cases of nonvisual dreaming. Case 1 presented with a classic prosopagnosic deficit. She recognized familiar people only by way of their voices or clothing. Her behavior on the ward was consistent with the diagnosis of prosopagnosia, and a disorder of familiar-face recognition was formally demonstrated by means of an improvised Famous Faces Test (using local newspapers and magazines). By contrast, although Case 2 also claimed that he found it difficult to recognize familiar faces, this claim was not verified on objective assessment. The patient was able to identify all photographs of famous faces that were presented to him. However, a severe deficit in the judgment of *un*familiar faces was documented on formal testing. In other words, whereas Case 1 suffered true prosopagnosia (defective face recognition) it seems that Case 2 suffered defective face perception.

Negative Cases

Aside from these two cases, the series yielded three cases of patients with prosopagnosia who did not report cessation or restriction of visual dream-imagery. However, once again, all three of these patients reported global cessation of dreaming. We are therefore unable to confirm the observations of

Pallis (1955), Brown (1972), and Schanfald et al. (1985), all of whom reported prosopagnosic cases where visual dream-imagery was preserved. Our cases are summarized very briefly here.

   Case 7: Global Cessation of Dreaming (Patient No. 139).   This patient (who was described previously) lived in a remote rural village with a very small population. He frequently mistook people for one another. (This information was supplied by the patient's mother.)

   Case 8: Global Cessation of Dreaming (Patient No. 207).   This man (also already described) was unable to identify photographic portraits of his favorite football stars nor could he identify famous political figures (despite a keen pre-morbid interest in politics). The patient himself confirmed that he frequently misrecognized friends and family members.

   Case 10: Global Cessation of Dreaming (Patient No. 346).   According to his wife, this patient (also already described) often failed to recognize family members and neighbors. This was confirmed on assessment, where he failed even to recognize a photograph of himself.

Considered together, these findings suggest that nonvisual dreaming is commonly but not invariably associated with prosopagnosia. Although statistically reliable statements cannot be made on the basis of such a small number of cases, these findings are at least broadly consistent with the trend observed in the literature, in which only 73% of cases with nonvisual dreaming suffered prosopagnosia (Table 4.1). However, because our series yielded only one case with complete cessation of nonvisual dreaming, and since prosopagnosia was present in that case, the possibility cannot be excluded that prosopagnosia has a stronger relationship with complete cessation of visual dream-imagery than with some partial variants of this disorder.

TOPOGRAPHICAL AMNESIA AND AGNOSIA

These symptoms, too, were not present in both cases. Case 1 reported that she frequently lost her way in familiar environments. Her behavior on the ward was consistent with this claim. It was never formally determined whether this disorder had an agnostic or an amnestic basis. Topographical functions were entirely spared in Case 2.

Negative Cases

Our series yielded 13 cases of topographical amnesia who did not report cessation or restriction of visual dream-imagery. Eight of these patients reported global cessation of dreaming (Patients No. 22, 49, 58, 139, 207, 209, 224 & 346).[2] In the other 5 cases, visual dream-imagery was preserved (Patients No. 4, 13, 235, 246, & 343).[3] In addition, our series included one case with true topographical agnosia. This patient reported global cessation of dreaming. We are therefore unable to confirm Pallis' (1955) observation to the effect that topographical agnosia is compatible with normal dream-imagery. Our case is reported below.

Case 11: Global Cessation of Dreaming (Patient No. 234).   This patient was a 77-year-old dextral male; he was a highly educated rabbi. He was admitted with a history of progressive visual disturbance:

> It started with the vision. I could see that the vision has changed terribly. I came to the Princess [a Nursing Home where he frequently visited members of his congregation]. It's a place where I came to a million times. And I look; "Is this the place?" All of a sudden I have doubts about the place; a place where I come to every day. I understand it must be my eyes. All of a sudden I don't recognize the place. I had to look at the sign above the entrance and I see; "Yes, it's still the Princess." But it's not the same. I see it's a radical change.

Various similar experiences were described. For example, the patient once asked for directions to the railway station when he was already in the station. He first sought medical advice when he noticed progressive difficulty in reading. Clinical neurological examination elicited nothing other than a positive Babinski response and fixed (left) hemianopia. Neurobehavioral assessment revealed subtle signs of (left) hemispatial neglect, including intermittent paralexia. Apart from the perceptual abnormality already described, no other deficits of visual recognition were documented. The patient gave accurate verbal descriptions of the routes to and from the various places he failed to recognize. Revisualization and color perception were normal. There were no other cognitive features of note. A CT scan demonstrated right parieto-occipital hyperdensity. This was identified as an infiltrating glioma at biopsy. This patient stated emphatically that he had not had a single dream for at least 3 months.

Considered together, the foregoing findings suggest that visual dreaming is preserved in approximately half of the patients with topographic agnosia or amnesia, and similarly, that topographical functions are spared in approximately half of the cases with nonvisual dreaming. This confirms the trend observed in the previous literature (see Table 4.1). Topographical amnesia and agnosia and nonvisual dreaming seem to be relatively independent disorders. However, as was the case for prosopagnosia, because our series yielded only one case with complete cessation of nonvisual dreaming (and because topographical disorientation was present in that case) the possibility cannot be excluded that topographical disorders have a stronger relationship with complete cessation of visual dream-imagery than with some partial variants of this disorder.

VISUAL OBJECT AGNOSIA

As was the case for prosopagnosia and topographical disorder, this symptom was present in only one of our Charcot-type cases. Case 1 had considerable difficulty recognizing complex visual scenes. None of the Poppelreuter figures could be identified. A photograph depicting a dinner party was described in terms of isolated, disparate elements, and the global significance of the scene was not recognized. Photographs of amorphous objects and scenes could not be identified. The patient herself complained that things sometimes appeared "dark" or "vague," although a primary deficit of visual acuity was not evident on formal testing. This clinical presentation resembles Wolpert's (1924) simultanagnosia. Case 2 described a visual imagery deficit that was analogous to simultanagnosia, but true visual agnostic features could not be demonstrated in this patient.

Negative Cases

In addition to Case 1, the series yielded 5 further cases of visual agnosia. One of these cases conformed to Lissauer's (1890) associative type and 4 cases conformed to the apperceptive type (see appendix). The associative case (viz., Case 6, described previously) reported global cessation of dreaming. One of the 4 apperceptive cases reported global cessation of dreaming (Case 5, also described previously). A second case of apperceptive agnosia (Patient No. 76, a case of chronic cysticercosis with multiple foci) reported preservation of dreaming, but with a marked decrease in dream frequency and an impaired recall of dreams. The other two apperceptive cases experienced normal dreaming and dream-imagery (Patient No. 287, diffuse calcific process of unknown etiology; Patient No. 60, high-velocity closed head injury). This confirms the theoretically important observations reported by Wilbrand (1887, 1892), Brain (1941), Brown (1972), Levine (1978), Morin et al. (1984), Goldenberg et al. (1985), Riddoch and Humphreys (1987), Schanfald et al. (1985), Jankowiak et al. (1992) and Behrmann et al. (1992), to the effect that visual agnosia (of all types) can occur independently of visual irreminiscence (see chapter 3). It also confirms the observations of Brain (1941), Brown (1972), and Schanfald et al. (1985), to the effect that visual agnosia (of all types) can occur independently of nonvisual dreaming.

In summary, our series yielded one case with apperceptive agnosia who reported nonvisual dreaming and one case with nonvisual dreaming who did not suffer from any form of agnosia. This is at least broadly consistent with the 50% incidence of visual agnosia recorded among cases with nonvisual dreaming in the previous literature (see Table 4.1). In addition, our series yielded one case with associative agnosia and one with apperceptive agnosia who reported global cessation of dreaming. Three further cases with apperceptive agnosia were negative in the stricter sense; they reported actual preservation of visual dream-imagery. Taken together, these findings suggest that visual agnosia and nonvisual dreaming are relatively independent disorders. This supports the views of Brain (1950, 1954), Humphrey and Zangwill (1951), Macrae and Trolle (1956), Basso et al. (1980), Murri et al. (1984, 1985), and Botez et al. (1985), who excluded visual agnosia from the classical Charcot–Wilbrand syndrome (cf. Adler, 1944, 1950; Boyle & Nielsen, 1954; Broughton, 1982; Gloning & Sternbach, 1953; Greenwood et al., 1977; Grünstein, 1924; Nielsen, 1946; Pötzl, 1928). However, as was the case with prosopagnosia and topographic agnosia and amnesia, the possibility cannot be excluded that visual agnosia has a stronger relationship with complete cessation of visual dream-imagery than with some partial variants of this disorder.

CONCLUSIONS

Considering the foregoing four symptoms in relation to the predictions advanced at the beginning of this chapter (Hypothesis 3), it is evident that visual irreminiscence is an essential clinical correlate of cessation or restriction of visual dream-imagery. This does not apply to the other elements of the classical Charcot–Wilbrand syndrome (see Table 13.1). Although all of the classical symptoms were present in Case 1 (with complete cessation of visual dream-imagery) numerous instances of complete cessation of visual dream-imagery in the absence of prosopagnosia, topographical agnosia and amnesia, and visual agnosia have been described in the existing literature. Only irreminiscence is an invariable correlate of cessation or restriction of visual dream-imagery. The latter two symptoms may therefore be described as the cardinal elements of the nonvisual variant of the Charcot–Wilbrand syndrome.

Qualitative variations in visual dream-imagery are accompanied by analo-

TABLE 13.1
Quality of Dreams in Cases with Irreminiscence, Prosopagnosia,
Topographical Agnosia or Amnesia, and Visual Agnosia

	Normal	Cessation or Restriction of Visual Imagery	Global Cessation
Irreminiscence	0[a]	2	3
Prosopagnosia	0	1	3
Topog. disorder	5	1	9
Visual agnosia	3[b]	1	2

[a]Assumes absence of deficit in Case 9.
[b]Includes Patient No. 76.

gous variations in the quality of waking imagery. It therefore seems appropriate to attribute the two cardinal symptoms of the nonvisual variant of the Charcot–Wilbrand syndrome to a single underlying deficit, and to conclude that they are two manifestations of the same underlying deficit, in sleep and wakefulness, respectively. The essential nature of the underlying deficit is, as yet, unclear. However, it is evident that it is a highly circumscribed deficit. It affects imagery only (i.e., it does not necessarily extend to the external perceptual process). Similarly, it affects visual imagery, or even specific aspects thereof, but it does not affect imagery in general (i.e., it is a modality-specific deficit). The theoretical implications of these conclusions will be considered in chapter 15.

The relatively high correlations between nonvisual dreaming and prosopagnosia, topographical agnosia and amnesia, and visual agnosia reflect the fact that these symptoms all arise from lesions in the same general anatomical region (namely, the ventral occipito-temporal axis). These symptoms do not share intrinsic mechanisms. This explanation neatly accounts for the greater co-incidence of these symptoms in cases with complete cessation of visual dream-imagery. Complete cessation of visual dream-imagery (like prosopagnosia, topographical agnosia, and visual agnosia) occurs more readily with bilateral medial occipito-temporal lesions than with unilateral lesions in this region (cf. chapter 12).

OTHER SYMPTOMS

Before concluding this chapter, I briefly consider three symptoms that were not included in the classical Charcot–Wilbrand syndrome but that are nevertheless of interest. These symptoms are central achromatopsia, hypoemotionality, and visuospatial short-term memory disorder.

Achromatopsia

This symptom was not present in either of the two symptomatic cases but it was present in two negative cases (Patients No. 207 & 346). Both of these negative cases suffered global cessation of dreaming. This is broadly consistent with the literature (see Table 4.1), and suggests that nonvisual dreaming and achromatopsia are independent symptoms. This neither adds nor subtracts from the conclusion reached in chapter 3, namely, that there was little reason to believe that central achromatopsia formed an integral part of the syndrome of nonvisual dreaming. The modest association between these two symptoms in the previous literature (Table 4.1) is explicable in the same way as the associations between nonvisual dreaming and prosopagnosia, topographic agnosia and amnesia, and visual agnosia (i.e., they arise from lesions in the same general anatomical region). These symptoms do not share intrinsic mechanisms with nonvisual dreaming (or visual irreminiscence).

Hypoemotionality

This symptom was present in one of the two symptomatic cases (Case 1), but in the other symptomatic patient (Case 2) there was an abundance of depressive emotion. Therefore, hypoemotionality was only present in our single case with complete cessation of visual dream-imagery; it was absent in our case with partial cessation (or restriction) of visual dream-imagery. In this respect hypoemotionality is no different from the classical Charcot–Wilbrand symptoms (with the exception of what we have described as its two cardinal elements). On the other hand, it is also possible that the terms *hypoemotionality* and *depression* describe two points on an affective continuum (cf. Schilder, 1934; Styron, 1990). The incidence of hypoemotionality and depression among negative cases was not specifically investigated in the present study. However, we have already considered the possible significance in this regard of the preponderance of limbic lesions among subclinical cases with reduced vivacity of visual dream imagery (see chapter 12).[4]

Visuospatial Short-Term Memory Disorder

This was the only other symptom (apart from irreminiscence) that was present in both Cases 1 and 2 (e.g., Case 1 scored only 36% on the immediate recall trial of the Complex Figure Test [9/25; delayed recall = 40%] and Case 2 scored 50% [16/32; delayed recall = 50%]). Visual working memory disorder might be considered a necessary consequence of visual irreminiscence, if mental images are "best viewed as short-term memory representations" (Kosslyn, 1994, p. 286). However, it is important to recognize that visual mental images are just *"one form* [italics added] of short-term memory representation" (Kosslyn, 1994, p. 324). Irreminiscence is not synonymous with short-term memory (STM) disorder. The phenomenon of unconscious priming (Schacter, 1987) demonstrates that long-term memories can be activated in STM without becoming conscious. This is confirmed by everyday clinical observation; visuospatial STM disorder (which is common) frequently occurs in the absence of visual irreminiscence (which is rare). Irreminiscence is an explicit disorder; it entails a subjective inability to generate and/or maintain conscious visual images (cf. chapter 9). However, the conceptual division between imagery and STM is by no means unambiguous. This important issue requires systematic investigations, beyond the scope of the present study.

NOTES

[1]Gloning and Sternbach (1953) reported a single case of nonvisual dreaming in the absence of irreminiscence. This observation has never been repeated.

[2]Patients 139, 207, and 346 were described above as Cases 7, 8, and 10.

[3]However, one of these patients (No. 246) did report a relative reduction in the vivacity of visual dream-imagery, in response to question 9 of the dream interview (cf. subclinical nonvisual dreaming, chapter 12).

[4]None of these subclinical cases reported irreminiscence, prosopagnosia, topographical agnosia, visual agnosia, or achromatopsia. Only 1 case (Patient No. 246) displayed topographical amnesia. None of the neurobehavioral symptoms and signs listed in Table 9.4 discriminated significantly between patients with and without reduced vivacity of dream-imagery, $p = .1$.

14

Some Incidental Observations on Modal Specificity

In the prototypical case report of nonvisual dreaming, Charcot (1883/1889) reached the following conclusions:

> This necessarily leads one to admit that the *different groups of memories have their seat in circumscribed regions of the encephalon* [italics added]. And this in turn becomes added to the proofs which go to establish that the hemispheres of the brain consist of a number of differentiated "organs," each of which possesses its proper function. (pp. 162–163)

As we saw in chapter 3, Charcot's explanation of nonvisual dreaming as a loss of stored modality-specific representations was elaborated by Grünstein (1924). Grünstein observed that whereas visual dream-imagery is lost in cases of visual agnosia and irreminiscence (i.e., in cases with damage to secondary visual cortex), it is not affected in cases of cortical blindness (i.e., in cases with damage to primary visual cortex). This confirmed Charcot's interpretation of nonvisual dreaming as a disorder of visual memory. Grünstein concluded on this basis that the syndrome of nonvisual dreaming is specifically associated with damage to visual association cortex. He then predicted that analogous modality-specific dream disorders should arise from damage to secondary cortex outside of the visual sphere. For example, patients with lesions in secondary auditory cortex should experience nonauditory (or nonverbal) dreams. Grünstein himself was unable to confirm this prediction in two cases of pure word-deafness, because both of them reported global cessation of dreaming (see Table 2.2). His hypothesis therefore remains of theoretical interest today, as it has still not been systematically investigated. It was not included in the 18 hypotheses formally investigated in the present study. However, the following incidental observations are of interest in this regard.

SPONTANEOUS REPORTS OF MODALITY-SPECIFIC DREAM DISORDERS

An open-ended question in the dream interview (question 13) invited spontaneous descriptions of modality-specific disorders of dreaming. This question was put to all 361 cases included in the study. It did not yield a single report of cessation or restriction of dreaming in any specific modality outside of the visual sphere. This is consistent with a trend that emerges from the existing literature. At least 15 cases with abnormalities of dream-imagery confined to the visual sphere have been reported, and 2 further cases of this type were identified in the present study. However, only 2 cases with analogous abnormalities in the other primary modalities have ever been reported. Grünstein (1924) reported a case of acoustic neuroma with increased auditory dream-imagery, and Gloning and Sternbach (1953) reported the case of a patient with cerebellar glioma with increased falling and flying imagery in his dreams. Neither of the latter two observations has ever been repeated, and they were not confirmed by the present study.[1]

PRIMARY SENSORY–MOTOR DEFICITS IN DREAMS

Selected patients were asked directly whether or not their dreams contained imagery in the particular modalities that were affected by their neurological illness. This question was posed to 40 patients with primary sensory–motor deficits (18 cases of hemiplegia with varying degrees of pre- and postcentral cortical involvement, 1 case of triplegia, 5 cases of cerebellar ataxia, 7 cases of hemianopia with varying degrees of striate cortical involvement, 1 case of cortical blindness, 2 cases of cerebral blindness with perichiasmic lesions, 5 cases of paraplegia with spinal lesions, and 1 case of quadriplegia). All but 2 of these patients reported that their sensory–motor deficits disappeared in their dreams. The somatosensory and motor functions of the hemiplegic patients were subjectively intact in their dreams, as were the visual fields of the hemianopic and cortically blind patients and the motor coordination of the cerebellar patients. Identical experiences were reported by the spinal patients vis-à-vis the functional capacities of their paretic and anesthetic limbs and genitals. However, two of these patients reported that they sometimes experienced paraplegia in their dreams, although they had not done so initially (i.e., in the first months of their illness). These findings are consistent with the existing literature. In fact, vivid visual dreaming is a common occurrence in the acute phase of cortical blindness (Brown, 1989; Hécean & Albert, 1978).[2]

Similarly, Mach (1906/1959) reported normal somatomotor dream-imagery in an autobiographical account of dense (right) hemiplegia:

> Optical and tactual motor-images persisted in my memory. Very often during the day I formed the intention to do something with my right hand, and had to think of the impossibility of doing it. To the same source are to be referred the vivid dreams which I had of playing the piano and writing, accompanied by astonishment at the ease with which I wrote and played, and followed by bitter disappointment on waking. (pp. 175–176)

Mach's poignant remark about "bitter disappointment on waking" was repeated by many of my own patients.

These observations pose serious questions for the influential activation–synthesis theory of dreams, proposed by Hobson and McCarley (1977), which suggests that dream-imagery is an isomorphic representation of the activation of central sensory and motor centers during REM sleep:

> As an example of the formal isomorphism approach, it may be reasonably assumed that subjective experience of visually formed imagery in dreams implicates activation of perceptual elements in the visual system during REM sleep. We may further assume that the visual-system activation of REM sleep must be formally similar to that of the waking state. We could not otherwise account for the clarity of our dream vision. Other details of psychophysiological correlation are assumed to obey the same general law; for example, the vivid hallucinated sensation of moving [in dreams] is assumed to be related to patterned activation of motor systems and of those central brain structures subserving one's perception of where one's body is in space. (Hobson, 1988, pp. 204–205)

The demonstrable preservation of visual and somatomotor imagery in dreams despite the physical destruction of perceptual elements in the visual and motor systems undermines the Hobson–McCarley assumption to the effect that central sensory–motor activation in REM sleep "must be formally similar to that of the waking state" (Hobson, 1988, p. 205). This issue is considered further in the following chapter.

VERBAL IMAGERY IN DREAMS

In view of my observation (in Case 2) that visual dream-imagery can be selectively impaired in cases with unilateral right-hemisphere lesions, I asked 10 patients with analogous unilateral left-hemisphere lesions whether or not they still experienced verbal imagery in their dreams. (This question was also put to 15 patients with unilateral right-hemisphere lesions, 9 with bilateral lesions, and 18 with diffuse lesions.) None of these patients reported cessation of verbal dream-imagery. (However, two of them were unsure as to whether or not their dreams had ever contained verbal imagery premorbidly.)

THE DREAMS OF APHASIC PATIENTS

In view of the argument expressed in the literature by some authors to the effect that an inability to generate language necessarily implies an inability to generate dreams (Anan'ev, 1960; Jakobson, 1973; Moss, 1972; Zinkin, 1959), I asked a small number of aphasic patients not only whether they still dreamed, but also whether they experienced aphasia in their dreams ($N = 12$). Four of these patients could not comprehend or respond meaningfully to this question. Five cases indicated in response that their dreams were completely unchanged, but they could not convey specific information about their audioverbal dream-imagery. Two of the latter patients were fluent aphasics (Patient No. 6, fronto-temporal empyema; Patient No. 50, parietal meningioma), and 3 of them were nonfluent aphasics (Patient No. 39, frontal infarct; Patient No. 45, fronto-parietal hemorrhage; Patient No. 287, diffuse calcific process). Only 3 patients provided specific information concerning dream-imagery. These patients all indicated that they were not aphasic in their dreams and that their dreams contained normal verbal imagery. This confirms the observations of Cathala et al. (1983) and Schanfald et al. (1985), who reported that aphasiacs with lesions in auditory and somatosensory association cortex are able to generate normal audioverbal dream imagery. My own 3 cases are described briefly here.

Case 12 (Patient No. 206). This patient was a 22-year-old dextral male; he was a policeman with 12 years' formal education. Following a thrombosis in the region of the left middle cerebral artery (in association with bacterial endocarditis), infarction of the left frontal lobe convexity and underlying basal ganglia was demonstrated on CT scan. At neurobehavioral assessment (20 weeks postictus), severe nonfluent aphasia and right upper limb paralysis were noted. The patient's speech was telegraphic, with better repetition than spontaneous production. However, his pragmatic communication was excellent. Examination of writing and reading revealed agrammatic paragraphia and literal alexia. Comprehension was essentially preserved but with some isolated instances of alienated word-meaning. Apart from moderate acalculia and limb-kinetic apraxia, there were no other focal signs. This patient mentioned spontaneously that his speech difficulty disappeared during his dreams. In this regard, on further questioning, he clearly and emphatically indicated that his dreams were entirely unchanged, that they still contained visual, auditory, and motor elements and that he was able to speak normally and to hear and understand speech in his dreams. He also reported that his hemiplegia disappeared in his dreams.

Case 13 (Patient No. 235).   This patient was a 49-year-old dextral, polyglot male. He was a highly educated professional. Eight years after insertion of a cardiac valve prosthesis, he suffered a series of massive embolic infarctions in the distributions of the left middle and posterior cerebral arteries. This resulted in an extensive cortical lesion, causing global aphasia, topographical amnesia, hemianopia, hemiplegia, and catastrophic reaction. Neurobehavioral assessment (several months later) was truncated. However, the following interchange suggested that the patient continued to dream, and that audioverbal dream-imagery was preserved. This interchange conveys something of the difficulties that are involved in an investigation of the dream-life of aphasic patients.

[*Do you sleep at night?*]
So-so [tearful].
[*Do you sleep well?*]
Yes and no [shrugs shoulders, resigned expression, but appears not to be understanding].
[*Do you still dream at night?*]
. . . [pause] Yes! Thank you! [very emphatic, indicates thumbs-up].
[*You are still dreaming at night?*]
Yes, yes [still thumbs-up but now less definite and looking unsure].
[*Have you stopped dreaming at night?*]
No, no [thumbs up, shakes head].
[*Do you still hear things in your dreams?*]
Yes, yes, fine, fine [thumbs up but looks unsure, expectant].
[*But can you hear words in your dreams?*]
Yes . . . fine, fine [hesitant, confused expression].
[*But speech {examiner indicates his mouth} can you hear words?*]
Yes, yes, fine, fine [smiling, emphatic thumbs-up].
[*Can you speak in your dreams?*]
Yes, yes, thank you, thank you! [very animated, pointing at examiner, looking pleased as if at last well-understood].
[*But you can't speak when you are awake?*]
. . . [no response, looks confused].
[*Can you speak {examiner indicates mouth} when you are awake? {indicating wide-open eyes}*]
. . . [pause] No, no [shakes head, becoming agitated].
[*Are you sure you can speak in your dreams?*]
Yes, yes, fine, fine! [annoyed].

[*And you can hear speech in your dreams?*]
Yes, yes [irritated tone and expression].
[*But not when you are awake*]
. . . [no response, dismissive gesture, as if to give up on the examiner].
[*I see, I understand*]
. . . [patient became tearful].

Case 14 (Patient No. 248). This patient was a 47-year-old dextral female; she was a homemaker with 12 years' formal education. An aneurysm in the left middle cerebral artery ruptured. A large hematoma was surgically evacuated and the aneurysm was clipped. A CT scan (7 months postictus) demonstrated extensive low density in the fronto-temporal cortex of the left hemisphere, extending subcortically as far as the anterior limb of the internal capsule. At the time of neuropsychological assessment (also 7 months postictus) the patient presented with severe nonfluent aphasia and right hemiplegia (affecting her face, arm, and leg). Speech production was very agrammatical and effortful, with abundant literal (perseverative) paraphasias. Repetition was similarly nonfluent and paraphasic. Phonemic hearing and audioverbal grammatical comprehension appeared entirely normal. Other signs included dense apraxic agraphia, literal alexia, dyscalculia, moderate limb-kinetic apraxia, motor non-fluency with perseveration, mild disinhibition, and adynamia with executive memory deficit (visual memory only was assessed). This patient indicated clearly (with the help of her daughter, an experienced interlocutor of her communications) that she was able to speak quite normally in her dreams but that her dreams as a whole had become more fragmentary.

CONCLUSIONS

The clinical observations reported in this chapter require further systematic investigation. Ideally, sleep-laboratory studies of patients with MRI-localized lesions should be undertaken. Nevertheless, the currently available data appear to support the following two conclusions. First, the data support Grünstein's (1924) hypothesis to the effect that disorders of dreaming are association cortex disorders; disorders of dreaming apparently do not occur with lesions in idiotypic (primary unimodal) cortex. However, second, the data disconfirm Grünstein's further prediction to the effect that modality-specific deficits in dream imagery—analogous to nonvisual dreaming of the Charcot type—accompany lesions in homotypical (unimodal association) cortex outside the visual sphere. Modality-specific deficits of dream-imagery are apparently confined to the visual sphere. A systematic study of this question would need to consider the possibility that the visual bias in the existing material merely reflects the predominantly visual quality of normal dream-imagery.

However, the available data with regard to the audioverbal modality, at least, do not support this interpretation. For example, Grünstein (1924) predicted specifically that patients with lesions in dominant-hemisphere auditory association cortex would not be able to generate audioverbal imagery in their dreams. The 3 cases reported earlier—together with those reported by Cathala et al. (1983) and Schanfald et al. (1985)—directly contradict this prediction. To date, the only observation of aphasic imagery in dreams was reported by Harrison (1981). In his case the onset of aphasia was heralded by transient alexia in a dream. Therefore in this case, too, the disorder was represented in the visual modality.

NOTES

[1] It might be significant in this regard that I did not specifically ask my patients with cerebellar lesions about falling and flying imagery in their dreams. Fremel and Schilder (1920) described vivid falling and flying dreams in patients with cerebellar lesions, without clarifying whether or not such dreams (which are common in the normal population) were unusual for the patients in question. Eisinger and Schilder (1929) described similar phenomena in cases with peripheral labyrinthine disease.

[2] Vivid visual dreaming has also been reported in cases of blindness due to perichiasmic lesions (Gloning & Sternbach, 1953; Sacks, 1995). There is even evidence to suggest that visual dream-imagery is unusually vivid (perhaps disinhibited) in both cortically and cerebrally blind patients (see chapters 7 and 21).

15

Initial Theoretical Remarks

The data reported in the previous chapter cast further light on the nature of the basic deficit that underlies the syndrome of nonvisual dreaming (cf. chapter 13). Thus far, the most robust finding of the present study was the observation that cessation or restriction of visual dream-imagery is invariably associated with a precisely analogous deficit in waking imagery. This striking association was noted in all but 1 of the 15 cases reported in the previous literature and in both of the cases in our own series. In all of these cases the deficit was confined to the visual modality. In some of them the deficit was even more specific and affected only circumscribed aspects of visual imagery.

A DOUBLE DISSOCIATION BETWEEN IMAGERY AND PERCEPTION

In selected cases, the parallel deficits in waking and dream imagery were associated with analogous deficits in visual *perception*. Thus, Tzavaras's (1967) case with absence of facial dream-imagery suffered prosopagnosia, Sacks and

Wasserman's (1987) case with loss of color imagery in dreams suffered central achromatopsia, and 50% of the cases with complete cessation of visual dream-imagery suffered visual (object) agnosia. Nevertheless, in common with most authors in the classical literature reviewed previously, we have thus far attributed the association between nonvisual dreaming and visual irreminiscence to an underlying deficit in visual memory (rather than visual perception). This attribution is supported by the apparent association between the syndrome of nonvisual dreaming and visuospatial short-term memory disorder. Moreover it is supported, first, by the numerous reports of cases cited previously in which nonvisual dreaming and irreminiscence occurred in the absence of perceptual impairments (of any type), and second, the numerous reports of cases in which perceptual impairments (of various types, both sensory and gnostic) occurred in conjunction with normal dream and waking imagery. These reports establish a double dissociation between visual imagery and visual perception.

As previously noted (chapter 3), this double dissociation poses problems for those cognitive theorists who, following Munk's (1878) classical model of central visual processing, claimed that perception and imagery involve bottom-up and top-down activation of the same visual representations (Farah, 1989a, 1989b; Finke, 1980; Hebb, 1968; Kosslyn, 1980, 1994; Shepard, 1978). Farah (1984) solved one of these problems by fractionating the dream-imagery process into two components; she proposed that dream and imagery deficits that occur in conjunction with agnosia should be interpreted as image representation disorders, and that dream and imagery deficits that occur in the absence of agnosia should be interpreted as image generation disorders (which spare the stored visual representations themselves). However, this solution did not account for the other half of the double dissociation; that is, it failed to account for the fact that agnosia can occur in the absence of dream or imagery deficits. The obvious solution to this remaining problem is to abandon the classical interpretation of associative agnosia as a disorder affecting stored visual representations (Dejerine, 1914; Lissauer, 1890; Nielsen, 1946; von Monakow, 1914) and to argue instead—as Farah did later—that "all of the agnosias seem to be attributable to faulty *perception* [italics added]" (Farah, 1990, p. 120). The latter argument dispenses with the need to postulate a distinct image generation module to account for loss of dreaming and imagery with preserved object recognition (for the preserved functions are now considered to be perceptual in nature). It is also consistent with the foregoing conclusion to the effect that the syndrome of nonvisual dreaming with irreminiscence is attributable to a disorder of visual memory (for a disorder of visual memory can occur independently of visual agnosia, which is a perceptual disorder).

THE LOCALIZATION OF THE "VISUAL BUFFER" IN V1 AND V2

However, a weighty problem still remains. The prevailing cognitive theory of imagery states not only that percepts and images activate the same stored representations; it also asserts that a *"visual buffer* [italics added] is shared by imagery and perception" (Kosslyn, 1994, p. 75). This buffer is conceptualized as the "medium in which [dream] images occur" (Farah, 1984, p. 249). The following authoritative statement summarizes this aspect of the theory:

> How are images formed? In some cases, one may have just seen an object, and can retain the image briefly. But in most cases the image is *generated* on the basis of information in memory . . . a visual memory representation is primed so much that it in turn primes the lower areas, forming the image. . . . Visual memories can [thus] be activated to form mental images, using the efferent connections from areas "higher" in the processing stream to topographically organized areas. The areas that appear to play a role in storing visual information in the inferior temporal lobe in monkeys[1] are not topographically organized (or have a very rough topographic organization at best; see Van Essen et al., 1990). Thus, imagery may be necessary to "unpack" the stored visual information, laying out the geometric relations inherent in shape. This is accomplished, I have suggested, by projecting information backward in the system—using the efferent connections—to evoke a pattern of activity in the visual buffer. (Kosslyn, 1994, p. 75)

Kosslyn's anatomical localization of the visual buffer is imprecise ("somewhere between areas V1 and V4"; Kosslyn, 1984, p. 86), but his remarks concerning its functional properties and topographical organization strongly implicate areas V1 and V2. Zeki (1993) firmly localizes a functional entity with identical properties in areas V1 and V2:

> The visual normality of dreams and hallucinations, their sense of reality, is so intense and compelling that all of us have experienced situations which we subsequently find difficult to ascribe to dreams or to reality. It is therefore difficult not to conceive of them as internally generated images which are fed back into the cortex as if they were coming from the outside. If this were so, one would naturally expect that the primary visual cortex might be involved, if only because in normal vision (to which dreams bear such a strong resemblance) the first cortical stage which the incoming visual signals enter is area V1. . . . There is another reason for this interest in V1 and the adjoining area V2. These are the two areas with the highest precision of mapping, in the sense that they contain highly detailed maps of the retina and hence of the field of view. In dreams and hallucinations, just as in normal vision, objects maintain their topographic position. One might expect therefore that, wherever the images in dreams and hallucinations are generated, they must be fed back into an area with high topographic precision. (p. 326)

These assertions are clearly at variance with the available data, which suggest that V1 is unnecessary for the generation and maintenance of normal dream-imagery (the same applies to V2, which is a thin strip of cortex directly adjacent to V1). This has important implications for contemporary theories of consciousness based upon notions of *backward projection* or *re-entry* (Crick, 1994; Edelman, 1989), for it seems to imply that the conscious representation of spatial relationships can be established without reference to topographically isomorphic cortex (Zeki, 1993, p. 343). Moreover, if V1 is unnecessary for normal dream-imagery, then the notion of a visual buffer that is shared by imagery and perception must be substantially revised. At the least, the visual buffer must be located deeper within the visual system, in the homotypical (unimodal association) cortex of the medial occipito-temporal region. This region is conventionally included among the modality-specific memory systems of the brain. If the visual buffer is localized within these systems, the fundamental distinction between perception and memory—a distinction on which the entire classical theory of higher vision was based—is undermined.

Can perception and memory be located in the same place? Kosslyn (1994) localized his preprocessing, motion relations encoding, and pattern activation modules in the medial occipito-temporal region. The first and third of these modules perform modality-specific mnemic functions. However, he also attributed perceptual functions to these modules, insofar as he acknowledged that modality-specific representations "are stored along with the processes that compute them in the first place" (p. 214).

Perhaps these problems do no more than demonstrate the weakness of a narrow localizationist approach to neuropsychology. It is certainly possible, for example, that the previously mentioned functional modules are localized within densely interdigitated and overlapping tissues. It is also possible that the visual buffer itself is a complex functional system that incorporates some tissues that are essential for externally derived perception but unnecessary for internally generated imagery, and vice versa. This is consistent with modern conceptualizations of V1 and V2. They are thought to act as segregators that parcel out signals in the different visual submodalities to the different specialized areas of V3, V3A, V4, V5, and V6 (Zeki, 1993). The loss of this channeling function would deprive the specialized areas of vital external signals, but it need not have any appreciable effect on internally generated images. The specialized areas, by contrast, which subserve complex forms of visual representation such as color, motion, depth, form, and face perception, are almost certainly implicated in hallucinatory dreaming. As we saw in previous chapters, functions such as these can be selectively disrupted in the syndrome of nonvisual dreaming.

THE BACKWARD PROJECTION OF DREAM IMAGES

Whatever the anatomical correlates of the visual buffer may be, the fact remains that if V1 is unnecessary for normal dreaming, then hallucinatory dreams are not in fact "internally generated images which are fed back into the cortex as if they were coming from the outside" (Zeki, 1993, p. 326). The available data are more consistent with a theory that conceptualizes dream images as attenuated object representations (Brown, 1989). According to this approach, dreams are something less than perceptions. Zeki (1993, p. 326) is probably wrong to emphasize the "sense of reality" and "visual normality" of dreams. Although it is true that topographic relationships are (for the most part) preserved in dreams, there is much about dream-imagery that is unreal and abnormal. Dream-imagery, in short, is underspecified and underconstrained by external reality. If V1 is the vehicle of these constraining influences, then it is inessential to the dream process.[2]

This difference between dreams and normal perception evokes an intriguing remark by Fechner (1889), which greatly impressed Sigmund Freud: "the scene of action of dreams is different from that of waking ideational life" (Freud, 1900/1953, p. 536). Fechner's remark prompted Freud to propose, like contemporary cognitive scientists are still proposing almost 100 years later,[3] that hallucinatory dreams differ from waking cognition in that they are generated by a process in which mnemic information is projected backward onto the perceptual systems:

> The only way in which we can describe what happens in hallucinatory dreams is by saying that the excitation moves in a *backward* direction. Instead of being transmitted towards the *motor* end of the apparatus it moves towards the *sensory* end and finally reaches the perceptual system. If we describe as "progressive" the direction taken by psychical processes arising from the unconscious during waking life, then we may speak of dreams as having a "regressive" character. This regression, then, is undoubtedly one of the psychological characteristics of the process of dreaming. . . . *In regression the fabric of the dream-thoughts is resolved into its raw material.* (Freud, 1900/1953, pp. 542–543)

This prescient statement reminds us that our analysis of the syndrome of nonvisual dreaming has, thus far, only dealt with the tip of a neuropsychological iceberg. Whatever the contribution (or lack of contribution) may be of various components of the cortical visual system to the perception of visual dream-imagery, the processes underlying dreaming itself ("dream-thoughts" in Freud's terminology) are generated elsewhere. The dreams of patients with medial occipito-temporal lesions are normal dreams in every respect, apart from their nonvisual character. Therefore, if we are justified in attributing backward directionality to the process that generates dreams, we have to place the perceptual experience of visual dream-images at the terminal end of a complex process. Accordingly we must look toward deeper components of the mental apparatus for an understanding of the mechanisms that generate dreams as opposed to visual dream-imagery. Thus far our only clue in this regard has been the surprising fact that unimodal (somatosensory–motor and auditory) cortex does not appear to be involved in the generation of dream-imagery outside of the visual modality.

The following four chapters, which consider the syndrome of global cessation of dreaming, reveal a good deal more about the process of dreaming itself.

NOTES

[1] Equivalent to medial occipito-temporal cortex in man (Zeki, 1993; Kosslyn, 1994).

[2] However, the dreaming mind apparently does retain subliminal (implicit) contact with reality through all sensory channels. There is much anecdotal and experimental evidence for the assertion that "sensory stimuli that reach us during sleep may very well become the sources of dreams" (Freud, 1900/1953, p. 23).

[3] See Nikolinakos (1992) for a comprehensive discussion of the Freudian antecedents of Kosslyn's theory of mental imagery.

16

Anatomical Correlates of Global Cessation of Dreaming

Cases with global cessation of dreaming were identified by question 2 of the interview schedule. Definite answers were given by 321 patients (11 were excluded due to equivocal responses). Of these, a full 112 patients reported that they had stopped dreaming completely since the onset of their illness. (In addition, 1 of the 29 control subjects reported global cessation of dreaming. This patient is discussed separately later.) This is an incidence of 34.9%, which is much higher than the 1.1% incidence recorded for nonvisual dreaming. Evidently Murri et al. (1984)—who did not distinguish between global cessation of dreaming and nonvisual dreaming—were both right and wrong when they remarked that the Charcot–Wilbrand syndrome may be "not as rare as it is presently considered to be" (p. 185). Certainly Wilbrand's variant of the syndrome is far from being rare.

The large number of patients presenting with this disorder makes it possible for us to begin the present chapter with a few simple statistical observations. Anatomical data for the 321 cases just mentioned are summarized in Table 16.1. Multivariate analysis of this data revealed, first, that parietal lobe involvement discriminated highly significantly between dreamers and non-

TABLE 16.1
Anatomical Correlates of Global Cessation of Dreaming

Lesion Characteristics	Dreams Absent	Dreams Present
Quality		
Diffuse	48	78
Focal	64	131
Laterality		
Bilateral	12	30
Unilateral		
Left	27	39
Right	25	49
Localization[a]		
Brainstem	10 (0)	43 (14)
Limbic Lobe	18 (0)	40 (1)
Occipital Lobe	12 (0)	21 (2)
Parietal Lobe	47 (6)	47 (4)
Temporal Lobe	25 (0)	33 (4)
Frontal Lobe	9 (4)	81 (18)

[a]These lesion sites are not exclusive. Pure cases are given in parentheses.
See Table 9.3 for definitions of anatomical categories.

dreamers, $F = 13.68$, $p = .0003$. Second, when the variance contributed by the parietal lobe was partialled out, the frontal lobes discriminated significantly between dreamers and nondreamers, $F = 5.19$, $p < .05$. No other lesion site discriminated between the two groups (at $p = .1$).

A glance at Table 16.1 shows that not all of the nondreaming patients had parietal or frontal involvement. Only 47 of them had definite parietal lesions and only 9 patients had definite frontal lesions. The lesion data for these two anatomical groups are summarized in Table 16.2 and Table 16.3, respectively. But what of the remaining 56 nondreaming patients? In fact, only a handful of them had focal lesions outside of the parietal lobe. Questions of localization obviously cannot be decided for the 48 patients with diffuse and nonlocalizable lesions (see Table 16.1). (These patients are discussed later.) This leaves only 8 nondreaming patients with nonparietal focal lesions. The pathological-anatomical data for these patients is summarized in Table 16.4 and Fig. 16.1. A close study of this table and figure reveals that all of the patients had lesions in close proximity to the parietal lobe, and in 7 of them the lesions were space-occupying. The possibility of parietal lobe involvement, therefore, cannot be excluded with any certainty in these nonparietal cases. It seems more reasonable to describe them as periparietal cases.

The nondreaming patients with focal lesions in our series therefore clearly fell into two anatomical groups, one involving the parietal and the other involving the frontal lobe. This is consistent with the hypothesis that we ad-

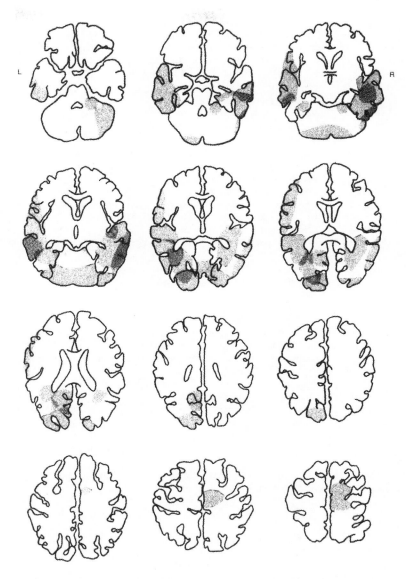

FIG. 16.1.   Combined facsimile of CT scans in eight cases with global cessation of dreaming caused by posterior space-occupying lesions, illustrating the proximity of the lesions to the parietal lobe (mass effects are not represented).

TABLE 16.2
Cases of Global Cessation of Dreaming With Parietal Lobe Lesions

Patient No.	Age/sex	Lesion
8	10-yr M.	R. med. par-temp. meningioma
17	36-yr M.	R. par-temp. stab-wound with intracerebral hemorrhage
23	28-yr F.	L. par-temp-limbic infarct following subarachnoid hemorrhage (L. mid. cereb. art. aneurysm)
27	29-yr F.	L. par-front. depressed fracture with abscess formation (assault)
43	22-yr F.	L. par. infarct (L. int. carotid art. traumatic occlusion)
44	44-yr F.	R. par-fro. meningioma (with R. mid. cereb. art. infarction)
48	42-yr M.	L. par-temp. arachnoid cyst
49	29-yr M.	R. lat. par-temp-fro. chronic subdural hemorrhage (MVA)
57	29-yr M.	R. lat. par-fro. chronic subdural hemorrhage (assault)
71	42-yr M.	L. deep par-temp. cyst (cysticercosis)
86	46-yr F.	L. par-fro. infarct following subarachnoid hemorrhage (L. mid. cereb. art. aneurysm)
87	60-yr M.	L. par-fro-limbic depressed fracture with abscess formation (assault)
99	34-yr M.	L. lat. par-fro-temp. acute subdural hemorrhage with L. fro. intracerebral extension
119	14-yr F.	R. deep par-temp-limbic astrocytoma
130	56-yr F.	R. par-fro. meningioma (with cortical infiltration)
134	54-yr F.	R. lat. par-temp. meningioma
143	27-yr M.	R. lat. par infarct (R. mid. cereb. art. thrombosis)
157	40-yr F.	L. lat. par-occip. infarct following subarachnoid & intracerebral hemorrhage (L. mid. cereb. art. aneurysm)
162	73-yr M.	R. deep par-occip. intracerebral hemorrhage (hypertension)
168	35-yr M.	L. par-temp-limbic astrocytoma
173	34-yr M.	Par-temp-limbic intracerebral hemorrhage (AVM fed by R. mid. cereb. art)
186	65-yr F.	L. lat. par-temp. meningioma
187	17-yr F.[a]	R. med. par. meningioma
191	33-yr F.	Bilat. par-fro. & L. temp. multiple intracerebral hemorrhages (lupus erythematosus)
224	39-yr F.	R. lat. par-fro-occip. infarct (R. mid. cereb. art. thrombosis)
234	77-yr M.	R. deep par-occip-temp-limbic glioma
238	63-yr F.	R. med. par-fro-limbic meningioma
241	18-yr M.	Bilat. lat. par-fro-occip. dermoid cyst with R. fro. chronic subdural hemorrhage
244	77-yr M.	L. deep par-occip. metastatic carcinoma
268	67-yr M.	R. lat. par-fro. subdural empyema
273	27-yr M.	L. par-fro. open head injury (MVA)
284	23-yr M.	R. par. open head injury (stab-wound)
285	18-yr M.	L. lat. par-fro. open head injury (gunshot wound)
286	31-yr F.	L. par. open head injury (stab-wound)
302	32-yr F.	L. lat. par-fro. infarct (L. mid. cereb. art. thrombosis)
303	25-yr M.	L. lat. par-fro. acute subdural hemorrhage (MVA)
305	58-yr M.	R. lat. par-temp-fro. infarct (L. mid. cereb. art. thrombosis)
306	33-yr F.	L. lat. par-temp. infarct (L. mid. cereb. art. thrombosis)
312	59-yr M.	R. lat. par-temp-fro. infarct (R. mid. cereb. art. thrombosis)

(Continued)

TABLE 16.2
(Continued)

Patient No.	Age/sex	Lesion
321	35-yr M.	R. lat par-temp-fro. infarct (mid. cereb. art) following subarachnoid hemorrhage (ant. comm. art. aneurysm)
327	44-yr F.	R. deep par. intracerebral hemorrhage
336	77-yr M.	L. lat. par-fro metastatic carcinoma
338	54-yr M.	L. deep par. astrocytoma
341	18-yr M.	L. lat. par-fro. acute subdural hemorrhage (MVA)
345	43-yr M.	R. lat. par-fro. acute subdural hemorrhage (MVA)
349	63-yr F.	L. med. par-fro. meningioma
353	50-yr M.	R. lat. par-fro. subdural–extradural hemorrhage (assault)

[a]Ambidextrous patient.

vanced in this regard in chapter 5 (Hypothesis 7): Global cessation or reduction of dreaming indicates either (a) a left posterior cortical lesion or (b) a deep bilateral frontal lesion. I now consider the two components of this hypothesis separately, in relation to the two anatomical groups.

POSTERIOR CORTICAL LESIONS

One of the central controversies in the literature regarding the pathological anatomy of global cessation of dreaming was the question as to whether this disorder occurred more frequently with right- or with left-hemisphere lesions (see chapter 4). Perusal of Table 16.2 and Table 16.4 immediately demonstrates that our provisional conclusion in this regard (Hypothesis 7), which favored the left-dominant theory, cannot be supported. Forty-five of the 47 nondreaming patients with definite parietal involvement had unilateral lesions, and the laterality of these lesions was evenly distributed between the two hemispheres, $\chi^2 = 1.40, p > .4$. This demonstrates that global cessation of dreaming arises with equal frequency with left and right posterior cortical lesions.[1] This contradicts the views of Bogen (1969), Galin (1974), and Stone (1977) to the effect that "the right hemisphere is the dreamer" (Bakan, 1976, p. 66), as well as the opposing views of Farah (1984) and Greenberg and Farah (1986) to the effect that "a region of the dominant posterior hemisphere is critical for dreaming" (Greenberg & Farah, 1986, p. 319). Instead, the results of the present study support the views of Doricchi and Violani (1992), who argued that simple right-dominant versus left-dominant theories of dreaming are "too generic and potentially misleading" (p. 121; similar views were expressed by Antrobus, 1987; Foulkes, 1978, 1985; and Kerr & Foulkes, 1981. Recent findings on image generation in general also suggest that "both hemi-

TABLE 16.3
Cases of Global Cessation of Dreaming With Frontal Lobe Lesions

Patient No.	Age/Sex	Lesion
9	13-yr F.	Bilat. deep fro-thalam. glioma (glioblastoma multiforme)
129	14-yr M.	Bilat. deep frontal abscess
150	58-yr F.	Suprasellar pituitary tumor with med. fro-limbic-ventricular extension (prolactinoma-macroadenoma)
181	35-yr M.	L. deep fro. abscess and intracerebral hemorrhage; R. med. fro. intracerebral hemorrhage & subdural empyema
214	18-yr M.	L. basal fro. intracerebral hemorrhage; R. carotid-cavernous fistula
261	62-yr M.	Bilat. med. frontal meningioma
280	63-yr F.	Bilat. calloso-fro-limbic glioma (glioblastoma multiforme)
281	44-yr F.	Bilat. med. fro-limbic subarachnoid & intracerebral hemorrhage (ant. comm. art. aneurysm)
291	21-yr F.	L. med. fro-limbic-diencephalic abscess (stab wound)

TABLE 16.4
Cases of Global Cessation of Dreaming With Periparietal Lesions

Patient No.	Age/Sex	Lesion
122	37-yr M.[a]	Bilat. occip. subdural & cerebellar extradural hemorrhages (assault)
174	29-yr M.	Vertex & L. temp. stab wounds with medial L hemispheric subarachnoid and temp. intracerebral hemorrhages (pericallosal traumatic aneurysm)
189	49-yr F.[b]	Bilat. med. occip-temp multiple lacunar infarctions (region of post. cereb. art.)
217	42-yr F.	Pontine–cerebellar (acoustic neuroma); postsurgery R. occip-temp. intracerebral hemorrhage
263	43-yr F.	L. med. occip-temp-limbic meningioma
288	67-yr F.	L. fro-temp. subdural & intracerebral hemorrhages (assault)
289	35-yr M.	R. temp. & cerebellar intracerebral hemorrhages & shrapnel/bone (bomb blast)
299	54-yr M.	L. occip-temp-limbic glioma (astrocytoma)

[a]Sinistral patient; described in extenso in chapter 12 (Case 4).
[b]Described in extenso in chapter 12 (Case 5).

spheres can generate images," Kosslyn, 1994, p. 319.) The question as to whether or not the results of the present study support the further arguments of some of these authors, to the effect that the right hemisphere provides the "perceptual 'hard grain' . . . which is probably indispensable for the sensorial vividness of the dream experience" (Doricchi & Violani, 1992, p. 121), whereas the left hemisphere provides the "cognitive decoding of the dream during its actual nocturnal development" (p. 122), is considered in chapters 19, 24, and 25.

The other prediction of Hypothesis 7 concerning posterior cortical lesions was upheld by the present study. Our data support the conclusions of Cathala et al. (1984), Murri et al. (1984), Murri et al. (1985), and Doricchi and Violani (1992), to the effect that global cessation of dreaming is more commonly associated with posterior than anterior cortical lesions (see Table 4.3). In fact our data go further and suggest that global cessation of dreaming is commonly associated not only with posterior cortical lesions in general, but specifically with lesions in the parietal lobe.

An additional question now arises: Does global cessation of dreaming occur with lesions anywhere in the parietal (or periparietal) region, or is it possible for us to identify a more precise localization of this symptom? Cases of thrombotic (nonhemorrhagic) infarction are particularly suitable for such purposes (Damasio & Damasio, 1989; Damasio & Geschwind, 1985; Frederiks, 1985; Kertesz, 1983). Our series included 6 nondreaming patients with lesions of this type. It is seen from Fig. 16.2 that all of these patients sustained damage to the lateral surface of the inferior parietal lobule, and specifically to the supramarginal gyrus (Brodmann's area 40). This suggests that global cessation of dreaming is associated not only with parietal lobe lesions in general but specifically with lesions in the region of the parieto–occipito–temporal junction. However, this conclusion is based on a small number of cases and it must therefore be treated with caution.

The cases listed in Table 16.4 suggest that the same syndrome might sometimes arise with occipito-temporal lesions that spare the inferior parietal lobule. This is supported by autopsy data in some of the previously published cases (Ettlinger et al., 1957; Gloning & Sternbach [case L. Josef], 1953; Wilbrand, 1892). However, it is reasonable to conclude, at least on the basis of the data now available, that cessation of dreaming is associated with parietal lobe lesions in the vast majority of cases.

Negative Cases

If the syndrome of global cessation of dreaming is so closely tied to parietal lobe damage, then why did so many parietal patients in our series continue to dream (see Table 16.1)? These negative cases could be accounted for in one of two ways. They could differ from the symptomatic cases either in terms of the type of pathology or in terms of the chronicity of illness. The first of these possibilities was not supported by the available data. The dreaming and nondreaming patients with parietal lesions in our series could not be discriminated by pathology type, $p = .1$. However, there was a difference between the two groups in regard to the chronicity of their illness. The mean number of weeks elapsed since the last neurological insult was somewhat lower for the nondreaming patients than the dreaming patients, $t = 1.70$, $p < .1$, nondreaming $\bar{x} = 30.8$ wks; dreaming $\bar{x} = 97.2$ wks. This suggests that some of the

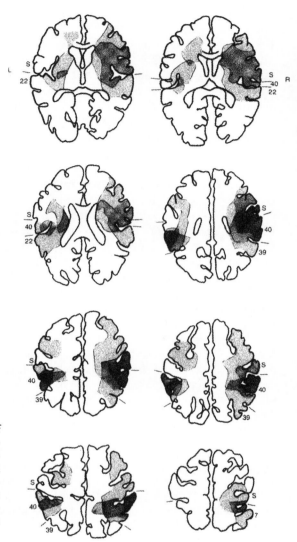

FIG. 16.2.   Combined facsimile of CT scans in 6 cases with global cessation of dreaming caused by thrombotic infarctions of the parietal lobe, illustrating the strong involvement of the lateral surfaces of the inferior lobule, and of the supramarginal gyrus (Brodmann's area 40) in particular.

dreaming subjects with parietal lesions may in fact have been nondreamers at an earlier stage of their illnesses. This introduces the issue of recovery from cessation of dreaming—an issue which warrants direct investigation.

In order to explore the natural history of global cessation of dreaming following parietal lobe damage, I followed up 13 of the symptomatic cases for varying lengths of time (Patients No. 27, 48, 119, 130, 157, 173, 241, 273, 286,

303, 305, 306, & 312). Ten of these patients (77%) started dreaming again within 1 year of the last neurological insult, $\bar{x}$ = 16.3 wks, s = 20.0 wks. The 3 patients who did not report recovery of dreaming (Patients No. 241, 305, & 306) were not followed up for a full year. However, it is certain that at least some patients with parietal lobe lesions did suffer persistent cessation of dreams; Patients No. 44, 49, and 321 reported chronic absence of dreams when interviewed at 98, 553, and 108 weeks postinsult, respectively. All three of these cases had massive right hemisphere lesions (see Table 16.2). Three of the periparietal cases (Table 16.4) were also followed up, but none for more than 1 year. These cases (Patients No. 263, 288, & 289) all reported persistent absence of dreams within the limited follow-up period. These findings suggest that most (but not all) posterior–cortical cases with cessation of dreaming recover within 1 year. The fact that those who did not recover all had right hemispheric lesions is consistent with unpublished data cited by Doricchi and Violani (1992). Out of 22 patients originally classified as non-dreamers in experimental studies by Murri and colleagues (Murri et al., 1984; Murri et al., 1985), only 5 showed absence of dream recall 2 to 4 years later. All of these patients had right posterior lesions. The right-dominant theory of dreaming might, therefore, have limited credibility after all.

FRONTAL LESIONS

Anatomical data for this group was presented in Table 16.3. Eight of the 9 cases had deep bilateral frontal lesions. The one exception (Patient No. 291) had a deep unilateral frontal space-occupying lesion, where the possibility of bilateral mass-effect could not be excluded. These data support the second part of our hypothesis: Global cessation of dreaming is indeed associated with deep bilateral frontal lesions.

This part of Hypothesis 7 was based primarily upon psychosurgical evidence to the effect that prefrontal leukotomy commonly results in global cessation of dreaming (see Table 5.1). Closer analysis of the lesions in our cases demonstrates that precisely the same region was involved in them as was targeted by the various modifications of Freeman and Watts's prefrontal leukotomy procedure ("a circumscribed lesion just anterior to the frontal horn of the ventricle, in the lower medial quadrant of the frontal lobe;" Walsh, 1994, p. 177). As can be seen from Fig. 16.3, the white matter just anterior to the frontal horns of the lateral ventricles was compromised in all of our cases. This suggests that bilateral periventricular white matter involvement is critical for global cessation of dreaming in frontal cases. Although our series yielded only a small number of nondreaming patients with lesions in this area, the same localization has been demonstrated in such a large number of cases in the psychosurgical literature that I consider it to be conclusively established (see Table 5.1).

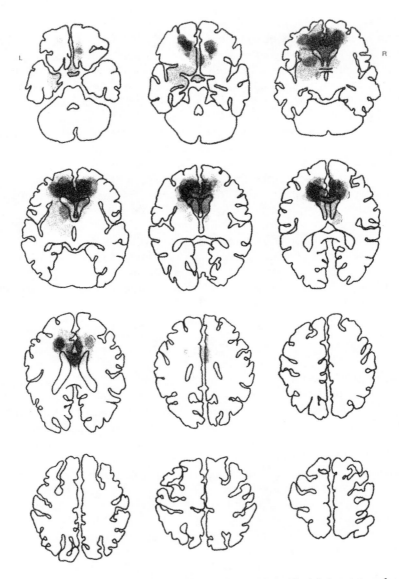

FIG. 16.3. Combined facsimile of CT scans in nine cases with global cessation of dreaming caused by deep frontal lesions, illustrating the strong involvement of the white matter surrounding the frontal horns of the lateral ventricles.

My own cases (together with Gloning and Sternbach's, 1953, Case, Sch. Gertrude) do no more than remove any lingering doubt that the symptom occurs only in patients with severe psychopathology requiring prefrontal leukotomy.

Negative Cases

Our series also included 15 patients with bifrontal lesions who reported preservation of dreaming (negative cases). Table 16.5 and Fig. 16.4 illustrate that in the majority of these cases a different aspect of the frontal lobes was involved, namely the cortical convexity. This strongly supports the interpretation given in chapter 5 to explain the contradiction in the literature between those authors who described the relative preservation of dreaming with frontal lesions as their "most robust and consistent conclusion" (Doricchi & Violani, 1992, p. 118) and those who described "poverty or entire lack of dreams" as a common result of prefrontal leukotomy (Frank, 1946, p. 508). Our supposition was that the authors who reported a low incidence of loss of dreaming among frontal cases studied only patients with unilateral and/or convexity lesions (Cathala et al., 1983; Humphrey & Zangwill, 1951; Murri et al., 1984; Murri et al., 1985), whereas those who reported a high incidence of loss of dreaming among frontal cases studied only patients with bilateral, white matter lesions (Frank, 1946, 1950; Jus et al., 1973; Partridge, 1950; Piehler, 1950; Schindler, 1953).

TABLE 16.5
Cases of Preserved Dreaming With Bifrontal Lesions

Patient No.	Age/sex	Lesion
2	12-yr M.	Bilat. deep frontal abscess
100	44-yr F.	Bilat. fro. gliosis (assault, cranial fracture, meningitis)
102	45-yr M.	L. med. fro. meningioma; R. lat. fro. extradural hemorrhage
108	15-yr F.	Bilat. frontal interhemispheric empyema
121	33-yr M.	Bilat. dorsal frontal missile wound
163	22-yr F.[a]	L. fro. herniation; R. fro. extradural hemorrhage; L. post. cereb. art. infarction (MVA)
183	40-yr M.	L. lat. fro. intracerebral hemorrhage (L. mid. cereb. art.), followed by R. deep fro. intracerebral hemorrhage (R. mid. cereb. art.)
213	53-yr F.	Bilat. fro. atrophy (clinical diagn. Pick's disease)
233	70-yr M.	Bilat. polar frontal missile wound
245	26-yr M.	Bilat. basal fro. gliosis (ant. fossa missile injury)
259	22-yr F.	Suprasellar pituitary tumor with fro-diencephalic extension (macroadenoma)
324	18-yr M.	Bilat. med. fro-limbic subarachnoid hemorrhage with intracerebral extension (ant. com. art. aneurysm)

[a]Sinistral patient.

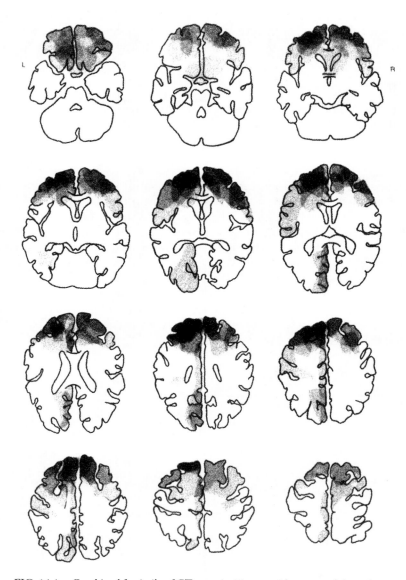

FIG. 16.4. Combined facsimile of CT scans in 14 cases with preserved dreaming with bifrontal lesions, illustrating the relative preponderance of cortical convexity involvement (excludes the scan of Patient No. 264, which could not be meaningfully represented).

However, in two of our own cases of frontal lobe lesions with preserved dreaming (Patients No. 2 & 324) the apparently critical region of periventricular white matter was involved. These two negative cases were not essentially different from the nondreaming cases. No pathological–anatomical explanation for this anomaly was evident from the available data. However, it is noteworthy that both of these cases experienced a gross reduction in the frequency and duration of dreams. In other words, these two cases may have experienced a subclinical form of the disorder of global cessation of dreaming (i.e., global reduction of dreaming). This is consistent with the observations of Frank (1946, 1950) to the effect that prefrontal leukotomy produces not only cessation of dreaming but also poverty or infrequency of dreams.

As regards the question of recovery, only two nondreaming patients in the small frontal group could be followed up over time (Patients No. 150 & 281). Neither of these patients recovered during the brief period over which they were studied (12 & 10 weeks, respectively). We were therefore unable to confirm the observations of Piehler (1950, Cases 1 & 3) and Gloning and Sternbach (1953, Case K. Franz) to the effect that reduced frequency, intensity, and complexity of dreaming follows recovery from global cessation of dreaming in bifrontal cases. However, no firm conclusions can be drawn in this regard from our limited data. (The issues of reduced frequency, complexity, and intensity of dreaming are addressed in chapter 24.)

Considering the foregoing two groups together, the following general conclusion seems justified: Global cessation of dreaming is associated with either (a) an inferior parietal lesion or (b) a deep bifrontal lesion.

DIFFUSE AND NONLOCALIZABLE LESIONS

I now briefly describe the 48 nondreaming patients with diffuse and nonlocalizable lesions. Thirty-three of these cases displayed clinical evidence of both parietal and frontal pathology. Nineteen of them were cases of hydrocephalus. Fourteen of them sustained high-velocity closed head injuries. One was a low-velocity open head injury (assault) with a fracture across the anterior fossa, complicated by meningitis and left frontal abscess formation with air in the frontal horns of both lateral ventricles. One patient had multiple sclerosis.

Parietal lobe involvement was suggested by the clinical presentations of 13 of the remaining cases. Seven of them were cases of ruptured cerebral aneurysm where no circumscribed hemorrhagic or thrombotic focus could be identified on CT or MRI scans. Two of these were aneurysms of the left internal carotid artery, 1 was an aneurysm of the right internal carotid, 2 were aneurysms of the left middle cerebral artery, and 2 were aneurysms of the left posterior communicating artery. In addition, this group included 1 case of left internal carotid artery thrombosis, 1 of left and 1 of right middle cerebral artery thrombosis, and 1 of ruptured AVM draining from the left middle cerebral artery. The lesions in these cases were localized by angiogram; CT and MRI data were not available. This group also included a patient with a low-velocity closed head injury (multiple assault). The CT scan, which was subsequently lost, indicated multiple intracranial hemorrhages and a clinical picture of global cerebral impairment implicating at least both medial surfaces of the hemisphere and the right dorsolateral convexity. Another patient in this group sustained a low-velocity closed head injury (assault) with surgical observation of left-sided acute subdural hematoma extending fronto-parietally and with a clinical presentation of significant left fronto-temporal dysfunction (scan not available).

Clinical evidence of parietal or bifrontal involvement was lacking in the final two cases, but the possibility of such involvement cannot be excluded. One of these patients had a low-velocity closed head injury in the right frontal region (suspected assault), with normal CT scan but clinical evidence of right fronto-temporal and bilateral medial occipito-temporal dysfunction. The other patient sustained a low-velocity open head injury (assault, uncertain history of previous cerebral trauma) with multiple hemorrhagic lesions.

Six cases in the diffuse and nonlocalizable category reported continued absence of dreams more than 1 year after the last neurological insult. In all but 1 of these cases (high velocity closed head injury), there was clinical evidence of significant right hemispheric involvement.

I conclude this chapter by considering the control subject who reported global cessation of dreaming. He was a highly suggestible patient with hysterical features.

CASE 16 (PATIENT NO. 218)

This 35-year-old male was a security guard with 9 years' formal education. His hospital records indicated that he had previously fallen from a moving vehicle and fractured his cervical spine. He spent a few months in a rehabilitation unit and was reported to have made a full functional recovery. Exactly one year later he was admitted through our casualty department with bilateral lower limb paresis. The patient claimed that he had lost consciousness earlier that day for approximately 30 minutes and then awoke in his present, inexplicable, paraplegic condition. There were no wounds suggestive of trauma. On examination, the consultant neurosurgeon noted an unusual and inconsistent pattern of deficits. The myelogram was considered normal.

At neurobehavioral assessment (1 week later) this patient was informed that he would be asked to perform a number of psychological tests, as the neurosurgeons were unable to detect any evidence of a spinal lesion. Therefore the question of a brain lesion, and other possibilities, had to be explored. The patient gave a lucid history of the events leading up to his admission (including a vivid description of the day of the admission itself, up to and including the actual moments of loss and recovery of consciousness). On examination he displayed a multiplicity of pseudoneurological deficits. These ostensible deficits were incompatible with the patient's behavior on the ward since his admission 8 days earlier, and they were not consistent with any established neuropsychological syndrome. For example, the patient was unable to write his own name and could not read the word *cat* ("I can't make it out, is it 'hat' . . . or 'cow' or something?") and he misidentified individual letters of the alphabet, despite the fact that there were no clinical signs of aphasia. Also, he had previously completed and signed numerous hospital admission and consent forms without apparent difficulty. Similarly, formal assessment of memory suggested dense global amnesia (he was disoriented in time; digits forward = 3; Hidden Objects Test = 0/4), but there was no evidence of daily forgetfulness, and the patient gave a clear account of the events leading up to his hospitalization. Further examples abounded. This patient evidently produced deficits on an ad hoc basis according to his perceptions of what the examiner expected. When asked whether or not he was dreaming, he reported that he had not had a single dream since the day of admission.

This case confirms Styron's (1990) report to the effect that subjective cessation of dreaming—unlike nonvisual dreaming—can occur in purely functional conditions. Goodenough et al. (1959) demonstrated that the subjective absence of dreams in neurotic subjects is disconfirmed on REM awakening. However, this does not apply to organic cases reporting global cessation of dreaming (Michel & Sieroff, 1981; Schanfald et al., 1985). These findings suggest an objective method for distinguishing between functional and organic cases.

NOTE

[1]The possibility that right parietal cases of global cessation of dreaming were underrepresented due to anosognosia is considered in chapter 18.

17

Are Dreams Generated by Brainstem Mechanisms?

I stated in the previous chapter that all the patients with focal lesions in the present study who reported global cessation of dreaming sustained either parietal (or periparietal) or bifrontal lesions. The lesions in these cases were not necessarily limited to the parietal or frontal lobes; in most cases they involved other structures as well. Nevertheless, multivariate statistical analysis revealed that the parietal and frontal components of the lesions were responsible for the dream disorder; no other lesion site discriminated significantly between dreamers and nondreamers.

These findings are consistent with my review of the literature, which revealed that almost all previously reported cases with loss of dreaming sustained damage to neocortical structures and connections (see chapter 6). This was a very striking finding, in view of the widespread assumption in the physiological literature to the effect that the subjective experience of dreams is generated (literally *turned on*) by brainstem mechanisms. It followed from this assumption that global cessation of dreaming should result from lesions in the REM-on nuclei of the pontine reticular formation rather than the lobes of the cerebral hemispheres. But the clinical evidence suggested the opposite; in only two of the large number of cases listed in Tables 2.2, 4.2, 4.3, and 5.1 could the cessation of dreaming be attributed to a disruption of the REM cycle or the destruction of brainstem nuclei (viz., Feldman, 1971; Schanfald et al., 1985). This surprising finding led to the realization that, despite the vast literature that has accumulated around the phenomenon of REM sleep, it has in fact never been demonstrated that the abolition of REM is accompanied by a cessation of the subjective experience of dreaming. Conversely, it was repeatedly demonstrated that the cessation of subjective dreaming following parietal or frontal lesions is compatible with a normal REM cycle (Benson & Greenberg, 1969; Brown, 1972; Efron, 1968; Jus et al., 1973; Kerr et al., 1978; Michel & Sieroff, 1981; Schanfald et al., 1985).

These facts prompted me to conclude (in chapter 6) that although there is a strong statistical correlation between the physiological state of REM sleep and the conscious state of dreaming, the neural mechanisms that produce REM are neither necessary nor sufficient for the conscious experience of dreaming. In order to confirm this apparent double dissociation between REM and dreaming, it is necessary not only to demonstrate that REM persists in patients with cessation of dreaming (which was already demonstrated), but also that dreaming persists in patients with cessation of REM (which has not yet been demonstrated). The outstanding critical experiment requires sleep laboratory studies of nondreaming patients with brainstem lesions. Such experiments transcend the stated aims and methods of the present study. Nevertheless, I resolved to make a preliminary contribution to the solution of this important theoretical problem, using clinico-anatomical methods, by testing the following interrelated predictions (Hypothesis 8): Deep brainstem lesions are not commonly associated with global cessation of dreaming, and global cessation of dreaming is not commonly associated with deep brainstem lesions.

CLINICO-ANATOMICAL OBSERVATIONS

The REM-on center is traditionally localized to the medial pontine reticular formation. This localization has been repeatedly confirmed in human cases (Adey, Bors, & Porter, 1968; Chase et al., 1968; Cummings & Greenberg, 1977; Feldman, 1971; Freemon et al., 1974; Guilleminault et al., 1973; Lavie et al., 1984; Markand & Dyken, 1976; Osorio & Daroff, 1980). However, new evidence from single-unit recording and chemical microinjection experiments in animals and from human clinical studies has led some leading authorities to suggest that the "REM sleep generator zone . . . is an anatomically distributed population of neurons (REM-on cells) in the brain stem" (Hobson, Lydic, & Baghdoyan, 1986, p. 374). In order to test Hypothesis 8, it therefore seemed prudent to begin with a broad definition of the REM generator. Our series included 61 cases with lesions affecting any part of the medulla oblongata, pons, cerebellum, midbrain, hypothalamus, or thalamus. The lesion was confined to these structures in 11 cases but included telencephalic structures in the remaining 50 of them (Table 9.3). Fifty-three of these patients with brainstem lesions were able to provide clear information as to whether or not they still dreamed. The vast majority of them (including all those with pure lesions) reported a preservation of the subjective experience of dreaming $(N = 43)$. In 18 of these (dreaming) cases the damage was largely restricted to the nonspecific nuclei of the medulla oblongata, pons, midbrain, hypothalamus and thalamus. Figure 17.1 and Table 17.1 summarize the pathological anatomical data for these cases. These data demonstrate the extent to which damage to structures that are implicated in current theories of REM generation is compatible with normal dreaming.

Ten patients with brainstem involvement (broadly defined) reported global cessation of dreaming. These were not pure brainstem cases. The pathological–anatomical data for these patients are summarized in Tables 16.2, 16.3, and 16.4 (Patients No. 9, 150, 173, 181, 191, 217, 280, 281, 289, & 291). The parietal lobes and/or deep bifrontal region were also involved in all cases. It is therefore reasonable to attribute the cessation of dreaming in these cases to the telencephalic component of the lesions. This was confirmed by multivariate statistical analysis, where the brainstem component of the lesion did not dis-

TABLE 17.1
Cases of Preserved Dreaming With Deep Brainstem Lesions

Patient No.	Age/Sex	Lesion
26	25-yr F.	Ventral cervical spinal–medullary meningioma (with hydroceph.)
30	60-yr M.	Rostral midbrain intracerebral hemorrhage (with hydroceph.)
37	24-yr F.	Anterior thalamic–hypothalamic intracerebral hemorrhage
67	M.	Pontine–medullary–cerebellar glioblastoma multiforme
84	18-yr M.	Hypothalamic astrocytoma (with hydroceph.)
91	25-yr F.	Fourth ventricle cyst (cysticercosis — with hydroceph.)
135	32-yr F.	Third ventricle oligodendroglioma (with hydroceph.)
172	27-yr M.	Ventral pontine granuloma
239	61-yr F.	Pituitary adenoma
264	55-yr F.	Pituitary adenoma
269	55-yr F.	Pituitary adenoma
278	21-yr M.	Deep midbrain intracerebral hemorrhage
295	72-yr M.	Lateral medullary thrombosis
316	12-yr M.	Pineal–thalamic dysgerminoma (with hydroceph.)
329		Pituitary adenoma
339	71-yr F.	Pituitary adenoma
356	44-yr F.[a]	Pituitary adenoma
359	25-yr M.	Medullary–pontine–midbrain–cerebellar medulloblastoma

[a]Ambidextrous patient.

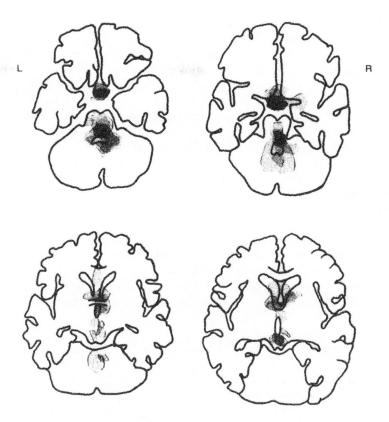

FIG. 17.1.   Combined facsimile of CT scans in 17 cases of preserved dreaming with brainstem lesions, illustrating the extent to which significant brainstem pathology can coexist with normal dreaming (excludes the scan of Patient No. 326, which could not be meaningfully represented).

criminate between dreamers and nondreamers, $F = 0.65, p > .4$; controlling for variance contributed by parietal and frontal lobes, $F = .03, p > .8$.

A Preliminary Experiment

The series also included 10 nondreaming cases with space-occupying brainstem lesions in association with obstructive hydrocephalus (Patients No. 16, 33, 75, 77, 103, 105, 132, 160, 176, & 354). These cases were classified as diffuse in chapter 16. Hydrocephalus, by its very nature, leads to significant neocortical dysfunction, and to deep bifrontal dysfunction in particular. Compression of the white matter surrounding the frontal horns of the lateral ventricles is a prominent feature of hydrocephalic pathophysiology (Adams &

Victor, 1985). Because it was already established (in chapter 16) that this region of the frontal lobes is critical for the preservation of dreaming, it is likely that the cessation of dreaming in my cases of patients with hydrocephalus was attributable to telencephalic mechanisms. However, the possibility cannot be excluded that it was caused by the brainstem mechanisms, especially because brainstem lesions that produce hydrocephalus are frequently located in structures that are thought to be critical for REM-sleep generation (e.g., in the region of the fourth ventricle).

Because hydrocephalus is a treatable condition, this possibility could be tested directly. If compression of telencephalic white matter surrounding the lateral ventricles caused the cessation of dreaming in these cases, then surgical amelioration of the hydrocephalus (by ventriculo-peritoneal [VP] shunting) should result in a recovery of dreaming. If, on the other hand, the underlying brainstem lesions caused the cessation of dreaming in these cases, then the dream disorder should persist despite successful treatment of the hydrocephalus. These alternatives were tested in 5 patients. Table 17.2 illustrates that all 5 cases recovered normal dreaming within 4 weeks of VP shunting. This strongly suggests that the cessation of dreaming in these cases was caused by the telencephalic component of their lesions rather than the brainstem component.

CONCLUSIONS

Considering all of these findings together, it seems reasonable to uphold Hypothesis 8 and to conclude that dreams are generated by telencephalic mechanisms. This is a finding of great theoretical importance, which casts consider-

TABLE 17.2
Global Cessation of Dreaming in Cases With Hydrocephalus
Before and After Ventriculo-Peritoneal Shunting

Patient No.	Age/Sex	Lesion	Dreams	
			Preshunt	Postshunt
16	14-yr M.	Pontine–medullary–cerebellar pilocystic astrocytoma	Absent	Present within 2 wks
63	19-yr M.	L. int. carotid art. aneurysm (subarachnoid hemorrhage)	Absent	Present within 4 wks
105	9-yr M.	Posterior third ventricle tumor (unclassified)	Absent	Present within 1 wk
148	31-yr F.	Idiopathic hydrocephalus	Absent	Present within 1 wk
354	27-yr M.	Third ventricle colloid cyst	Absent	Present within 1 wk

able doubt on conventional assumptions regarding the relationship between REM sleep and dreaming. Unless it can be demonstrated (by the requisite sleep laboratory studies already described) that dreams persist in cases with both brainstem lesions and demonstrable cessation of REM, we cannot conclude that dreams are generated exclusively by telencephalic mechanisms (or that they do not also involve brainstem mechanisms).

The statistical observation remains that the two phenomena (dreams and REM) tend to co-occur in the normal subject. However, the fact that global cessation of dreaming is commonly associated with telencephalic lesions (and that REM in demonstrably preserved in these cases) shows that the subjective experience of dreams themselves depends on telencephalic mechanisms. Moreover, the fact that the critical telencephalic lesions occur in specific locations (namely, the inferior parietal lobule and bifrontal white matter), and that damage in other locations (e.g., V1, S1, and M1) has no effect upon dreams, shows that the subjective experience of dreams depends on specific telencephalic mechanisms. This suggests that dreams cannot simply be attributed to brainstem activation of the neocortex as a whole during REM sleep (cf. Hobson, 1988; Hobson & McCarley, 1977). Dream-imagery is clearly not generated by a nonspecific process. The following question therefore arises: What specific functions are performed by the parietal and frontal lobes which are so crucial to the normal dream process? An analysis of the neuropsychological syndromes in which the loss of dreaming is embedded in cases with parietal and frontal lesions should cast some light on this question.

18

Clinical Correlates of Global Cessation of Dreaming

On the basis of the previous literature, a number of hypotheses were advanced in chapter 4 regarding the neurobehavioral correlates of global cessation of dreaming. It was predicted, first, that global cessation or reduction of dreaming has no special relationship with any element of the classical Charcot–Wilbrand syndrome (Hypothesis 4). Second, it was proposed that global cessation or reduction of dreaming is a primary phenomenon, independent of any disturbance of memory (Hypothesis 5). Third, it was stated that global cessation or reduction of dreaming is commonly (but not invariably) associated with aphasia (Hypothesis 6). Fourth, it was suggested that the incidence of cessation of dreaming in right hemisphere lesions might have been underestimated in the literature due to the tendency of patients with right hemisphere lesions to deny their symptoms; in other words, it was suggested that there may be an inverse relationship between cessation of dreaming and anosognosia. (This was not a formal hypothesis.) Finally, as regards the function of dreams (and specifically, the sleep-protection theory of dreams) it was predicted in chapter 6 that global cessation of dreaming is typically associated with disrupted sleep (Hypothesis 9).

The findings pertinent to these hypotheses are reported under separate headings.

THE CLASSICAL
CHARCOT–WILBRAND SYMPTOMS

None of the classical Charcot–Wilbrand symptoms discriminated significantly between dreamers and nondreamers, $p < .1$. Only 3 of the 112 nondreaming patients reported irreminiscence (i.e., 2.7% of the series), only 3 reported prosopagnosia (2.7%), only 8 reported topographical amnesia (7.1%), only 1 reported topographical agnosia (.9%), and only 2 patients reported visual (object) agnosia (1.8%). Some of these patients were described in extenso in chapter 13 (Cases 7–11). These incidences are considerably lower than those reported in the previous literature (cf. Table 4.1). The discrepancy is probably explained by the fact that ours was an unselected series, whereas most of the cases in the literature were reported precisely because they suffered unusual disorders of visual mental imagery or perception. The low incidence of the classical Charcot–Wilbrand symptoms (and especially of irreminiscence) among our global as opposed to visual nondreaming patients strongly supports Hypothesis 4 and underlines our previous conclusion to the effect that global cessation of dreaming and nonvisual dreaming are distinct disorders. This is also consistent with the distinct lesion sites that we have found to be associated with the two variants of the classical syndrome.

However, although global cessation of dreaming is clearly not commonly accompanied by the classical Charcot–Wilbrand symptoms, the converse does not apply. The low incidence of these (rare) symptoms among cases with the (relatively common) symptom of global cessation of dreaming masks the fact that most patients with any of the classical Charcot–Wilbrand symptoms suffer either nonvisual dreaming or global cessation of dreaming (see Table 13.1). In other words, although global cessation of dreaming is not commonly accompanied by the classical Charcot–Wilbrand symptoms, the classical Charcot–Wilbrand symptoms are commonly accompanied by global cessation of dreaming. The fact that a small but significant subgroup of cases with global cessation of dreaming do suffer the classical Charcot–Wilbrand symptoms reinforces our earlier conclusion to the effect that there is a degree of overlap between the two variants of the classical syndrome. These facts probably go some way towards explaining the conflation of the two variants of the syndrome in the previous literature.

MEMORY DISORDER

Long-term memory disorder (both anterograde and retrograde) did not discriminate significantly between dreamers and nondreamers, $F = 2.35, p > .1$.

The incidence of this disorder among nondreaming patients was 25%, which is comparable to the 21% incidence we inferred from the existing clinical literature (Table 4.1). Most of the truly amnestic patients in my series stated that they were unsure of whether or not they were dreaming. These findings suggest that subjective cessation of dreaming cannot be dismissed as an artifact of recent memory disorder as some authors have suggested (see chapter 4).

This conclusion is consistent with the REM-awakening findings reported by Michel and Sieroff (1981) and Schanfald et al. (1985), and with the most recent neuropsychological findings reported by Murri et al. (1985). However, it is contradicted by the reports of Cathala et al. (1983), who reported strongly positive correlations between various graded tests of visual and verbal memory on the one hand and frequency and informative richness of dream-recall on the other, and of Arena et al. (1984), who found that absence of dreaming was related to poor long-term verbal recall. These discrepancies are probably explicable in terms of the methodological differences (and consequent definitional differences) between the latter studies and the present one, as discussed in chapters 4 and 9. (It is important to note that Arena et al. also found that absence of dream recall was related to aphasia, which could well explain his finding that absence of dream recall correlated with poor verbal long-term memory but not visual long-term memory performances.)

Audioverbal short-term (immediate) memory disorder also did not discriminate between the dreaming and nondreaming patients in our series, $F = .02, p > .8$. However, dreamers and nondreamers were significantly different in relation to visuospatial short-term memory performance, as measured by the immediate recall trial of the Complex Figure Test. This difference emerged both in terms of raw scores, $t = 2.48, p < .02$; dreamers $\bar{x} = 14/36$, nondreamers $\bar{x} = 11.1/36$, and in terms of percentage recall scores,[1] $t = 2.06, p < .05$; dreamers $\bar{x} = 49.2\%$, nondreamers $\bar{x} = 41.8\%$. When the parietal and bifrontal lesion groups were considered separately, it emerged that this difference applied only to the parietal group, parietal nondreamers $\bar{x} = 10/36$ (41.37%); parietal dreamers $\bar{x} = 13.5/36$ (49.3%); bifrontal nondreamers $\bar{x} = 11.6/36$ (38.7%); bifrontal dreamers $\bar{x} = 11.1/36$ (39.4%). Notwithstanding the lack of overlap in terms of lesion site, this finding suggests that in cases of parietal lobe lesion, the two variants of the syndrome do overlap with regard to visuospatial short-term memory. In this limited respect, Hypothesis 5 was not supported. This is consistent with our conclusion regarding the limited overlap between the two variants of the classical syndrome in regard to irreminiscence, prosopagnosia, topographical amnesia and agnosia, and visual (object) agnosia. The theoretical implications of this overlap are discussed in chapter 19.

A second difference that emerged only when the parietal and bifrontal lesion groups were considered separately was that the bifrontal nondreamers (unlike parietal nondreamers) were significantly less likely to suffer long-term memory disorders than their dreaming counterparts, $\chi^2 = 4.97, p < .05$. This suggests that the axial fronto-limbic structures crucial to normal long-term memory functioning were typically spared in cessation of dreaming of bifrontal origin. This interpretation is consistent with the anatomical data reported in chapter 16 (see Fig. 16.2). However, it is inconsistent with the report of Jus et al. (1973), who found no difference in the mnestic abilities of dreaming and nondreaming prefrontal leukotomy patients.

APHASIA

The incidence of aphasia among the nondreaming patients in our series was 25%, which is much lower than the 52% incidence that we inferred from the literature (Table 4.1). The discrepancy is probably attributable to the fact that many previous authors specifically investigated aphasic populations (e.g., Epstein & Simmons, 1983). Forty-one percent of the confirmed aphasic patients in our series reported cessation of dreaming. Nondreamers were not significantly different to dreamers in relation to the incidence of aphasia, $F = .30, p > .8$. The same applied to agraphia, $F = .64, p > .4$, and to alexia, $F = .21, p > .6$. Subdivision of the aphasic cases into parietal and frontal lesions and fluent and nonfluent disorder subgroups also did not produce significant differences between dreamers and nondreamers, $p > .1$. Hypothesis 6 must therefore be rejected; language disorder is no more common among nondreamers than dreamers.

The high incidence of preserved dreaming among our aphasic patients confirms the findings of Cathala et al. (1983), Murri et al. (1984), and Schanfald et al. (1985) and demonstrates that loss of the ability to generate language does not necessarily imply loss of the ability to generate dreams (cf. Anan'ev, 1960; Broughton, 1982; Doricchi & Violani, 1992; Epstein & Simmons, 1983; Foulkes, 1978; Jakobson, 1973; Moss, 1972; Zinkin, 1959). However, the possibility that cessation of dreaming is linked to more subtle semantic disorders that are "functionally linked to language" (Doricchi & Violani, 1992, p. 122) cannot be excluded. In this respect, special investigations of the semantic capacities of dreamers versus nondreamers are required. However, if our conclusion in chapter 16 to the effect that cessation of dreaming is commonly associated with parieto–occipito–temporal junction lesions is correct, then the likelihood that cessation of dreaming is associated with semantic impairments (at least in those cases with *left* parieto–occipito–temporal lesions) must be considered to be high.

ANOSOGNOSIA

This symptom did not discriminate between dreamers and nondreamers, $F = .003, p > .9$. Moreover, it was no more common among unilateral right hemispheric patients who reported cessation of dreaming than those who reported preservation of dreaming, $\chi^2 = 2.52, p > .1$. It is therefore unlikely that the incidence of cessation of dreaming among right-hemisphere patients was underestimated in the present study due to the tendency of these patients to deny their symptoms.

OTHER SYMPTOMS AND SIGNS

Before proceeding to the theoretical question (concerning the function of dreams) raised by Hypothesis 9, I must consider what other symptoms and signs—not predicted by any hypothesis derived from the previous literature—might have discriminated significantly between the dreaming and nondreaming patients in our series. In fact there were 5 disorders of this type. They were *right–left disorientation, F = 2.77, p < .1, finger agnosia, F = 2.77, p < .1, perseveration, F = 21.15, p < .001, disinhibition, F = 5.28, p < .05*, and *adynamia, F = 3.02, p < .1*. These disorders have acknowledged localizing correlates that tally closely with the two critical lesion sites identified in chapter 16.

The Gerstmann Syndrome

Right–left disorientation and finger agnosia form part of the classical syndrome of Gerstmann (1924, 1927, 1930, 1940), which is unequivocally associated with lesions involving the angular and supramarginal gyri of the left parietal lobe (Mazzoni, Pardoni, Giorgetti, & Arena, 1990; Morris, Lüders, Lesser, Dinner, & Hahn, 1984; Roeltgen, Sevush, & Heilman, 1983; Varney, 1984). The individual symptoms making up this syndrome can occur (in isolation) with lesions elsewhere in the brain; therefore they only acquire precise localizing significance when they occur together (Strub & Geschwind, 1983). Until recently (Benton, 1992) the low intercorrelation between finger agnosia, right–left disorientation, agraphia, and acalculia among patients with lesions elsewhere in the brain prompted some neuropsychologists to dismiss Gerstmann's classical syndrome altogether (Benton, 1961, 1977). However, this was based on a misunderstanding of the syndrome concept:

> The essence of a medical syndrome is that a collection of signs or symptoms, when all present, indicate the presence of a specific disease. The correlation between elements in a syndrome may be low, high or in-between. . . . Indeed, a syndrome is most useful as a diagnostic tool precisely when the elements usually are not found together. When they are found together, this strongly points to some special pathological process. (Strub & Geschwind, 1983, p. 318; cf. Strub & Geschwind, 1974)

Benton (1992) now accepts that the full Gerstmann tetrad indicates a lesion in the left interior parietal lobule.

The correlation among our own cases between cessation of dreaming and finger agnosia in isolation and between cessation of dreaming and right–left disorientation in isolation can therefore only be validly linked with (left) inferior parietal lesions if it can be demonstrated that the full Gerstmann syndrome discriminates between dreamers and nondreamers. In fact, the full syndrome discriminated more significantly between the dreaming and nondreaming patients in my series than the individual elements did, $F = 7.31$, $p <$ .01. (The low correlation between the symptoms with lesions elsewhere in the brain explains the modest discriminative power of the individual elements.) It therefore seems reasonable to conclude that global cessation of dreaming in (left) inferior parietal cases is commonly associated with elements of the Gerstmann syndrome.

The Right Hemisphere Syndrome

The puzzling fact that cessation of dreaming does not appear to correlate significantly with any classical right parietal symptoms and signs (e.g., anosognosia, hemineglect, or constructional apraxia) is probably explained by the fact that right hemisphere functions are more diffusely organized than left-hemisphere functions are (Teuber, 1960). As a result, right parietal and right nonparietal lesions give rise to similar neuropsychological disorders. However, visuospatial short-term memory deficit, which is considered to be a right parietal symptom by some authors (e.g., Butters, Barton, & Brody, 1970; McCarthy & Warrington, 1990), did discriminate significantly between right parietal dreamers and nondreamers.

The Frontal Lobe Syndrome

The remaining symptoms that discriminated significantly between dreamers and nondreamers in our series can clearly be linked to the bifrontal lesion site (viz., perseveration, disinhibition, and adynamia). These symptoms are classically associated with frontal lobe dysfunction. However the frontal lobe syndrome is now conventionally divided into two variants, the mediobasal and dorsolateral frontal syndromes (Luria, 1973, 1980). Disinhibition and adynamia are included in the mediobasal variant and perseveration is included in both variants (Luria, 1965). Considered together with the anatomical data reported in chapter 16 (cf. Figs. 16.2 and 16.3), the fact that cessation of dreaming correlates with these symptoms suggests that the frontal lobe syndrome in nondreaming patients is of the mediobasal variety. This is consistent with the fact that cessation of dreaming was a common consequence of modified prefrontal leukotomy, which specifically targeted the subcortico-cortical fibers passing the anterior tip of the lateral ventricles bilaterally (see chapter 5).

It is of interest to note that the rationale for this procedure was based on the belief

> that leukotomy becomes the treatment of choice in a patient with the symptom complex of what Arnot (1949) termed "a fixed state of tortured self-concern," where this has been unrelieved over a long period by other methods. The concept of "self-concern" as a favourable indication had also been referred to by others (Poppen, 1948; Freeman & Watts, 1950). . . . We agree with Robinson and Freeman (1954) that . . . [the various reasons given for the procedure] are all aspects of concern over the self, the continuity of which can be modified by psychosurgery so that guilt-laden rumination about the past and fearful anticipation of the future are reduced in the direction of living more fully and contentedly in the present. (Walsh, 1994, pp. 179–180)

Whatever it was about the psychosurgical lesions that prevented these patients from lapsing into "guilt-laden rumination about the past and fearful anticipation of the future" also deprived them of the ability to generate dreams (cf. Ostow, 1954a, 1955). These remarks suggest that it is not only disinhibition, adynamia, and perseveration that characterize nondreaming patients with frontal lobe lesions, but probably also something else that is more difficult to pin down clinically and is therefore not reflected in the results of the present study.

The theoretical implications of these findings are discussed in the next chapter.

SLEEP

I conclude this chapter by considering the final hypothesis mentioned at the outset of the chapter. This hypothesis was prompted by the realization (in chapter 6) that the clinical phenomenon of global cessation of dreaming provides unique opportunities to isolate the effects of dream deprivation from those of REM and sleep deprivation and therefore to investigate the function of dreaming directly. Freud's (1900/1953) original assertion that dreams are the guardians of sleep seemed to be an appropriate place to start these investigations. Hypothesis 9 therefore predicted that global cessation of dreaming is associated with disrupted sleep.

This hypothesis could only be tested in a preliminary way in the present study, due to its exclusive reliance upon clinical methods of investigation. Therefore, in question 1 of the dream interview, patients were asked whether or not their sleep had been affected by their illness. Responses were classified under four headings; sleep was considered to be (a) *better*, (b) *disrupted*, or (c) *unaffected* since the onset of illness, or patients were (d) *unsure* of whether or not there had been any change in the quality of sleep. The responses to this question are classified in Table 18.1.

TABLE 18.1
Quality of Sleep in Cases With Global Cessation of Dreaming

Dreams	Sleep	
	Disrupted	*Not Disrupted*[a]
Absent	49	52
Present	59	127

[a]I.e., *better* or *unaffected.*

The nondreaming patients experienced significantly more disturbed sleep than the dreaming patients, $\chi^2 = 7.87, p < .01$. This was a counterintuitive finding; one would expect nondreamers to sleep better than dreamers (because their sleep would be unadulterated by dreams). Nevertheless, pending the outcome of objective (sleep laboratory) studies, which may or may not confirm the subjective reports, the sleep-protection theory of dreams is provisionally supported. Conversely, this result fails to support Partridge's (1950) hypothesis to the effect that cessation of dreaming (following prefrontal leukotomy) can be attributed to increased depth of sleep (see chapter 5).

NOTE

[1]Percentage recall scores were calculated on Snow's (1979) formula, which controls for the effects of visuo-constructive disability.

19

Further Theoretical Remarks

The knowledge gained in the previous three chapters can now be integrated with the theoretical formulations advanced in chapter 15. The mechanism of nonvisual dreaming was relatively self-evident. The dream imagery deficits were regularly accompanied by exactly analogous deficits of waking visual imagery. It was therefore possible to conclude with some confidence that these patients were unable to visualize in their dreams because they were unable to visualize in general. Global nondreamers do not present clinically with a corresponding (global) deficit of waking thought. Nevertheless, an analysis of the syndrome of cessation of dreaming should provide a working definition of the particular aspect of cognition that is lost in nondreaming patients. This definition should in turn make it possible to isolate one of the most essential factors in dream mentation, for the loss of this factor leads to a complete cessation of dreaming as a whole. In fact, there should be two (or three) such factors, corresponding to the two (or three) anatomical regions that we have associated with global cessation of dreaming.

PARIETAL MECHANISMS UNDERLYING
CESSATION OF DREAMING

The inferior parietal region is considered first. Three symptoms associated with lesions in the parietal lobes discriminated statistically between dreamers and nondreamers. These were right–left disorientation, finger agnosia, and visuospatial short-term memory deficit. The first two of these symptoms are elements of the Gerstmann syndrome, which is associated with angular gyrus and supramarginal gyrus lesions in the left parietal lobe. The four combined elements of this syndrome discriminated more significantly between dreamers and nondreamers than did right–left disorientation and finger agnosia alone. Is there a common underlying factor which cessation of dreaming shares with the Gerstmann syndrome?

Left Parietal Mechanisms

Various interpretations of this syndrome have been advanced, including an underlying disturbance of the body scheme (Gerstmann, 1930), of spatial orientation (Stengel, 1944), of spatiotemporal processing (Kinsbourne & Warrington, 1964) and of language mechanisms (Poeck & Orgass, 1966). However, most authorities would agree that patients with inferior parietal lesions of the left (speech-dominant) hemisphere "have difficulty in the analysis not only of concrete [spatial], but also of symbolic relationships" (Luria, 1973, p. 151). This observation is traditionally related to the fact that the cortex of the parieto–occipito–temporal junction does not receive direct afferents from sensory organs, but rather re-represents inputs from the modality-specific sensory and motor analyzers (and from limbic and thalamic association nuclei) and combines them into the heteromodal syntheses that are necessary for abstract (symbolic) processes.

> Within heteromodal areas, the modality specificity of information is lost in favor of intermodal associations. Even the distinction between what is sensory and what is motor is no longer present. For example, many cells in heteromodal areas increase firing not only in response to sensory input but also in phase with motor output. It could be argued that during the process of gaining awareness of the world, sense organs are not passive portals for sensory input. Instead, they could be considered to act as tentacles or feelers for the active scanning and updating of a dynamically shifting inner representational map. At this level, the building blocks of awareness are as much motor as they are sensory phenomena, and this is clearly reflected in the physiology of the heteromodal areas. At least two transformations are likely to occur in heteromodal areas. First, these areas provide a neural template for intermodal associations necessary for many cognitive processes, especially language. . . . Second, they provide the initial interaction between extensively processed sensory information and limbic-paralimbic

input. Thus, another distinction that is lost in heteromodal areas is that between limbic and nonlimbic. (Mesulam, 1985a, p. 25)

This classical theory has been questioned in recent years, on the grounds that heteromodal cells are in a minority in the region of the parieto–occipito–temporal junction in subhominid primates (e.g., Zeki, 1993, pp. 304–305). However, it is questionable whether cortex that is homologous to the human supramarginal and angular gyri (Brodmann's areas 39 and 40) exists in these species (Creuzfeldt, 1995). Brodmann, von Economo, and Vogt are all of the view that areas 39 and 40 are "reduced to rudimentary areas in subhominid primates, and would therefore constitute a new addition in the human brain" (Creuzfeldt, 1995, p. 373). This distinction is important, considering that the heteromodal symbolic processes attributed to these areas by clinical researchers are considered to be "the most complex and specifically human forms of gnostic activity" (Luria, 1973, p. 151). Only von Bonin and Bailey (1947) believed that a delineation of areas 39 and 40 is possible in the monkey (see also Bailey, von Bonin, & McCulloch, 1950). Nevertheless, few would disagree that "whichever path is taken in this homologization, the specific symbolic–linguistic capacities of the human brain depend upon a proper functioning of the lateral parietal lobe (i.e., of areas 39 and 40 of the posterior perisylvian cortex of the speech-dominant hemisphere)" (Creuzfeldt, 1995, p. 373).

If we accept that representations derived from modality-specific cortex are re-represented in the form of quasispatial syntheses within the left inferior parietal region, and if we combine this notion with the theory of backward projection advanced in chapter 15 (on the basis of our analysis of the syndrome of nonvisual dreaming), then the following extension of that theory seems justified. Because dreams are endogenous perceptions that are generated by a process which reverses the normal perceptual sequence, in dreams the heteromodal (inferior parietal) level of cortical processing precedes the unimodal (medial occipito-temporal) level of processing.

The implications of this formulation become clear if one considers the following description of the contribution made by the left inferior parietal region to the normal perceptual process:

> The tertiary zones of the posterior cortical regions is . . . essential, not only for the successful integration of information reaching man through his visual system, but also for the transition from direct, visually represented syntheses to the level of symbolic processes—or operations with word meanings, with complex grammatical and logical structures, with systems of numbers and abstract relationships. It is because of this that the tertiary zones of the posterior cortical region play an essential role in the conversion of concrete perception into abstract thinking, which always proceeds in the form of internal schemes, and for the memorizing of organized experience or, in other words, not only for the reception and coding of information, but also for its storage. (Luria, 1973, p. 74, italics deleted)

According to my extension of the backward projection theory, dreams reverse this process. This implies that dreams involve a transition from the level of abstract (heteromodal) memories and symbolic re-representations to the level of concrete visual representations. In short, in dreams abstract thinking is converted into concrete perceptions.

In addition, this formulation implies that heteromodal (symbolic) representation is more fundamental to the dream process than is unimodal (visual) representation, a postulate that is consistent with the clinical fact that inferior parietal lesions prevent the development of dreams as a whole whereas medial occipito-temporal lesions prevent the development only of visual dream imagery. The primacy of heteromodal cortex in dreaming also makes sense of our observation that modality-specific disorders of dreaming apparently do not occur with lesions in unimodal (primary and secondary) somatosensory, auditory, and motor cortex. Because all modalities are re-represented in inferior parietal cortex, it is at least theoretically possible for any aspect of human experience to be generated in simultaneous consciousness by parieto-occipital mechanisms.[1] However, on this view, it is difficult to explain why modality-specific imagery disorders *do* occur with lesions in unimodal (secondary) visual cortex. It is therefore important to recall the possibility (mentioned in chapter 15) that the visual bias in the existing clinical material might merely reflect the predominantly visual quality of normal dream imagery. Nevertheless, the essential point remains: In dreams one represents oneself in various perceptual situations but one is not actually perceiving anything. Dream perceptions are not perceptions; they are representations of perceptions, derived from past experience.[2]

Right Parietal Mechanisms

Since cessation of dreaming also occurs with right parietal lesions, the same considerations should apply to this region. In fact heteromodal synthetic functions are attributed to the inferior parietal region of both hemispheres in the classical theory cited above, that is, both parietal lobes "play a basic role in the organization of complex simultaneous (spatial) syntheses" (Luria, 1973, p. 147, italics deleted). Also, "Appreciable differences [between the hemispheres] begin to appear only when from studying disturbances in *concrete* space we move on to more complex forms of disturbance of orientation in logical 'quasi-spatial' relationships" (Luria, 1973, p. 151). In other words, whereas global cessation of dreaming in left parietal cases is attributable to disturbances of symbolic quasispatial functions, the same disorder in right parietal cases is attributable to disturbances of concrete spatial functions. The latter functions (which also depend on heteromodal synthesis) are evidently just as fundamental to the process of dreaming as symbolic functions are.

Our observation that global cessation of dreaming is commonly associated with visuospatial short-term memory disorder might therefore best be understood in terms of an underlying disorder of spatial representation. Loss of the ability to represent information spatially or quasispatially could well disrupt both dream generation and visuospatial working memory (cf. the visuospatial scratch-pad of Baddeley, 1986). This implies that a disorder of spatial cognition is the *Grundstörung* underlying the syndrome of cessation of dreaming, analogous to the disorder of visual imagery underlying the syndrome of nonvisual dreaming.[3] On this basis we could say that the visuospatial scratch-pad is to global cessation of dreaming what the visual buffer of Kosslyn (1980) was to nonvisual dreaming. Spatial cognition would then become the "medium" within which dream-thoughts (as opposed to visual dream-images) are represented.

However, this formula implies an equation of spatial cognition with Baddeley's scratch-pad, which is a much narrower concept. Because Kosslyn's associative memory is certainly the cognitive homologue of the heteromodal parietal functions that were discussed above (Kosslyn attributed identical functions to this module and he localized it to the same cortical region; see Kosslyn, 1994)[4] this also implies an equation of spatial cognition with Kosslyn's associative memory, which is a much broader concept. Nevertheless, leaving aside the vagaries of contemporary cognitive models, the essential point is that heteromodal spatial and quasispatial cognition, which is the medium of "the most complex and specifically human forms of gnostic activity" (Luria, 1973, p. 151), is also the medium of dreams.

I conclude this section by pointing out that this formulation can explain our observation (in chapter 16) to the effect that the right hemisphere seems to play a marginally dominant role in dreaming. Assuming that the right parietal region is indeed (at least relatively) dominant for visuospatial short-term memory—which I am equating with concrete spatial representation—then it is possible that the relatively greater severity of the syndrome of cessation of dreaming with right parietal lesions is attributable to a relatively more severe disorder of concrete spatial representation. For although it is conceivable that concrete spatial dreams can occur perceptually in the absence of quasispatial (symbolic) operations, it is difficult to imagine how symbolic dreams could occur perceptually without being grounded in a medium of concrete spatial representation. This conclusion is broadly consistent with Doricchi and Violani's (1992) formulation to the effect that the right hemisphere provides the "perceptual 'hard grain' . . . which is probably indispensable for the sensorial vividness of the dream experience" (p. 121), whereas the left hemisphere provides the "cognitive decoding of the dream [thought] during its actual nocturnal development" (p. 122).[5]

FRONTAL MECHANISMS UNDERLYING
CESSATION OF DREAMING

I turn now to the bifrontal variant of the syndrome of global cessation of dreaming. This takes us still deeper into the components of the mental apparatus which generate dream-thoughts as opposed to dream-imagery. Frank (1946, 1950), who discovered the bifrontal variant of the syndrome of loss of dreaming, attributed it to the emotional asymbolia that follows the prefrontal leukotomy procedure. Gloning and Sternbach (1953) similarly attributed it to a disconnection of affective impulses (supposedly generated in the dorsomedial nuclei of the thalamus) from areas 9, 10, 11, and 12 of the frontal lobes. (Schindler, 1953, and Greenberg et al., 1968, expressed similar views.) On this basis Gloning and Sternbach predicted (a) that complete, bilateral lesions of the dorsomedial thalamus or its frontal projections would produce global cessation of dreaming, due to ablation or disconnection of the primary instigator of dreams, and (b) that incomplete or unilateral thalamo-frontal disconnections would produce reduced frequency and emotional intensity of dreaming, due to an incomplete disruption of the same mechanisms.[6]

Only the first of these predictions concerns us here. Although we cannot support the idea that affective impulses are generated in the dorsomedial thalamus, we certainly do have reason to believe that frontal subcortico–cortical fiber pathways play an important role in emotional life. Panksepp's (1985) authoritative review of the neuroanatomy of affective mechanisms included these fiber pathways in the "curiosity-interest-expectancy command systems of the brain . . . which instigate goal-seeking behaviors and an organism's appetitive interactions with the world" (p. 273). According to Panksepp (1985):

> These expectancy circuits include cell groups situated in the ventral tegmental area of Tsai, at the ventromedial transition zone between mesencephalon and diencephalon where the source cells for mesolimbic and mesocortical dopamine systems are situated. . . . The system ascends through the forebrain bundles of the lateral hypothalamus, through basal forebrain areas (synapsing on many systems along the way, including nucleus basalis, bed nucleus of the stria terminalis and orbito-frontal cortical areas). Descending components of this emotive system probably arise from the latter brain areas, and there is reason to believe they are influenced strongly through cholinergic agents. (p. 273)

The probability that the effects of prefrontal leukotomy are attributable to disruption of this dopaminergic appetitive circuit is suggested by Panksepp's further remark to the effect that "the widely held view that antipsychotic medications [dopamine blockers] yield chemical lobectomies (Breggin, 1980) is arguably supported by the anatomy of the dopamine systems" (Panskepp, p. 273). Panksepp continued:

That the major psychological effect of antipsychotic medication in normals is a loss of interactive interest in the world (Lehmann & Hanrahan, 1954)—an observation that has been so apparent as to dissuade analysis—affirms the fundamental role of these systems in mediating psychological processes characterized by curiosity and exploration. Furthermore, stimulant drugs which promote activity in catecholamine systems increase approach behaviors, investigatory activities, and curiosity to a point where even the most mundane object can sustain attention, albeit in a very stereotyped way (Angrist & Sudilovsky, 1978). It is generally thought that these circuits participate in the overstimulated mood changes of acute schizophrenic breakdowns and amphetamine psychoses. (Panskepp, 1985, p. 273)

The notion that damage to dopaminergic expectancy circuits results in "loss of interactive interest in the world" is consistent with Walsh's remarks to the effect that prefrontal leucotomy prevents patients from lapsing into "guilt-laden rumination about the past and fearful anticipation of the future" (1994, p. 180).

Because these patients are simultaneously prevented from generating dreams, these remarks suggest that "loss of interactive interest in the world" might also be the cause of cessation of dreaming in patients with deep bifrontal lesions. This interpretation—which is broadly consistent with Gloning and Sternbach's (1953) notion that loss of dreaming following deep bifrontal lesions is caused by damage to the instigator of dreams (and with the views of Jus et al., 1973, to the effect that loss of dreaming in frontal cases might be due to a failure of active searching behavior)—is supported from three directions. First, the symptom of adynamia discriminated significantly between dreamers and nondreamers in our series. *Adynamia* is defined as an inability to initiate and sustain volitional motivation (see Appendix). This suggests that the underlying deficit that produces loss of dreaming also causes loss of the ability to initiate and sustain volitional motivation. Second, drugs that excite the curiostity–interest–expectancy pathways described previously (e.g., L-dopa, amphetamines, cocaine) are known to stimulate excessive, unusually frequent, and vivid dreaming (Sacks, 1990, 1991).[7] This suggests that these pathways are implicated in the generation of dreams. The link between hallucinogenic substances and excessive dreaming is consistent with the widely held notion that dreaming is akin to psychosis (which implies that they share common neural mechanisms). Third, drugs that block the dopaminergic appetitive pathways (e.g., haloperidol) are known to inhibit excessive, unusually frequent, and vivid dreaming (Sacks, 1985, 1991). This confirms the suggestion that these pathways are implicated in the generation of dreams. The notion that reduced excitation of dopaminergic circuits inhibits dreaming is also broadly consistent with the observation that severe endogenous depression can provoke cessation of dreaming (Styron, 1990).

These considerations justify the conclusion that dreams are generated by frontal subcortico-cortical systems that "instigate goal-seeking behaviors and an organism's appetitive interactions with the world" (Panksepp, 1985, p. 273). This conclusion casts doubt on the prevalent notion—based on simple generalizations from the mechanism of REM sleep—that "the primary motivating force for dreaming is not psychological but physiological" (Hobson & McCarley, 1977, p. 1346). If psychological forces are equated with higher cortical structures and functions, then both our anatomical and our clinical data are inconsistent with this generalization. It is difficult to reconcile the notion that dreams are random physiological events generated by primitive brainstem mechanisms with our observations to the effect that cessation of dreaming is associated with telencephalic lesions resulting in spatial, symbolic, or motivational disorders. On the contrary, this evidence suggests that dreams are critically mediated by some of the highest mental mechanisms.

The association between cessation of dreaming and the symptoms of perseveration and disinhibition suggests that the basal ganglia and descending components of the cortico–subcortical pathways already discussed are also critically implicated in the generation of dreams. Disinhibition and perseveration are in some respects necessary corollaries of the disturbances of volitional activation that occur with damage to the ascending component of these pathways. Mediobasal frontal cortex does not only elaborate stereotyped appetitive drives activated by brainstem and diencephalic–limbic mechanisms into adaptive and voluntary goal-seeking behaviors; it also exerts powerful descending influences over those same brainstem and diencephalic–limbic mechanisms. These descending influences facilitate adaptive and voluntary activity by giving the "activating impulses [of the deeper structures] their differential character, and making them conform to the dynamic schemes of behavior which are directly formed with the frontal cortex" (Luria, 1973, p. 86). Differential influences of this type have been repeatedly demonstrated by physiological experiments (see Perecman, 1987; Pribram & Luria, 1973). In other words, the mediobasal divisions of the frontal lobes are associated not only with the elaboration of appetitive drives, but specifically with the *differential* elaboration of those drives. On this basis it is generally agreed that

> the orbital sector of the frontal lobe contains a variety of structures that "gate" diencephalic function. They can override a variety of primary hypothalamic mechanisms of response, substituting more elaborate forms of action suitable to complex social behaviors. (Damasio, 1985, p. 369)

Accordingly, disinhibition and perseveration are interpreted as failures of mediobasal–frontal "gating" mechanisms. This renders *adaptive* "interactive interest in the world" impossible (Panksepp, 1985, p. 273). The motivational aspect of this appetitive interest is usually attributed to the medial sector of the frontal lobes, whereas the inhibitory aspect is attributed to the basal sector (e.g., Damasio, 1985; Luria, 1973). However, both aspects depend on the rec-

iprocal subcortico–cortical pathways that surround the frontal horns of the
lateral ventricles.

It seems reasonable to conclude that dreams are generated by frontal subcortico-cortical systems that "instigate goal-seeking behaviors and an organism's appetitive interactions with the world," and that dreams are therefore
impossible to generate without the active participation of some of the highest
regulatory mechanisms of the mind.

A SPECULATIVE SYNTHESIS

In view of my (tentative) support for Freud's sleep-protection theory of the
function of dreams, one could speculate that the disorder of adaptive behavior
associated with the cessation of dreaming in deep bifrontal cases undermines
the function of dreams. In doing so, it is tempting to equate the inhibitory and
regulatory mechanisms just mentioned with the censorship of Freud (1900/
1953), which plays such an important role in the formation of dreams in his
theory. The sleep-protection theory conceptualizes dreams as compromise
formations. The compromise is struck between instinctual (appetitive) strivings on the one hand, which threaten to disturb sleep, and the censorship on
the other hand, which only allows the appetitive strivings to be fulfilled in a
disguised (and hallucinatory) form. The hallucinatory format is achieved by
the mechanism of regression (i.e., backward projection; discussed in chapter
15), and the disguise is achieved through symbolic transformations of the primary impulses. In this way the censorship deflects the appetitive impulses
away from the motor systems and protects the rest of the sleeper. On this theory, dreams certainly would be impossible to produce without the active participation of the highest inhibitory and regulatory mechanisms of the mind.

I would be going too far beyond the available data if I were to firmly link
Freud's censorship with the inhibitory functions of the mediobasal frontal region[8] and the symbolic transformations of appetitive impulses with the rerep-
resentational functions of the inferior parietal lobules.[9] However, in drawing
these tentative links we are at least paving the way for experimental tests of
Freud's classical theory on objective (neuropathological) material.

NOTES

[1]It is of interest in this regard to note that some authorities equate reflexive consciousness itself with symbolic representation. According to Otto Creuzfeldt, for example:

A unified consciousness is closely connected with the capacity for symbolic representation.
. . . Human consciousness emerged after the peripheral apparatus had appeared in evolution and the attached cerebral control apparatus for language with its symbolic compe-
tence. This does not preclude transitional states, a "dawn of consciousness" in some subhominid primates such as apes. We cannot make any statement about a consciousness

which cannot represent its experience in symbols of that experience . . . the basis of conscious experience . . . [is] the representation of symbols." (Creuzfeldt, 1995, pp. 561–562)

In this view, dream consciousness is dependent on a form of symbolic representation that is analogous to but different from language. This underlines the need for systematic investigations of the broader semantic functions of nondreaming patients (cf. chapter 18).

[2]The following remark by Fischer (1954) is cited by Zeki (1993, p. 325): "It is entirely possible that the dream work cannot compose a new visual structure any more than it can a new speech."

[3]In a quantitative study, Cathala et al. (1983) found the preserved dreams of patients with parietal lesions to be less spatially elaborated than those of controls.

[4]Kosslyn (1994) describe *associative memory* as "a subsystem at a relatively late stage of processing that receives input from multiple sensory modalities and stores associations among facts about objects" (p. 216). He added that

the contents of associative memory are more abstract than those of the modality-specific pattern activation subsystems; associative memory not only stores associations among individual perceptual representations, but also organizes "conceptual" information that may not be directly derived from the senses (e.g., mathematical truths, meanings of abstract terms, and so on). (p. 215).

Kosslyn localized this subsystem to the "posterior superior temporal cortex [and] temporal–occipital–parietal junction" (p. 381).

[5]However, I would substitute the function of *spatial cognition* for Doricchi and Violani's *perceptual hard grain*, and I would attribute the latter to the medial occipito-temporal region of both hemispheres. I would also substitute *inferior parietal lobule* for the term *hemisphere* in their formulation.

[6]On this view therefore—as was discussed in chapter 7—reduced frequency and emotional intensity of dreaming was considered to be a subclinical form of global cessation of dreaming. This viewpoint is indirectly supported by our observation (in chapter 16) to the effect that the deep bifrontal cases in our series with preserved dreaming experienced a gross reduction in the frequency and duration of their dreams. (However, see chapter 24 for a full discussion of reduced frequency and emotional intensity of dreaming.)

[7]Alterations in dreaming are often the first sign of response to L-dopa in patients with ordinary Parkinson's disease, as well as in those with post-encephalitic syndromes. Dreaming typically becomes more vivid (many patients remark on their dreaming, suddenly, in brilliant color), more charged emotionally (with a tendency towards erotic dreams and nightmares) and more prone to go on all night. Sometimes their "realness" is so extraordinary that they cannot be forgotten or thrown off after waking. . . . Excessive dreaming of this sort—excessive both in visual and sensory vividness, and in activation of unconscious psychic content; dreaming akin to hallucinosis—is common in fever, and after many drugs (opiates, amphetamines, psychedelics); during (or at the start of) certain migraines and seizures; in other organic excitements; and sometimes at the beginning of psychoses. (Sacks, 1990, pp. 154–155)

[8]Cf. Freud (1900/1953, p. 540):

We found reasons for identifying the critical agency [the "censorship"] with the agency which directs our waking life and determines our voluntary, conscious actions. If, in accordance with our assumptions, we replace these agencies by systems, then our last conclusion must lead us to locate the critical system at the motor end of the apparatus.

[9]Cf. Doricchi and Violani (1992, pp. 120–121):

Looking at the striking consequences of semantic disorders on dream recall [with posterior cortical lesions] one is led to the apparently paradoxical conclusion that the appearance of the visual–semantic incongruencies that so often characterize normal dreaming is strictly conditioned to the perfect and complete functioning of the processes subserving meaning-recognition during waking.

20

Ten Patients
With Varying Degrees of Confusion
Between Dreams and Reality

The responses of my patients to various questions concerning the frequency and vivacity of their dreams (questions 7, 9, 10, & 11) fell into two distinct categories. The first category included patients who experienced a radical change in their relationship to their dreams, which closely resembled the syndrome that was described in our review of the previous literature under the heading of increased frequency and vivacity of dreaming (see Table 7.1). Most of the patients who fell into this category described these changes spontaneously as soon as the subject of dreaming was broached. Others among them were incapable of participating in a structured interview (for reasons that will soon become obvious), but nevertheless they clearly indicated in various ways that their dream-life had undergone a radical change of this kind.

In the second category were patients who reported—in response to questions 7 and 9—that there had been a relative increase in the frequency and/or vivacity of their dreams, but the changes were not impressive. None of these patients reported actual confusion between dreams and reality, and none of them reported the phenomenon of continuous dreaming (see chapter 7). Changes of

176

this order were also reported by controls. They can therefore not reasonably be described as clinical disorders of dreaming. In this chapter, I report only the cases that fell into the first of these two categories. The second category of patients is described at the end of chapter 21.

It is difficult to define the incidence of the putative syndrome of increased frequency and vivacity of dreaming with any precision. It is a complex entity, with different aspects of the syndrome predominating in different patients. Accordingly, I argue later in this chapter that there are grounds for dividing it into a number of interrelated disorders. Nevertheless, 10 patients reported gross changes in their dreaming that at least closely approximated those reported by previous authors. If the sample from which these patients were drawn is taken to be all those cases who were able to give definite answers to any of the four questions mentioned earlier ($N = 189$),[1] then the incidence of this disorder in the present series was 5.3%. The cases in question are described briefly here.

CASE 17: INCREASED REALITY OF DREAMING WITH GLOBAL FANTASY–REALITY CONFUSION (PATIENT NO. 106)

This patient was a 62-year-old dextral male; he was an engineer with 16 years' formal education. He was admitted following a subarachnoid hemorrhage, which resulted in left lower limb paresis and severe mental confusion. A CT investigation (4 days postictus) revealed blood in the anterior interhemispheric fissure. An aneurysm of the anterior communicating artery (with spasm of right anterior and middle cerebral arteries) was demonstrated by angiogram. A follow-up CT scan (performed 1 month later) showed bilateral medial frontal low density in the anterior limbic system (cingulate gyrus and basal forebrain) which extended on the right side to include the right anterior cerebral artery and right middle cerebral artery distributions (see Fig. 20.1).

The neurobehavioral assessment (14 weeks postinsult) documented a severe confabulatory amnestic syndrome (Wechsler Memory Scale: Logical Memory Subtest, Story A = 8/23, Story B = 0/23, with strong proactive interference effect; Associate Learning Subtest = 3,0; 4,1; 5,0; Visual Reproduction Subtest = 0/14). There was substantial retrograde autobiographical-memory loss (extending backwards for approximately 10 years). The patient was disoriented, his insight was reduced, he was disinhibited, and his emotional state fluctuated wildly. It was difficult to assess higher cortical functions in this context but the following deficits were unmistakably present: hemispatial (left) neglect in all modalities, reduplicative paramnesia for persons and places, and severely deficient visuospatial judgment and cognition (e.g., Judgment of Line

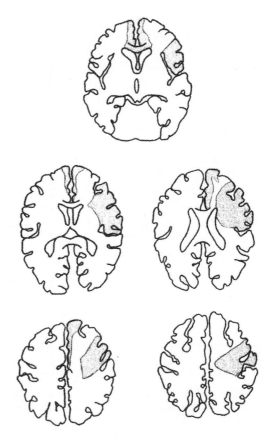

FIG. 20.1. Facsimile of the second CT scan in Case 17 (increased reality of dreaming with global fantasy–reality confusion) illustrating the approximate location and extent of the anterior limbic and frontal lobe infarction.

Orientation Test = 2/30; Face Recognition Test = 28/54; Three-Dimensional Block Construction Test = 0/29). Language-based cognitive functions were essentially preserved.

In lengthy discussions with this patient it emerged that he regularly confused his dreams with reality. For example, on the first day of his admission to our rehabilitation unit he insisted that he was dead and wanted to know whether he (and the other patients) were in Heaven or Hell. He was agitated and he lamented the fact that he had not managed to arrange his financial affairs properly before his death. It was impossible to convince him by logical argument that he was still alive. However, in the process of discussing his predicament the patient reported that a priest had visited him the night before, "at the pearly gates," and had told him that he was dead. Asked whether this had been a dream or an actual occurrence, the patient conceded that it was "probably" a dream. A few days later he told several members of the nursing staff that he had spent the previous night driving his car around the vicinity of the hospital. In a discussion of this recollection later in the day, he conceded that it "must have been a dream" and remarked that "my mind is playing tricks on me again." He then added, "I expect I shall have to give it [driving] up completely."

A few days later he stated that he had slept at home the night before and that his wife had left in the middle of the night to attend a conference (neither of which were true). Later on that same day he said that he had dreamed that his wife had gone to a conference. When asked whether or not he still believed that he had slept at home on the previous night, he said, "You had better ask B—— [his wife], she's more clear about this sort of thing than I am. You can trust her to give you an objective opinion."

He would typically describe his fantastical experiences, even when they were not clearly recognized as dreams, as having occurred the night before. Furthermore, the nursing staff observed that his confusion and disorientation was at its worst in the early morning. Sometimes this patient also mistook waking thoughts and daydreams for real experiences. For example on one occasion he asked angrily, "Where has B—— got to now? She was here just a minute ago!" When asked if he was sure that she had actually been there, he said, "Oh no, not again! My mind is playing tricks on me. I was just *thinking* about her." (His wife had not visited him for a few days).

It was not possible to obtain a clear and direct account from this patient as to whether or not he was dreaming more frequently or vividly than before, and so on, but it seems likely that (embedded in a generally confused mental state) he frequently mistook dream experiences for real events.

CASE 18: INCREASED REALITY AND FREQUENCY OF DREAMING WITH CIRCUMSCRIBED FANTASY– REALITY CONFUSION (PATIENT NO. 136)

This patient was a 32-year-old dextral male. He was a businessman with 12 years' formal education. He was admitted semiconscious (GCS = 10/15), with an open wound at the vertex of the cranium following a motor vehicle accident. The brain was herniated and a sequestrectomy was performed. A postsurgical CT scan demonstrated bilateral paracentral low density extending inferiorly to the level of the corpus callosum (including both cingulate gyri), anteriorly to the premotor cortex, and posteriorly to the superior parietal lobule on the left and occipital pole on the right (involving most of the right parieto-occipital convexity; see Fig. 20.2). The clinical sequelae of this lesion included triplegia (sparing the right upper limb) and a left visual-field scotoma, with visual hallucinations (of insects and small animals) in the left field arising from the scotoma (cf. chapter 13). At neurobehavioral assessment (5 weeks

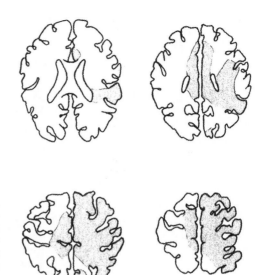

FIG. 20.2. Facsimile of the CT scan in Case 18 (increased reality and frequency of dreaming with circumscribed fantasy/reality confusion) illustrating the approximate location and extent of the limbic and right-hemispheric damage.

posttrauma) the patient was anosodiaphoric. He was inappropriately unconcerned about his sudden and devastating loss of motor function, and he was jocular and garrulous. A mild premotor syndrome (motor perseveration and nonfluency), mild unilateral (left) visual neglect, and severe constructional apraxia were noted. There were no other localizing symptoms or signs.

The patient reported that in the first few days after his accident, his dreams changed radically. He had never paid much attention to his dreams before (indeed he had barely been aware of them), but after the accident they became extremely vivid and realistic. He also dreamed far more frequently than before, and he sometimes had the impression that he was dreaming all night. The dreams seemed to be generally unpleasant and disturbing in content. Also, the patient reported that he sometimes had the experience of a dream continuing across intervening periods of wakefulness. He once dreamed that there was a corpse in his bed, and when he awoke he was surprised to discover that he was alone in bed; he then went back to sleep and continued to dream the same dream, namely, that there was a corpse in his bed. Subsequently his dreams returned to normal. Later the patient had the impression that dreaming might have ceased altogether. He attributed this to Valium and other medications, which made him "sleep dead."

At a follow-up examination (6 months posttrauma), this patient reported that his dreams had once again undergone a radical transformation. He was unsure as to whether he was dreaming or hallucinating at night. He explained this confusion as follows. He would frequently wake up during a dream, but the dream would continue; he would then think that he was having a real ex-

perience rather than a dream, until his wife reoriented him to reality and convinced him that there was nothing there. He could not determine whether
he was actually awake during these experiences, which he described as "terrifyingly real." The dreams varied in content. He frequently dreamed of ghosts.
However, some of these dreams, at least, were similar to his earlier visual-
hallucinatory experiences. For example, he sometimes imagined that he saw
small animals and other creatures crawling about the room when he woke up
at night. The patient's wife corroborated his reports. She also stated that he
was "far more placid" in his outlook on life than he had been premorbidly.

CASE 19: INCREASED REALITY OF DREAMING
WITH GLOBAL FANTASY/REALITY CONFUSION
(PATIENT NO. 147)

This patient was a 30-year-old dextral female. She was a homemaker with 9
years' formal education. Admission followed a subarachnoid hemorrhage. An
aneurysm of the anterior communicating artery was demonstrated on angiogram. After the aneurysm was wrapped, the patient's condition deteriorated
and she developed left lower limb paresis. A MRI scan demonstrated right
mediobasal frontal infarction (in the region of the anterior cerebral artery).
The area of low density extended posteriorly to include the basal forebrain
(see Fig. 20.3). Despite rapid physical recovery, mental confusion persisted. At
the neurobehavioral assessment (which was conducted 8 weeks postictus) the
patient was disoriented for time and place, she was disinhibited (with wildly
fluctuating mood), and she was extremely logorrheic and concrete. A severe
confabulatory amnestic syndrome was documented (Wechsler Memory Scale,
Associate Learning Subtest = 2,0; 4,0; 4,0; Visual Reproduction Subtest = 3/
14). There was massive intertest contamination and inert stereotypy. Anosognosia and reduplicative paramnesia for place and persons were also present.
    This patient was incapable of participating (reliably) in a formal dream in-
terview. However, her behavior on the ward, and a few fortuitous comments
she made, strongly suggested that—embedded in her generally confused
mental state—she regularly mistook dreams for reality. She consistently reported that she did not sleep in the hospital but rather that she went home
every night. She described various fantastical activities and experiences that
were supposed to have taken place there. On one occasion she claimed that
her husband had visited her during the night and thrown a wild party for her,
but later she admitted that the party had been "just a dream." On another occasion the patient said that she had gone home the night before to attend a
New Year's Eve dinner party. Moments later she wondered aloud whether this
had truly happened, and she realized that it might have been a dream. (She was
aware that a temporary discharge from the rehabilitation unit to allow her to

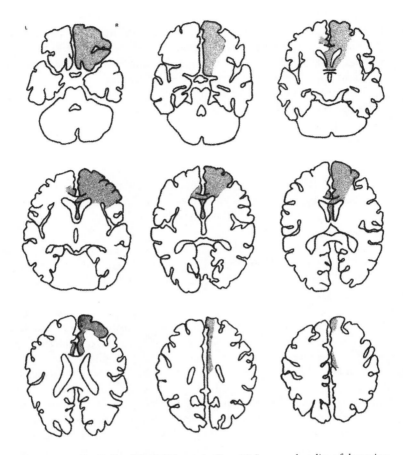

FIG. 20.3.   Facsimile of the MRI scan in Case 19 (increased reality of dreaming with global fantasy–reality confusion) illustrating the approximate location and extent of frontal–limbic infarction.

be with her family over the holiday period was currently under consideration.) This patient herself reported later, in a psychotherapy session with a colleague, that she confused her dreams with reality.

CASE 20: INCREASED REALITY OF DREAMING WITH GLOBAL FANTASY–REALITY CONFUSION (PATIENT NO. 194)

The patient was a 30-year-old highly educated professional male. This was a case of high grade astrocytoma (arising from the right medial thalamus). The clinical progression was initially slow (with headaches, drowsiness, and forgetfulness), and his condition was treated conservatively. Thereafter hydrocephalus developed and a ventriculo-peritoneal (VP) shunt was inserted. (Also at this point the tumor was biopsied.) After a period of remission, the patient's condition relapsed. He then traveled to a foreign country, where the tumor was debulked. On his return home, his condition deteriorated rapidly. The terminal phase of the disease produced left hemiplegia, hemianopia, amnesia, mental confusion, and finally, stupor.

This patient was assessed neuropsychologically at an early stage of his illness. At that stage, in addition to mild hypoarousal, there were only subtle indications of dyschronogenesis and of left hemineglect. The patient then traveled abroad for specialist treatment. He deteriorated rapidly upon his return, and further formal assessments were not undertaken. However, the patient's wife reported that she first recognized that the period of remission had come to an end when the patient began to confuse dreams with reality. For example, he dreamed one night that he and his wife went to "a very beautiful place." He reminisced with her about it afterwards, apparently not realizing that she had not really shared the experience with him. She indicated to him that she had no recollection of the events that he was describing, and the patient then realized with some embarrassment that he had mistaken a dream for a real event. As the illness advanced the patient became more and more reluctant to accept his wife's version of events. Simultaneously, paranoid ideation developed and he began to accuse his wife of lying and attempting to confuse him. Later, accusations regarding waking events occurred as well. The patient clearly mistook fantastical happenings for reality. Ultimately, he slept most of the day and remained in an oneiroid state even when awake. There were, however, moments of lucidity in which the patient himself would describe "a very plastic type of thinking" and "vivid and fantastic dreams." (These were usually highly pleasurable dreams with idealized content.)

CASE 21: INCREASED REALITY AND FREQUENCY OF DREAMING WITHOUT FANTASY/REALITY CONFUSION (PATIENT NO. 239)

This patient was a 61-year-old dextral female; she was a shop assistant with 10 years' formal education. Admission followed a 5-week history of deteriorating vision with headache. The diagnosis was Cushing's disease. A large suprasellar pituitary adenoma extending into the infundibular region up to the level of the splenium (see Fig. 20.4) was excised transnasally. Postsurgically the patient was massively disinhibited with fluctuating affect and amnesia (e.g., Auditory Verbal Learning Test = 5/4/5/8/3/(4)/2; Complex Figure Test = 33/36 copy, 15/36 immediate recall). During the neurobehavioral assessments (at 3 weeks postsurgery, and 7 weeks postsurgery) the patient reported a marked increase

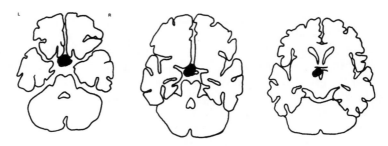

FIG. 20.4.   Facsimile of a CT scan in Case 21 (increased reality and frequency of dreaming without fantasy–reality confusion) illustrating the approximate location and extent of the suprasellar pituitary tumour.

in the frequency and reality of her dreams. She made it clear that this constituted a very dramatic change in her dreams. She stated that she also experienced more frequent nightmares than were normal for her. However, there was no indication in this case of actual fantasy–reality breakdown, nor of dreamlike thinking extending into waking life.

CASE 22: INCREASED REALITY OF DREAMING WITH GLOBAL FANTASY/REALITY CONFUSION; RECOVERY (PATIENT NO. 281)

This patient was a 44-year-old dextral female, a homemaker with 12 years' formal education. She was admitted following a subarachnoid hemorrhage from an anterior communicating artery aneurysm. The aneurysm was identified on angiogram. A left mediobasal frontal intracerebral hemorrhage and interhemispheric blood were seen on CT scan. Following a brief period of hallucinatory mental confusion (visual hallucinations, reduplicative paramnesia for place, and increased reality of dreaming with associated fantasy–reality breakdown) the clinical picture improved. The aneurysm was clipped 3 months later. Transient nonfluent dysphasia and a (persistent) left-superior quadrantanopia were observed postsurgically. A follow-up CT scan revealed low density in the left mediobasal frontal lobes, extending upwards and across into both anterior cingulate gyri and the basal forebrain (see Fig. 20.5). At the neurobehavioral assessment (2 weeks after surgery), mildly defective recall of complex verbal material was observed. This did not constitute a true amnestic syndrome (Wechsler Memory Scale: Associate Learning Subtest = 5,2; 6,2; 6,4; Visual Reproduction Subtest = 12/14). Other features of note included mild unilateral (left) visual neglect and defective visuospatial judgement (e.g., Line Orientation Test = 17/30).

During the neurobehavioral assessment the patient gave a lucid retrospective account of her preoperative confusion. Initially, she had experienced actual visual hallucinations (small lizards, chameleons, snakes, mice, etc.), but these rapidly passed. This was followed by a somewhat longer period of reduplicative paramnesia, which the patient described vividly:

> I had the impression that the hospital was built in my house. I even told the doctor that it was. Now I realize that was impossible nonsense—it was my imagination. But at the time it all seemed perfectly reasonable. Sometimes I thought the clinic was in a different part of my house, and then at night I would go back to the old part. I thought I went through this routine every day. Another time I thought that the hospital had taken over my house. So I asked my daughter: "Go and make sure its still there." So I think she humored me, and she looked and it [the house] was still there. But I just couldn't believe it. "How can it be there and here at the same time?," I thought. It seems I thought that it was there and here at the same time, and that this was the hospital but it was *also* my house. Even when I realized, when I knew that this was a hospital, the hospital and not my house, then at night sometimes I would go to the toilet and I would think "Where have they moved the toilet to?"—because the toilet should be over there, like it is in my house, but now it was somewhere else. So I still got the two places mixed up, even when I knew that my house was still somewhere else. Now it all seems totally crazy, a crazy mix-up. . . . Also, my [recently deceased] husband; I couldn't stop thinking he's alive, even though I knew he was dead. I even said to my daughter, "Watch him," you know, "Make sure he doesn't go after the ladies." But then later I said to my brother-in-law, "Tell me the truth"—then I realized it's all in my imagination.

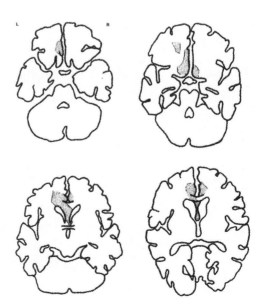

FIG. 20.5. Facsimile of the follow-up CT scan in Case 22 (increased reality and frequency of dreaming with global fantasy–reality confusion) illustrating the approximate location and extent of frontal–limbic infarction.

In addition to such experiences, the patient experienced her thoughts as real events, especially at night.

> I wasn't actually dreaming at night, but sort of thinking in pictures. It's as if my thinking would become real—as I would think about something, so I would see it actually happening before my eyes and then I would also be very confused and I wouldn't know sometimes what had really happened and what I was just thinking.
>
> [*Were you awake when you had these thoughts?*]
>
> It's hard to say. It's as if I didn't sleep at all, because so much was happening to me. But of course it wasn't really happening, I was just dreaming these things; but they weren't like normal dreams either, it was as if these things were really happening to me. . . . [For example] I had a vision of my husband; he came into my room and gave me medicine, and spoke some kind things to me, and the next morning I asked my daughter: "Tell me the truth, is he really dead?" and she said "Yes Mama." So it must have been a dream. . . . [Another example:] One night I was sleeping and it seems I thought a "Visitor" came [by "Visitor" the patient meant "alien;" she was referring to a science-fiction television series]. And then I saw that my brother-in-law was there—he had come to do something electrical, some electrical job—and I yelled at him: "Watch out! Go away!" I remember it very clearly still now today. I can picture exactly what he was wearing. Then the next morning I thought, "Can it really be?" So I asked my daughter, and she said "No Mama," he did no electrical jobs at the hospital. Of course not! How could it really be!

On other occasions such phenomena occurred during the day, when the patient was more certainly awake:

> I was lying in my bed thinking, and then it sort of just happened that my husband was there talking to me. And then I went and bathed the children, and then all of a sudden I opened my eyes and "Where am I?"—and I'm alone!
>
> [*Had you fallen asleep?*]
>
> I don't think so, it's as if my thoughts just turned into reality.

Such experiences were described by the patient as being qualitatively different from the hallucinations that she had experienced at an earlier stage in her illness:

> It wasn't just seeing things. It was as if it was real—as if it was really happening—and many times I couldn't make out what did happen from what didn't. I really believed it! It's not just seeing little things crawling around that can't be real.

CASE 23: INCREASED REALITY AND FREQUENCY OF DREAMING WITH CIRCUMSCRIBED FANTASY-REALITY CONFUSION (PATIENT NO. 354)

This patient was a dextral male. He was a 27-year-old university student. The illness started with a series of drop-attacks, of which there were three over a

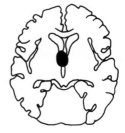

FIG. 20.6.   Facsimile of the CT scan in Case 23 (increased reality and frequency of dreaming with circumscribed fantasy–reality confusion) illustrating the approximate location and extent of the colloid cyst (mass effects are not represented).

period of 9 months. The third attack was accompanied by incontinence and a 1-hour period of disorientation, after which the patient suffered persistent headache and repeated clonic seizures. On admission (11 months postonset) there were mild (left) lower-limb paretic signs and there was papilloedema. Hydrocephalus was demonstrated on CT scan, with a ring-enhancing mass in the anterior aspect of the third ventricle. This was identified as a colloid cyst (see Fig. 20.6). After insertion of a VP shunt, there was good symptomatic improvement. At the neurobehavioral assessment (which was conducted 1 week after the insertion of the shunt) the patient described recent-onset forgetfulness, absent mindedness, loss of libido, lack of motivation, and irritability. He was fully oriented, there was little objective evidence of memory impairment on formal testing, and no other neurocognitive deficits could be detected.

This patient reported that more or less simultaneously with the onset of his drop-attacks, his dreams underwent a radical transformation. He had never been a "big dreamer" before, but he gradually became aware that he was (almost nightly) having very vivid and realistic dreams. Then all dreaming suddenly stopped. Two nights after insertion of the VP shunt, vivid, realistic dreams returned. He gave the following example. He dreamed that he had found a signet ring that his mother had previously given him but which he had (in reality) lost. The dream was extremely vivid and "real." When he awoke the next morning he did not realize at first that he had not actually found this ring, and a mood of mild euphoria persisted. He then noticed that the ring was not on his finger, and recognized (to his disappointment and amazement) that the entire episode had been a dream.

CASE 24: INCREASED REALITY OF DREAMING WITHOUT FANTASY–REALITY CONFUSION (PATIENT NO. 356)

This patient was a 44-year-old ambidextral (shifted sinistral) female. She was a homemaker with 10 years' formal education. She was admitted with a 4-month history of deteriorating vision in the left eye, excessive thirst, and fluctuating temperature. On MRI scan, a craniopharyngioma was seen, extending

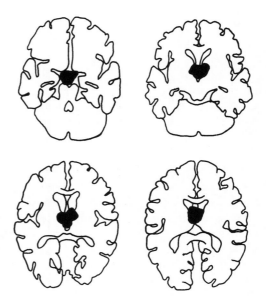

FIG. 20.7. Facsimile of the MRI scan in Case 24 (increased reality of dreaming without fantasy–reality confusion) illustrating the approximate location and extent of the craniopharyngioma (mass effects are not represented).

into the pituitary fossa and upwards into the third ventricle (see Fig. 20.7). At the neurobehavioral assessment (1 week after admission) the patient was disoriented for time and place, and there was moderate achronogenesis and fluctuating affect (without true disinhibition). Her conversation was inconsistent and illogical, and she denied her visual deficit.

This patient spontaneously reported realistic dreams that disturbed her greatly and made it impossible for her to sleep. She described these dreams as extremely vivid, and she stated that they frequently woke her up and prevented her from going back to sleep. She remarked in response to a direct question that she was also having far more nightmares than was usual for her. It appears that the content of these nightmares varied. It was impossible to elicit a fuller description from this patient.

CASE 25: INCREASED FREQUENCY AND REALITY OF DREAMING WITH CIRCUMSCRIBED FANTASY–REALITY CONFUSION; RECOVERY (PATIENT NO. 357)

This patient was a 32-year-old dextral female. She was a secretary with 10 years' formal education. She was attacked by a mob during a political riot. A brick that was thrown through her car window struck her on the forehead. She sustained an open fracture, with brief loss of consciousness followed by a 2-

day period of post-traumatic amnesia. After a sequestrectomy, the CT scan revealed an extensive medial frontal lesion. The area of low density extended posteriorly to include the anterior aspect of both cingulate gyri, but it was more extensive on the right (Fig. 20.8). Air was present in the anterior horns of both lateral ventricles. The patient made an excellent physical recovery but there were residual second and eighth nerve lesions (on the right). Cranioplasty was performed 3 months later. At the neurobehavioral assessment (which was conducted 1 week after the last surgery) fluctuating affect with encapsulated paranoid ideation and decreased libido and drive were noted, but neither true amnesia nor a classical frontal syndrome could be demonstrated.

This patient reported that in the first weeks after her injury she experienced frequent and vivid nightmares, which, although bizarre, were very much more realistic than her normal dreams. She had always been a vivid dreamer but she experienced these dreams as being "utterly different." She felt that her dream recall was greatly enhanced, and she stated that she had considerable difficulty

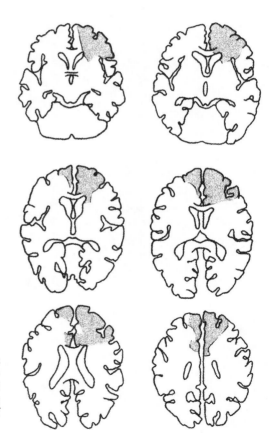

FIG. 20.8.   Facsimile of the CT scan in Case 25 (increased frequency and reality of dreaming with circumscribed fantasy–reality confusion) illustrating the approximate location and extent of frontal–limbic damage.

TABLE 20.1

Cases With Increased Reality and Frequency of Dreaming

Case	Age/Sex	Lesion[a]	Relevant Symptoms and Signs	Dreams
Case 17	62-yr M.	Bilat. med. front., cingulate g., basal forebrain; R. lat. front-tempar. (ant. comm. aneurysmal rupture with ant. & mid. cereb. spasm)	Disorientation, confabulatory amnesia, disinhibition, fluctuating affect, reduplicative paramnesia, neglect, reduced insight	Increased reality in context of global fantasy/reality breakdown
Case 18	32-yr M.	Bilat. cingulate g., postcentral, precentral & premotor g., R. lat. par-occip. (open head injury)	±Disinhibition, euphoria/placidity, visual hallucination, neglect, anosodiaphoria	Increased reality & frequency with circumscribed fantasy/reality breakdown (and with repetitive nightmares)
Case 19	30-yr M.	R. med. front., cingulate g., basal forebrain (ant. comm. aneurysmal rupture with ant. cereb. spasm)	Disorientation, confabulatory amnesia, disinhibition, fluctuating affect, reduplicative paramnesia, anosognosia	Increased reality in context of global fantasy/reality breakdown
Case 20	30-yr M.	R. med. thalamic astrocytoma[b]	Torpor/stupor, disorientation, confabulatory amnesia, paranoia, neglect, reduced insight[c]	Increased reality in context of global fantasy/reality breakdown
Case 21	61-yr F.	Hypothalam. (suprasellar pituitary adenoma)	Disinhibition, fluctuating affect, reduced insight	Increased reality and frequency (with increased frequency of nightmares)
Case 22	44-yr F.	L. med. front., bilat. cingulate g., basal forebrain (ant. comm. aneurysmal rupture with front. intracerebral hemorrhage extension)	±Amnesia, visual hallucination, reduplicative paramnesia, neglect[c]	Increased reality in context of global fantasy/reality breakdown and recovery

(Continued)

TABLE 20.1
(Continued)

Case	Age/Sex	Lesion[a]	Relevant Symptoms and Signs	Dreams
Case 23	27-yr M.	Bilat. med. thalam. (colloid cyst of the third ventricle)	Torpor, ±amnesia, irritability.[c]	Increased reality & frequency with circumscribed fantasy/reality breakdown
Case 24	44-yr F.[d]	Hypothalam., bilat. med. thalam. (craniopharyngioma)	Disorientation, amnesia, fluctuating affect, anosognosia	Increased reality (& frequency of nightmares)
Case 25	32-yr F.	Bilat. med. frontal, cingulate g. (open head injury with ? R. ant. cereb. infarct)	Torpor, fluctuating affect, paranoia	Increased reality and frequency with circumscribed fantasy/reality breakdown (with repetitive nightmares) and recovery

[a]All lesions localized by in vivo imagery.
bSubsequent lesion data not available.
[c]Patient not assessed at time of dream disorder.
[d]Ambidextral (shifted sinistral) patient.

191

convincing herself that the dreams were not real. She would typically dream of snakes, of needles (being stuck into her), and of vampires, and the dreams were always unpleasant. For example, she dreamed one night that there was something wriggling about in her "knickers," so she put her hand down and found (to her extreme horror) a green snake. She then felt something else was there and discovered three smaller snakes. Finally a black snake crawled up into her vagina. She awoke in terror and searched the bed for snakes. She knew that she had been dreaming, but she still could not resist the urge to check. On other occasions she would awake from dreams and feel compelled to check all around the house, and she once asked her boyfriend to search outside for vampires. On one occasion she awoke from a dream and was astonished to find that she was not in hospital, as she felt sure that a drip had just been inserted into her arm and that someone had given her an injection in her buttocks. These experiences stopped within 2 months of the assault, and her dreams returned to normal.

The essential features of the above reports are summarized in Table 20.1.

The following isolated case did not report increased frequency and vivacity of dreaming. However, she reported the phenomenon of continuous dreaming, which is a variant of the foregoing syndrome.

CASE 26: CONTINUITY OF DREAMS ACROSS INTERVENING PERIODS OF WAKEFULNESS (PATIENT NO. 98)

This patient was a 27-year-old dextral female. She was a homemaker with 8 years' formal education. She collapsed suddenly, 10 days postpartum. She was unconscious on admission, with right hemiplegia. A CT scan demonstrated a left antero-basal temporal lobe intracerebral hemorrhage (see Fig. 20.9). The

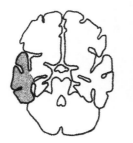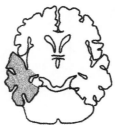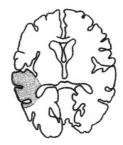

FIG. 20.9.   Facsimile of the follow-up CT scan in Case 26 (continuity of dreams across intervening periods of wakefulness) illustrating the approximate location and extent of right temporal infarction.

angiogram was considered to be normal. A craniotomy (for removal of the hematoma) was performed 10 days after admission. No arterio-venous abnormality could be demonstrated. The final diagnosis was cryptic AVM. At neurobehavioral assessment (5 months postsurgery) the patient presented with a moderate verbal-specific recent and immediate memory deficit, nonfluent aphasia, and dyscalculia. She reported that she was sleeping and dreaming normally, and she specifically denied any increase in the vivacity or frequency of her dreams. However, she noticed that if she awoke from a dream and then went back to sleep again, the same dream would continue from where she had left off. This had become a common occurrence for her, although it had never occurred premorbidly.

NOTE

[1]The reader is reminded that the 112 patients who reported global cessation of dreaming were excluded by definition. (Controls are considered separately.)

21

Clinico-Anatomical Correlates of the Confusion Between Dreams and Reality

CLINICAL ASPECTS:
A DISORDER OF REALITY MONITORING

The dramatic phenomena reported in the previous chapter are highly reminiscent of those discussed in the literature review under the heading of increased frequency and vivacity of dreaming. However, the defining feature of our cases appears to be "difficulty distinguishing dreams from reality and vice versa" (Morris et al., 1992, p. 1834), rather than increased frequency and vivacity of dreaming per se. The essential difficulty that we observed is exemplified by the following episode described in the literature:

> [The patient] reportedly woke from dreams and believed that they were real events. On one occasion, after dreaming that he had been bitten by a poisonous snake, the patient's wife had to seek the help of neighbors to calm the patient. He was convinced that this had actually occurred and was demanding to be taken to hospital. (Morris et al., p. 1834)

The phrase *increased frequency and vivacity of dreaming* might therefore be a misnomer. Many of these patients did not experience increased frequency or vivacity of dreaming as such but rather a difficulty in distinguishing their dreams from real perceptions.

In chapter 7, on the basis of the previous literature, the hypothesis was advanced that increased frequency and vivacity of dreaming typically occurs in conjunction with disturbed reality monitoring, affective disinhibition or cerebral blindness (Hypothesis 15). In my series, disorders of reality monitoring clearly predominated. They were present in all cases but one (Case 21). These disorders were variously characterized by fantasy–reality confusion, confabulatory amnesia, reduplicative paramnesia, formed visual hallucinations, anosognosia, and hemineglect.

Fantasy–reality confusion is of particular theoretical interest. This disorder was present to varying degrees in most of our cases (Cases 17, 18, 19, 20, 22, 23, 24, & 25). Case 22 provided an unusually lucid description of it: "It's as if my thinking would become real—as I would think about something, so I would see it actually happening before my eyes and then I would also be very confused and I wouldn't know sometimes what had really happened and what I was just thinking." Case 17 experienced this phenomenon as "my mind playing tricks on me." However, most of the patients were unable to reflect rationally on such experiences, which were embedded within a generalized oneiroid state. Identical phenomena were reported in the literature. Whitty and Lewin (1957) provided particularly clear examples. Damasio et al. (1985, p. 269) aptly described them as *waking dreams*.

A Possible Mechanism: Excessive Backward Projection

These phenomena evoke the regressive (or backward projection) mechanism of normal dreaming, which was described in chapter 19 as "abstract thinking being converted into concrete perception." In the cases reported in chapter 20, the normal dream process of regression apparently occurred excessively, and the patients experienced their abstract thoughts as concrete perceptions not only during dreams but also during waking cognition. The same mechanism can explain the phenomenon of continuous dreaming; in these cases the abstract thought processes that normally occur throughout non-REM sleep (Foulkes, 1972) are converted into continuous perceptual processes. Increased frequency of dreaming, too, can be attributed to an excessive tendency to backward projection during sleep. Thus, a single pathophysiological mechanism can explain all the characteristic features of this syndrome, namely fantasy–reality confusion, continuous dreaming, and increased frequency of dreaming. On this view, the confusion between dreams and reality in these cases is a specific instance of a general tendency to confuse thoughts and reality. Considering the vivid perceptual quality of normal dreams, patients with a tendency toward excessive backward projection would in fact be more likely to confuse dreaming with reality than other forms of thinking with reality. Also noteworthy in this regard is Johnson's (1991) observation that if the perceptual qualities of imagined events are unusually vivid, they are more difficult to discriminate retrospectively from perceived events.

Associated Symptoms

It is likely that the primary symptom of dream–reality confusion is exacerbated by associated amnestic and executive disorders. Johnson (1991) attributed the common association between reality monitoring disorders and amnesia to the fact that "supporting memories for events occurring both before and after a target event are used to help specify the origin of a memory. Anything that makes such supporting events more difficult to retrieve (e.g., disrupted reflective retrieval operations) should disrupt reality monitoring." Similar considerations apply to executive disorders in general: "Anything that differentially reduces the amount of contextual information that usually is associated with perceived events or that differentially increases the contextual information associated with imagined events would make reality monitoring more difficult" (p. 184).

Negative Cases

Disorders of reality monitoring were absent in only two of our cases. In one case (Case 26), increased frequency and vivacity of dreaming itself was absent, and the syndrome was characterized by relatively pure continuous dreaming. In the other case (Case 21), the dream disorder was associated with severe optic atrophy, causing partial cerebral blindness (cf. Hypothesis 15). This case was reminiscent of two patients reported in the previous literature in whom increased frequency and vivacity of dreaming were associated with cerebral blindness, in the absence of manifest fantasy–reality confusion (Gloning & Sternbach's, 1953, case M. Johanna; Grünstein's, 1924, Patient N.).

Cerebral visual defects were present in a total of five cases in our series (Cases 18, 20, 21, 22, & 24). It is well known that deafferentation of the cortical visual system can provoke visual hallucinations (see chapter 3). The physiological conditions prevailing during sleep are especially apt to release such phenomena. Therefore, in these cases, too, increased frequency and vivacity of dreaming might be attributable to pathological backward projection. This is consistent with Johnson's remark—cited previously—to the effect that imagined events with unusually vivid perceptual qualities are difficult to discriminate from perceived events. It is also consistent with her remark to the effect that "anything that differentially reduces the amount of contextual information that usually is associated with perceived events . . . would make reality monitoring more difficult" (Johnson, 1991, p. 184; cf. Anton, 1899). My suggestion in chapter 7 to the effect that the syndrome of increased frequency and vivacity of dreaming might have a different mechanism in cases with cerebral blindness is therefore only partly supported. Evidently cerebral visual defects, like amnestic (retrieval) and other executive disorders, provoke or exacerbate an underlying tendency to reality monitoring disorders.[1]

ANATOMICAL ASPECTS:
A FRONTAL–LIMBIC DISORDER

Johnson (1991, p. 190) reduced all disorders of reality monitoring to disturbances of the "reflective" systems of the brain, which she localized to the frontal lobes. This anatomical conceptualization is broadly consistent with the hypothesis we advanced in chapter 7 on the basis of our review of the literature, namely, that the syndrome of increased frequency and vivacity of dreaming occurs with lesions—usually but not exclusively bilateral—in the anterior parts of the limbic system (Hypothesis 14).

All but one of the cases in our series had lesions in the frontal limbic region. The exception was Case 26, who presented with continuous dreaming in the absence of reality monitoring disorders. In this case temporal–limbic structures were involved. However, even the frontal–limbic cases did not form an homogeneous group. Medial prefrontal cortex was involved in 5 cases (Cases No. 17, 19, 22, 23, & 25), the anterior cingulate gyrus was involved in 5 cases (Nos. 17, 18, 19, 22, & 25), the basal forebrain nuclei were involved in 4 cases (Nos. 17, 19, 22, & 24), and antero-medial diencephalic nuclei were involved in 4 cases (Nos. 20, 21, 23, & 24). It is perhaps noteworthy that the most severe examples of fantasy–reality confusion were cases in which medial frontal cortex was extensively involved (Cases 17, 19, & 22). These patients were incapable of reflecting on their experiences, and the dream disorder was imbedded within a generalized oneiroid state. However, oneiroid states are also observed in diencephalic cases (e.g., Case 20).

There appear to be grounds for a further subdivision of these cases according to more detailed anatomical criteria. However, the dense interdigitation of the structures in question makes this difficult in practice. At present it is possible to conclude only that increased frequency and vivacity of dreaming is invariably associated with anterior limbic lesions. Hypothesis 14 is thereby supported.

Negative Cases

Fourteen patients in our series with extensive frontal–limbic lesions did not experience increased frequency and vivacity of dreaming. Most of these patients reported global cessation or reduction of dreaming (Patients No. 9, 150, 171, 179, 212, 280, 281, 291, 324, & 339). The fact that frontal–limbic damage can globally inhibit or prevent dreaming in some cases and disinhibit or stimulate it in others is very striking. It is possible that antagonistic neuro-transmitter pathways are involved in the two symptoms. Our analysis of the former symptom in chapter 19 suggested that damage to subcortico-cortical dopaminergic pathways produces global cessation of dreaming, and con-versely that the administration of dopamine agonists produces increased fre-quency and vivacity of dreaming. This suggested a reciprocal relationship be-tween the two conditions.

Further Consideration of Possible Mechanisms

Damasio et al. (1985) and Morris et al. (1992) suggested that the confusional syndrome associated with basal forebrain lesions is attributable to cholinergic denervation of the hippocampus. This accounts for the amnesia in their cases. The occurrence of continuous dreaming in one of our cases with a hippo-campal lesion (Case 26) is broadly consistent with this hypothesis. However, fantasy–reality confusion was absent in that case (and it is rare with hippocam-pal lesions in general). Also, it is questionable whether basal forebrain patients are truly amnestic. In some respects these patients could even be described as hypermnestic. This undermines the premise of the hippocampal denervation hypothesis. The essential memory deficit with basal forebrain lesions does not appear to be one of forgetting, or inability to remember, but rather an inabil-ity to *select* the appropriate memory from a bewildering array of possibilities. Memory is, as it were, disinhibited. In this sense these patients are hyper-mnestic. The hippocampal cholinergic denervation hypothesis therefore leaves some essential features of the syndrome of dream–reality confusion un-explained. Moreover, in some of our patients (e.g., Cases 20 & 23) and in some cases reported in the literature (e.g., Lugaresi et al., 1986; Whitty & Lewin, 1957) the critical cholinergic basal forebrain nuclei were spared. In these cases the lesion was restricted either to the anterior cingulate or to antero-medial diencephalic nuclei.

Disturbances of consciousness with antero-medial diencephalic lesions are often attributed to arousal mechanisms rather than to memory mechanisms (see Gallassi, Morreale, Montagna, Gambetti, & Lugaresi, 1992, and Guille-minault, Quera-Salva, & Goldberg, 1993, for reviews). Such patients are often described as being "lost in the transition between wakefulness and sleep" (Guilleminault et al., 1993, p. 1549). Moreover, some authors (e.g., Luria, 1973, 1980) attributed the amnestic syndrome associated with basal forebrain lesions, too, to a disturbance of arousal. For example, Luria (1973) described the syndrome associated with ruptured anterior communicating artery aneurysms as a "disturbance of the selectivity of mental processes":

The first and most important consequence of a lesion in these brain zones is a *sharp decrease in cortical tone*, leading to *disturbance of the waking state* and sometimes to the appearance of *oneiroid states*, characteristic of lesions of the limbic region. A special feature of these states of diminished wakefulness arising in lesions of the medial zones of the frontal lobes is that they take place against a background of a *diminished critical faculty* characteristic of frontal lobe pathology or, in other words, against the background of a *disturbance of the action acceptor [reflective] apparatus*, providing the essential control over the performance of conscious processes. The principal symptom found in patients with lesions of the medial frontal zones is thus one which I have described as *disturbance of the selectivity of mental processes* (Luria, Homskaya, Blinkov, & Critchley, 1967), in which the patient is no longer clearly oriented relative to his surroundings or to his past, he utters uncontrollable confabulations, and his *consciousness* becomes unstable and is sometimes profoundly disturbed. A second aspect of this syndrome is the gross *disturbances of memory* found in these patients, with a well-marked phenomenon of "equalization of excitability" of traces, leading to a state of confusion and to the production of confabulations. (p. 224)

These remarks seem to cover all the essential features of the syndrome associated with dream–reality confusion.

The notion of equalization of excitability of traces suggests that the fantasy–reality confusion associated with basal forebrain lesions could be attributed to equalized activation of hippocampal mechanisms by damaged basal forebrain structures, or equalized interpretation of the reciprocal hippocampal innervations. An intact hippocampus would thereby be rendered dysfunctional (cf. Johnson, 1994). However, in my view, the resultant disorder should be described as an agnosia rather than an amnesia; these patients misrecognize and misidentify their internal perceptions (memories, fantasies) just as patients with posterior lesions misrecognize and misidentify their external perceptions.[2]

I am unable to support Whitty and Lewin's (1957) suggestion to the effect that dream–reality confusion may be attributable to discharging lesions in the temporal lobe. A seizure disorder was demonstrated in only one of our cases with this syndrome (Case 23). Although there appears to be an increased incidence of vivid nightmares among patients with the syndrome of dream–reality confusion (see Cases 18, 21, 24, & 25), only 2 patients reported recurring nightmares of the type that are associated with epilepsy (cf. Table 7.2). It therefore seems likely that the syndrome of dream–reality confusion is attributable to a structural lesion in the reflective systems themselves, rather than a discharging lesion in the memory systems of the brain. (This assertion is qualified in the final section of this chapter.)

CONCLUSIONS

In conclusion, the foregoing considerations suggest that the diverse neurobehavioral symptoms and signs associated with increased vivacity and frequency of dreaming can be reduced to a single basic deficit, namely, disturbed selectivity of mental processes. Disturbed selectivity of mental processes apparently underlies the pathological tendency to backward projection in these cases. It is normal for backward projection to occur to a far greater degree during sleep than waking ideational life. This results in normal dreaming (which does not occur when one is awake). Excessive backward projection provokes excessive dreaming during sleep and dreamlike thinking during waking ideational life. The connections which bind current volitional intentions with specific stored representations seem to lose their selective character, and as a result "the fabric of thinking is resolved into its raw material" (Freud, 1900/1953, p. 543; cf. chapter 15, this volume). The cardinal element of the resultant syndrome—namely dream–reality confusion—is part of a more general tendency to fantasy–reality (or thought–reality) confusion. This tendency is exacerbated by amnestic (retrieval) and other executive deficits, which combine to produce generalized disorders of reality monitoring. Affective disinhibition and cerebral blindness have a similar effect, but they are not essential elements of this syndrome (cf. Hypothesis 15). The essential elements of the syndrome are associated with anterior limbic lesions. The frontal limbic region inhibits dreaming and dreamlike thinking. This implies that some of the fundamental differences between dreaming and waking cognition mentioned in chapter 15 are attributable to functional differences in frontal limbic activity. This simple inference goes a long way towards explaining Fechner's (1889) remark to the effect that "the scene of action of dreams is different from that of waking ideational life" (Freud, 1900/1953, p. 536). The state of mind that is generated by frontal limbic lesions and the state of mind that characterizes normal dreaming are almost identical.

PATIENTS WITH INCREASED FREQUENCY OR VIVACITY OF DREAMING

We turn now to the subclinical cases mentioned at the beginning of chapter 20. Our series included 27 such cases who reported relatively increased dream frequency in response to question 7 of the interview (19.9% of an effective sample of 136). The series also included 31 such cases who reported relatively increased dream vivacity in response to question 9 (26.7% of an effective sample of 116). These subclinical changes were also reported by control subjects. Three controls reported a relative increase in dream frequency (13.6% of an effective sample of 22) and 7 reported a relative increase in dream vivacity (38.8% of an effective sample of 18). None of these patients reported actual confusion between dreams and reality in response to question 10. Nor did any of them report the phenomenon of continuous dreaming in response to question 11. The fact that changes in dream frequency and vivacity occurred with control subjects demonstrates that these factors can be influenced by purely functional factors. (We reached a similar conclusion in chapter 12.) Changes of this order are therefore clinically unreliable.

No anatomical site or neurobehavioral symptoms discriminated significantly between the subclinical cases and those not reporting increased vivacity or frequency of dreaming, $p = .1$. However, these patients were significantly different with regard to the incidence of epilepsy. Epilepsy was more common in both subclinical groups (increased dream frequency, $\chi^2 = 7.41$, $p < .01$; increased dream vivacity, $\chi^2 = 7.72$, $p < .01$). This provides limited support for the Whitty–Lewin hypothesis that we rejected before (see also Cases 18 & 25). Apparently, relatively increased frequency or vivacity of dreaming is provoked by epilepsy in some (but by no means all) cases. (Limbic tissue is highly susceptible to epileptiform irritation.) The subclinical group also included three patients with cerebral blindness (Patients No. 21, 201, & 320), all 3 of whom reported both increased frequency and increased vivacity of dreaming. This confirms the observations already reported.

NOTES

[1]These remarks qualify the formulation advanced in chapter 15 to account for the apparent indifference of the dream process to V1 lesions. Damaged primary visual cortex evidently does not only remove reality constraints, which play no part in the dream process, it might also positively release endogenous imagery processes (which play a part in the generation of dreams) and undermine reality monitoring processes (which play a part in the retrospective differentiation of dreams and perceptions).

[2]It is of historical interest to note that Flechsig (1896) speculated on anatomical grounds that posterior association mechanisms interpret the world around us, whereas frontal mechanisms interpret the internal world.

22

Nine Patients With Recurring Nightmares

The term *recurring nightmares* refers to the repeated experience of the same dream, or to the repeated experience of dreams with a stereotypical theme. Cases presenting with this phenomenon were identified by question 6 of the interview schedule, to which 114 patients gave a definite answer.[1] Nine of these patients reported recurring nightmares. This is an incidence of 7.9%. In addition, 17 patients reported increased frequency of nightmares in general. These were not recurring nightmares. One control patient reported the same phenomenon. The 9 patients with recurring nightmares are described briefly in the following sections. The patients with nonrecurring nightmares are discussed at the end of the next chapter.

CASE 9: FREQUENT NIGHTMARES WITH A STEREOTYPED THEME (PATIENT NO. 200)

This patient was described in chapter 20. She was a 33-year-old dextral artist with 15 years' formal education. She had a lifelong history of poorly controlled idiopathic complex-partial epilepsy. There was a right temporal lobe focus on EEG. After one generalized seizure in childhood there had been transient left hemianesthesia and hemianopia. The patient complained of episodic depersonalization and derealization experiences. She also complained of confusional episodes and occasional "horrifying" visual and auditory hallucinations. Her typical hallucinations involved the sound of a baby crying, the illusion of floating above the ground, scenes of blood, and an image of a black dog. The psychiatric history was eventful and the patient had made repeated attempts at suicide. Neurological and neuropsychologial examinations did not demonstrate any definite abnormalities.

For as long as this patient could remember she experienced frequent nightmares. There was not a single, repetitive dream but rather a stereotypical theme. The nightmares always revolved around the subject of death (usually her own death). As far as the patient was aware she did not experience the hallucinatory aurae described above in her dreams. However, she reported frequent sleep-onset hypnogogic hallucinations in which she typically saw a disembodied face.

CASE 18: FREQUENT AND VIVID HALLUCINATORY NIGHTMARES WITH A STEREOTYPED THEME (AND WITH CIRCUMSCRIBED FANTASY–REALITY CONFUSION) (PATIENT NO. 136)

This patient was described in chapter 20. He was a 32-year-old dextral businessman with 12 years' formal education. He presented with an open wound at the vertex of the cranium (with herniation of the brain) following a motor vehicle accident. A sequestrectomy was performed. The postoperative CT scan demonstrated bilateral paracentral low density, which extended inferiorly to the level of the corpus callosum (including both cingulate gyri), anteriorly to the premotor cortex, and posteriorly to the occipito-parietal sulcus on the left and the occipital pole on the right. Clinical symptoms and signs included triplegia, left visual-field scotoma and visual hallucinations arising from the scotoma in the left field. At neurobehavioral assessment 5 weeks posttrauma the patient presented with euphoric mood, jocularity, garrulousness and anosodiaphoria. He had a mild premotor syndrome (motor perseveration and nonfluency), mild unilateral (left) visual neglect, and severe constructional apraxia. There were no other localizing features.

Some months after his accident, this patient was unsure as to whether he was dreaming or hallucinating at night. He would frequently wake up during a dream, but the dream would continue. The patient would think that it was a real experience rather than a dream until his wife reoriented him and convinced him that there was nothing there. He could not determine whether or not he was actually awake during these experiences, which were described as "terrifyingly real." The dreams varied in content but some at least were similar to his earlier visual-hallucinatory experiences (small animals and insects in the left visual field). On more than one occasion this patient woke up and saw small animals and insects crawling about his room. He dreamed frequently of ghosts. An EEG record was not available.

CASE 25: FREQUENT AND VIVID NIGHTMARES WITH A STEREOTYPED THEME (AND WITH CIRCUMSCRIBED FANTASY–REALITY CONFUSION); RECOVERY (PATIENT NO. 357)

This patient also was described in chapter 20. She was a 32-year-old dextral secretary with 10 years' formal education. A brick was thrown at her while she was the passenger in a moving car. She was struck on the forehead and sustained an open fracture. After she had undergone a sequestrectomy, a CT scan revealed bilateral medial frontal low density extending backwards to include the anterior cingulate gyri and most of the right mediobasal frontal area. There was air in the frontal horns of the lateral ventricles. She made an excellent physical recovery and was left with residual second and eighth nerve lesions on the right. Cranioplasty was performed 3 months later. On neurobehavioral assessment (1 week after cranioplastic surgery) fluctuating affect with encapsulated paranoid ideation, decreased libido, and decreased drive were noted. Classical signs of frontal lobe disorder could not be demonstrated. Memory functions appeared normal.

This patient reported that, in the first weeks after her trauma, she experienced frequent and vivid nightmares that (although bizarre) were very much more realistic than her normal dreams. She had always been a vivid dreamer but she experienced these dreams as being utterly different. She felt that her dream recall was much enhanced and she stated that she had great difficulty convincing herself that the dreams were not real. She would typically dream of snakes, of needles (being stuck into her), and of vampires. The dreams were always unpleasant. She once had a terrifying dream about snakes after which (on awakening) she searched the bed for snakes. She knew that she had been dreaming, but she still could not resist the urge to check. On other occasions she would awaken from dreams and feel compelled to check around her house for snakes or vampires. Her dreams returned to normal within a few weeks. An EEG record was not available.

CASE 27: RECURRING NIGHTMARES
INCORPORATING EPILEPTOGENIC
HALLUCINATORY IMAGERY (PATIENT NO. 230)

This patient was a 24-year-old dextral male. He was a university student. There was a 4-year history of progressive motor neuron disease, with an anoxic episode 2 years postonset. Since then, the patient suffered dense amnesia and complex-partial epilepsy. An MRI scan revealed lacunae in the posterior hippocampal region of both hemispheres. Bitemporal epileptiform foci were demonstrated on sleep EEG.

By the time of the neurobehavioral assessment, this patient was quadriplegic and on a ventilator. He was disoriented for time but not for place. A very severe material nonspecific anterograde amnesia, with a 2-year retrograde extension, was documented. Remote and immediate memory were intact. Insight was preserved and his mood was depressed. Localizing symptoms and signs other than the amnesia could not be demonstrated. There was no evidence of medial occipito-temporal neocortical involvement, there were no cortical-convexity signs, and there was no evidence of intellectual decline.

The seizures typically occurred during sleep. The patient awoke with facial twitching, masticatory movements, vivid visual hallucinations, and, occasionally, fluent jargon aphasia (word salad). According to the parents of this patient (who were nursing him at home) his hallucinations were sometimes of the simple variety (e.g., shooting stars) but more commonly they were complex, formed hallucinations involving horrific scenes of traffic accidents with dismembered bodies. The parents based their descriptions of the hallucinations upon statements which the patient made immediately postictus. At assessment the patient himself had no recollection of the content of these hallucinations, but he did seem to be at least vaguely aware that he was given to frightening seizures. He frequently expressed the fear that he might die during his sleep, and he became very anxious whenever he was left alone.

His parents also described recurring nightmares. To the extent that they were able to determine the content, the nightmares apparently consisted of the same imagery as the hallucinations described above. (The parents drew a distinction between nightmares and hallucinations on the basis of the presence or absence of associated motor signs. However, it seems likely that both phenomena were epileptogenic.) On more than one occasion he awoke from a nightmare and reported visions of "broken bodies strewn across the road" and other scenes of dismembered bodies in traffic accidents. The patient himself was aware that he suffered frequent nightmares but could not recall their content.

Both the seizures and the nightmares were partially controlled by various combinations of anticonvulsant medications. There was no special premorbid propensity to nightmares in this case.

CASE 28: RECURRING NIGHTMARES
(PATIENT NO. 304)

This patient was a 25-year-old dextral female with 11 years' formal education. She was unemployed. She was a passenger in a bus accident. There was brief loss of consciousness, followed by protracted stupor and torpor. One week posttrauma the patient suffered her first fit. A left parieto-temporal fracture was seen on X-ray but the CT scan was considered normal. A diffuse EEG abnormality was recorded, with occasional asymmetrical temporal spikes (which were more pronounced on the left than the right). At neurobehavioral assessment (3 years posttrauma) the patient complained of sleepiness and forgetfulness. Fluctuating arousal and adynamia were observed. No higher cortical symptoms or signs could be demonstrated. The seizures (which were usually generalized, but sometimes consisted of aggressive rages with amnesia) persisted. The patient described an aura of visual flashes or stars (without any lateralized component), epigastric sensations, dizziness, and a "funny feeling" that she could not describe. She also reported a recurring, stereotyped nightmare of being dead. She dreamed frequently that "people are at my funeral." Also, she very frequently dreamed that "a horrible thing is chasing me." She was not given to nightmares premorbidly.

CASE 29: RECURRING UNPLEASANT DREAMS
INCORPORATING EPILEPTOGENIC PHENOMENA
(PATIENT NO. 308)

This patient was a 47-year-old dextral female. She was a homemaker with 12 years' formal education. Following a sudden drop-attack, with left anterobasal temporal low density evident on CT scan, a diagnosis of CVA was made. There was a second attack 6 months later. ("I smelt something burning and started to talk in circles.") A repeat CT scan and biopsy were performed, revealing an oligodendroglioma. There was a third drop-attack 2 weeks later, 1 week after the biopsy. This consisted of a tingling sensation around the mouth, a musty taste, and "an awful smell, like someone being cremated." The hallucinations were followed by generalized (tonic–clonic) convulsions. Neurobehavioral assessment (presurgery) revealed no deficits. This patient reported that over the past few months she frequently awoke from dreams which had culminated in an unpleasant smell. She could not recall the content of these dreams, but she considered them to be highly unusual. She believed that the smell "wiped out" the dreams. After successful surgery, normal dreaming and dream recall returned. An EEG was not performed in this case.

CASE 30: RECURRING NIGHTMARES INCORPORATING EPILEPTOGENIC PHENOMENA (PATIENT NO. 311)

This patient was a 12-year-old dextral female, a sixth-grade student. She was struck by a car and suffered right fronto-temporal lacerations and a brief loss of consciousness. X-ray and CT scan were normal. At the neurobehavioral assessment (4 months later) she complained of headaches and of recurring nightmares of "being chased by someone that I'm afraid of." She also complained of "hearing voices" while she was sleeping—usually of someone calling her name. These dreams sometimes incorporated unpleasant olfactory sensations and dizziness. Nocturnal enuresis was also noted. More recently, together with her headaches, the patient had begun to experience dizziness, phosphenes ("twinkles"), olfactory hallucinations ("something rotten"), and occasional auditory hallucinations ("people calling my name"). Her parents also described episodes suggestive of absence attacks. A nonspecific abnormality was recorded on EEG. At 6-month follow-up it transpired that the headaches and associated symptoms were well controlled by anticonvulsant medication and that the nightmares had ceased.

CASE 31: RECURRING UNPLEASANT DREAMS (PATIENT NO. 331)

This patient was a 46-year-old dextral male. He was an artisan. A craniotomy was performed to clip an aneurysm of the right middle cerebral artery after he had suffered an intracerebral hemorrhage (2 weeks previously). The patient made a good physical recovery. Postsurgical CT scan revealed a patch of lateral fronto-temporal low density on the right. At the neurobehavioral assessment (5½ months later) the patient appeared agitated, restless, and aggressive. He was oriented and alert, and his memory appeared normal. Dense left hemispatial neglect and severe constructional apraxia were observed. The patient complained of claustrophobia (which was not present premorbidly). During the assessment his wife described an episode of "peculiar behavior," which had occurred during the first weeks of his convalescence. This took place before he was discharged from hospital in Johannesburg (an inland city). He was listening to a radio broadcast of a surfing event taking place in Durban (a coastal city). He thought to himself that his wife and family (who lived in Johannesburg) would no longer be able to visit him, because he was in Durban.

TABLE 22.1
Cases with Recurring Nightmares

Case	Age/Sex	Lesion	Relevant Symptoms & Signs	Dreams
Case 9	33-yr F.	R. temp. focus on EEG (idiopathic)	Complex-partial (and occasional generalized) seizures	Frequent nightmares with repetitive theme
Case 18	32-yr M.	Bilat. paracentr. fro-par, R. occip-par, Bilat. cingulate g. (open head injury)	±Disinhibition, euphoria, placidity, visual hallucination, neglect, anosodiaphoria	Increased reality & frequency with circumscribed fantasy/reality breakdown and repetitive nightmares
Case 25	32-yr F.	Bilat. med. frontal/ant. cingulate g. (open head injury)	Torpor, fluctuating affect, paranoia	Increased reality and frequency with circumscribed fantasy/reality breakdown and repetitive nightmares
Case 27	24-yr M.	Bitemporal foci on EEG (anoxic episode)	Simple & complex-partial seizures, amnesia, depression	Recurring stereotypical nightmare incorporating epileptogenic hallucinatory imagery
Case 28	25-yr F.	Bitemporal foci on EEG, L. > R. (closed head injury)	Generalized & complex-partial seizures, torpor, adynamia/aspontaneity	Recurring stereotypical nightmare
Case 29	47-yr F.	L. ant.-basal temp (oligodendroglioma)	Simple & complex-partial seizures (with occasional 2° generalization)	Recurring incorporation of epileptogenic olfactory image
Case 30	12-yr F.	Nonspecific abn. on EEG (closed head injury)	Simple & complex-partial seizures (with occasional 2° generalization)	Recurring nightmare incorporating epileptogenic hallucinatory imagery and aura
Case 31	46-yr M.	R. lat. fro-temp. (aneurysmal rupture)	Disinhibition, affective abn., neglect, ?reduplicative paramnesia	Recurring stereotypical dream
Case 32	50-yr M.	L. deep par-temp. (glioblastoma multiforme)	±Fluent aphasia	Recurring stereotypical nightmare (with increased frequency & vivacity)

He thought that he was in Durban despite the fact that his wife and family visited him quite regularly. Later that day, during visiting hours, he was very surprised to see his wife. He asked her if she could arrange for his bed to be placed nearer to the window "because he wanted to have a view of the sea." It is likely that this paramnestic event was an isolated occurrence for (although the patient was not examined neuropsychologically at the time) there was no mention in his progress notes of mental confusion, disorientation, or amnesia.

During the assessment the patient also reported the following recurring dream, which he experienced frequently ever since his illness:

> I am being chased around by this bloody bull. There's no stopping the little bugger.
>
> [*Is the dream frightening?*]
>
> No, but it has fucking long horns.
>
> [*Would you describe it as a nightmare?*]
>
> It's not really frightening. It just keeps coming at me: a really persistent little bugger.

There were no other changes in this patient's dreams. An EEG record was not available.

CASE 32: RECURRING NIGHTMARES
(PATIENT NO. 342)

This patient was a 50-year-old male. He was a shopkeeper with 12 years' formal education. The notes recorded a 2-year history of episodic headaches and blurred vision. A deep left parieto-temporal infiltrating mass (observed on MRI scan) was identified as a glioblastoma multiforme by tissue biopsy. The neurobehavioral assessment was conducted 2 days after the biopsy was performed. The patient presented with mild word-finding difficulty in spontaneous speech, with anomia on confrontation testing, receptive dysgrammatism, hesitant verbal repetition, occasional literal and verbal paraphasias, aphasic dysgraphia, severe acalculia, and right-left disorientation. Reading was unaffected. This patient had never been particularly aware of his dreams in the past, but over the past 3 years he suffered frequent, vivid, repetitive nightmares. As this patient was gravely ill, further information was not elicited.

These case reports are summarized in Table 22.1.

NOTE

[1]Due to global cessation of dreaming, 112 patients were excluded. A further 106 patients gave equivocal responses to question 6.

23

Clinico-Anatomical Correlates of Recurring Nightmares

It was not possible to identify any specific neurobehavioral correlates of recurring nightmares in our review of the literature. Nevertheless it was evident that recurring nightmares are frequently associated with seizure disorder (Hypothesis 16). The literature also pointed to a definite localization of the seizure foci responsible for this disorder: Recurring nightmares indicate a discharging lesion in the region of the right temporal lobe (Hypothesis 17).

CLINICAL ASPECTS: A SEIZURE DISORDER

Five of the 9 cases described in the previous chapter presented with definite epilepsy (Cases 9, 27, 28, 29, & 30). The causal nature of the link between recurring nightmares and seizure disorder was suggested by the fact that simple and complex-partial seizure phenomena were incorporated into the content of the nightmares in three of these cases (Cases 27, 28, & 29). Moreover, the recurring nightmares responded to anticonvulsant medication in 2 cases (Cases 27 & 30) and to surgical removal of the irritative focus in one case (Case 29).

210

These observations confirm those of Penfield and Erickson (1941), who first demonstrated the causal link between recurring nightmares and seizure disorder from a different point of view.

The diagnosis of seizure disorder cannot be excluded with certainty in the other 4 cases (Cases 18, 25, 31, & 32). Unfortunately some of them were not adequately investigated in this respect. Sleep EEG studies (preferably with depth electrodes) are required. It is possible that nocturnal seizure activity was present in Cases 18 and 32, but there is little evidence for this in Cases 25 and 31. The latter 2 cases experienced repetitive nightmares with a stereotyped theme rather than true recurring nightmares. In addition, in these 2 cases the unpleasant dreams formed part of a broader disorder characterized by increased frequency and vivacity of dreaming with fantasy–reality confusion. Increased frequency and vivacity of dreaming were also reported in Case 32. Moreover nightmares were commonly reported by the patients with the syndrome of dream–reality confusion described in chapters 20 and 21.

Relationship with the Syndrome of Dream–Reality Confusion

These findings, together with those discussed in chapter 21, suggest that the syndrome of recurring nightmares overlaps with the syndrome of dream–reality confusion. This conclusion is consistent with our observation in chapter 7 to the effect that it was difficult to classify some of the previously published cases; they seemed to belong in both of these categories. With this qualification, Hypothesis 16 can be upheld: In most cases recurring nightmares are caused by seizure disorder, but in some cases the latter diagnosis is uncertain. In the uncertain cases the syndrome is less well defined and it overlaps with the syndrome of dream–reality confusion. It could be said that the syndromes of recurring nightmares and of dream–reality confusion represent two extremes on a nosological continuum; the boundary between them is blurred, but as the dreams become more repetitive in content and more unpleasant in emotional tone, so the likelihood of an underlying seizure disorder increases. The link between these two syndromes is probably attributable to the low seizure threshold and dense interdigitation of limbic tissues. These remarks confirm our qualified support for Whitty and Lewin's (1957) hypothesis to the effect that the syndrome of dream–reality confusion is sometimes caused by discharging lesions in the temporal lobe. We may speculate that seizure activity anywhere in the limbic system is apt to generalize within that system and overwhelm the frontal-limbic mechanisms that inhibit dreams and dreamlike thinking (cf. chapter 21). This fits neatly with the classical observation of "dreamy states" in temporal lobe epileptics (Jackson, 1879/1931). (It is noteworthy that this directly contradicts the hippocampal denervation hypothesis, discussed above in chapter 21; dreamy states are evidently associated with hippocampal *over*activity.)

ANATOMICAL ASPECTS:
A TEMPORAL–LIMBIC DISORDER

As regards the pathological–anatomical correlates of this syndrome, limbic system involvement could be demonstrated in most but not in all cases (Cases 9, 18, 25, 27, 28, & 29). An extralimbic localization of the primary lesion or focus (in an essentially physiological disorder) does not, of course, preclude limbic involvement. In this regard it is noteworthy that the phenomenology of the seizures or dreams themselves in all of our cases was suggestive of limbic mechanisms. The involvement of temporal lobe mechanisms in particular is suggested by the fact that recurring nightmares are invariably marked by anxiety (Tyrer & Seivewright, 1985). These observations provide indirect support for the hypothesis that temporal–limbic mechanisms are implicated in the syndrome of recurring nightmares (cf. Hypothesis 17).

However, the (rightward) lateral bias predicted by Hypothesis 17 did not emerge in our cases. There were 2 patients with unilateral right hemisphere lesions or foci (Cases 9 & 31), 2 with unilateral left hemisphere lesions (Cases 29 & 32), and 5 with bilateral lesions or foci (Cases 18, 25, 27, 28, & 30). This does away with a contradiction noticed in our review of the previous literature (chapter 7); investigators of cases with structural lesions concluded that dreams were generated by left-posterior neocortical mechanisms, and investigators of cases with discharging lesions concluded that dreams were generated by right temporal–limbic mechanisms. Our observations on the syndromes of nonvisual dreaming, global cessation of dreaming, dream–reality confusion, and recurring nightmares, all suggest that both hemispheres are involved in the generation of dreams (albeit asymmetrically, in some respects).

PATIENTS WITH NONRECURRING NIGHTMARES

As already mentioned, in addition to the 9 cases reported in chapter 22, 17 patients in our series (14.9% of the effective sample) reported increased frequency of nightmares in general, in response to question 5 of the dream interview (Patients No. 10, 12, 25, 72, 104, 131, 142, 184, 198, 208, 239, 245, 256, 264, 292, 310, & 356). These were nonrecurring nightmares, and the incidence of epilepsy was not higher in this group than it was among those who did not report increased frequency of nightmares. (Only 4 of these patients suffered epilepsy.) The clinical usefulness of this phenomenon is therefore questionable, especially in view of the fact that it was also reported by one control patient (Patient No. 7, a paraplegic). On the other hand, the incidence of frequent nightmares was slightly higher in the cerebrally impaired group than it was in the control group (3.4%), $\chi^2 = 2.97$, $p < .1$, and it did correlate significantly with limbic system involvement, $\chi^2 = 5.13$, $p < .05$. A clear lateral bias did not emerge, but the incidence of anosognosia was slightly raised among the patients who denied increased frequency of nightmares, $F = 3.69$, $p < .1$. The latter finding is difficult to interpret, but it may be added to our (equally unimpressive) observations with respect to global cessation of dreaming, which suggested a marginal and subtle dominance of right hemisphere mechanisms in dream generation.

THEORETICAL SPECULATIONS

I conclude this chapter with some further theoretical speculations. The fact that nocturnal seizures are causally linked to dream generation suggests that we should situate the mechanisms involved at the initiating end of the dream process. This is consistent with Penfield and Erickson's (1941) cryptic remark to the effect that "one may be said to dream with his temporal lobe" (p. 133). However this remark assigns too exclusive a role to the temporal lobe. Other mechanisms that appear to be implicated in the initiation of dreams are the curiosity–interest–expectancy circuits arising from dopaminergic tegmental and diencephalic–limbic nuclei, and the REM-generation circuits arising from cholinergic pontine nuclei. The frontal–limbic structures that appear to differentially inhibit the process of backward projection may be situated somewhere in between these initiating mechanisms and the spatial, quasispatial, and visual mechanisms that we have placed at the terminal end of the dreaming process (see chapters 15 and 19, this volume). The latter mechanisms are implicated in the elaboration and representation of dream imagery.

It is unlikely that REM-generation mechanisms are mandatory in the initiation of dreaming (see chapters 6 and 17), although the probability that dreams can occur in the absence of REM has not yet been conclusively demonstrated. On the other hand, whether a mandatory causal link between REM and dreaming exists or not, the fact still remains that there is a very high statistical correlation between these two phenomena. This fact requires explanation. An explanation might be found in the causal link just demonstrated between limbic seizure activity and dreaming. That is, REM might cause dreaming for the same reason that nocturnal seizures cause dreaming.[1] What REM sleep and limbic seizures have in common is the fact that they are states of arousal. This suggests that the dream process is triggered by arousal mechanisms. If this inference is correct, it would be consistent with the sleep-protection theory of dreams, which predicts that anything that threatens sleep is apt to trigger the process of dreaming. This explains both the high correlation between REM and dreaming and our putative observation that dreams can occur in the absence of REM. In this view, the cyclical state of REM is but one among many arousal stimuli (albeit a common one) that disturb sleep and thereby cause dreaming; limbic epileptiform discharge is another such stimulus (albeit a pathological one). External sensory stimulation (above a certain threshold) might be yet another frequent disturber of sleep. There are likely to be many more. All such stimuli probably activate a final common arousal mechanism, which in turn triggers the process of dreaming itself. The curiosity–interest–expectancy circuits in the ventromesial forebrain are a likely candidate for this final common pathway, because the ablation of these circuits prevents all dreaming.

NOTE

[1] It is unlikely that nocturnal seizures are triggered by REM, as most nocturnal seizures occur during NREM sleep (Janz, 1974).

24

Miscellaneous Observations (Including Normal Dreaming)

In this chapter I report miscellaneous observations arising from the structured dream interview. Most of them—apart from the observations reported at the end of the chapter (concerning normal dreaming)—are of little scientific interest.

REDUCED FREQUENCY OF DREAMING

Fifty-two patients in our series (from an effective sample of 136 patients) reported reduced frequency of dreaming in response to question 7 of the interview schedule. This was an incidence of 38.2%, which was not significantly different from the 40.9% incidence in the control group, $N = 9$; $\chi^2 = .04, p > .1$. The patients who did and did not report reduced frequency of dreaming could not be differentiated in terms of lesion site or neurobehavioral symptomatology, $p > .1$. Reduced frequency of dreaming is therefore of little diagnostic value.

There was no evidence to suggest that reduced frequency of dreaming was more common with parietal and frontal lobe lesions than with other sites of lesion. This suggests that reduced frequency of dreaming is not a subclinical form of global cessation of dreaming, as reduced vivacity of visual dream-imagery was in relation to nonvisual dreaming (cf. chapter 12). Also, reduced frequency of dreaming was not more common with parietal than frontal lesions, $\chi^2 = .16, p > .6$. This suggests that chronic reduction in dream frequency is not especially characteristic of parietal lesions (as was suggested in chapter 7). Hypotheses 10 and 11 are thereby confirmed: Reduced frequency of dreaming has no localizing significance, and reduced frequency of dreaming has no specific neurobehavioral correlates.

On the other hand, reduced frequency of dreaming did have limited lateralizing significance. This phenomenon was slightly more common with right hemisphere lesions than with left hemisphere lesions, $\chi^2 = 2.76, p < .1$. This is a further indication that the right hemisphere might be marginally dominant for dream generation. Patients with bilateral lesions were also more likely to report this phenomenon than were unilateral cases, $\chi^2 = 5.85, p < .02$.

In addition, the incidence of reduced frequency of dreaming among recovered nondreamers (100%) was significantly greater than it was in the clinical series as a whole (38.2%), $\chi^2 = 14.4, p < .001$. This suggests that reduced frequency of dreaming is a chronic form of global cessation of dreaming (which usually recovers within 1 year). Similar observations were reported in chapter 16.

REDUCED NARRATIVE COMPLEXITY AND EMOTIONAL INTENSITY OF DREAMING

Twenty-three patients in our series (from an effective sample of 118 patients) reported this phenomenon in response to questions 4 and 5 of the interview schedule. This was an incidence of 19.5%, which was not significantly different from the 22.2% incidence in the control group, $N = 4; \chi^2 = .01, p > .9$. The patients who did and did not report reduced narrative complexity and emotional intensity of dreaming could not be differentiated in terms of lesion site or neurobehavioral symptomatology, $p > .1$. This phenomenon, too, is therefore of little diagnostic value.

There was no evidence to suggest that reduced narrative complexity and emotional intensity of dreaming was more common with frontal and parietal lobe lesions than other sites of lesion. This suggests that this phenomenon, too, is not a subclinical form of global cessation of dreaming. In addition, reduced narrative complexity and emotional intensity of dreaming was not more common with frontal than parietal lesions. This suggests that chronic reduction in dream complexity and intensity is not especially characteristic of frontal lesions (as was suggested in chapter 7). Hypotheses 12 and 13 are thereby supported: Reduced narrative complexity and emotional intensity of dreaming has no localizing significance, and reduced narrative complexity and emotional intensity of dreaming has no specific neurobehavioral correlates.

However, as was the case with reduced frequency of dreaming, this phenomenon did have slight lateralizing significance; left hemisphere patients were marginally more likely to report reduced narrative (or symbolic) complexity and emotional intensity of dreaming than were right hemisphere patients, $\chi^2 = 3.18$, $p < .1$. Taken together with the finding that right hemisphere lesions are more commonly associated with reduced frequency of dreaming, this (equally modest) finding is consistent with the hypothesis of Doricchi and Violani (1992) to the effect that the left hemisphere provides the "cognitive decoding of the dream during its actual nocturnal development" (p. 122), whereas the right hemisphere provides the "perceptual 'hard grain' . . . which is probably indispensable for the sensorial vividness of the dream experience" (p. 121).

Similarly, these findings are consistent with my own hypothesis to the effect that the left parietal region contributes symbolic (quasispatial) mechanisms to the dream process whereas the right parietal region contributes concrete spatial mechanisms. These findings are also broadly consistent with the hypothesis of Kerr and Foulkes (1981) to the effect that the narrative structure of dreaming is contributed by the left frontal lobe whereas the visual-imagistic components of dreaming are mediated by the posterior divisions of the right hemisphere (see also Antrobus, 1987; Foulkes, 1978, 1985). However, I report a further observation in the final section of this chapter that suggests that it is unlikely that the left frontal convexity contributes significantly to dreaming.

From the point of view of recovery from global cessation of dreaming, only a small number of recovered nondreamers were available for study ($N = 4$). Two of these patients reported a reduction in the complexity and intensity of their postrecovery dreaming compared with their subjective premorbid norm. This is not significantly greater than the incidence of such reports in the clinical series as a whole, $\chi^2 = 2.33$; $p > .1$. The small sample size makes it difficult to interpret this finding.

CESSATION OF RECENT MNEMIC CONTENT IN DREAMS

Torda (1969) proposed that the dreams of amnestic patients were characterized by the absence of recent mnemic material. This aspect of dreaming was assessed by question 12 of the structured interview. None of the patients or controls in our series reported a cessation of recent mnemic material in their dreams. In fact most subjects (70.9%) found this question impossible to answer.

Any attempt to investigate the dreams of amnestic patients (and especially the mnemic content of their dreams) is bound to be unreliable. Only 51 of the patients with long-term memory disorder included in my series were sure that they were dreaming at all (most of the truly amnestic patients were *unsure* in this regard). Of the 51 patients, 33 reported a gross reduction in dream recall in general. Sixteen of them (31.3%) stated that their dreams did include recent mnemic material. Thirty-five were *unsure* of whether or not their dreams included recent mnemic material.

DECREASED DREAM-DURATION

The subjective duration of dreams was investigated by question 11 of the dream interview, to which 106 patients provided a definite answer. Of these, 47 patients (44.3%) reported decreased duration of dreams. This incidence is significantly higher than it was for controls (11.1%), $\chi^2 = 7.08$, $p < .01$. However, specific lesion sites and neuropsychological deficits did not discriminate significantly between those who did and those who did not report decreased dream duration, $p > .1$. This appears to be a nonspecific complaint akin, perhaps, to slowness and the like.

OTHER CHANGES

Question 13 of the interview schedule asked patients to describe any changes in their dreaming that might not have been covered by the structured interview. This question did not yield any interesting observations. We are therefore unable to support Hypothesis 18, which predicted that a variety of neuropathologically significant dream phenomena exist that have not yet been identified in the literature.

The responses to question 13 can be classified into two groups. First, there were changes in dreaming that the patient could not define. These patients ($N = 16$) reported that their dreams had changed in some indefinite way since the onset of their illness. Despite careful (and often leading) questioning, the patients were unable to articulate the nature of these changes, although they were certain that their dreams had definitely changed. Interestingly, almost all of the patients in this category had mediobasal frontal lesions, and they were either mildly adynamic or mildly disinhibited (Patients No. 2, 5, 10, 15, 24, 61, 70, 82, 102, 105, 128, 158, 163, 170, 276, & 294). Whether this observation refers to a distinctive change that is unusually difficult to describe or to a range of disparate phenomena which are united only by associated self-reflective or motivational (or other) deficits, is difficult to determine.

Second, many patients reported changes in their dreaming that were of an obviously idiosyncratic nature. For example, one patient reported that he dreamed more about a certain friend of his, another that he dreamed a lot more about football, and so on. Such remarks do not warrant classification and systematic study. Hypothesis 18 was therefore not supported.

NORMAL (COMPLETELY UNCHANGED) DREAMING

The question as to whether or not (and under what circumstances) dreaming can remain entirely unaffected by brain damage has not previously been investigated. The existing reports of neurological patients with preserved dreaming (and dream-imagery) were summarized in Tables 2.3a and 2.3b. However, preserved dreaming is not synonymous with normal dreaming. As the previous chapters amply demonstrate, the preserved dreams of the brain-damaged patient are sometimes highly abnormal dreams. In the absence of a systematic clinico-anatomical study of truly normal dreaming, we do not know what (if any) neuroanatomical structures and neuropsychological functions are inessential to the dream process. The data presented in this section shed some light on this theoretically important question.

Only 24 of the patients in our series (8.6% of the effective sample) experienced absolutely normal dreams. That is, only 24 patients reported that there had been no change at all in their dreams following the onset of cerebral pathology. The pathological–anatomical and clinical data for these cases are summarized in Table 24.1. In addition, 10 of the 29 control subjects reported no change at all in their dreams (Patients No. 52, 56, 74, 182, 199, 267, 325, 330, 333, & 355). The incidence of normal dreaming among controls (34.5%) was significantly greater than it was in the clinical population, $\chi^2 = 17.93$, $p < .001$. The latter finding is not surprising. The low incidence of completely normal dreaming among the clinical cases is consistent with the observations reported above and in the literature; it suggests that dreaming depends on a network of anatomical structures that are widely distributed in the brain.

Anatomical Correlates of Normal Dreaming

Eight normal dreamers had diffuse or nonlocalizable lesions. In the 16 focal cases, a significant lateralizing tendency emerged. Twelve cases (85.7% of the effective sample) had unilateral left hemisphere lesions, whereas only 1 case (6.3%) had a unilateral right-sided lesion. The incidence of normal dreaming was therefore significantly higher with left than with right hemisphere lesions, $\chi^2 = 8.93$, $p < .005$ (see Table 24.2 & Fig. 24.1). (Two of the 16 focal cases had cerebellar lesions and were therefore excluded from the laterality analysis. The remaining focal case had a bilateral lesion.) This provides further evidence for the notion that the right hemisphere is relatively dominant for

TABLE 24.1

Cases with Normal (Entirely Unchanged) Dreaming

Patient No.	Age/Sex	Lesion	Relevant Symptoms and Signs
6	13-yr M.	L. lat. fro-temp. (subdural empyema)	Fluent aphasia
29	54-yr M.	Cerebellum (metastatic carcinoma)	Hypoarousal, disorientation
39	26-yr F.	L. lat fro. (L. int. carot. art. aneurysmal rupture with L. mid. cereb. art. 2° infarct)	Nonfluent aphasia
45	32-yr M.	L. lat. fro-par. subdural hemorrhage (low-velocity closed head injury)	Short-term (modality nonspecific) memory deficit, adynamia, disinhibition, motor perseveration, nonfluent aphasia
50	55-yr M.	L. med. par. (meningioma)	Partial (simple) epilepsy, short-term (verbal) memory deficit, fluent aphasia, constructional apraxia, hemispatial (right) neglect
51	60-yr F.	L. lat. fro. (meningioma)	Perseveration
60	21-yr M.	Diffuse (high velocity closed head injury)	Disorientation, long-term (modality nonspecific) memory deficit, adynamia, disinhibition, ideomotor apraxia, visual (apperceptive) agnosia, alexia, agraphia, constructional apraxia, hemispatial (left) neglect, anosognosia
94	38-yr M.	L. lat. fro-temp. (post. comm. art. aneurysmal rupture with L. mid. cereb. art. 2° infarction)	Short-term (modality nonspecific) memory deficit, adynamia, disinhibition, problem-solving deficit
96	28-yr M.	Diffuse (high velocity closed head injury)	Nil
101	38-yr F.	Nonlocalizable [no visible focal lesion] (ant. comm. art. aneurysmal rupture)	Adynamia, disinhibition
109	25-yr M.[a]	Diffuse (high velocity closed head injury)	Adynamia, acalculia
122	28-yr M.	Non-localizable (AVM draining from R. mid. cereb. art.)	Partial (complex) epilepsy, hypoarousal

TABLE 24.1
(Continued)

Patient No.	Age/Sex	Lesion	Relevant Symptoms and Signs
127	23-yr M.	Diffuse (high velocity closed head injury)	Disinhibition
141	51-yr F.	L. lat. fro. (mucocoele)	Perseveration, problem-solving deficit
151	21-yr M.	Cerebellum (abscess)	Nil
159	18-yr M.	R. lat. fro. (subdural empyema)	[Truncated neuropsychological assessment]
161	28-yr M.	L. lat. fro. (low velocity open head injury)	Perseveration
178	25-yr M.	Bilat. par., R. med. occip-temp-limbic (low velocity open head injury with 2° intracerebral hemorrhage)	Ideomotor apraxia, agraphia, finger agnosia, constructional apraxia, neglect
180	34-yr M.	L. occip-par. (open head injury with abscess formation)	Nil
206	22-yr M.[b]	L. lat. fro. (L. mid. cereb. art. thrombosis)	Limb-kinetic apraxia, nonfluent aphasia, agraphia, alexia, acalculia
233	70-yr M.	Bilat. ant. fro. (high velocity open head injury)	Disorientation, long-term (modality nonspecific) memory deficit, adynamia, disinhibition, perseveration and non fluency, problem-solving deficit, hemineglect, anosognosia
274	24-yr M.	Nonlocalizable [no visible focal lesion] (low velocity closed head injury)	Partial (complex) epilepsy, short-term (visual specific) memory deficit
287	48-yr F.[a]	Diffuse (unclassified calcific process)	Visual (apperceptive) agnosia, fluent aphasia, alexia, agraphia, neglect
323	14-yr M.[a]	Nonlocalizable (intraventricular hemorrhage with hydrocephalus)	Hypoarousal

[a]Sinistral or ambidextral patient.
[b]Case 12.

221

TABLE 24.2
Laterality of Lesions in Cases With Normal Dreaming[a]

	Laterality of Lesion		
Dreaming	Left	Right	Bilat
Normal (unchanged)	12	1	1
Abnormal (changed)	56	60	32

[a]Excludes diffuse and nonlateralizable cases.

TABLE 24.3
Dorsolateral Frontal Lesions in Cases With Normal Dreaming[a]

	Lateral Frontal Lesion	
Dreaming	Present	Absent
Normal (unchanged)	12	4
Abnormal (changed)	56	98

[a]Excludes diffuse and nonlocalizable cases.

dreaming (see prior discussion). Normal dreaming also correlated significantly with dorsolateral frontal lobe involvement. Twelve of the 16 focal cases (75% of the effective sample) had dorsolateral frontal lobe lesions. The incidence of dorsolateral frontal lesions among focal cases with abnormal dreaming was 36.4%. This is significantly lower than it was among normal dreamers, $\chi^2 = 9.02, p < .005$ (see Table 24.3 & Fig. 24.1).

Clinical Correlates of Normal Dreaming

A variety of neurobehavioral symptoms and signs—notably aphasia ($N = 12$), problem-solving deficits ($N = 17$), and perseveration ($N = 18$)—were prominent among patients with normal dreaming, but these correlations did not reach statistical significance, $p > .1$. These correlations are consistent with my observations (reported in chapter 14) to the effect that hemiplegic patients experience normal movement in their dreams and nonfluent aphasic patients speak normally in their dreams. Evidently motor imagery in dreams is not dependent upon cortical (i.e., dorsolateral frontal) motor systems.

Theoretical Speculations on Normal Dreaming

These findings suggest that the dorsolateral frontal region (and perhaps the left dorsolateral prefrontal region in particular) plays no essential role in the normal dream process. This is compatible with the observations reported in

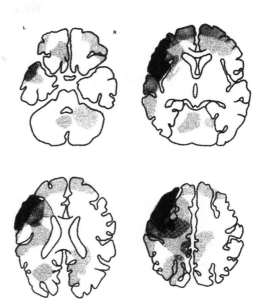

FIG. 24.1. Combined facsimile of CT scans in 15 cases of normal (entirely unchanged) dreaming, illustrating the relative preponderance of left hemispheric and frontal convexity lesions (excludes the scan of Patient No. 150, which could not be meaningfully represented).

chapter 16 to the effect that frontal white-matter lesions disrupt dreaming whereas frontal convexity lesions do not (cf. Figs. 16.2 & 16.3). However, it contradicts the hypothesis of Kerr and Foulkes (1981) to the effect that the narrative structure of dreaming is contributed by the left frontal lobe. In fact it seems that the left prefrontal lobe—the part of the brain that is most concerned with narrative structure—is precisely the part of the brain that is least essential to the dream process. Considering the erratic narrative structure of most dreams, this is perhaps not surprising.

This reminds us that dreams differ from other forms of visual imagery in many important respects, and it suggests that some of the striking differences between dreaming and waking cognition might be explained by the lack of any substantial contribution to dreaming by the dorsolateral prefrontal convexity. More than any other region, the prefrontal convexity provides thinking with its characteristic propositional structure, logical coherence, and volitional purpose. This applies especially to the left prefrontal convexity, which imbues thinking with the predicative and abstract properties of language. In Kosslyn's (1994) model of mental imagery, the prefrontal convexity is the location of the property lookup systems, which constrain perceptual possibilities on the basis of established knowledge of the world. In fact, the prefrontal convexity is involved in the planning, regulation, and verification of voluntary motor activity in general, and for this reason it is often conceptualized as the upper end of the motor system—the gateway from thought to action (Luria, 1980; Passingham, 1993). If there is indeed a "scene of action of waking ideational life," as Fechner (1889, pp. 520–521) and Freud (1900/1953, p. 536) suggested (see chapter 15), then the left prefrontal convexity would be the best candidate for the job. The lack of a substantial contribution by this brain region to the dream process would greatly undermine adaptive mentation in dreams, it would release perceptual imagery from knowledge based constraints, and it would obstruct the passage from thinking to motor activity. These considerations go a long way towards explaining some of the striking differences between dreaming and waking imagery. In our dreams we all appear to suffer, not only from the confusional state associated with anterior limbic lesions (cf. chapter 21), but also from the dorsolateral variant of the frontal lobe syndrome.

Inconsistent with the formulation that motor activity in dreams is blocked by dorsolateral frontal inhibition is the fact that pyramidal tract neurons discharge at high levels during REM sleep, and that muscular activity is blocked at the spinal level during REM through pontine–medullary inhibition of alpha motoneurons (Pompeiano, 1979). However, the motor disorder in the dorsolateral prefrontal syndrome is not characterized by paralysis; it is characterized by a "curious dissociation between knowing and doing" (Teuber, 1964). These patients can move normally, but they cannot implement their volitional intentions. Moreover, if dreams occur outside of REM sleep—as I argue they can and often do—then an alternative mechanism is required to explain the inhibition of volitional action during NREM dreams. Inhibition of the prefrontal region could be this alternative mechanism. If this speculation is correct, one could say that the prefrontal convexity is inhibited during dreams and that the central scene of action of ideational life shifts to the inferior parietal and medial occipito-temporal regions. Presumably the frontal convexity is inhibited during dreams because volitional motor activity would disturb sleep. (The mechanism of prefrontal inhibition might be linked with the mediobasal frontal and frontal-limbic mechanisms discussed in chapters 19 and 21.) This suggests that anything that disinhibits the prefrontal convexity during sleep would undermine the function of dreams. Conversely, damage to the prefrontal convexity itself should have no appreciable effect on dreaming. This is precisely what I found.

25

Summary of Results and Nosological Conclusions

This study began with the observation that certain neurological patients complained of specific changes in their dreams, the onset of which they dated to the beginning of their illness. I said at the outset that I considered this observation to be a simple clinical fact, as deserving of serious attention as any other. I argued that there was no a priori reason to doubt the veracity of these patients' reports nor the reality of the experiences they described. I suggested that we should treat their reports as we would any other clinical complaint, and then attempt to discover whether or not they displayed a degree of uniformity and whether or not typical subjective descriptions co-occurred with particular clinical presentations and pathological–anatomical findings. Only then, I argued, would it be possible for us to form a considered opinion on the scientific value of such reports.

In order to prepare the ground for some conclusions in this regard, I briefly summarize the results of this study in relation to the pertinent questions.

DID THE REPORTED SUBJECTIVE CHANGES
IN DREAMING DISPLAY A DEGREE OF UNIFORMITY?

Four major changes in dreaming, consistent with those reported in the previous literature, were observed in the present study. From a series of 332 cases with cerebral lesions, 2 patients reported cessation of visual dream imagery (although this was restricted to the kinematic aspect of visual imagery in one case), 112 patients reported global cessation of dreaming, 9 patients reported (or appeared to experience) confusion between dreams and reality, and 9 patients reported recurring nightmares.

Because some patients in the original sample were unable to provide unequivocal descriptions of the relevant aspects of their dreams, the incidences of these disorders were calculated as percentages of the number of cases who adequately described the aspect of dreaming in question, rather than of the number of cases in the series as a whole. This approach yielded the following figures; 1.1% of the effective sample reported cessation or restriction of visual dream imagery, 34.9% reported global cessation of dreaming, 5.3% reported varying degrees of confusion between dreams and reality, and 7.9% reported recurring nightmares. There was a degree of overlap between the last two groups, that is, some patients reported both dream–reality confusion and recurring nightmares (or, at least, both increased frequency and vivacity of dreaming and increased frequency of nightmares). There were suggestive grounds for a further division of these cases into clinical and anatomical subgroups, but due to the paucity of suitable material this was not possible.

The major changes in dreaming just enumerated were reported far more frequently in the cerebrally impaired population than they were among the 29 control subjects. In fact the incidence among controls of all but one of these disorders was 0%, the exception being global cessation of dreaming, which was reported by a single control subject—a case of hysteria.

The remaining cases in the original series did not describe completely normal dreaming. They reported a range of subtle changes in their dreams, some of which were qualitatively similar to the gross changes already described. These were not clinical disorders of dreaming that were clearly recognizable as such by both patient and investigator alike. Instead they seemed to represent normative tendencies in the direction of those disorders, that is, relative changes in aspects of dream phenomenology that were grossly affected in the clinical disorders. Where other links could be established between these normative changes and the full-blown disorders, these changes were described as subclinical variants of the disorders.

This approach yielded the following seven groups: Thirty-one percent of the effective sample reported reduced vivacity of visual dream-imagery (a subclinical variant of cessation of visual dream-imagery), 38.2% and 19.5% reported reduced frequency of dreaming and reduced narrative complexity and emotional intensity of dreaming, respectively (possible subclinical variants of global cessation of dreaming), 26.7% and 19.9% reported increased vivacity of dreaming and increased frequency of dreaming, respectively (possible subclinical variants of the confusion between dreams and reality), 14.9% reported increased frequency of (nonrecurring) nightmares (a possible subclinical variant of recurring nightmares), and 44.3% reported reduced duration of dreams (a phenomenon without apparent links to any of the established disorders). There was considerable overlap between most of these phenomena, particularly with regard to vivacity of dreaming, frequency of dreaming, and nightmares. In addition, changes of this (relative) type were commonly reported by control subjects. Only reduced vivacity of visual dream-imagery (which was reported by 15.7% of controls), increased frequency of nonrecurring nightmares (reported by 3.5% of controls), and decreased duration of dreams (reported by 11.1% of controls), were significantly more common in the cerebrally impaired population than they were in the control group. Changes of the subclinical type are therefore of limited diagnostic value, although they are of scientific interest.

Apart from the specific visual changes already mentioned, no other modality-specific or material-specific disorders of dreaming were observed in the present study. On the contrary, a number of patients with specific deficits in various modalities (ranging from paraplegia and hemiplegia to cortical blindness and aphasia) reported a positive preservation of their impaired functions in their dreams.

Finally, one form of dreaming that occurred significantly more commonly among the control subjects than the cerebrally impaired patients was completely normal dreaming. Of the controls, 34.5% reported no changes in their dreams since the onset of their physical symptoms. However, completely normal dreaming was also reported by 8.6% of the cerebrally impaired patients.

DID THE TYPICAL DESCRIPTIONS OF SUBJECTIVE CHANGES IN DREAMING CO-OCCUR WITH SPECIFIC PATHOLOGICAL-ANATOMICAL FINDINGS?

The four major disorders of dreaming described previously all correlated with specific sites or types of lesion. This was not the case for the subclinical changes in dreaming.

Cessation of Visual Dream Imagery

In both of our cases who reported cessation of visual dream-imagery (or an aspect of visual dream-imagery) the medial occipito-temporal region was involved. The lesion was bilateral in the case with complete cessation of visual dream imagery and right-sided in the case with akinematic dream imagery. No cases with bilateral lesions in the medial occipito-temporal area reported preservation of visual dream imagery, although a number of them did report global cessation of dreaming (which necessarily implies cessation of visual dream imagery). The same general anatomical region was implicated in the subclinical form of this disorder, namely the limbic–occipital axis. (The limbic lobe discriminated more than the occipital lobe did.) Most of these lesions were unilateral.

Global Cessation of Dreaming

The large group of patients who reported global cessation of dreaming fell into two distinct anatomical subgroups. The majority of these cases had parietal lobe lesions (or space-occupying lesions in close proximity to the parietal lobe). There was no lateral bias between the hemispheres. The others had deep bifrontal lesions (or space-occupying deep frontal lesions). Further study of selected cases in these subgroups suggested that involvement of the inferior parietal lobule and the white matter immediately anterior to the frontal horns of the lateral ventricles, respectively, might be the critical lesion sites.

However, a substantial number of other patients with lesions in these supposedly critical regions reported preserved dreaming. A possible explanation for this anomaly was found in the further observation that dreaming and nondreaming patients in these lesion groups were significantly different in terms of the chronicity of their neurological illness. A shorter period of time had elapsed since the last neurological insult in the cases that reported cessation of dreaming than in those who reported preserved dreaming. This suggested that the factor of recovery might have played an important role in the latter group. This possibility was supported by a study of the natural history of global cessation of dreaming in selected patients. The majority of nondreaming (parietal) patients that were followed up recovered within a period of 1 year. The small group of patients that did not recover within 1 year were marked by substantial right hemisphere involvement. (The natural history of cessation of dreaming with bifrontal lesions could not be adequately characterized, due to a paucity of such cases. The possibility that different mechanisms applied in the bifrontal subgroup therefore could not be excluded.)

For theoretical reasons, we investigated the possibility that global cessation of dreaming might also be associated with deep brainstem lesions. All of the patients in our series with deep brainstem lesions ($N = 18$) reported preservation of dreaming. The question then arose as to whether or not cessation of dreaming in brainstem cases had perhaps been masked by the fact that many of them suffered from hydrocephalus, and were therefore classified as diffuse.

This possibility was excluded by obtaining dream reports from a small sample of hydrocephalic patients with primary brainstem lesions before and after VP shunting (a surgical procedure that relieves the hydrocephalus but has no effect upon the primary lesion). All of these patients reported recovery of dreaming within 4 weeks of surgery. We concluded that the cessation of dreaming had been caused by the telencephalic (hydrocephalic) component of the lesions in all cases.

Questions surrounding reduced frequency of dreaming and reduced narrative complexity and emotional intensity of dreaming were not resolved conclusively. Reduced frequency of dreaming was significantly correlated with bilateral lesions and, less significantly, with right hemisphere lesions. There was no significant relationship between reduced frequency of dreaming on the one hand and parietal or frontal lesions on the other. This suggested that reduced frequency of dreaming should not be considered to be a subclinical variant of global cessation of dreaming. However, in those cases in which the natural history of global cessation of dreaming was documented, the patients invariably reported reduced frequency of dreaming upon recovery. This suggested that reduced frequency of dreaming is a chronic form of global cessation of dreaming (which is an acute condition). As regards reduced narrative complexity and emotional intensity of dreaming, the weight of the evidence went against the notion that this was a subclinical variant of global cessation of dreaming. There was no significant relationship between this condition and parietal or frontal lesions. However reduced narrative complexity and emotional intensity of dreaming was (modestly) correlated with left hemisphere lesions in general. Reduced duration of dreams did not correlate with any particular lesion site.

Confusion Between Dreams and Reality

The confusion between dreams and reality, by contrast, had definite localizing significance. Nine of the 10 patients in this clinical group had lesions in the anterior limbic region, although these lesions were not homogenous. (The 10th case had a posterior limbic lesion, but the clinical picture was significantly different in that case.) In some of these cases the medial frontal cortex was involved, in some the anterior cingulate gyrus, in some the basal forebrain nuclei, and in some the antero-medial aspect of the thalamus; however, no single structure was involved in all cases. It seemed likely that an anatomical subdivision of the cases in this group would have been possible if more precise pathological–anatomical material had been available. The putative subclinical variants of this disorder (increased frequency and/or vivacity of dreaming) possessed no localizing significance at all. However, the incidence of epilepsy was significantly raised in these cases. This (together with the fact that many of these patients reported frequent, vivid nightmares) suggested an overlap between the syndrome of dream–reality confusion and the syndrome of recurring nightmares.

Recurring Nightmares

Recurring nightmares had the least robust localizing significance among the four major disorders of dreaming that were identified in the present study. The radiological evidence suggested that recurring nightmares were commonly, but by no means always, associated with structural lesions of the limbic system (in either hemisphere). The physiological and clinical evidence suggested that limbic–temporal epileptiform discharge (in either hemisphere) was highly characteristic of this group. However, seizure activity was not conclusively demonstrated in some cases. In those cases the dream disorder was marked by increased frequency and vivacity of nightmares rather than by recurring nightmares sensu strictori. This confirmed the overlap between the present syndrome and the previous one.

Normal Dreaming

I mentioned already that completely normal dreaming correlated with the absence of cerebral pathology. However, within the small group of cerebrally impaired patients that also reported completely normal dreaming, dorsolateral frontal lesions were common. In addition, there was a significant (leftward) lateralizing tendency in this group.

DID THE TYPICAL SUBJECTIVE CHANGES IN DREAMING CO-OCCUR WITH CHARACTERISTIC CLINICAL PRESENTATIONS?

The four major disorders of dreaming just enumerated all correlated with characteristic clinical presentations. This did not apply to the subclinical changes in dreaming.

Cessation of Visual Dream-Imagery

Cessation or restriction of visual dream-imagery was associated with visual irreminiscence. Moreover, the quality of the irreminiscence directly paralleled the quality of the dream imagery disorder. The other classical Charcot–Wilbrand symptoms (prosopagnosia, topographical disorder, and visual agnosia) were present in our single case with complete cessation of visual dream-imagery but not in the case with partial cessation of visual dream-imagery (loss of kinematic imagery). The same applied to hypoemotionality. Neither of our 2 cases had achromatopsia.

Global Cessation of Dreaming

The classical Charcot–Wilbrand symptoms were also present in a small number of patients with global cessation of dreaming, which necessarily implied cessation of visual dreaming. In this respect, the syndromes of nonvisual dreaming and global cessation of dreaming appeared to overlap. Similar considerations applied to visuospatial short-term memory disorder, which was a significant correlate of both syndromes. In addition to visuospatial short-term memory disorder, global cessation of dreaming in cases with parietal leasions was correlated with right–left disorientation and finger agnosia (and with Gerstmann's syndrome as a whole). In the bifrontal cases global cessation of dreaming correlated significantly with adynamia, disinhibition, and perseveration. Loss of dreaming was not significantly correlated with aphasia or amnesia (nor with anosognosia). Interestingly, however, there was a significant relationship with subjectively disturbed sleep. There were no regular neuropsychological correlates of reduced frequency of dreams, reduced narrative complexity and emotional intensity of dreams, or reduced duration of dreams.

Confusion Between Dreams and Reality

Confusion between dreams and reality was associated with a wide range of neurobehavioral disorders, such as fantasy–reality confusion, confabulatory amnesia, reduplicative paramnesia, formed visual hallucinations, anosognosia, and hemineglect. The common denominator in these disorders appeared to be defective reality monitoring. Dream–reality confusion was sometimes complicated by executive disorders, cerebral blindness, and affective disinhibition, but the latter symptoms did not appear to be essential elements of the syndrome.

Normal Dreaming

Normal dreaming was linked with a number of symptoms and signs typically associated with (left) dorsolateral frontal lesions (aphasia, defective problem-solving, perseveration) but these associations did not reach statistical significance.

CONCLUSIONS

We are now in a position to form an opinion on the question that was posed at the outset. In my view, the summarized findings justify the conclusion that there are four major changes in dreaming that deserve to be treated as valid neuropsychological syndromes. These phenomena are no different in their essence from the classical aphasias, apraxias, and agnosias. Changes in dreaming differ from the aphasias, apraxias, and agnosias in that the neuroscientific investigator cannot observe them directly. With the exception of some cases of dream–reality confusion, we were wholly dependent on the patients' description of the phenomena that were the primary object of this investigation. However, the veracity of the patients' reports in regard to the four major disorders mentioned earlier was supported by three objective considerations; (a) different patients independently described the same subjective experiences; (b) the typical descriptions of subjective changes in dreaming correlated with specific pathological–anatomical findings; and (c) the typical subjective changes correlated with characteristic clinical presentations. The objective reality of the syndromes in question was further confirmed by the fact that they were broadly consistent with similar observations reported by independent investigators in a widely dispersed body of literature over a period of more than 100 years.

The major disorders of dreaming that I suggest should be treated as valid neuropsychological syndromes were surrounded by an indefinite number of subtle changes in dreaming that do not warrant the same status. Although many cerebrally impaired patients reported these changes in response to direct questions about aspects of their dreams, many control patients without cerebral impairment reported the same changes. These reports did not correlate reliably with established neurobehavioral symptoms and signs. In addition, although some of them correlated statistically with broad pathological–anatomical categories (such as left vs. right hemisphere lesions), the site of the lesions in individual cases could not be reliably predicted from the subjective reports. Such probabilistic correlations are of scientific interest, but of little clinical value.

These relative deviations from normal dreaming probably represent subclinical tendencies in the direction of the major disorders of dreaming in some cases, but they also represent nonspecific reactions to cerebral pathology, as well as purely functional effects in other cases. They therefore fall somewhere between the major changes in dreaming and completely normal dreaming. The major changes are caused by damage to parts of the brain that are presumed to be centrally involved in the dream process. Completely normal dreaming presumably occurs when these critical parts of the brain are completely spared. At best, the subtle changes that lie between these two extremes reflect the influence of brain structures and functions that are peripherally involved in the process of dreaming. However, they also reflect other influences, such as nonspecific effects and purely functional factors. These phenomena are therefore of little nosological value.

I can only draw reliable nosological conclusions with regard to the four major disorders of dreaming mentioned above. These conclusions are based on the results of the present study, when they are combined with the generic picture that emerged from the existing literature.

The Syndrome of Nonvisual Dreaming

The cardinal element of this syndrome is a loss of visual dream imagery, or an aspect of visual dream imagery, in the context of otherwise normal dreaming. It arises exclusively from damage to the medial occipito-temporal region. There are at least four variants:

Complete Cessation of Visual Dream-Imagery. This variant arises from bilateral medial occipito-temporal lesions and was first described by Charcot (1883). It is typically accompanied by complete visual irreminiscence and visuospatial short-term memory deficit. Commonly it also co-occurs with pro-sopagnosia and some form of visual agnosia, topographical agnosia, and/or topographical amnesia. However, the latter symptoms are not invariable correlates. Complete cessation of visual dream-imagery might also be accompanied by hypoemotionality.

Cessation of Facial Dream-Imagery. This variant, which arises from lesions within the same general area (presumably more circumscribed, involving the fusiform gyrus bilaterally), was first described by Tzavaras (1967). It is typically accompanied by facial irreminiscence and prosopagnosia. The former symptom is probably an invariable correlate of cessation of facial dream-imagery.

Cessation of Color Dream-Imagery. The third variant arises from lesions within the same general area (presumably lying more posteriorly in the fusiform gyrus bilaterally). This variant, first described by Sacks and Wasserman (1987), is typically accompanied by chromatic irreminiscence and central achromatopsia. The former symptom is probably an invariable correlate.

Cessation of Kinematic Dream-Imagery. The last variant arises from lesions in the same general area, but the lesion involves only the right hemisphere. This variant was first described by Kerr and Foulkes (1981). It is typically accompanied by impoverished kinematic imagery (kinematic irreminiscence) and visuospatial short-term memory deficit. The former symptom is probably an invariable correlate. Cessation of kinematic dream-imagery co-occurs with a reduction of visual dream-imagery in general.

The Syndrome of Global Cessation of Dreaming

The cardinal element of this syndrome is a total loss of dreaming. Loss of dreaming is an acute symptom that typically recovers within 1 year. However, some cases, usually with extensive right hemisphere damage, do not recover within that period (if ever). Global cessation of dreaming is a frequent concomitant of hydrocephalus, and it may be useful in the clinical diagnosis and monitoring of that condition. Recovery is typically followed by decreased frequency of dreaming. The loss of dreaming occurs in the context of two (or three) distinct syndromes.

First, it occurs with parietal (probably inferior parietal) lesions of either hemisphere. It also occurs with lesions in close proximity to this area (the region of the parieto–occipito–temporal junction). Global cessation of dreaming within the context of this syndrome was first reported by Wilbrand (1887), and more certainly, by Müller (1892). In cases with left parietal involvement, global cessation of dreaming co-occurs with elements of Gerstmann's syndrome and with visuospatial short-term memory deficits. In cases of right parietal lesions, it co-occurs with various apractagnosic symptoms and signs, but only visuospatial short-term memory deficit is an invariable feature.

Second, global cessation of dreaming occurs with deep bifrontal lesions. The lesion involves the white matter immediately surrounding the anterior horns of the lateral ventricles. Global cessation of dreaming in the context of this syndrome was first reported by Frank (1946), who described it as a common consequence of prefrontal leukotomy. In the case of bifrontal lesions, loss of dreaming co-occurs with adynamia, disinhibition, and perseveration.

The Symptom-Complex of Dream–Reality Confusion

The cardinal element in this complex of symptoms is a difficulty in distinguishing dreams from reality. This difficulty is typically (but not invariably) accompanied by an increase in the frequency of dreams. Continuation of dreams across intervening periods of wakefulness is a closely related symptom. It can also be associated with increased incidence of nightmares. Confusion between dreams and reality was first described by Whitty and Lewin (1957). This complex of symptoms occurs with anterior limbic (limbic–frontal) lesions. Subtle changes of this type can be an early sign of pathology in the region of the third ventricle (e.g., colloid cyst). The changes in dreaming are typically accompanied by various manifestations of defective reality monitoring. They also commonly co-occur with executive disorders, affective disinhibition, and cerebral blindness, all of which may exacerbate the primary disorder of reality monitoring. There are possible grounds for a fractionation of this symptom-complex into a number of more specific syndromes, which cannot as yet be specified.

The Syndrome of Recurring Nightmares

This syndrome is characterized by recurring nightmares or by frequent nightmares with a repetitive theme. The nightmares are often accompanied by increased frequency and vivacity of dreaming. This syndrome occurs with temporal–limbic seizure activity. In verified cases of epilepsy, recurring night-mares may be considered to be complex-partial seizure equivalents. In the absence of independent corroboration, however, recurring nightmares should not be considered pathognomonic of epilepsy. In cases with nondischarging lesions, the nightmares are less stereotyped, and the clinical picture overlaps with that described previously under the heading of dream–reality confusion. Epilepsy was linked with recurring nightmares by various authors since ancient times, but a causal link was first established by Penfield and Erickson (1941).

Nomenclature

It is clear from the foregoing remarks that the classic nosological concept in the neuropsychology of dreams, the Charcot–Wilbrand syndrome, is no longer tenable. The Charcot–Wilbrand concept conflates at least two distinct syndromes, each of which admits of further subdivisions. It is also clear that a number of distinctive changes in dreaming exist that have nothing to do with the Charcot–Wilbrand syndrome. These other symptoms have been given different descriptive epithets by different authors, some of which are rather unwieldy. I would therefore like to propose a simplified nomenclature for these disorders.

If we replace the descriptive phrase *loss of dreaming* with a single word, *anoneira* — which is the privative form of the Greek noun ὄυειρα (dreams) — then the following simple names are generated for the major disorders of dreaming that we have identified.

1. For the condition that I have been calling *nonvisual dreaming, cessation or restriction of visual dream-imagery*, and the like, the term *visual anoneira* (or *Charcot's anoneira*) seems appropriate. If this term is reserved for complete cessation of visual dream imagery — in other words for Charcot's variant of the Charcot–Wilbrand syndrome — then the following three terms seem appropriate for the more circumscribed variants of this syndrome: *facial anoneira*, *color anoneira*, and *kinematic anoneira*. Similar descriptive terms can be used for additional variants of this syndrome if they are described in future.

2. For the condition that I have been calling *loss of dreaming, global cessation of dreaming*, and *Wilbrand's variant of the Charcot–Wilbrand syndrome*, the term *global anoneira* (or *Wilbrand's anoneira*) seems appropriate.

3. The diverse phenomena previously designated by phrases such as *increased frequency and vivacity of dreaming, confusion between dreams and reality, vivid daydreaming*, etc., cannot be subsumed under a single term. However, at the risk of introducing another cacophonous word into neuropsychological nosography, the designation *anoneirognosis* seems appropriate for the core feature of this symptom-complex.

4. There is no compelling reason to replace the simple descriptive phrase *recurring nightmares* by another term.

In the next and final chapter I return to a speculative line of thought and attempt to integrate the theoretical inferences that I have made throughout this book on the basis of the clinico-anatomical findings. In constructing a speculative model such as this, I hope that I am paving the way for systematic experimental research into some of the more interesting and important questions that have arisen out of this clinical-descriptive investigation into the neuropsychology of dreams.

26

Final Theoretical Remarks: A Model of the Normal Dream Process

The findings of this research suggest that the following parts of the human brain are centrally implicated in the normal process of dreaming: the limbic system, the medial occipito-temporal cortex, the inferior parietal convexity, and the connections between mediobasal frontal cortex and brainstem and diencephalic–limbic structures. Damage to these regions of the brain produces definite and specific effects on the subjective experience of dreams. On the other hand, the following parts of the nervous system appear to be inessential to the normal dream process, or even to be inhibited during dreaming: the spinal and peripheral sensory-motor systems, primary (idiotypic) sensory-motor cortex, unimodal (homotypical) isocortex outside of the visual sphere, and dorsolateral prefrontal cortex. Damage to these structures has no appreciable effect upon the subjective experience of dreams. The following formulation can be advanced on the basis of these findings: the essential nature of the dream process is determined by the concerted functioning of the former group of structures in the absence of a contribution from the latter group of structures. The role of the remaining regions of the brain is unclear, but it seems likely that activation or inhibition of these regions does not play a fundamental role in the normal process of dreaming.

COMPLEMENTARY EVIDENCE
FROM A POSITRON EMISSION TOMOGRAPHY (PET) STUDY

These conclusions, based on the clinico-anatomical evidence, are broadly consistent with the available PET evidence. I am aware of only a single study of regional metabolic rates in the human brain during dreaming versus dreamless sleep. Heiss, Pawlik, Herholz, Wagner, & Weinhard (1985) compared the cerebral glucose uptake of 3 subjects during dreamless sleep with that of a single subject who experienced "an extended frightening dream with intimidating figures moving around and towards him" (p. 363). According to this study, the following parts of the brain were significantly more active during dreaming than dreamless sleep: limbic and paralimbic cortex, medial occipital cortex, inferior parietal cortex, and superior frontal cortex. In addition, basal frontal white matter was more active during dreaming than posterior (occipito-parietal) white matter.

The only significant discrepancy between these findings and our clinico-anatomical findings pertains to the superior frontal cortex. According to our findings, superior frontal cortex should be inactive, or inhibited, during dreams. However, according to Heiss et al. (1985), the superior frontal region is highly activated during dreams. There are three possible explanations for this discrepancy.

First, it is impossible to determine whether the increased superior frontal activity observed by Heiss et al. was excitatory or inhibitory. (This interpretive difficulty applies to all PET studies.) If it was inhibitory activation, then increased superior frontal activity would be consistent with our hypothesis to the effect that the prefrontal convexity is inhibited during the process of dreaming.

Second, even if the increased activity was excitatory, it is unclear from the published report whether Heiss et al. observed increased superior *pre*frontal activity or increased activity in Brodmann's area 8 (the frontal eye fields). Although Heiss et al. distinguished between premotor and inferior and superior frontal areas, it is unclear whether they classifed area 8 as premotor or superior frontal (cf. Passingham, 1993, p. 103). If the increased superior frontal activity they observed was in area 8, it might well have been caused by the saccadic eye movements which characterize REM sleep.[1] Increased activity in area 8 would therefore not contradict our hypothesis to the effect that the prefrontal convexity is inactive or inhibited during dreaming sleep, and consequently that volitional motor activity is suppressed.

Third, it is unclear from the published report whether Heiss et al. observed increased activity in the superior medial frontal cortex or the superior dorso-lateral frontal cortex.[2] If the increased activity was in the superior medial frontal region, it could reflect inhibitory activation of the supplementary motor area. This would be consistent with our hypothesis to the effect that the cortical gateway to volitional motor activity is blocked during dreaming.

Nevertheless, whichever of these explanations of the superior frontal activation is correct, in all other respects the findings of Heiss et al. (1985) provide striking confirmation of the results of the present study. Of particular interest in this regard is the fact that the brainstem was far less activated during dreaming than were the cortical regions mentioned at the beginning of this chapter. In fact, the brainstem was not significantly more activated than was the brain as a whole (i.e., than all regions weighted for size). This is consistent with our clinico-anatomical finding to the effect that extensive brainstem lesions are compatible with the preservation of normal dreaming.

THE FUNCTIONAL ANATOMY
OF THE NORMAL DREAM PROCESS

If we accept that the essential nature of the dream process is determined by the concerted functioning of the limbic system, the medial occipito-temporal cortex, the inferior parietal convexity, and the connections between mediobasal frontal cortex and brainstem and diencephalic–limbic structures, then the following question arises: What is the contribution of each of these structures to the process of normal dreaming? Presumably each structure contributes a particular factor to the overall process, and the special contribution of each can be inferred from the manner in which the global process breaks down when that structure is damaged. The inferred factors should also account for the neuro-behavioral changes that regularly co-occur with the various changes in dreaming. On the basis of these classical clinico-anatomical assumptions, the following conclusions are suggested by the results of the present study.

Medial Occipito-Temporal Structures

The medial occipito-temporal region contributes a factor of visual representability to the overall process of dreaming. With damage to this region, dreams occur that are normal in every respect apart from the fact that they are lacking in visual imagery (or aspects of visual imagery). Our analysis of the neuropsychological syndrome associated with nonvisual dreaming (visual anoneira) suggested that modality-specific memory systems were implicated in this aspect of the normal dream process. These systems apparently include the preprocessing, motion relations encoding, and pattern activation modules of Kosslyn's (1994) model, but they also perform some of the functions that

Kosslyn attributed to the visual buffer. The critical components of the cortical visual system probably include V3, V3A, and V4, but not V5 and V6. The role of V2 is questionable. The apparent lack of any contribution by primary visual cortex (V1) to the normal dream process led me to the additional conclusion that the visual imagery of normal dreaming is generated internally rather than externally. That is, I concluded (like almost all other theorists) that dreams are generated by a process of backward projection. This conclusion, together with the circumscribed nature of the dream abnormality associated with this syndrome, suggested that the factor of visual representability should be placed at the terminal end of the dream-generation process.

Inferior Parietal Structures

The inferior parietal region contributes a factor of spatial cognition to the overall process of dreaming. With damage to this region (of either hemisphere) the subjective experience of dreaming stops completely. This suggests that the factor of spatial cognition is fundamental to the overall process of dreaming. Spatial cognition depends on the heteromodal syntheses that are generated in the region of the parieto-occipito-temporal junction. An equivalent function is performed by the associative memory system in Kosslyn's (1994) model:

> The contents of associative memory are more abstract than those of the modality-specific pattern activation subsystems; associative memory not only stores associations among individual perceptual representations, but also organizes "conceptual" information that may not be directly derived from the senses (e.g., mathematical truths, meanings of abstract terms, and so on). (p. 215)

The homologous functional component of the cortical visual system in contemporary models—derived from animal research—is probably area STP (van Essen, Felleman, De Yoe, Olavarria, & Knierim, 1990). However, it is questionable whether a precisely homologous function exists in subhominid primates. In classical cytoarchitectural maps, Brodmann's areas 39 and 40 are critically implicated in heteromodal functions. Our analysis of the neuropsychological syndromes associated with cessation of dreaming (global anoneira) following left and right inferior parietal lesions suggested that different aspects of spatial cognition were contributed by each hemisphere. In cases of right parietal lesions the specific factor appeared to be concrete spatial cognition; in left parietal cases it was symbolic (quasispatial) cognition. Both of these factors were evidently essential for the subjective experience of dreams. However, there was also evidence to suggest that the concrete spatial factor was more essential for normal dream experience than the quasispatial one. I therefore concluded that concrete spatial cognition (the visuospatial scratchpad of Baddeley) is the grounding medium within which the quasispatial (symbolic) operations occur. Combining these inferences with the backward projection formulation outlined previously, I concluded that dreams involve an abstract (symbolic) synthesis of stored representations, which are grounded in heteromodal (spatial) perception before they are projected onto a visual buffer. In this way, in dreams, abstract thinking is converted into concrete perception.

Basal Forebrain Pathways

The connections between mediobasal frontal cortex and brainstem and diencephalic–limbic nuclei contribute a factor of appetitive interest to the overall process of dreaming. With bilateral damage to these connections, dreaming stops completely. Our analysis of the neuropsychological syndrome associated with the bifrontal form of global anoneira, together with the psychosurgical and psychopharmacological evidence, suggested that the "curiosity–interest–expectancy command systems of the brain . . . which instigate goal-seeking behaviors and an organism's appetitive interactions with the world" (Panksepp, 1985, p. 273) are implicated in this aspect of the normal dream process.

> These expectancy circuits include cell groups situated in the ventral tegmental area of Tsai, at the ventromedial transition zone between mesencephalon and diencephalon where the source cells for mesolimbic and mesocortical dopamine systems are situated. . . . The system ascends through the forebrain bundles of the lateral hypothalamus, through basal forebrain areas (synapsing on many systems along the way, including nucleus basalis, bed nucleus of the stria terminalis and orbito-frontal cortical areas). Descending components of this emotive system probably arise from the latter brain areas. (p. 273)

The fact that these circuits "instigate goal-seeking behaviors and an organism's appetitive interactions with the world" (p. 273), the fact that chemical excitation of these circuits stimulates excessive, unusually frequent and vivid dreaming (and vice versa), and the fact that damage to these circuits produces a complete cessation of dreaming together with a "loss of interactive interest in the world" (p. 273), led us to the conclusion that these circuits are centrally implicated in the instigation (rather than the representation) of dreams.

The fact that the descending components of these circuits are also associated with the gating of appetitive drives, and the fact that global anoneira with deep bifrontal lesions is associated not only with adynamic but also with disinhibitory symptomatology, led to the further conclusion that normal dreaming is impossible without the active contribution of some of the highest regulatory and inhibitory mechanisms of the mind.

These conclusions cast doubt on the prevalent notion—based on simple generalizations from the mechanism of REM sleep—that "the primary motivating force for dreaming is not psychological but physiological" (Hobson &

McCarley, 1977, p. 1346). If *psychological forces* are equated with *higher cortical functions*, it is difficult to reconcile the notion that dreams are random physiological events generated by primitive brainstem mechanisms, with our observation that global anoneira is associated not with brainstem lesions resulting in basic arousal disorders, but rather with parietal and frontal lesions resulting in spatial–symbolic and motivational–inhibitory disorders. These observations suggest that dreams are both generated and represented by some of the highest mental mechanisms.

Frontal–Limbic Structures

The frontal–limbic region contributes a factor of mental selectivity to the overall process of dreaming. This region is included in the reflective systems in Johnson's (1991) model of reality monitoring. The critical structures appear to be the anterior cingulate gyrus, anterior and dorsomedial thalamus, basal forebrain nuclei, and medial frontal cortex. Damage to these structures leads to excessive dreaming and dreamlike thinking.

Our analysis of the neuropsychological symptom-complex associated with the cardinal feature of this dream disorder (anoneirognosis) led us to the conclusion that the normal dream mechanism of backward projection is selectively inhibited and regulated by this region. The striking similarities between the state of mind that is generated by frontal–limbic lesions and the state of mind that characterizes normal dreaming suggested that some of the fundamental differences between dreaming and waking cognition are attributable to physiological changes in this region. On this basis, we equated excessive dreaming and dreamlike thinking with an excessive tendency to backward projection. This tendency results in patients experiencing their abstract thoughts as concrete perceptions not only during sleep (and sometimes excessively during sleep) but also during waking cognition. In other words, due to a physiological alteration in the frontal–limbic region during sleep, "the scene of action of dreams is different from that of waking ideational life" (Fechner, 1889, pp. 520–521). Combining this simple inference with the formulations outlined in the foregoing discussion, we may conclude that perceptual attention during waking ideational life is directed selectively towards externally generated perceptions, whereas during sleep it is directed equally towards internally generated perceptions.

It is also possible that frontal–limbic structures selectively inhibit external perceptual attention (primary perceptual cortex) during normal sleep, and that this mechanism breaks down with frontal–limbic lesions. (The anterior cingulate gyrus, in particular, is implicated in most models of selective attention; Mesulam, 1990; Posner & Driver, 1992; Posner & Peterson, 1990.) If we accept the hypothesis that dreams protect sleep against disturbing stimuli (a hypothesis that was tentatively supported by our data) then this further inference would simultaneously explain the increased frequency and vivacity of dreaming that is typically associated with the symptom of anoneirognosis, and the apparent lack of a contribution from primary cortical regions to normal dreaming. The possibility that the frontal–limbic region exerts a similar inhibitory influence over cortical motor systems during normal sleep is supported by the striking fact that lesions in this area (anterior and dorsomedial thalamus) cause some patients to act out their dreams (Gallasi et al., 1992; Julien, Vital, Deleplanque, Lagueny, & Ferrer, 1990; Lugaresi et al., 1986). The inference that the frontal–limbic region inhibits cortical motor systems during normal sleep is consistent with our observation that the dorsolateral frontal region, like the modality-specific perceptual zones outside the (secondary) visual sphere, make no obvious contribution to the normal experience of dreaming.

The lack of a contribution by this region (and especially by the left prefrontal convexity) further accounts for the many differences between dreaming and waking imagery. In Kosslyn's (1994) model of waking imagery, the prefrontal convexity is the location of the property lookup systems, which constrain perceptual possibilities on the basis of established knowledge of the world. The prefrontal convexity is also the scene of action of intentional activity in general. For this reason the prefrontal convexity is often conceptualized as the upper end of the motor system—the gateway from thought to action. The lack of a substantial contribution by this brain region to the dream process greatly undermines adaptive thinking in dreams, it releases perceptual imagery from knowledge-based constraints, and it blocks the passage from intentions to motor actions. Combining these considerations with our conclusion to the effect that perceptual attention during waking ideational life is directed selectively toward real external perceptions whereas during sleep it uncritically accepts internal hallucinatory perceptions, we may similarly conclude that motor intentionality during waking ideational life is directed selectively towards real external goals, whereas during dreams it is discharged uncritically in internal hallucinatory representations. This explains my observation to the effect that M1 lesions apparently do not have any effect on motor activity in dreams; in dreams one represents oneself doing various things but one is not actually doing anything. Dream actions are not actions; they are representations of actions derived from past experience.

Temporal–Limbic Structures

Excitatory activity in the limbic system contributes a factor of affective arousal to the overall process of dreaming. Seizure activity in this region leads to frequent and recurring nightmares. Our analysis of this syndrome (and the dreamy states associated with temporal–limbic seizures during waking ideational life) suggested that excessive limbic discharge can overwhelm the inhibitory and regulatory frontal–limbic backward projection mechanisms described previously. This results in excessive dreaming and dreamlike thinking, similar to that which occurs with frontal–limbic lesions.

The fact that dreams associated with limbic seizures are invariably marked by anxiety reflects the specific involvement of temporal–limbic structures in these nightmares, the stimulation of which is known to generate fear and anxiety. It might also reflect a failure of the normal function of dreams, in that nocturnal seizure activity overwhelms the sleep-protection mechanisms described earlier.[3] The recurring content of these nightmares reflects the specificity of some of the mental mechanisms that initiate dreaming. The demonstrable fact that temporal–limbic mechanisms cause dreams (albeit dreams of a particular type) suggests that this region should be placed at the initiating end of the dream process.

This adds further weight to our conclusion that dreams are not initiated (or not exclusively initiated) by the brainstem mechanisms that initiate REM sleep. The clinical fact that some dreams are initiated by limbic seizure activity (which typically occurs during NREM sleep), combined with the statistical fact that other dreams (perhaps most dreams) occur during REM sleep (and therefore apparently are initiated by brainstem arousal mechanisms), combined with the psychopharmacological fact that stimulation of dopaminergic appetitive circuits can stimulate excessive dreaming, suggests that anything that arouses the sleeping brain can initiate the process of dreaming. The additional fact that ablation of the latter circuits prevents all dreaming, whereas ablation of temporal–limbic and brainstem tissues apparently does not have this effect, further suggests that the frontal dopaminergic circuits are the final common pathway for the diverse arousing stimuli that can initiate the process of dreaming. Presumably, if these appetitive-interest circuits are not activated (or not activated above a certain threshold) then dreaming will not ensue.

A SPECULATIVE MODEL
OF THE NORMAL DREAM PROCESS

I can now synthesize the foregoing conclusions in the form of a speculative model of the normal dream process: Any arousing stimulus capable of activating appetitive interest, which under normal circumstances would lead to the execution of a motor act (or perhaps even to a sufficiently developed intention to execute such an act), cannot run its conventional course during sleep. This is because volitional motor activity and the wish to sleep are mutually incompatible states. For this reason the sleeping brain is equipped with various contrivances that are designed to prevent the occurrence (or at least the registration) of arousing stimuli and the execution of volitional motor activity.

This adaptive arrangement is reflected in the development of two basic neuropsychological contrivances. (a) The primary sensory zones and the receptor apparatuses attached to them are deactivated or inhibited during sleep. Physiologically, apart from the closing of the eyelids, this probably involves a withdrawal of preactivation from these zones by way of frontal–limbic selective attention mechanisms. (There is evidence to suggest that the anterior cingulate gyrus, in particular, is involved in this aspect of attentional inhibition.) This reduces the potential for external stimulation. (b) The entire motor system (including the frontal cortical convexity) is similarly deactivated or inhibited. Physiologically, this probably involves not only brainstem inhibition of spinal motoneurons, but also anterior limbic inhibition of the prefrontal convexity. (There is evidence to suggest that anterior and dorsomedial thalamic nuclei, in particular, are involved in this aspect of motor inhibition.) This prevents the implementation of volitional intentions and reduces the potential for motor activity in general.

Withdrawal of attention from the outside world and the blocking of goal-directed activity do not, however, completely eliminate the potential for nocturnal arousal, for at least three obvious reasons: (a) Anecdotal and experimental evidence demonstrates that external sensory stimulation, although reduced, is not entirely abolished during sleep. (b) It is unclear what becomes of pre-existing volitional intentions and motor programs during sleep (day residues). (c) Various types of endogenous stimulation occur spontaneously and relentlessly during sleep. In addition to hunger and thirst and the like, REM activation is the best example of nocturnal stimulation of this kind. There may be many more examples. Limbic irritation due to seizure activity is a pathological equivalent. Endogenous stimulation is probably the most significant source of nocturnal arousal, because the contrivances just listed (inhibition of sensory and motor systems) offer no protection against endogenous stimuli.

The dream process thus arises, on the one hand, partly as a result of the failure of contrivances that cannot protect the sleeper against external stimuli above a certain threshold, and, on the other hand, partly out of their inability to block the arousing effects of endogenous stimuli occurring during sleep. If these stimuli activate the curiosity–interest–expectancy (appetitive) circuits in the mediobasal frontal region, then the dream process proper begins. This process is a third contrivance designed to protect the state of sleep. Like the other two contrivances, the dream process fails under certain conditions (cf. anxiety dreams).

The organization of the dream process is primarily determined by the requirement that it must not terminate in volitional motor activity. That is to say, it is shaped fundamentally not only by the inhibition of spinal motoneurons but also by the inhibition of the dorsolateral–frontal convexity. If an appetitive process cannot terminate in the activation of dorsolateral-frontal motor systems (as it normally does in waking ideational life) then severe restrictions will have been placed on the neuropsychological processes to which it can ultimately give rise. All subsequent developments in the process of dreaming will carry with them the lack a contribution from those parts of the brain which normally imbue human thought and action with logical coherence, propositional structure, and volitional purpose.

As appetitive interest is inhibited in the direction of volitional motor action, it proceeds regressively in the direction of perceptual hallucination. The perceptual–mnestic systems abutting directly on the limbic system (that is, inferior parietal and medial occipito-temporal cortex) thereby become the scene of action of the manifest dream. During waking ideational life regressive activation of perceptual–mnestic cortex is inhibited by frontal–limbic attentional mechanisms and constrained by external sensory information. However, these inhibitory constraints are weakened during sleep, when attentional preactivation is withdrawn and external stimulation is blocked. A pattern of perceptual–mnestic activity that is primed under the influence of nocturnal appetitive interest thereby reaches hallucinatory intensity, and it is mistaken for a real perception by the weakened frontal reflective systems.

The hallucination proper is apparently constructed by a 3-stage process, in which the appetitive program formulated by mediobasal–frontal mechanisms is represented symbolically by left parietal mechanisms, rerepresented concretely (in a spatial medium) by right parietal mechanisms, and then converted into a complex kinematic visual perception by bilateral occipito-temporal mechanisms. The bizarre quality of the resultant perceptual experience is caused by the lack of external perceptual (primary cortical) and executive (dorsolateral frontal) constraints, and perhaps also by the descending influence of mediobasal frontal mechanisms (censorship).

The formulation just presented can be summarized thus: An arousing stimulus that awakens appetitive interest during sleep does not awaken the sleeper because various inhibitory (dorsolateral and mediobasal frontal) mechanisms prevent it from being converted into volitional motor activity, because various perceptual and mnestic (occipito–temporo–parietal) mechanisms transform it symbolically and represent it concretely in the form of a visuospatial hallucination, and because various (frontal–limbic) reflective mechanisms fail to distinguish the resultant hallucination from reality.

CONCLUDING REMARKS

I hope that the foregoing attempt to model the complex neuropsychological process of dreaming will not be misunderstood. It is a speculative model that aims to synthesize the results of a systematic clinico-anatomical study and to integrate them with existing knowledge. I hope that my attempt to provide a simple, perspicacious, and coherent model will not be mistaken for theoretical recklessness. I am painfully aware of both the incompleteness of my knowledge of how the process of dreaming is organized in the brain and of the many gaps and inconsistencies in the formulation that I have presented. However, rather than "shrink in horror at the thought of investigating what appears so impenetrable a problem" (Zeki, 1993, p. 343), on completing this initial survey I have permitted myself the pleasure of formulating some educated guesses as to the implications of my findings for the normal dream process. I fully realize that a great deal more research is required before these conjectures are transformed into knowledge. However, I believe I have achieved the modest theoretical goals that I set for this clinical study if my model has at least posed a set of rational questions for future experimental research.

This research might begin with quantitative laboratory studies of the amount and continuity of sleep in dreaming versus nondreaming patients, REM-awakening studies of modality-specific dream imagery in patients with unimodal sensory-motor deficits outside the visual sphere, REM-awakening studies of visual dream imagery in cortically blind patients with complete V1 and V2 lesions, sleep-awakening studies of the subjective experiences of brainstem patients with demonstrable loss of REM, PET studies of regional activation in the frontal lobes during dreaming sleep, and detailed neuropsychological studies of visuospatial short-term memory and semantic functions in patients with visual and global anoneira. I sincerely hope that colleagues with access to suitable material and technology will take up some of these suggestions or other questions raised by the research that I have reported in this book. They will thereby devote to the problem of dreaming the detailed neuroscientific attention that it deserves. *Nihil simul inventum est et perfectum.*

NOTES

[1]Starr (1967) linked the depression of subjective dreaming in a case of Huntington's disease with the absence of saccadic eye movements during (otherwise normal) paradoxical sleep.

[2]The table printed on p. 363 of the report distinguishes between the cingulate gyrus and superior frontal cortex but not between medial and dorsolateral superior frontal cortex. The figure printed on p. 365 of the report suggests that it was the former rather than the latter region that was activated during dreaming.

[3]It is of theoretical interest to note that the acting out of dreams that occurs with anterior and mediodorsal thalamic lesions also occurs with the recurring anxiety dreams associated with post-traumatic stress disorder (cf. chapter 7).

Appendix:
Glossary of Nosological Terms

Acalculia. This is an acquired disorder of numerical or mathematical ability. I do not make the diagnosis of acalculia in cases with generalized attentional, problem-solving, or intellectual impairments (see relevant entries). When examining mathematical ability I follow the approach of Hécaen and his coworkers, who distinguished three forms of acalculia (Hécaen, 1969; Hécaen et al., 1961).

The first form is based on alexia or agraphia for numbers and can be called an *aphasic acalculia*. These patients cannot comprehend or write numbers or arithmetical signs as language entities. Paraphasic substitution is a common feature. This form of acalculia is frequently associated with aphasia, alexia, and agraphia.

The second form is a disorder of *spatial* organization where the rules for setting written digits in their proper order and position are not followed. The patient cannot align numbers in columns for addition or multiplication, cannot place decimal points, and so on. This interferes with complex calculations, even though the patient is competent in basic arithmetical operations. This form of acalculia is commonly associated with other visual–spatial disorders.

248

The third form of acalculia is *anarithmetria*. This is a primary impairment of the ability to perform arithmetical operations. These patients correctly recognize and reproduce individual numbers, know their value, and can handle numbers in space, but they cannot perform computations (apart from automatized ones). This form of acalculia is extremely rare when distinguished from disturbed problem-solving in general (see relevant entry). It can occur in pure form, in the absence of linguistic and spatial disorders.

The clinical characteristics of the above three syndromes are succinctly described by Levin and Spiers (1985). When assessing for acalculia, I first require patients to read and write numbers and arithmetical signs and to distinguish between larger and smaller numbers (with and without decimal points). The numbers are presented first aurally and then visually. I then ask patients to perform a series of simple (single-digit) calculations, which are presented first aurally and then visually. I require patients to read aloud the visually presented items. Finally, I present a series of progressively more complex written calculations designed to elicit both spatial and sequential errors.

Adynamia.   The following definition is derived from Walsh (1994). The term *adynamia* refers to a general lack of spontaneity and voluntary action. There is frequently an associated impoverishment of spontaneous speech and a reduction in the patient's conversational replies—which are often limited to passive responses to direct questions. These responses usually have an echolalic quality. In mild cases the patient is less active than usual, with little spontaneous speech. In moderate cases the patient is generally akinetic and will remain in one situation for long periods of time; no spontaneous comment is proferred but the patient will reply cogently to others' conversation and will carry out actions without any difficulty—even when these are of a high level of complexity. The patient lapses back into inactivity once the external stimulus is removed. In severe cases the syndrome of akinetic mutism is observed. The latter syndrome is defined as "a disorder of consciousness characterized by unresponsiveness but with the superficial appearance of alertness. The patient's eyes are open but he neither speaks nor moves, nor is the examiner able to communicate with the patient" (Freemon, 1971, p. 693). The essential feature for the diagnosis of adynamia is an inability to initiate and sustain one's own motivation—it is a defect of voluntary regulation of arousal. This latter feature distinguishes adynamia from primary hypoarousal (described below). I use Benton and Hamsher's (1989) Word Fluency Test, Benton et al.'s (1983) Motor Impersistence Test, and the Digit–Symbol subtest of the WAIS (Wechsler, 1981) to formally document and quantify this disorder; however, the diagnosis itself is based entirely upon clinical observation.

Agraphia.   I define *agraphia* as a disorder of written language production which is not attributable to primary perceptual or motor impediments. Unlike many authorities, I exclude the diagnosis of agraphia in disorders of arousal, attention, and general intellect (cf. Benson & Cummings, 1985; Benson & Geschwind, 1985). Some authorities include extraneous disorders of writing such as unilateral paragraphia, paretic agraphia, and micrographia under the rubric of agraphia (e.g., Benson & Cummings, 1985). I classify such cases under the headings of *hemineglect* and *movement disorder.* I reserve the term *agraphia* for cases in which the disorder of written language is clearly attributable to intrinsic linguistic, praxic, or gnostic mechanisms.

When assessing for agraphia I begin by asking the patient to write his or her own name. This automatized skill is seldom impaired and is therefore useful in distinguishing between agraphia and primary motor impediments to writing. This task also provides a useful baseline in hemiparetic patients who are forced to write with the nondominant hand. Next, I examine spontaneous writing, by asking the patient to compose a brief paragraph describing the weather or their job. I then assess specific features of writing by asking the patient to produce to dictation spatially ambiguous letters, short and long words, regular and irregular words, common and uncommon words, and sentences. Finally, I ask the patient to copy letters, words, and sentences from visual models.

On the basis of these tasks I distinguish three broad clinical types of agraphia —aphasic, constructional, and apraxic—which can coexist in a single patient. In the aphasic group spelling, semantic, and grammatical errors abound. This category includes numerous distinctive subtypes, such as the agraphias that typically accompany fluent and nonfluent aphasia, respectively. These are fully described by Benson and Cummings (1985) and Benson and Geschwind (1985). Disturbances of the spatial relationships intrinsic to writing underlie constructional agraphia (Leischner, 1969). Letters and words are formed clearly enough but they are wrongly arranged on the page. The letters and words may be superimposed, written diagonally, in haphazard arrangements, from right to left, or reversed in various planes. In apraxic agraphia language formulation is correct and the spatial arrangement of letters and words is respected but there is loss of the skilled movements required to form letters and words. There may be an uncertainty as to how the pen should be held and applied to paper, and handwriting becomes a scrawl (Adams & Victor, 1985).

Alexia.   This term refers to an inability to comprehend language through the visual sense when this inability is not due to primary sensory loss, to unfamiliarity with the language, to a disorder of focused attention, nor to a lack of general intelligence. Alexia is frequently accompanied by visual perceptual impairments, but, as with the visual agnosias (see the relevant entry), the diagnosis is only excluded if visual acuity is inadequate to permit recognition. The diagnosis of aphasia does not exclude the diagnosis of alexia, even if a single mechanism produces both disorders. In classical definitions of alexia, emphasis is placed on the impairment of visual–linguistic comprehension (Benson & Geschwind, 1969). Oral reading tasks are therefore of little value in the diagnosis of alexia.

When assessing written language comprehension I begin with a letter recognition task, by asking the patient to match upper- and lower-case letters. Next I assess word recognition by means of an improvised word–picture association test. I assess comprehension of more abstract words by using an odd word out test—similar to the one used by Albert, Yamadori, Gardner, & Howes (1973)—in which the patient is presented with a list of five words, four of which belong to the same semantic category. Finally, I assess sentence comprehension by requiring the patient to perform written commands. If apraxia is suspected I ask the patient to point to sentences that correspond to various pictures, and in severe cases I use a fill-in-the-missing-word paradigm. Paragraph comprehension is tested by asking the patient to answer questions about a written paragraph.

I do not routinely assess the cognitive basis of alexia, but rather specify the clinical syndrome in accordance with traditional nosological criteria (*pure alexia, alexia with agraphia* [central alexia], and *literal alexia*). The clinical features of these syndromes are succinctly described by Benson and Geschwind (1985, p. 217).

Anosognosia.   This term refers to the failure to recognize illness. Its normal clinical usage implies a failure to perceive a defect or the denial of a defect. Patients with this disorder may rationalize their failures. In less severe cases patients admit that they are impaired but they appear unconcerned about their loss (*anosodiaphoria*). Classically, the term *anosognosia* denotes a denial of hemiplegia (Babinski, 1914). However, like most modern practitioners, I use the term more broadly to denote unawareness of or marked unconcern about any obvious neurological impairment (e.g., blindness, Anton, 1899; Wernicke's aphasia, Lebrun, 1987).

Aphasia.   This term refers to an impairment in the comprehension or expression of the symbolic content of language when the impairment is not due to purely sensory or motor deficits or to generalized intellectual impairment. I include generalized disorders of arousal under the latter heading. Accordingly, I do not make the diagnosis of aphasia in cases with global adynamia or akinetic mutism. However, I do include specific disorders of the impetus to speak under the heading of aphasia (cf. Luria, 1980).

When examining speech and language functions, I begin with an assessment of spontaneous or conversational output, which I classify as either *fluent* or *nonfluent.* I define nonfluent speech as being sparse (under 50 words per minute), effortful, and poorly articulated. Nonfluent speech is associated with short phrase length, marked dysprosody, and the preferential use of substantives. Agrammatism is another salient feature—that is, a tendency to omit syntactically significant function words and syntactic endings such as verb tense and plurals. I define fluent speech as being abundant (usually well above 50 words per minute), effortless, and well articulated. Fluent speech is associated with normal phrase length (averaging 5 to 8 words per phrase) and normal prosodic quality. Aphasic patients with fluent speech tend to omit lexically significant substantives (empty speech) and to utter meaningless words (paraphasia). In extreme cases the patient produces rapid sequences of well-articulated but paraphasic words (jargon). On the basis of these simple criteria, I distinguish between fluent and nonfluent aphasia.

In problematical cases, I follow the differential diagnostic criteria of Benson and Geschwind (1985). I obtain a standard sample of speech output by asking the patient to describe the cookie theft picture from the Boston Diagnostic Aphasia Examination (Goodglass & Kaplan, 1983).

When paraphasia is present I distinguish between verbal and literal subtypes. I then examine comprehension, repetition, and naming in order to further specify the type of aphasia. I begin the examination of comprehension by asking the patient to follow increasingly complex verbal commands. I formally document any deficits using a modified Token Test (de Renzi & Faglioni, 1978). If the patient fails to carry out verbal commands I take care to exclude ideomotor apraxia (see relevant entry). I also ask the patient to point to various objects in a visual array that I identify verbally (using names initially and then increasingly vague functional descriptions).

If a comprehension deficit is demonstrated I attempt to qualify the nature of the deficit (phoneme discrimination, verbal–visual association, acoustico-mnestic retention, logico-grammatical analysis) using the clinical techniques of Luria (1980). Next, I assess repetition, starting with the simple repetition of single-syllable words and building up to the repetition of complex sentences. I formally document repetition deficits using Benton and Hamsher's (1989) Sentence Repetition Test. Finally, I assess confrontation naming, using the Boston Naming Test (Kaplan et al., 1983). On the basis of the patient's performances on the different aspects of this examination I classify the specific aphasic syndrome (e.g., *Broca, Wernicke, conduction, global, transcortical motor, transcortical sensory, mixed transcortical, anomic*) according to conventional criteria. The clinical characteristics of these well-known syndromes are succinctly described by Benson (1985) and Benson and Geschwind (1985).

Apraxia.   Most clinicians would agree with Dejerine's (1914) maxim to the effect that it is easier to say what apraxia is not than to say what it is. Accordingly apraxia is diagnosed by exclusionary criteria—as a disorder of skilled movement that cannot be accounted for by paresis, deafferentation, abnormal tone or posture, movement disorder (such as ataxia, tremor, or chorea), defective comprehension or perception, uncooperativeness, or generalized dementia (cf. Ajuriaguerra & Tissot, 1969; Geschwind & Damasio, 1985; Heilman & Rothi, 1985; Walsh, 1994). A disorder defined in this way inevitably covers a wide range of different manifestations.

In the present study I have reserved the term *apraxia* for the classic ideo-motor type of apraxia. These patients have difficulty performing a skilled movement to verbal or visual command (with either hand) although they are capable of performing the same movement under automatic or fortuitous conditions. I assess praxis by conventional clinical methods; first I ask the patient to perform a variety of symbolic gestures (both to verbal command and to imitation), then I ask the patient to use a variety of objects (both imagined and real) first to verbal command and then to imitation. I use the gestures and objects recommended by Heilman and Rothi (1985). I make the diagnosis of apraxia only if these tasks present significant difficulties that cannot be accounted for by any of the exclusionary disorders listed above.

In this study I have classified focal cases with ideational apraxia under the heading of *disturbed problem-solving* (see the relevant entry). Alternatively, ideational apraxia is subsumed under the rubric of dementia. The so-called motor or kinetic apraxias (including gait apraxia) have a dubious status in relation to the exclusionary criteria. I classify constructional apraxia separately (see the relevant entry). I assess buccofacial praxis in the context of Broca's aphasia (see relevant entry). I do not formally assess dressing praxis (see Weintraub & Mesulam, 1985).

Central Achromatopsia. This term signifies an acquired difficulty in perceiving color. Patients with achromatopsia generally complain about their loss of color vision and they describe their world as "black and white," "all gray," "washed out" or "dirty" (Bauer & Rubens, 1985, p. 204). This usually affects both visual fields but it can affect only one (hemiachromatopsia). More circumscribed color-field defects do not occur. However, the perception of some colors—usually the reds—may be preserved (incomplete achromatopsia). Although central achromatopsia is almost invariably associated with an upper-field scotoma and is commonly associated with prosopagnosia and topographical agnosia or amnesia, patients with central achromatopsia usually perceive well (i.e., they have normal acuity, form, and depth perception). I assess for achromatopsia using simple hue discrimination and color matching tasks, and I formally document any defects with Ishihara plates and the Munsell Farnsworth 100-Hue Test. These tests readily distinguish between achromatopsia and color anomia (patients with color anomia can discriminate hues nonverbally).

Constructional Apraxia. Following Kleist's (1923) classic definition, I reserve this term for cases with visuoconstructive impairments that cannot be reduced to modality-specific perceptual or motor mechanisms. *Constructional* *apraxia* is a heteromodal disturbance "in formative activities such as assembling, building, and drawing, in which the spatial form of the product proves to be unsuccessful, without their being apraxia of single movements [or inadequate visual perception]" (Kleist, 1923).

This definition differs from that of many modern neuropsychologists, who use the term to refer to almost any disorder of visuoconstructional ability. I use a wide variety of clinical tasks to assess constructional praxis. I usually begin by asking the patient to copy simple line-drawings of a star, a house, and a three-dimensional cube before presenting the complex figure of Rey (1941). This is followed by simple and complex two-dimensional constructional tasks, such as the Stick Test of Butters and Barton (1970) and the Block Design subtest of the WAIS (Wechsler, 1981), which I administer without time limits. Thereafter, I require the patient to copy simple and complex three-dimensional block constructions (after Hécaen, Ajuriaguerra, & Massonnet, 1951, and Benton et al., 1983). Finally, I ask the patient to produce drawings from memory (a person, a bicycle). When significant incompetency can be demonstrated in comparison with purely visual and motor tasks, the diagnosis of constructional apraxia is made.

Disinhibition.   I use this term only where there is a lack of learned adaptive and social constraints on impulsive behaviors and affective displays. I do not use the term to describe more specific disorders of inhibition such as hypermetamorphosis, perseveration, or pathological laughter and crying. Disinhibition in the behavioral and affective spheres is frequently—if not invariably—associated with secondary disturbances of cognition. Harlow's classical description of the case of Phineas Gage is as good as any modern definition of the primary (behavioral and affective) features of this disorder:

> the equilibrium or balance, so to speak, between [the patient's] intellectual faculties and animal propensities, seems to have been destroyed. He is fitful, irreverent, indulging at times in the grossest profanity (which was not previously his custom), manifesting but little deference to his fellows, impatient of restraint or advice when it conflicts with his desires, at times pertinaciously obstinate but yet capricious and vacillating, devising many plans for future operation which no sooner are arranged than they are abandoned in turn for others appearing more feasible. (Harlow, 1868, p. 389)

Luria defined the secondary cognitive disturbances that are typically associated with disinhibition as follows:

> Although gnosis, praxis, and speech remain largely intact, these patients often show increased impulsiveness during tests of their praxis, usually without any sign of pathological inertia of established motor stereotypes, but often their motor responses arise impulsively (sometimes even in the form of premature movements). The same impulsiveness is revealed in their memorizing and intellectual

activity; they often give fragmentary, impulsive responses when recalling series of words, when assessing the meaning of a thematic picture, and during arithmetical operations, although the operations themselves remain potentially intact. (p. 362)

I typically use Luria's tests (Christensen, 1974) to document the effects of this disorder, but the primary clinical changes in the affective and behavioral spheres cannot be meaningfully measured.

> ***Disorientation for Time, Person, or Place.*** Disoriented patients may or may not be hypoaroused (see the relevant entry). In the former case the disorientation may be attributable to the hypoarousal. The diagnoses are not mutually exclusive. Like hypoarousal, disorientation is a nonspecific symptom; it is not attributable to a disorder of formal cognitive operations.

> Perhaps the most important fact is that, against the background of this clearly abnormal state of consciousness, the special higher cortical functions of these patients remain intact. They may have no difficulty in performing tests of praxis, repeating given movements, recognizing pictures, repeating sounds or words, or reading and writing, and they can perform relatively simple arithmetical operations. (Luria, 1980, p. 367)

Amnesia has a special place in this respect. Disorientation is almost always accompanied by a degree of amnesia, and amnesia is frequently accompanied by some form of disorientation. In the latter case the disorientation may be attributable to amnesia; the diagnoses are not mutually exclusive. When assessing orientation I typically ask the questions listed by Christensen (1975), and I pay particular attention to the differential-diagnostic pitfalls discussed by Luria (1980) and Christensen (1974).

> ***Disturbed Problem-Solving.*** As is the case with most higher mental functions, problem-solving can be disturbed for a variety of different reasons. I assess problem-solving by means of two complex tests: the Austin Maze (Walsh, 1991) and the Tower of London (Shallice, 1982). I use the qualitative features of a defective performance, together with a variety of simpler tasks, to isolate the basic factor underlying the disorder (Christensen, 1974; Luria, 1980). I classify the basic factors, following McCarthy and Warrington's (1990) analysis, under five headings: (a) focused attention, (b) higher order inferences, (c) formulation of strategies, (d) flexibility, and (e) evaluation of outcome. I only make the diagnosis of disturbed problem-solving if one of the latter four factors can be isolated; if the complex problem-solving disorder is reducible to a disorder of focused attention, I do not make the diagnosis. Such cases are classified under hyperarousal, adynamia, or disinhibition (see relevant entries).

> ***Finger Agnosia.*** Traditionally the patient with this sign cannot recognize

which of their fingers has been touched by the examiner. The deficit is typically most pronounced for the three middle fingers. Patients are usually unaware of the deficit and therefore make no attempt to correct their errors. Because somatosensory impairment and aphasia can obviously interfere with this ability, I examine finger gnosis in a variety of different ways. This approach is consistent with Gerstmann's (1957) classical definition of finger agnosia as a heteromodal disorder:

> It consists in a primary disturbance or loss of the ability to recognize, identify, differentiate, name, select, indicate, and orient as to the individual fingers of either hand, the patient's own, as well as those of other persons. . . . [It is often accompanied by] restriction in their separate kinetic realization. (p. 866)

When examining finger gnosis, I begin by pointing to specific fingers and combinations of fingers on the patient's dominant hand. If the patient fails to identify them correctly I exclude primary somatosensory impairment by assessing the other hand. If necessary I switch to a drawing of the hand. If the patient continues to misidentify fingers, I exclude aphasic misnaming. If this is present I require the patient to point to or move fingers that I name. If the patient continues to fail, and the failure cannot be sufficiently accounted for by aphasia, the diagnosis of finger agnosia is made.

Hemispatial Neglect. In patients with hemispatial neglect, sensory events in one half of space (usually the left) differentially lose their impact on awareness, especially when competing events are taking place in the other half of space. The most obvious demonstration of this occurs when patients who respond perfectly well to unilateral stimulation from either the left- or the right-hand side consistently ignore left-sided stimuli under conditions of bilateral simultaneous stimulation. Especially when it occurs in more than one modality the phenomenon of sensory extinction suggests that left hemispace is neglected despite intact central reception of the relevant sensory stimulation (Mesulam, 1985a, p. 142).

Extinction can be subtle or severe and it can be demonstrated in a great many different ways by varying stimulus and response parameters. I usually begin with direct unilateral and bilateral stimulation in the visual, tactile, and auditory modalities, taking care to exclude split-brain phenomena (Mesulam, 1985b). This is followed by horizontally oriented drawing tasks (such as the Scene Test of Gainotti, Messerli, & Tissot, 1972), by line bisection, and by item cancellation tasks that provide formal measurements of the disorder (Schenkenberg, Bradford, & Ajax, 1980; Gauthier, Dehaut, & Joanette, 1989).

Hypoarousal. This term refers to a primary disturbance of the level of wakefulness. Although the condition may fluctuate in response to factors such as fatigue and the general intellectual demands of a task, it is an entirely non-specific symptom from the cognitive point of view. These patients

> show no symptoms of a disturbance of gnosis and praxis; they retain their speech, and are able to perform relatively elementary intellectual operations. The only symptom clearly manifested by these patients may be a certain lowering of the tone of psychological processes, a certain slowness and proneness to fatigue, which is equally manifested in all spheres of their activity. (Luria, 1980, p. 366)

The clinical techniques that I employ to assess level of consciousness are outlined in Strub and Black (1985). I define anything less than full alertness (i.e., lethargy, somnolence, obtundation, stupor, and semicoma) as *hypoarousal*. These terms are precisely defined in Strub and Black (1985).

Long-Term Memory Disorder. Long-term memory disorder is frequently confused with remote memory disorder and retrograde amnesia (e.g., Devinsky, 1992). The following definition is derived from Walsh (1994). In clinical practice the term *long-term memory disorder* refers primarily to a disorder of recent memory, that is, to a difficulty in acquiring new information. Information that appears to have been apprehended cannot be recalled after the passage of an unusually brief period. As nothing new is learned there develops an increasing period of anterograde amnesia. Retrograde memory loss may or may not be an associated feature; if it is, a temporal gradient can usually be demonstrated (the amount of information decreases as questions move closer in time to the present). Confabulation may be present but it is not a constant feature. The rate of forgetting and the degree of disorganization of remembered material may vary. However, many aspects of memory are preserved (see Moscovich, 1982). Verbal and visuospatial memory may be dissociated. An essential feature is the preservation of short-term memory (the audioverbal span being around 7 units and the visuospatial span around 6 units).

Clinical examination reveals no inherent difficulties with speech, language, gesture, well-practiced skills, and general knowledge. Implicit learning (learning without conscious awareness) and procedural (sensory-motor) learning can frequently be demonstrated. The presence of an executive disorder does not exclude the diagnosis of amnesia if the above configuration can be demonstrated (see entries for *adynamia, disinhibition,* and *disturbed problem-solving*). In such cases more information can be elicited by direct questioning, by cuing, and by recognition paradigms, than the patient can recall spontaneously.

I use a wide variety of clinical tests to examine the multiple aspects of long-term memory. I select the appropriate tests according to the unfolding clinical picture. However, I usually begin with a simple Hidden Objects Test (Strub & Black, 1985) and follow up any signs of abnormality with systematic tests of rote verbal and visual learning—using the Auditory Verbal Learning Test of Rey (1964), the Associate Learning subtest of the Wechsler Memory Scale (Wechsler, 1945), the Seven/Twenty-Four Test of Barbizet and Cany (as described by Rao, Hammeke, & McQuillen, 1984), and the block-tapping task of Corsi (as described by Milner, 1971). Thereafter, I typically assess more complex aspects of recent memory by means of Babcock's (1930) Story Recall Test, the Logical Memory subtest of Wechsler's Memory Scale (1945), the Complex Figure Test of Rey (1941), and Benton's Visual Retention Test (1955), with the addition of distractor tasks, recognition trials, and delayed recall trials wherever appropriate. I evaluate these tests in terms of the qualitative features of the performances (as described by Signoret, 1985). I assess remote memory informally by questioning patients about significant public events and popular television programs. Standardized tests of remote memory are notoriously unreliable (Weintraub & Mesulam, 1985).

Perseveration.   In the present study I use this term to denote the disorder that Luria (1973) described under the heading of *elementary motor perseveration:* "If the patient is asked to draw a shape, such as a circle, he easily begins to do so but cannot stop at the right time and goes on repeating the movement over and over again" (p. 182).

In these cases it is clear that the intention to perform the movement as well as the general plan of its execution remains intact, but the movement itself becomes freed from the restraining effect of the program. I do not make the diagnosis in cases of ideational perseveration, in which the intention or the general plan of action, rather than the individual movements, exhibit pathological inertia (see Luria, 1965). In the present study I included cases of this type under the heading of *disturbed problem-solving,* where they are classified under the subheading of *flexibility* (see relevant entry). I use a variety of simple, repetitive drawing and tapping tasks to elicit motor perseveration (Christensen, 1974; Luria, 1980).

Prosopagnosia.   This is a distinct form of visual agnosia that notably affects the recognition of familiar human faces (Damasio & Damasio, 1983). Prosopagnosia is distinguished from visual agnosia (see the relevant entry) by virtue of the fact that the patient can recognize a face as a face—and can if requested point to its several components—but he or she is unable to identify particular, individual faces. In other words prosopagnosia comprises the recognition of a previously well-known, specific member within a class, although recognition of the class itself is not impaired (Damasio & Damasio, 1983). The co-occurrence of other class-specific agnosias (e.g., for particular items of furniture, cars, or animals) does not preclude the diagnosis of prosopagnosia. Also, prosopagnosia and visual agnosia are not mutually exclusive diagnoses.

I make the diagnosis of prosopagnosia on the basis of significant everyday difficulties in the recognition of familiar faces, taking care in the clinical situation to exclude nonvisual cues to recognition. In addition to informal observation, I systematically examine the patient using the famous faces paradigm. However, I do not make the diagnosis of prosopagnosia on the basis of defective performances on standardized tests alone. I use standardized tests for purposes of formal documentation and measurement of the symptom. The failure to distinguish between the clinical syndrome of prosopagnosia and relative difficulty with various tests of facial perception and recognition has led to some confusion in the neuropsychological literature (Walsh, 1994, p. 313).

Right–Left Disorientation. I do not assess for this symptom in cases of hemineglect. This symptom is demonstrated by asking the patient to show his right or left hand and to point at right or left body parts on himself and the examiner. If the patient answers correctly, cross-pointing is requested. When significant incompetency can be demonstrated in comparison with other verbal–praxic tasks, the diagnosis of right–left disorientation is made (Benson & Geschwind, 1985). I formally document the disorder using Benton's et al.'s (1983) standard battery.

Short-Term Memory Disorder. Short-term memory is frequently confused with recent memory (e.g., Devinsky, 1992). I use the term in a narrow sense, to indicate a modality or material-specific disorder of immediate memory. The diagnosis is therefore not made in cases with global attentional disorder (e.g., hypoarousal, adynamia, disinhibition). However, the presence of aphasia—and especially of conduction aphasia—does not preclude the diagnosis of (audioverbal) short-term memory disorder. I use the Digit Span subtest of the WAIS and WMS batteries (Wechsler, 1945, 1981) to assess the audioverbal span, and I use Corsi's blocks to assess the visuospatial span (Milner, 1971). I apply cutoff scores of 6 and 5 respectively. I do not always examine working memory, which can be impaired for a great many different reasons. However, in cases where a circumscribed STM defect results in a marked impairment of working memory, I formally document the disorder using the concurrent task paradigm of Baddeley (1986).

Topographical Agnosia. This is a distinctive form of visual agnosia (see the relevant entry) that affects the recognition of familiar places. Topographical agnosia is distinguished from visual agnosia by virtue of the patient's failure to identify individual places despite retained ability to recognize the broad category (e.g., a hill, a church) to which they belong (de Renzi, 1982, p. 214). In other words, like prosopagnosia, topographical agnosia comprises the recognition of a previously well-known, specific member within a category, although recognition of the category itself is not impaired. The co-occurrence of other category-specific agnosias does not preclude the diagnosis of topographical agnosia. Also, topographical agnosia and visual agnosia are not mutually exclusive diagnoses.

I make the diagnosis of topographical agnosia on the basis of significant everyday difficulties in the recognition of familiar places. These patients describe distinctive experiences of knowing intellectually where they are and yet feeling that the (previously familiar) place looks strange and unfamiliar. When assessing topographical gnosis I take care to distinguish between the immediate perceptual experience of familiarity and the compensatory strategy of identifying familiar places by means of deductive reasoning. I also distinguish between topographical agnosia and reduplicative paramnesia (de Renzi, 1985). The clinical distinction between topographical agnosia and topographical amnesia is discussed next.

Topographical Amnesia.   This disorder is characterized by an inability to find one's way about in surroundings with which one was previously familiar, due to a specific loss of spatial memory. The disorder may also affect the acquisition of new topographical knowledge. However, I do not make the diagnosis of topographical amnesia if it is indistinguishable from a general amnestic syndrome (see the relevant entry). The diagnosis of topographical amnesia is also not made if the disorder can be attributed to impaired perceptual analysis of the environment (e.g., erroneous appreciation of distance, defective scanning, hemineglect). Topographical amnesia is a heteromodal disorder. These criteria distinguish topographical amnesia from topographical agnosia (Paterson & Zangwill, 1945). However, topographical amnesia and topographical agnosia can coexist (de Renzi, 1985).

I assess topographical memory in accordance with de Renzi's recommendations (1983). Detailed descriptions of the tests I use can be found in de Renzi (1982). I ask the patient to provide verbal descriptions of more or less familiar routes, to locate places and to trace paths on blank maps, to identify photographs of famous landmarks and buildings, and (where possible) to lead the way in surroundings that were known before and after the onset of illness. In the latter cases I take care to distinguish topographical memory based on knowledge of concrete spatial relationships from route-finding ability based on abstract reasoning processes.

Visual Agnosia.   Like apraxia, *visual agnosia* is defined by exclusionary criteria. It is an inability to recognize objects through the visual sense when this inability is not due to primary sensory loss, to unfamiliarity with the object, to a disorder of focused attention, to aphasic misnaming, to modality nonspecific semantic impairments, or to generalized dementia.

The patient with visual agnosia does not respond appropriately to visually presented material even though visual sensory processing, language, and general intellectual functions are preserved to sufficient levels so that their impairment cannot account individually or in combination for the failure to recognize. Poor recognition is usually limited to the visual sphere, and appropriate responses occur when the patient is allowed to handle the object or hear it in use. (Bauer & Rubens, 1985, p. 190)

I assess this function in a simple clinical fashion by asking the patient to name a variety of objects and pictures of objects and complex visual arrays. The pictures include veridical and degraded images of objects (unusual perspectives, uneven lighting, blurred photographs, incomplete drawings, overlapping drawings). However, I do not make the diagnosis of visual agnosia if the patient can easily recognize real objects and is only deficient on the recognition of relatively degraded images on formal testing. If visual recognition presents everyday difficulties for the patient, I exclude primary sensory loss by confrontation testing and by asking the patient to draw objects or pictures which he or she cannot name. I also ask patients to match identical objects and pictures. Preserved acuity can be strikingly demonstrated in some cases by slowly moving the objects that the patient cannot name across the field of vision. However, intact primary vision can sometimes only be demonstrated by asking the patient to name bright, saturated colors.

When assessing the significance of primary visual defects, a degree of clinical judgment is called for. I use a simple rule of thumb; the failure to identify objects visually must be attributable to persistent misrecognition of the meaning of patterns of visual stimuli rather than to nonawareness of the stimuli themselves (cf. Williams, 1970, p. 58). I exclude aphasic misnaming by examining object use and multiple choice pointing, and I exclude modality nonspecific semantic impairments by assessing recognition through the tactile and auditory modalities. Generalized dementia is excluded clinically and documented formally by psychometric testing. If the patient is unable to identify objects visually and is able to perform all the latter tasks with relative ease, I make the diagnosis of agnosia regardless of whether or not primary visual defects can also be demonstrated. "The concurrent presence of visual sensory defect and visual agnosia cannot by itself be used as evidence that in the individual patient the visual defect is *sufficient* to result in the failure of recognition" (Bauer & Rubens, 1985, p. 193).

Having made the diagnosis of visual agnosia, I assess specific aspects of higher vision (e.g., perception of form, contrast, depth, part–whole integration, and spatial relationships) in an attempt to isolate the visual basis of the agnosia. If I am able to do so I designate the agnosia as *apperceptive* in accordance with Lissauer's (1890) classification. I include Wolpert's (1924) *simultanagnosia* under this heading. If the recognition disorder cannot be reduced to modality-specific perceptual defects of this type, and it appears instead to arise from a dissociation between the visual modality and semantic memory ("a normal percept stripped of its meaning;" Teuber, 1968), then I designate the agnosia as *associative*. Despite its problems, the distinction between perceptually and nonperceptually based agnosias is clinically valid and useful.

Visual Irreminiscence. This is an explicit and entirely subjective complaint that is defined as "the symptom whereby a patient loses the power to conjure up visual images" (Critchley, 1953, p. 311). Irreminiscence can affect visual mental imagery in general or specific aspects thereof (imagery for color, faces, spatial relationships, etc).

> It is uncertain how frequent this irreminiscence (as Nielsen calls it) occurs clinically, for some victims . . . are unlikely to complain spontaneously of such a defect. Nor can a patient whose sensorium is clouded be expected to give an altogether objective answer when a leading question is directly put to him as to the presence or absence of visual images. However, there are exceptional cases where the patient is a subject of high intelligence, not materially blunted by the cerebral lesion, and can give a convincing account of impaired imagery. The symptom is all the more arresting if the patient formerly possessed a vivid and predominantly visual type of imagery. (p. 311)

In recent years numerous objective tests have been developed from which the examiner may infer the presence or absence of imagery defects. The relationship between the functions measured by these tests and the classical symptom of irreminiscence is uncertain (see Goldenberg, 1989). Although a subjective loss of the ability to revisualize should produce defective performances on such tests, the converse need not apply; low scores on imagery-dependent tests are not necessarily attributable to defective explicit revisualization. These tests are therefore helpful in the formal documentation and measurement of imagery-related deficits, but their diagnostic value in regard to irreminiscence sensu strictori is problematic. When assessing revisualization the examiner is ultimately "at the mercy of the patient's own description of events" (Critchley, 1953, p. 299).

I assess for irreminiscence clinically by asking patients to close their eyes and bring various images to mind (e.g., a canary, a bicycle, a church, the face of Adolf Hitler, an upside-down letter K, the American flag). I then ask them to describe what they "see," using drawings if necessary (Lissauer, 1890). If the responses are impoverished in any respect (color, form, spatial relationships, etc.) I point this out to the patient and ask for more perceptual detail. I exclude optic dysphasia and similar phenomena by requiring the patient to describe real objects and pictures that are presented to them visually. I likewise exclude constructional dyspraxia by asking the patient to draw real objects from models. I pay careful attention to the patient's own opinion as to whether or not their revisualization is defective.

References

Adams, R., & Victor, M. (1985). *Principles of Neurology* (3rd ed.). New York: McGraw-Hill.

Adey, W., Bors, E., & Porter, R. (1968). EEG sleep patterns after high cervical lesions in man. *Archives of Neurology, 24*, 377–383.

Adler, A. (1944). Disintegration and restoration of optic recognition in visual agnosia: Analysis of a case. *Archives of Neurology and Psychiatry, 51*, 243–259.

Adler, A. (1950). Course and outcome of visual agnosia. *Journal of Nervous & Mental Diseases, 111*, 41–51.

de Ajuriaguerra, J., & Tissot, R. (1969). The apraxias. In G. Vinken and H. Bruyn (Eds.), *Handbook of clinical neurology* (Vol. 4, pp. 48–66). Amsterdam: North Holland.

Albert, M., Yamadori, A., Gardner, H., & Howes, D. (1973). Comprehension in alexia. *Neurology, 27*, 685–688.

Anan'ev, B. (1960). *Psixologija cuvstvennogo poznanija* [The psychology of learning through experience]. Moscow: Academy of Pedagogical Science.

Anton, G. (1899). Über die Selbstwahrnehmung der Herdkrankungen des Gehirns durch den Kranken bei Rindenblindheit und Rindentaubheit [On self-perception of focal symptoms of the brain by patients with cortical blindness and cortical deafness]. *Archiv für Psychiatrie, 32*, 86–127.

Antrobus, J. (1987). Cortical hemisphere asymmetry and sleep mentation. *Psychological Review, 94*, 359–368.

Antrobus, J., & Bertini, M. (Eds.). (1992). *The neuropsychology of sleep and dreaming.* Hillsdale, NJ: Lawrence Erlbaum Associates.

Antrobus, J., Ehrlichman, H., & Weiner, M. (1978). EEG asymmetry during REM and NREM: Failure to replicate. *Sleep Research, 7,* 24.

Arena, R., Murri, L., Piccini, P., & Muratorio, A. (1984). Dream recall and memory in brain lesioned patients. *Research Communications in Psychology, Psychiatry and Behavior, 9,* 31–42.

Aserinsky, E., & Kleitman, N. (1953). Regularly occurring periods of eye motility and concurrent phenomena during sleep. *Science, 118,* 273–274.

Aserinsky, E., & Kleitman, N. (1955). Two types of ocular motility during sleep. *Journal of Applied Physiology, 8,* 1–10.

Babcock, H. (1930). An experiment in the measurement of mental deterioration. *Archives of Psychology, 117,* 105.

Babinski, J. (1914). Contribution à l'étude des troubles mentaux l'hémiplégie organique cerebrale (anosognosie) [Contribution to the study of mental symptoms in organic cerebral hemiplagia (anosognosia)]. *Revue Neurologique, 27,* 845–847.

Baddeley, A. (1986). *Working memory.* Oxford: Clarendon Press.

Bailey, P., von Bonin, G., & McCulloch, W. (1950). *The neocortex of the chimpanzee.* Chicago: University of Illinois Press.

Bakan, P. (1976). The right brain is the dreamer. *Psychology Today, 10,* 66–68.

Bakan, P. (1977–1978). Dreaming, REM sleep and the right hemisphere: A theoretical integration. *Journal of Altered States of Consciousness, 3,* 285–307.

Basso, A., Bisiach, E., & Luzzatti, C. (1980). Loss of mental imagery: A case study. *Neuropsychologia, 18,* 435–442.

Bauer, R. (1982). Visual hypoemotionality as a symptom of visual-limbic disconnection in man. *Archives of Neurology, 39,* 702–708.

Bauer, R., & Rubens, A. (1985). Agnosia. In K. Heilman & E. Valenstein (Eds.), *Clinical neuropsychology* (2nd ed, pp. 187–241). New York: Oxford University Press.

Bay, E., & Lauenstein, O. (1948). Zum Problem der optischen Agnosie [On the problem of optic agnosia]. *Deutsche Zeitschrift für die Nervenheilkunde, 158,* 107–210.

Behrmann, M., Wincour, G., & Moscovitch, M. (1992). Dissociation between mental imagery and object recognition in a brain-damaged patient. *Nature, 359,* 636–637.

Benson, D. F. (1985). Aphasia. In K. Heilman & E. Valenstein (Eds.), *Clinical neuropsychology* (2nd ed., pp. 17–47). New York: Oxford University Press.

Benson, D. F., & Cummings, J. (1985). Agraphia. In P. Vinken, G. Bruyn, H. Klawans, & J. Frederiks (Eds.), *Handbook of clinical neurology,* (Vol. 45, pp. 457–472). Amsterdam: Elsevier.

Benson, D. F., & Geschwind, N. (1969). The alexias. In G. Vinken and H. Bruyn (Eds.), *Handbook of clinical neurology* (Vol. 4, pp. 112–140). Amsterdam: North Holland.

Benson, D. F., & Geschwind, N. (1985). Aphasia and related disorders: A clinical approach. In M.-M. Mesulam (Ed.), *Principles of behavioral neurology* (pp. 193–238). Philadelphia: F. A. Davis.

Benson, D. F., & Greenberg, J. (1969). Visual form agnosia: A specific defect in visual discrimination. *Archives of Neurology, 20,* 82–89.

Benton, A. (1955). *The Visual Retention Test.* New York: The Psychological Corporation.

Benton, A. (1961). The fiction of the "Gerstmann syndrome." *Journal of Neurology, Neurosurgery and Psychiatry, 24,* 176–181.

Benton, A. (1977). Reflections on the Gerstmann syndrome. *Brain and Language, 4,* 45–62.

Benton, A. (1992). Gerstmann's syndrome. *Archives of Neurology, 49,* 445–447.

Benton, A., & Hamsher, K. (1989). *Multilingual Aphasia Examination.* Iowa: AJA Associates.

Benton, A., Hamsher, K., Varney, N., & Spreen, O. (1983). *Contributions to neuropsychological assessment: A clinical manual.* New York: Oxford University Press.

Berger, R., & Oswald, I. (1962). Effects of sleep deprivation on behavior, subsequent sleep, and dreaming. *Journal of Mental Science, 108*, 457–465.

Berti, A., Arienta, C., & Papagno, A. (1990). A case of amnesia after excision of the septum pellucidum. *Journal of Neurology, Neurosurgery & Psychiatry, 53*, 922–924.

Bertini, M., & Violani, C. (1992). The postawakening testing technique in the investigation of cognitive asymmetries during sleep. In J. Antrobus & M. Bertini (Eds.), *The neuropsychology of sleep and dreaming* (pp. 47–62). Hillsdale, NJ: Lawrence Erlbaum Associates.

Bogen, J. (1969). The other side of the brain: II. An appositional mind. *Bulletin of the Los Angeles Neurological Society, 34*, 135–162.

Boller, F., Wright, D., Cavalieri, R., & Mitsumoto, H. (1975). Paroxysmal "nightmares": Sequel of a stroke responsive to diphenylhydantoin. *Neurology, 25*, 1026–1028.

von Bonin, G., & Bailey, P. (1947). *The neocortex of Macaca mulatta*. Chicago: University of Illinois Press.

Botez, M. In collaboration with Botez, T., & Olivier, M. (1985). Parietal lobe syndromes. In P. Vinken, G. Bruyn, H. Klawans, & J. Frederiks (Eds.), *Handbook of clinical neurology* (Vol. 45, pp. 63–85). Amsterdam: Elsevier.

Botez, M., Olivier, M., Vézina, J.-L., Botez, T., & Kaufman, B. (1985). Defective revisualization: Dissociation between cognitive and imagistic thought. Case report and short review of the literature. *Cortex, 21*, 375–389.

Boyle, J., & Nielsen, J. (1954). Visual agnosia and loss of recall. *Bulletin of the Los Angeles Neurological Society, 19*, 39–42.

Brain, R. (1941). Visual object-agnosia with special reference to the Gestalt theory. *Brain, 64*, 43–62.

Brain, R. (1950). The cerebral basis of consciousness. *Brain, 73*, 465–479.

Brain, R. (1954). Loss of visualization. *Proceedings of the Royal Society of Medicine, 47*, 288–290.

Broughton, R. (1982). Neurology and dreaming. *Psychiatric Journal of the University of Ottowa, 7*, 101–110.

Brown, J. W. (1972). *Aphasia, apraxia, agnosia: Clinical and theoretical aspects*. Springfield, IL: Thomas.

Brown, J. W. (1989). Essay on perception. In J. W. Brown (Ed.), *Neuropsychology of visual perception* (pp. 233–255). Hillsdale, NJ: Lawrence Erlbaum Associates.

Butters, N., Barton, M., & Brody, B. (1970). Role of the right parietal lobe in the mediation of cross-modal associations and reversible operations in space. *Cortex, 6*, 174–190.

Cathala, H., Laffont, F., Siksou, M., Esnault, S., Gilbert, A., Minz, M., Moret-Chalmin, C., Buzaré, M., & Waisbord, P. (1983). Sommeil et rêve chez des patients atteints de lésions pariétales et frontales [Sleep and dreams in patients with parietal and frontal lesions]. *Revue Neurologique, 139*, 497–508.

Charcot, J.-M. (1883). Un cas de suppression brusque et isolée de la vision mentale des signes et des objets, (formes et couleurs) [On a case of sudden isolated suppression of the mental vision of signs and objects (forms and colors)]. *Progrès Médical, 11*, 568–571.

Charcot, J.-M. (1886). *Neue Vorlesungen über die Krankheiten des Nervensystems insbesondere über Hysterie* [New lectures on the diseases of the nervous system, particularly on hysteria] (S. Freud, Trans.). Leipzig: Töplitz & Deuticke. (Original work published 1890)

Charcot, J.-M. (1889). *Clinical lectures on diseases of the nervous system* (Vol. 3). (T. Savill, Trans.). London: The New Sydenham Society. (Original work published 1883)

Chase, T., Moretti, L., & Prensky, A. (1968). Clinical and electroencephalographic manifestations of vascular lesions of the pons. *Neurology, 18*, 357–368.

Christensen, A.-L. (1974). *Luria's neuropsychological investigation: Text*. Copenhagen: Munksgaard.

Christensen, A.-L. (1975). *Luria's neuropsychological investigation: Manual.* Copenhagen: Munksgaard.

Cogan, D. (1973). Visual hallucinations as release phenomena. *Archives of Clinical Ophthalmology, 188,* 139–150.

Corda, F. (1985). *Esperienza onirica in pazienti portatori di lesioni cerebrali unilaterali* [Oneiric experience in patients with lateral brain damage]. Unpublished thesis, University of Rome.

Clarke, L. P. (1915). The nature and pathogenesis of epilepsy. *New York Medical Journal, 101,* 522, 567–573, 623–628.

Creuzfeldt, O. (1995). *Cortex cerebri: Performance, structural and functional organization of the cortex.* Oxford: Oxford University Press.

Crick, F. (1994). *The astonishing hypothesis: The scientific search for the soul.* London: Simon & Schuster.

Critchley, M. (1953). *The parietal lobes.* London: Edward Arnold.

Cummings, J., & Greenberg, R. (1977). Sleep patterns in the "locked in" syndrome' *Electroencephalography and Clinical Neurophysiology, 43,* 270–271.

Dahlberg, C., & Jaffe, J. (1977). *Stroke: A doctor's personal story of his recovery.* New York: Norton.

Damasio, A. (1985). The frontal lobes. In K. Heilman & E. Valenstein (Eds.), *Clinical neuropsychology* (2nd ed., pp. 339–375). New York: Oxford University Press.

Damasio, A., Damasio, H. (1983). Localization of lesions in achromatopsia and prosopagnosia. In A. Kertesz (Ed.), *Localization in neuropsychology* (pp. 417–428). New York: Academic Press.

Damasio, A., & Geschwind, N. (1985). Anatomic localization in clinical neuropsychology. In P. Vinken, G. Bruyn, H. Klawans, & J. Frederiks (Eds.), *Handbook of clinical neurology* (Vol. 45, pp. 7–22). Amsterdam: Elsevier.

Damasio, A., Graff-Radford, N., Eslinger, P., Damasio, H., & Kassell, N. (1985). Amnesia following basal forebrain lesions. *Archives of Neurology, 42,* 263–271.

Damasio, A., Yamada, T., Damasio, H., Corbett, J., & McKee, J. (1980). Central achromatopsia: Behavioral, anatomic and physiologic aspects. *Neurology, 30,* 1064–1071.

Damasio, H., & Damasio, A. (1983). Localization of lesions in conduction aphasia. In A. Kertesz (Ed.), *Localization in neuropsychology* (pp. 231–243). New York: Academic Press.

Damasio, H., & Damasio, A. (1989). *Lesion analysis in neuropsychology.* New York: Oxford University Press.

Dejerine, J. (1914). *Semiologie des affections du systeme nerveux* [Semiology of affections of the nervous system]. Paris: Masson.

Deleval, J., De Mol, J., & Noterman, J. (1983). La perte des images souvenirs [The loss of mnemic imagery]. *Acta Neurologica Belgica, 83,* 61–79.

Dement, W. (1960). Effect of dream deprivation. *Science, 131,* 1705–1707.

Dement, W. (1963). Perception during sleep. *Proceedings of the American Psychopathological Association Symposium on Psychopathology of Perception.* New York: American Psychopathological Association.

Dement, W., & Kleitman, N. (1957a). Cyclic variations in EEG during sleep and their relation to eye movements, body mobility and dreaming. *Electroencephalography and Clinical Neurophysiology, 9,* 673–690.

Dement, W., & Kleitman, N. (1957b). The relation of eye movements during sleep to dream activity: An objective method for the study of dreaming. *Journal of Experimental Psychology, 53,* 89–97.

Dement, W., Henry, P., Cohen, H., & Ferguson, J. (1967). Studies on the effects of REM-deprivation in humans and animals. In K. Pribram (Ed.), *Brain and behavior.* Harmondsworth, England: Penguin.

Devinsky, O. (1992). *Behavioral neurology: 100 maxims.* London: Edward Arnold.

Doricchi, F., & Violani, C. (1992). Dream recall in brain-damaged patients: A contribution to the neuropsychology of dreaming through a review of the literature. In J. Antrobus & M. Bertini

(Eds.), *The neuropsychology of sleep and dreaming* (pp. 99–140). Hillsdale, NJ: Lawrence Erlbaum Associates.

Edelman, G. (1989). *The remembered present: A biological theory of consciousness*. New York: Basic Books.

Efron, R. (1968). *What is perception? Boston studies in the philosophy of science*. New York: Humanities Press.

Eisinger, K., & Schilder, P. (1929). Träume bei Labyrinthläsionen [Dreams with labyrinthine lesions]. *Monatschrift für Psychiatrie & Neurologie, 73*, 314–329.

Epstein, A. (1964). Recurrent dreams: Their relationship to temporal lobe seizures. *Archives of General Psychiatry, 10*, 49–54.

Epstein, A. (1967). Body image alterations during seizures and dreams of epileptics. *Archives of Neurology, 16*, 613–619.

Epstein, A. (1973). The typical dream: Case studies. *Journal of Nervous & Mental Disease, 156*, 47–56.

Epstein, A. (1979). Effect of certain cerebral hemispheric diseases on dreaming. *Biological Psychiatry, 14*, 77–93.

Epstein, A., & Ervin, F. (1956). Psychodynamic significance of seizure content in psycho-motor epilepsy. *Psychosomatic Medicine, 18*, 43–55.

Epstein, A., & Freeman, N. (1981). The uncinate focus and dreaming. *Epilepsia, 22*, 603–605.

Epstein, A., & Hill, W. (1966). Ictal phenomena during REM sleep of a temporal lobe epileptic. *Archives of Neurology, 15*, 367–375.

Epstein, A., & Simmons, N. (1983). Aphasia with reported loss of dreaming. *American Journal of Psychiatry, 140*, 108–109.

van Essen, D., Felleman, D., De Yoe, E., Olavarria, J., & Knierim, J. (1990). Modular and hierarchical organization of extrastriate visual cortex in the macaque monkey. *Cold Spring Harbor Symposia on Quantitative Biology, 55*, 679–696.

Ettlin, T., Beckson, M., Benson, D., Langfitt, J., Amos, E., & Pineda, A. (1992). Prosopagnosia: A bihemispheric disorder. *Cortex, 28*, 129–134.

Ettlinger, G., Warrington, E., & Zangwill, O. (1957). A further study of visual-spatial agnosia. *Brain, 80*, 335–361.

Farah, M. (1984). The neurological basis of mental imagery: A componential analysis. *Cognition, 18*, 245–272.

Farah, M. (1989a). The neuropsychology of mental imagery. In J. Brown (Ed.), *Neuropsychology of visual perception* (pp. 183–201). Hillsdale, NJ: Lawrence Erlbaum Associates.

Farah, M. (1989b). The neuropsychology of mental imagery. In F. Boller & J. Grafman (Eds.), *Handbook of neuropsychology* (Vol. 2, pp. 395–413). New York: Elsevier.

Farah, M. (1990). *Visual agnosia: Disorders of object recognition and what they tell us about normal vision*. Cambridge, MA: MIT Press.

Farah, M., Levine, D., & Calvanio, D. (1988). A case study of mental imagery deficit. *Brain & Cognition, 8*, 147–164.

Farrell, B. (1969). *Pat & Roald*. London: Hutchinson.

Fechner, G. (1889). *Elemente der Psychophysik* [Elements of psychophysics]. (2nd ed.). Leipzig: Breitkopf & Härtel.

Feldman, M. (1971). Physiological observations in a chronic case of "locked-in" syndrome. *Neurology, 21*, 459–478.

Finke, R. (1980). Levels of equivalence in imagery and perception. *Psychological Review, 87*, 113–132.

Fischer, C. (1954). Dreams and perception. *Journal of the American Psychoanalytic Association, 2*, 389–445.

Flechsig, P. (1896). *Gehirn und Seele* [Brain and mind]. (2nd ed.). Leipzig: von Veit.

Foulkes, D. (1972). Nonrapid eye movement mentation. *Experimental Neurology, 19*, 28–38.

Foulkes, D. (1978). *A grammar of dreams*. New York: Basic Books.

Foulkes, D. (1985). *Dreaming: A cognitive-psychological analysis*. Hillsdale, NJ: Lawrence Erlbaum Associates.

Frank, J. (1946). Clinical survey and results of 200 cases of prefrontal leucotomy. *Journal of Mental Science, 92*, 497–508.

Frank, J. (1950). Some aspects of lobotomy (prefrontal leucotomy) under psychoanalytic scrutiny. *Psychiatry, 13*, 35–42.

Frederiks, J. (1985). Clinical neuropsychology: The neuropsychological symptom. In P. Vinken, G. Bruyn, H. Klawans, & J. Frederiks (Eds.), *Handbook of clinical neurology* (Vol. 45, pp. 1–6). Amsterdam: Elsevier.

Freeman, W., & Watts, J. (1942). *Psychosurgery*. Springfield, IL: Thomas.

Freeman, F. (1971). Akinetic mutism and bilateral anterior cerebral artery occlusion. *Journal of Neurology, Neurosurgery and Psychiatry, 34*, 693–698.

Freemon, F., Salinas-Garcia, R., & Ward J. (1974). Sleep patterns in a patient with a brain stem infarction involving the raphe nucleus. *Electroencephalography and Clinical Neurophysiology, 36*, 657–660.

Fremel & Schilder, P. (1920). Zur Symptomatologie der Kleinhirnwurmerkrankungen [On the symptomatology of cerebellar vermis pathology]. *Wiener klinische Wochenschrift, 47*, 314–329.

Freud, S. (1953). The interpretation of dreams. In J. Strachey (Ed. & Trans.), *The standard edition of the complete psychological works of Sigmund Freud* (vols. 4 & 5). London: Hogarth Press & The Institute of Psycho-Analysis. (Original work published 1900)

Gainotti, G., Messerli, P., & Tissot, R. (1972). Qualitative analysis of unilateral neglect in relation to laterality of cerebral lesions. *Journal of Neurology, Neurosurgery and Psychiatry, 35*, 545–550.

Galin, D. (1974). Implications for psychiatry of left and right cerebral specialization: A neurophysiological context for unconscious processes. *Archives of General Psychiatry, 31*, 572–583.

Gallassi, R., Morreale, A., Montagna, P., Gambetti, P., & Lugaresi, E. (1992). Fatal familial insomnia: Neuropsychological study of a disease with thalamic degeneration. *Cortex, 28*, 175–187.

Gauthier, L., Dehaut, F., & Joanette, Y. (1989). The bells test: A quantitative and qualitative test for visual neglect. *International Journal of Clinical Neuropsychology, 11*, 49–54.

Gerstmann, J. (1924). Fingeragnosie: Eine umschriebene Störung der Orientierung am eigener Körper [Finger agnosia: A circumscribed disorder of orientation to one's body]. *Wiener klinische Wochenschrift, 37*, 1010–1012.

Gerstmann, J. (1927). Fingeragnosie und isolierte Agraphie, ein neues Syndrom [Finger agnosia and pure agraphia: A new syndrome]. *Zeitschrift für die gesamte Neurologie und Psychiatrie, 108*, 381–402.

Gerstmann, J. (1930). Zur Symptomatologie der Hirnläsionen im Übergangsgebiet der unteren Parietalen und mittleren Occipitalwindung [On the symptomatology of brain lesions in the transitional zone of the inferior parietal and middle occipital gyrus]. *Nervenarzt, 3*, 691–695.

Gerstmann, J. (1940). Syndrome of finger agnosia, disorientation for right and left, agraphia and acalculia. *Archives of Neurology and Psychiatry, 44*, 398–408.

Gerstmann, J. (1957). Some notes on the Gerstmann syndrome. *Neurology, 7*, 866–869.

Geschwind, N., & Damasio, A. (1985). Apraxia. In P. Vinken, G. Bruyn, H. Klawans, & J. Frederiks (Eds.), *Handbook of clinical neurology* (Vol. 45, pp. 423–432). Amsterdam: Elsevier.

Gloning, K., & Sternbach, I. (1953). Über das Träumen bei zerebralen Herdläsionen [On dreams with focal cerebral lesions]. *Wiener Zeitschrift für die Nervenheilkunde, 6*, 302–329.

Goethe, J. (1988). The metamorphosis of plants. In D. Miller (Ed. & Trans.), *Goethe: Scientific Studies*. New York: Suhrkamp. (Original work published 1790)

Goldenberg, G. (1989). The ability of patients with brain damage to generate mental visual images. *Brain, 112*, 305–325.

Goldenberg, G. (1993). The neural basis of imagery. *Ballière's Clinical Neurology, 7*, 265–286.

Goldenberg, G. Mamoli, B., & Binder, H. (1985). Die Simultanagnosie als Symptom der Schädigung extrastriaterer visueller Rindenfelder - eine Fallstudie [Simultanagnosia as a symptom of extrastriate visual cortical damage: A case study]. *Nervenärzt, 56,* 682–690.

Goldstein, L. Burdick, J., & Lazslo, M. (1970). A quantitative analysis of the EEG during sleep in normal subjects. *Acta Physiologica Academiae Scientiarum Hungaricae, 37,* 291–300.

Goldstein, L., Stoltzfus, N., & Gardocki, J. (1972). Changes in interhemispheric amplitude relationships in the EEG during sleep. *Physiology & Behavior, 8,* 811–815.

Goodenough, D., Shapiro, A., Holden, M., & Steinschreiber, L. (1959). A comparison of "dreamers" and "nondreamers": Eye movements, electroencephalograms, and the recall of dreams. *Journal of Abnormal and Social Psychology, 59,* 295–302.

Goodglass, H. (1992). Diagnosis of conduction aphasia. In S. Kohn (Ed.), *Conduction aphasia* (pp. 39–49). Hillsdale, NJ: Lawrence Erlbaum Associates.

Goodglass, H., & Kaplan, E. (1983). *Assessment of aphasia and related disorders* (2nd ed.). Philadelphia: Lea & Febiger.

Gottschaldt, K. (1928). Über den Einfluss der Erfahrung auf die Wahrnehmung von Figuren [On the influence of experience upon the perception of figures]. *Psychologische Forschung, 8,* 18–317.

Green, G., & Lessell, S. (1977). Acquired cerebral dyschromatopsia. *Archives of Ophthalmology, 95,* 121–128.

Greenberg, M., & Farah, M. (1986). The laterality of dreaming. *Brain & Cognition, 5,* 307–321.

Greenberg, R., Pearlman, C., Brooks, R., Mayer, R., & Hartmann, E. (1968). Dreaming and Korsakoff's psychosis. *Archives of General Psychiatry, 18,* 203–209.

Greenwood, P., Wilson, D., & Gazzaniga, M. (1977). Dream report following commissurotomy. *Cortex, 13,* 311–316.

Grünstein, A. (1924). Die Erforschung der Träume als eine Methode der topischen Diagnostik bei Großhirnerkrankungen [Investigation of dreams as a method of topical diagnosis in cerebral disease]. *Zeitschrift für die gesamte Neurologie & Psychiatrie, 93,* 416–420.

Guilleminault, C., Cathala, J., & Castaigne, P. (1973). Effects of 5-hydroxytryptophane on sleep of a patient with a brain-stem lesion. *Electroencephalography and Clinical Neurophysiology, 34,* 177–184.

Guilleminault, C., Quera-Salva, M., & Goldberg, M. (1993). Pseudo-hypersomnia and pre-sleep behaviour with bilateral paramedian thalamic lesions. *Brain, 116,* 1549–1563.

Habib, M., & Sirigu, A. (1987). Pure topographical disorientation: A definition and anatomical basis. *Cortex, 23,* 73–85.

Harlow, J. (1868). Recovery from the passage of an iron bar through the head. *Proceedings of the Massachusetts Medical Society, 2,* 329–347.

Harrison, M. (1981). Dysphasia during sleep due to an unusual vascular lesion. *Journal of Neurology, Neurosurgery and Psychiatry, 44,* 739.

Hebb, D. O. (1968). Concerning imagery. *Psychological Review, 75,* 466–479

Hécaen, H. (1969). Aphasic, apraxic and agnosic syndromes in right and left hemisphere lesions. In G. Vinken & H. Bruyn (Eds.), *Handbook of clinical neurology* (Vol. 4, pp. 291–311). Amsterdam: North Holland.

Hécaen, H., de Ajuriaguerra, J., & Massonnet, J. (1951). Les troubles visuo-constructifs par lésion parieto-occipitale droite [Visual constructional disorders with right parieto-occipital lesions]. *Encéphale, 40,* 122–179.

Hécaen, H., & Albert, M. (1978). *Human neuropsychology.* New York: Wiley.

Hécaen, H., Angelergues, R., & Houillier, S. (1961). Les variétés cliniques des acalculies au cours des lésions rétro-rolandiques: approche statistique du problème [The clinical varieties of acalculia with retrorolandic lesions: A statistical approach to the problem]. *Revue Neurologique, 105,* 85–103.

Heilman, K., & Rothi, L. (1985). Apraxia. In K. Heilman & E. Valenstein, *Clinical neuropsychology* (2nd ed., pp. 131–150). New York: Oxford University Press.

Heiss, W.-D., Pawlik, G., Herholz, K., Wagner, R., & Weinhard, K. (1985). Regional cerebral glucose metabolism in man during wakefulness, sleep, and dreaming. *Brain Research, 327*, 362–366.

Hirschkowitz, M., Ware, J., & Karacan, I. (1980). Integrated EEG amplitude asymmetry during early and late REM and NREM periods. *Sleep Research, 9*, 291.

Hobson, J. A. (1988). *The dreaming brain*. New York: Basic Books.

Hobson, J. A., Lydic, R., & Baghdoyan, H. (1986). Evolving concepts of sleep cycle generation: From brain centers to neuronal populations. *Behavioral and Brain Sciences, 9*, 371–448.

Hobson, J. A., & McCarley, R. (1977). The brain as a dream-state generator: An activation-synthesis hypothesis of the dream process. *American Journal of Psychiatry, 134*, 1335–1368.

Hoppe, K. (1977). Split brains and psychoanalysis. *Psychoanalytic Quarterly, 46*, 220–244.

Hume, D. (1739). *Treatise on human nature*. London: Dent.

Humphrey, M., & Zangwill, O. (1951). Cessation of dreaming after brain injury. *Journal of Neurology, Neurosurgery & Psychiatry, 14*, 322–325.

Jackson, J. H. (1931). Lectures on the diagnosis of epilepsy. In J. Taylor (Ed.), *Selected writings of John Hughlings Jackson* (Vol. 1, pp. 276–307). London: Hodder & Stroughton. (Original work published 1879)

Jakobson, R. (1973). Towards a linguistic classification of aphasic impairments. In H. Goodglass & S. Blumstein (Eds.), *Psycholinguistics & aphasia* (pp. 29–47). Baltimore: Johns Hopkins University Press.

Jankowiak, J., Kinsbourne, M., Shalev, R., & Bachman, D. (1992). Preserved visual imagery and categorization in a case of associative visual agnosia. *Journal of Cognitive Neuroscience, 4*, 119–131.

Janz, D. (1974). Epilepsy and the sleep-waking cycle. In G. Vinken & H. Bruyn (Eds.), *Handbook of clinical neurology* (Vol. 45, pp. 457–490). Amsterdam: North Holland.

Johnson, M. (1991). Reality-monitoring: Evidence from confabulation in organic brain disease patients. In G. Prigatano & D. Schacter (Eds.), *Awareness of deficit after brain injury* (pp. 176–197). New York: Oxford University Press.

Johnson, M. (1994). Binding complex memories: The role of reactivation and the hippocampus. In D. Schacter & E. Tulving (Eds.), *Memory systems 1994* (pp. 311–350). Cambridge, MA: MIT Press.

Jouvet, M. (1973). Essai sur le rêve [Essay on dreams]. *Archives Italiennes dê Biologie, 111*, 564–576.

Julien, J., Vital, C., Deleplanque, B., Lagueny, A., & Ferrer, X. (1990). Atrophie thalamique subaigue familiale: Troubles mnesique et insomnie totale [Familial subacute thalamic atrophy: Memory disorders and total insomnia]. *Revue Neurologique, 146*, 173–178.

Jus, A., Jus, K., Villeneuve, A., Pires, A., Lachance, R., Fortier, J., & Villeneuve, R. (1973). Studies on dream recall in chronic schizophrenic patients after prefrontal lobotomy. *Biological Psychiatry, 6*, 275–293.

Kaplan, E., Goodglass, H., & Weintraub, S. (1983). *The Boston Naming Test* (2nd ed.). Philadelphia: Lea & Febiger.

Kardiner, A. (1932). The bio-analysis of the epileptic reaction. *Psychoanalytic Quarterly, 1*, 375–483.

Kerr, N., Foulkes, D., & Jurkovic, G. (1978). Reported absence of visual dream imagery in a normally sighted subject with Turner's syndrome. *Journal of Mental Imagery, 2*, 247–264.

Kerr, N., & Foulkes, D. (1981). Right hemispheric mediation of dream visualization: A case study. *Cortex, 17*, 603–610.

Kertesz, A. (1983). Issues in localization. In A. Kertesz (Ed.), *Localization in neuropsychology* (pp. 1–24). New York: Academic Press.

Kinsbourne, M., & Warrington, E. (1962). A study of finger agnosia. *Brain, 85*, 47–66.

Kleist, K. (1923). Kriegverletzungen des Gehirns in ihrer Bedeutung für die Hirnlokalisation und Hirnpathologie [War injuries of the brain and their significance for cerebral localization and cerebral pathology]. In O. von Schjerning (Ed.), *Handbuch der Ärztlichen Erfahrung im Weltkriege, 1914/1918* (Vol. 4). Leipzig: Barth.

Kosslyn, S. (1980). *Image and mind.* Cambridge, MA: Harvard University Press.

Kosslyn, S. (1994). *Image and brain.* Cambridge, MA: MIT Press.

Kramer, M., Roth, T., & Trinder, J. (1975). Dreams and dementia: A laboratory exploration of dream recall and dream content in chronic brain syndrome patients. *International Journal of Aging & Human Development, 6,* 169–178.

Labruzza, A. (1978). The activation-synthesis hypothesis of dreams: A theoretical note. *American Journal of Psychiatry, 135,* 1536–1538.

Lance, J. (1976). Simple formed hallucinations confined to the area of specific visual field defect. *Brain, 99,* 719–734.

Lange, J. (1936). Agnosien und Apraxien [Agnosias and apraxias]. In O. Bumke & O. Foerster (Eds.), *Handbuch der Neurologie* (Vol. 6, pp. 807–960). Berlin: Springer.

Lavie, P., Pratt, H., Scharf, B., Peled, R., & Brown, J. (1984). Localized pontine lesion: Nearly total absence of REM sleep. *Neurology, 34,* 118–120.

Lebrun, Y. (1987). Anosognosia in aphasics. *Cortex, 23,* 251–263.

Leischner, A. (1969). The agraphias. In G. Vinken & H. Bruyn (Eds.), *Handbook of clinical neurology* (Vol. 4, pp. 141–180). Amsterdam: North Holland.

Levin, H., & Spiers, P. (1985). Acalculia. In K. Heilman & E. Valenstein, *Clinical neuropsychology* (2nd ed., pp. 97–114). New York: Oxford University Press.

Levine, D. (1978). Prosopagnosia and visual object agnosia: A behavioral study. *Brain and Language, 5,* 341–365.

Lewin, B. (1946). Sleep, the mouth and the dream screen. *Psychoanalytic Quarterly, 15,* 419–434.

Lewin, B. (1953). Reconsideration of the dream screen. *Psychoanalytic Quarterly, 22,* 169–199.

Lipowski, Z. (1990). *Delirium: Acute confusional states.* New York: Oxford University Press.

Lissauer, H. (1890). Ein Fall von Seelenblindheit nebst einem Beitrage zur Theorie derselben [A case of mind blindness with a contribution to theory]. *Archiv für Psychiatrie, 21,* 222–270.

Locke, J. (1959). *Essay concerning human understanding.* New York: Dover. (Original work published 1689)

Lugaresi, E., Medori, R., Montagna, P., Baruzzi, A, Cortelli, P., Lugaresi, A., Tinuper, P., Zucconi, M., & Gambetti, P. (1986). Fatal familial insomnia and dysautonomia with selective degeneration of thalamic nuclei. *New England Journal of Medicine, 315,* 997–1003.

Luria, A. R. (1965). Two kinds of motor perseveration in massive injury of the frontal lobes. *Brain, 88,* 1–10.

Luria, A. R. (1973). *The working brain: An introduction to neuropsychology.* Harmondsworth, England: Penguin.

Luria, A. R. (1980). *Higher cortical functions in man* (2nd ed.). New York: Basic Books.

Luria, A. R., & Majovski, L. (1977). Basic approaches used in American and Soviet clinical neuropsychology. *American Psychologist, 32,* 959–968.

Lyman, R., Kwan, S., & Chao, W. (1938). Left occipito-parietal tumour with observations on alexia and agraphia in Chinese and in English. *Chinese Medical Journal, 54,* 491–516.

Mach, E. (1959). *The analysis of sensations, and the relation of the physical to the psychical* (C. Williams & S. Waterlow, Trans.). (5th ed.). New York: Dover Publications. (Original work published 1906)

Macrae, D., & Trolle, E. (1956). The defect of function in visual agnosia. *Brain, 79,* 94–110.

Markand, O., & Dyken, M. (1976). Sleep abnormalities in patients with brain stem lesions. *Neurology, 26,* 769–776.

Mazzoni, M., Pardoni, L., Giorgetti, V., & Arena, R. (1990). Gerstmann syndrome: A case report. *Cortex, 26,* 459–467.

McCarthy, R., & Warrington, E. (1990). *Cognitive neuropsychology: A clinical introduction.* New York: Academic Press.

McFie, J. (1960). Psychological testing in clinical neurology. *Journal of Nervous and Mental Diseases, 131*, 383–393.

McFie, J., & Zangwill, O. (1960). Visual constructive disabilities associated with lesion of the left cerebral hemisphere. *Brain, 83*, 243–260.

Mesulam, M.-M. (1985a). Attention, confusional states, and neglect. In M.-M. Mesulam (Ed.), *Principles of behavioral neurology* (pp. 125–168). Philadelphia: F. A. Davis.

Mesulam, M.-M. (1985b). Patterns in behavioral neuroanatomy: Association areas, the limbic system, and hemispheric specialization. In M.-M. Mesulam (Ed.), *Principles of behavioral neurology* (pp. 1–70). Philadelphia: F. A. Davis.

Mesulam, M.-M. (1990). Large-scale neurocognitive networks and distributed processing for attention, language and memory. *Annals of Neurology, 28*, 597–613.

Michel, F., & Sieroff, E. (1981). Une approche anatomo-clinique des deficits de l'imagerie onei-rique, est-elle possible? [A clinico-anatomical approach to dream imagery deficits: Is it possible?] In *Sleep: Proceedings of an International Colloquium*. Milan: Carlo Erba Formitala.

Milner, B. (1971). Interhemispheric differences in the localization of psychological processes in man. *British Medical Bulletin, 27*, 272–277.

Moffitt, A., Hoffman, R., Wells, R., Armitage, R., Pigeau, R., & Shearer, J. (1982). Individual differences among pre- and post-awakening EEG correlates of dream reports following arousals from different stages of sleep. *Psychiatric Journal of the University of Ottawa, 7*, 111–125.

von Monakow, C. (1914). *Die Lokalisation im Großhirn und der Abbau der Funktion durch Corticale Herde* [Brain localization and the dissolution of function with cerebral foci]. Wiesbaden: Bergmann.

Montemurro, D., & Bruni, J. E. (1988). *The human brain in dissection* (2nd ed.). New York: Oxford University Press.

Morin, P., Riurain, Y., Eustache, F., Lampert, J., & Courtheoux, P. (1984). Agnosie visuelle et agnosie tactile [Visual agnosia and tactile agnosia]. *Revue Neurologique, 140*, 271–277.

Morris, H., Lüders, H., Lesser, R., Dinner, D., & Hahn, J. (1984). Transient neuropsychological abnormalities (including Gerstmann's syndrome) during cortical stimulation. *Neurology, 34*, 877–883.

Morris, M., Bowers, D., Chatterjee, A., & Heilman, K. (1992). Amnesia following a discrete basal forebrain lesion. *Brain, 115*, 1827–1847.

Moscovitch, M. (1982). Multiple dissociations of function in amnesia. In L. Cermak (Ed.), *Human memory and amnesia* (pp. 337–370). Hillsdale, NJ: Lawrence Erlbaum Associates.

Moss, C. S. (1972). *Recovery with aphasia: The aftermath of my stroke*. Urbana: University of Illinois Press.

Müller, F. (1892). Ein Beitrag zur Kenntniss der Seelenblindheit [A contribution to the knowledge of mind-blindness]. *Archiv für Psychiatrie & Nervenkrankheiten, 24*, 856–917.

Müller, R.-A. (1992). Modularism, holism, connectionism: Old conflicts and new perspectives in aphasiology and neuropsychology. *Aphasiology, 5*, 443–475.

Munk, H. (1878). Weitere Mittheilungen zur Physiologie des Grosshirnrinde [Further contributions to the physiology of the cerebral cortex]. *Archiv für Anatomie und Physiologie 2*, 161–178.

Murri, L., Arena, R., Siciliano, G., Mazzotta, R., & Murarorio, A. (1984). Dream recall in patients with focal cerebral lesions. *Archives of Neurology, 41*, 183–185.

Murri, L., Massetani, R., Siciliano, G., & Arena, R. (1985). Dream recall after sleep interruption in brain-injured patients. *Sleep, 8*, 356–362.

Naville, F., & Brantmay, H. (1935). Contribution à l'étude des équivalents épileptiques chez les enfant [Contribution to the study of epilepsy in infancy]. *Archives Suisses de Neurologie et de Psychiatrie, 35*, 96–122.

Neal, P., with Deneut, R. (1988). *As I am*. London: Century.

Newcombe, F. (1969). *Missile wounds of the brain*. Oxford: Oxford University Press.

Nielsen, J. (1946). *Agnosia, apraxia, aphasia: Their value in cerebral localization* (2nd ed.). New York: Hoeber.

Nielsen, J. (1955). Occipital lobes, dreams and psychosis. *Journal of Nervous & Mental Disease, 121,* 50–52.

Nikolinakos, D. (1992). Freud on dreams and Kosslyn on mental imagery. *Journal of Mind and Behavior, 13,* 397–411.

Osorio, I., & Daroff, R. (1980). Absence of REM and altered NREM sleep in patients with spinocerebellar degeneration and slow saccades. *Annals of Neurology, 7,* 277–280.

Osterrieth, P. (1944). Le test de copie d'une figure complexe [The complex figure test]. *Archives de Psychologie, 30,* 206–356.

Ostow, M. (1954a). A psychoanalytic contribution to the study of brain function: I. The frontal lobes. *Psychoanalytic Quarterly, 23,* 317–338.

Ostow, M. (1954b). Psychodynamic disturbances in patients with temporal lobe disorder. *Journal of the Mount Sinai Hospital, 20,* 293–308.

Ostow, M. (1955). A psychoanalytic contribution to the study of brain function: II. The temporal lobes. *Psychoanalytic Quarterly, 24,* 383–423.

Pallis, C. (1955). Impaired identification of faces and places with agnosia for colours: Report of a case due to cerebral embolism. *Journal of Neurology, Neurosurgery & Psychiatry, 18,* 218–224.

Panksepp, J. (1985). Mood changes. In P. Vinken, G. Bruyn, H. Klawans, & J. Frederiks (Eds.), *Handbook of clinical neurology* (Vol. 45, pp. 271–285). Amsterdam: Elsevier.

Partridge, M. (1950). *Pre-frontal leucotomy: A survey of 300 cases personally followed for 1½–3 Years.* Oxford: Blackwell.

Passingham, R. (1993). *The frontal lobes and voluntary action.* New York: Oxford University Press.

Paterson, A., & Zangwill, O. (1945). A case of topographical disorientation associated with unilateral cerebral lesion. *Brain, 68,* 188–211.

Pearlman, A., Birch, J., & Meadows, J. (1979). Cerebral color blindness: An acquired defect in hue discrimination. *Annals of Neurology, 5,* 253–261.

Peña-Casanova, J., Roig-Rovira, T., Bermudez, A., & Tolosa-Sarro, E. (1985). Optic aphasia, optic apraxia, and loss of dreaming. *Brain & Language, 26,* 63–71.

Penfield, W. (1938). The cerebral cortex in man: I. The cerebral cortex and consciousness. *Archives of Neurology & Psychiatry, 40,* 417–442.

Penfield, W., & Erickson, T. (1941). *Epilepsy and cerebral localization.* Springfield, IL: Thomas.

Penfield, W., & Rasmussen, T. (1955). *The cerebral cortex of man.* New York: MacMillan.

Perecman, E. (Ed.). (1987). *The frontal lobes revisited.* Hillsdale, NJ: Lawrence Erlbaum Associates.

Piehler, R. (1950). Über das Traumleben leukotomierter (Vorläufige Mitteilung) [On the dreamlife of the leukotomized (preliminary communication)]. *Nervenärzt, 21,* 517–521.

Pivik, R., Bylsma, F., Busby, K., & Sawyer, S. (1982). Interhemispheric EEG changes in relationship to sleep and dreams in gifted adolescents. *Psychiatric Journal of the University of Ottawa, 7,* 57–76.

Poeck, K., & Orgass, B. (1966). Gerstmann's syndrome and aphasia. *Cortex, 2,* 421–439.

Pompeiano, O. (1979). Cholinergic activation of reticular and vestibular mechanisms controlling posture and eye movements. In J. A. Hobson & M. Brazier (Eds.), *The reticular formation revisited* (pp. 473–572). New York: Raven.

Poppelreuter, W. (1917–1918). *Die psychischen Schädigungen durch Kopfschuss* [Mental disorders due to bullet wounds to the head]. Leipzig: Voss.

Posner, M., & Driver, J. (1992). The neurobiology of selective attention. *Current Opinion in Neurobiology, 2,* 165–169.

Posner, M., & Peterson, S. (1990). The attention system of the human brain. *Annual Review of Neuroscience, 13,* 25–42.

Pötzl, O. (1928). *Die Aphasielehre vom Standpunkt der klinischen Psychiatrie, I: Die optisch-agnosti-*

schen Störungen (die verschiedenen Formen der Seelenblindheit) [The aphasia doctrine from the standpoint of clinical psychiatry, I: Optic-agnosic disorders (the different forms of mind-blindness)]. Leipzig: Deuticke.

Pribram, K., & Luria, A. R. (Eds.). (1973). *Psychophysiology of the frontal lobes.* New York: Academic Press.

Rao, S., Hammeke, T & McQuillen, M. (1984). Memory disturbances in chronic progressive multiple sclerosis. *Archives of Neurology, 41,* 625–631.

Raven, J. (1960). *Guide to the standard progressive matrices.* London: H. K. Lewis.

de Renzi, E. (1982). *Disorders of space exploration and cognition.* New York: Wiley.

de Renzi, E. (1985). Disorders of spatial orientation. In P. Vinken, G. Bruyn, H. Klawans, & J. Frederiks (Eds.), *Handbook of clinical neurology* (Vol. 45, pp. 405–422). Amsterdam: Elsevier.

de Renzi, E., & Faglioni, P. (1978). Normative data and screening power of a shortened version of the Token Test. *Cortex, 14,* 41–49.

Rey, A. (1941). L'examen psychologique dans les cas d'encephalopathie traumatique [Psychological assessment in cases of traumatic encephalopathy]. *Archives de Psychologie, 28,* 286–340.

Rey, A. (1964). *L'examen clinique en psychologie* [Clinical assessment in psychology]. Paris: Presses Universitaires de France.

Riddoch, G. (1935). Visual disorientation in homonymous half fields. *Brain, 58,* 376–382.

Riddoch, M., & Humphreys, G. (1987). *To see but not to see—A case study of visual agnosia.* Hillsdale, NJ: Lawrence Erlbaum Associates.

Ritchie, D. (1959). *Stroke: A diary of recovery.* London: Faber & Faber.

Rodin, E., Mulder, D., Faucett, R., & Bickford, R. (1955). Psychologic factors in convulsive disorders of focal origin. *Archives of Neurology, 74,* 365–374.

Roeltgen, D., Sevush, S., & Heilman, K. (1983). Pure Gerstmann's syndrome from a focal lesion. *Archives of Neurology, 40,* 46–47.

Rosekind, M., Coates, T., & Zarcone, V. (1979). Lateral dominance during wakefulness, NREM stage 2 sleep and REM sleep. *Sleep Research, 8,* 36.

Sacks, O. (1985). *The man who mistook his wife for a hat.* London: Duckworth.

Sacks, O. (1990). *Awakenings* (Rev. ed.). New York: HarperCollins.

Sacks, O. (1991). Neurological dreams. *MD, February,* 29–32.

Sacks, O. (1995). *An anthropologist on Mars.* London: Picador.

Sacks, O., & Wasserman, R. (1987). The case of the colorblind painter. *New York Review of Books, 34* (18), 25–34.

Sakai, K. (1980). Some anatomical and physiological properties of ponto-mesencephalic tegmental neurons with special reference to the PGO waves and postural hypotonia during paradoxical sleep in the cat. In *The reticular formation revisited.* New York: Raven Press.

de Sanctis, S. (1896). *Il sogni e il sonno* [Dreams and sleep]. Rome: Dante Alighieri.

Schacter, D. (1987). Implicit memory: History and current status. *Journal of Experimental Psychology: Learning, Memory, and Cognition, 13,* 501–518.

Schacter, D., McAndrews, M., & Moscovitch, M. (1988). Access to consciousness: Dissociations between implicit and explicit knowledge in neuropsychological syndromes. In L. Weiskrantz (Ed.), *Thought without language* (pp. 242–278). Oxford: Clarendon.

Schanfald, D., Pearlman, C., & Greenberg, R. (1985). The capacity of stroke patients to report dreams. *Cortex, 21,* 237–247.

Schenkenberg, T., Bradford, D., & Ajax, E. (1980). Line bisection and unilateral visual neglect in patients with neurologic impairment. *Neurology, 30,* 509–517.

Schilder, P. (1934). Self-consciousness and optic imagination in a case of depression. *Psychoanalytic Review, 21,* 316–328.

Schilder, P. (1961). *Brain and personality: Studies in the psychological aspects of cerebral neuropathology and the neuropsychiatric aspects of motility schizophrenics.* New York: International Universities Press.

Schindler, R. (1953). Das Traumleben der Leukotomierten [The dream-life of the leukotomized]. *Wiener Zeitschrift für die Nervenheilkunde, 6,* 330.

Schröder, P. (1925). Über Gesichtshalluzination bei organischen Hirnleiden [On facial hallucinations in organic nervous diseases]. *Archiv für Psychiatrie und Nervenkrankheiten, 73,* 308–777.

Seguin, E. (1886). A clinical study of lateral hemianopsia. *Journal of Nervous and Mental Disease, 13,* 445–454.

Shallice, T. (1982). Specific impairments of planning. *Philosophical Transactions of the Royal Society of London, Series B, 298,* 199–209.

Shepard, R. (1978). The mental image. *American Psychologist, 33,* 125–137.

Shuttleworth, E., Syring, V., & Allen, N. (1982). Further observations on the nature of prosopagnosia. *Brain & Cognition, 1,* 302–332.

Signoret, J.-L. (1985). Memory and amnesias. In M.-M. Mesulam (Ed.), *Principles of Behavioral Neurology* (pp. 169–192). Philadelphia: F. A. Davis.

Snow, W. (1979). *The Rey-Osterrieth Complex Figure Test as a measure of visual recall.* Paper presented at the 7th Annual Meeting of the International Neuropsychological Society, New York.

Snyder, H. (1958). Epileptic equivalents in children. *Pediatrics, 18,* 308–318.

Solms, M., Kaplan-Solms, K., & Brown, J. W. (1996). Wilbrand's case of "mind-blindness." In C. Code, C.-W. Wallesch, Y. Joanette, & A.-R. Lecours (Eds.), *Classic cases in neuropsychology* (pp. 89–110). Hove, England: Psychology Press.

Sparr, S., Jay, M., Drislane, F., & Venna, N. (1991). A historic case of visual agnosia revisited after 40 years. *Brain, 114,* 789–800.

Starr, A. (1967). A disorder of rapid eye movements in Huntington's chorea. *Brain, 90,* 545–564.

Stengel, E. (1944). Loss of spatial orientation, constructional apraxia and Gerstmann's syndrome. *Journal of Mental Science, 90,* 753–760.

Stone, M. (1977). Dreams, free association, and the non-dominant hemisphere: An integration of psychoanalytical, neurophysiological, and historical data. *Journal of the American Academy of Psychoanalysis, 5,* 255–284.

Strub, R., & Black, F. W. (1985). *The mental status examination in neurology* (2nd ed). Philadelphia: F. A. Davis.

Strub, R., & Geschwind, N. (1974). Gerstmann syndrome without aphasia. *Cortex, 10,* 378–387.

Strub, R., & Geschwind, N. (1983). Localization in Gerstmann syndrome. In A. Kertesz (Ed.), *Localization in neuropsychology* (pp. 295–321). New York: Academic Press.

Stuss, D., & Benson, F. (1983). Frontal lobe lesions and behavior. In A. Kertesz (Ed.), *Localization in neuropsychology* (pp. 429–454). New York: Academic Press.

Styron, W. (1990). *Darkness visible.* London: Jonathan Cape.

Symonds, C., & Mackenzie, I. (1957). Bilateral loss of vision from cerebral infarction. *Brain, 80,* 415–455.

Talland, G. (1965). *Deranged memory: A psychonomic study of the amnesic syndrome.* New York: Academic.

Taylor, E. (1959). *The appraisal of children with cerebral deficits.* Cambridge, MA: Harvard University Press.

Temkin, O. (1971). *The falling sickness: A history of epilepsy from the Greeks to the beginning of modern neurology* (2nd ed.). Baltimore, MD: Johns Hopkins University Press.

Terman, L., & Merrill, M. (1937). *Measuring intelligence.* Boston, MA: Houghton Mifflin.

Teuber, H.-L. (1955). Physiological psychology. *Annual Review of Psychology, 6,* 267–296.

Teuber, H.-L. (1959). Some alterations in behavior after cerebral lesions in man. In A. Bass (Ed.), *Evolution of nervous control from primitive organisms to man.* Washington, D.C.: American Association for the Advancement of Science.

Teuber, H.-L. (1960). Perception. In J. Field, H. Magonn, & V. Hall (Eds.), *Handbook of Physiology* (Vol 3, pp. 1595–1668). Washington, DC: American Physiological Society.

Teuber, H.-L. (1964). The riddle of frontal lobe function in man. In J. Warren & K. Akert (Eds.), *The frontal granular cortex and behavior.* New York: McGraw-Hill.

Teuber, H.-L. (1968). Alteration of perception and memory in man. In L. Weiskrantz (Ed.), *Analysis of behavioral change.* New York: Harper & Row.

Thomayer, J. (1897). Sur la signification de quelques rêves [The meaning of some dreams]. *Revue Neurologique, 5,* 98–101.

Torda, C. (1969). Dreams of subjects with loss of memory for recent events. *Psychophysiology, 6,* 358–365.

Tyrer, P., & Seivewright, N. (1985). Anxiety. In P. Vinken, G. Bruyn, H. Klawans, & J. Frederiks (Eds.), *Handbook of clinical neurology* (Vol. 45, pp. 265–269). Amsterdam: Elsevier.

Tzavaras, A. (1967). *Contribution à l'étude de l'agnosie des physiognomies* [Contribution to the study of agnosia for faces]. Unpublished doctoral dissertaion, Faculté de Médicine de Université de Paris.

Varney, N. (1984). Gerstmann syndrome without aphasia: A longitudinal study. *Brain and Cognition, 3,* 1–9.

Vogel, G. (1978). An alternative view of the neurobiology of dreaming. *American Journal of Psychiatry, 135,* 1531–1535.

Walsh, K. (1991). *Understanding brain damage: A primer of neuropsychological evaluation* (2nd ed.). Edinburgh: Churchill Livingstone.

Walsh, K. (1994). *Neuropsychology: A clinical approach* (3rd ed.). Edinburgh: Churchill Livingstone.

Wapner, W., Judd, T., & Gardner, H. (1978). Visual agnosia in an artist. *Cortex, 14,* 343–364.

Warrington, E., & McCarthy, R. (1987). Categories of knowledge: Further fractionations and an attempted integration. *Brain, 110,* 1273–1296.

Warrington, E., & Rabin, P. (1970). Perceptual matching in patients with cerebral lesions. *Neuropsychologia, 8,* 475–487.

Warrington, E., & Shallice, T. (1984). Category-specific semantic impairments. *Brain, 107,* 829–854.

Wasserman, M. (1984). Psychoanalytic dream theory and recent neurobiological findings about REM sleep. *Journal of the American Psychoanalytic Association, 32,* 831–846.

Wechsler, D. (1945). A standardized memory scale for clinical use. *Journal of Psychology, 19,* 87–95.

Wechsler, D. (1981). *WAIS-R Manual.* New York: The Psychological Corporation.

Weinstein, E. (1963). The relationship to dreams of symbolic patterns following brain injury. In E. Adelson (Ed.), *Dreams in contemporary psychoanalysis* (pp. 67–95). New York: Society of Medical Psychoanalysts.

Weintraub, S., & Mesulam, M.-M. (1985). Mental state assessment of young and elderly adults in behavioral neurology. In M.-M. Mesulam (Ed.), *Principles of behavioral neurology* (pp. 71–123). Philadelphia: F. A. Davis.

Whitty, C., & Lewin, W. (1957). Vivid day-dreaming: An unusual form of confusion following anterior cingulectomy. *Brain, 80,* 72–76.

Whitty, C., & Lewin, W. (1960). A Korsakoff syndrome in the post-cingulectomy confusional state. *Brain, 83,* 648–653.

Wilbrand, H. (1887). *Die Seelenblindheit als Herderscheinung und ihre Beziehung zur Alexie und Agraphie* [Mind-blindness as a focal symptom and its relationship to alexia and agraphia]. Wiesbaden: Bergmann.

Wilbrand, H. (1892). Ein Fall von Seelenblindheit und Hemianopsie mit Sectionsbefund [A case of mind-blindness and hemianopia with autopsy results]. *Deutsche Zeitschrift für die Nervenheilkunde, 2,* 361–387.

Williams, M. (1970). *Brain damage and the mind.* Harmondsworth, England: Penguin.

Wolpert, I. (1924). Die Simultanagnosie: Störung die Gesamtauffassung [Simultagnosia: A disorder of global interpretation]. *Zeitschrift für die gesamte Neurologie & Psychiatrie, 93*, 397–415.

Zeki, S. (1990). A century of central achromatopsia. *Brain, 113*, 1721–1777.

Zeki, S. (1991). Cerebral akinetopsia (visual motion blindness). *Brain, 114*, 811–824.

Zeki, S. (1993). *A Vision of the brain.* Oxford: Blackwell.

Zinkin, N. (1959). *Psixologiceskaja nauka vSSSR* [Psychological science in the USSR]. Moscow: Academy of Pedagogical Science.

Index of Personal Cases

Author Index

Subject Index

287